Montesquieu's Liberalism and the Problem of Universal Politics

Dubbed "the oracle" by no less an authority than James Madison, Montesquieu stands as a theoretical founder of the liberal political tradition. But equally central to his project was his account of the relationship of law to each nation's particular customs and place, a teaching that militates against universal political solutions. This teaching has sometimes been thought to stand in tension with his liberal constitutionalism. In this book, Keegan Callanan argues that Montesquieu's political particularism and liberalism are complementary and mutually reinforcing parts of a coherent whole. In developing this argument, Callanan considers Montesquieu's regime pluralism, psychological conception of liberty, approach to political reform, and account of "the customs of a free people," including the complex interaction of religion and commerce. Callanan concludes that, by reorienting our understanding of liberalism and redirecting our attention toward liberty's distinctive preconditions, a return to Montesquieu's political philosophy leaves us better prepared to confront liberal democracy's contested claim to universality.

KEEGAN CALLANAN holds the Christian A. Johnson Junior Professorship in Political Thought at Middlebury College. His research and writing have appeared in publications such as *History of Political Thought*, *Political Research Quarterly*, and *The Wall Street Journal*. He has held visiting fellowships at the University of Virginia and Princeton University. A graduate of Bowdoin College, Callanan received his PhD from Duke University.

D1158587

Montesquieu's Liberalism and the Problem of Universal Politics

KEEGAN CALLANAN
Middlebury College

CAMBRIDGE
UNIVERSITY PRESS

CAMBRIDGE
UNIVERSITY PRESS

University Printing House, Cambridge CB2 8BS, United Kingdom

One Liberty Plaza, 20th Floor, New York, NY 10006, USA

477 Williamstown Road, Port Melbourne, VIC 3207, Australia

314–321, 3rd Floor, Plot 3, Splendor Forum, Jasola District Centre,
New Delhi – 110025, India

79 Anson Road, #06–04/06, Singapore 079906

Cambridge University Press is part of the University of Cambridge.

It furthers the University's mission by disseminating knowledge in the pursuit of
education, learning, and research at the highest international levels of excellence.

www.cambridge.org
Information on this title: www.cambridge.org/9781108428170
DOI: 10.1017/9781108617277

© Keegan Callanan 2018

This publication is in copyright. Subject to statutory exception
and to the provisions of relevant collective licensing agreements,
no reproduction of any part may take place without the written
permission of Cambridge University Press.

First published 2018

Printed in the United States of America by Sheridan Books, Inc.

A catalogue record for this publication is available from the British Library.

Library of Congress Cataloging-in-Publication Data
NAMES: Callanan, Keegan, 1981–
TITLE: Montesquieu's liberalism and the problem of universal politics / Keegan Callanan,
Middlebury College.
DESCRIPTION: Cambridge, United Kingdom ; New York, N.Y. : Cambridge University
Press, [2018] | Includes bibliographical references.
IDENTIFIERS: LCCN 2018009858 | ISBN 9781108428170 (hardback)
SUBJECTS: LCSH: Montesquieu, Charles de Secondat, baron de, 1689-1755. |
Liberalism–Philosophy. | Political culture–Philosophy.
CLASSIFICATION: LCC JC179.M8 C225 2018 | DDC 320.51–dc23
LC record available at https://lccn.loc.gov/2018009858

ISBN 978-1-108-42817-0 Hardback
ISBN 978-1-108-45023-2 Paperback

Cambridge University Press has no responsibility for the persistence or accuracy
of URLs for external or third-party internet websites referred to in this publication
and does not guarantee that any content on such websites is, or will remain,
accurate or appropriate.

For Rachel

Contents

Acknowledgments

In a 1748 letter to Monsignor Cerati, Montesquieu grumbled that work on *De l'esprit des loix* had whitened his hair. I am eager to thank many whose support and example have kept my labors over this book from exacting a similar toll on me. I begin with my undergraduate teachers, Paul Franco and Jean Yarbrough, who together introduced me not only to the study of political theory but also to genuinely liberal education. They provided a model of the scholar-teacher that continues to inspire. To my dissertation supervisor, Ruth Grant, and committee members, Michael Gillespie and Thomas Spragens, I owe warm thanks for their wise guidance and enthusiasm for this project from its inception.

My work on this study continued while I was teaching at the University of Virginia on a fellowship with the Program on Constitutionalism and Democracy. The program's director, Jim Ceaser, gave my project a place to flourish and encouraged me in the work, not least by his assurances (only half-ironic) that we are living in the "Montesquieuian moment."

Since joining the faculty of Middlebury College, I have received generous institutional support in many forms, including the provision of funding for research assistance and leave. The efficient staff of the Davis Family Library have filled streams of loan requests. Many fine colleagues in my department and beyond have welcomed me into the fold. Along the way, I have accrued a special debt to my friend and colleague, Murray Dry, for his unstinting support and careful comments on nearly the entire manuscript.

I completed the final stages of work on the manuscript as a visiting fellow with the James Madison Program in American Ideals and Institutions at Princeton University. My Madison year has afforded me time for sustained reflection on the manuscript within a congenial and vibrant community of scholars. The program directors, Robby George and Brad Wilson, have my sincere thanks.

Many friends, colleagues, and conference discussants have read and offered advice on portions of the manuscript. I thank William B. Allen, Erik Bleich, Paul Carrese, Jim Ceaser, Hank Clark, Daniel Doneson, Murray Dry, Peter Euben, Ben Hertzberg, Jack Knight, Michael Kraus, Bill McClay, Jeanne Morefield, Paul Rahe, Dennis Rasmussen, Jeremiah Russell, Joel Schlosser, David Schmitz, Matt Sitman, Allison Stanger, Sarah Stroup, Jim Stoner, Nick Troester, and Jean Yarbrough for their suggestions and encouragement. Deserving of special thanks for their constant readiness to offer sound counsel on this project are my twin brother and earliest collaborator, Brian Callanan, and my friends, Jed Atkins, Alex Duff, and Owen Strachan.

I wish to express my appreciation to my editor at Cambridge University Press, Robert Dreesen, for efficiently shepherding the manuscript through the review and publication process. My thanks also extend to Mr. Dreesen's assistant, Meera Seth; the press's external readers; and Pilar Wyman, who compiled the index. *History of Political Thought* and *Political Research Quarterly* allowed me to reprint material in Chapters 5 and 7, respectively, that originally appeared in articles.

It is a pleasure and point of pride to acknowledge my excellent students at Middlebury College, particularly my interlocutors in the Montesquieu and Tocqueville seminar. Our conversations around the text opened new vistas to me. Several students formed a capable corps of research assistants. For their partnership in this project, I would like to thank Lindsay Grigg, Wan Ning Seah, Meena Fernald, Courtney Cano, Michael Gao, Sam McEntire, and David Rubinstein. Four students worked with me not only during the academic year but also for a summer: many thanks to Taylor Custer, Rachel Frank, Max Kagan, and Malkie Wall. Ms. Wall, in particular, provided crucial aid in the final months before submission to the press. Duanyi Wang generously assisted while I was in residence at Princeton.

My deepest debts are to family. I am grateful for the love and support of my parents, Michelle and Rick – my first and best teachers. I thank my grandparents, brother, and sister for their proud encouragement. My children – Fiona, Claire, Liam, and Elise – have refreshed me daily, filling our evenings with laughter and light. Finally, it is a particular joy to thank Rachel, my wife, for her love and gracious wisdom. I dedicate the book to her.

Abbreviations

References to Montesquieu's works appear in the text with the following abbreviations:

EL   Charles-Louis de Secondat, baron de Montesquieu, *The Spirit of the Laws*, eds. Anne M. Cohler, Basia C. Miller, and Harold S. Stone (Cambridge University Press, 1989), cited by book, chapter, and, where appropriate, page number.

LP   Charles-Louis de Secondat, baron de Montesquieu, *Persian Letters*, ed. Andrew Kahn (Oxford University Press, 2008), cited by letter number.

MP   Charles-Louis de Secondat, baron de Montesquieu, *My Thoughts*, ed. Henry C. Clark (Indianapolis: Liberty Fund, 2012), cited by entry number.

Nagel   Charles-Louis de Secondat, baron de La Brède et de Montesquieu, *Oeuvres complètes de Montesquieu*, ed. André Masson (Paris: Les Éditions Nagel, 1950–1955), cited by volume and page number.

VF   Charles-Louis de Secondat, baron de La Brède et de Montesquieu, *Oeuvres complètes de Montesquieu*, eds. Jean Ehrard, Catherine Volpilhac-Auger, et al. (Oxford: Voltaire Foundation, 1998–), cited by volume and page number.

Introduction

One likes to establish elsewhere what is established at home.
Montesquieu, *EL* 6.29.27

One clear September day in 2010, hundreds of Afghan children gathered on Kabul's Nader Khan Hill.[1] They had come for kites on offer from the Americans. Outlawed under Taliban rule, kite-flying is a favorite pastime in Afghanistan, though it is customarily reserved for boys and men. A contractor for the United States Agency for International Development (USAID) had organized a kite giveaway as part of an initiative to "promote the use of Afghanistan's formal justice system." Kites emblazoned with slogans about women's rights and the rule of law would be given to boys and girls alike. Through play, they would begin to acquire ideas and habits of great political import. But the event did not go as planned. Afghan police took dozens of kites for themselves, and they beat the children with sticks and water bottles to keep them from crowding the distribution tent. In the commotion, very few girls sought or managed to get one of the thousand kites on offer. An aid worker succeeded in pushing her way through a throng of boys to give a kite to a girl. Triumphant, the little girl ran back to her father, who seized the kite and gave it to her brother. "He is my son and he should get the kite," the father explained. The event's chief organizer claimed success when the

---

[1] Rod Nordland, "Afghan Equality and Law, but With Strings Attached," *The New York Times*, September 25, 2010. www.nytimes.com/2010/09/25/world/asia/25kite.html; Tim Gaynor, "U.S. Project Flies Democracy Message on Afghan Kites," *Reuters*, September 24, 2010. www.reuters.com/article/us-afghanistan-kites-idUSTRE68N2SS20100924.

kites were gone. But one aid worker, responsible for administering the "kite event effectiveness survey," expressed doubt. "That's not a very good example of the rule of law," said Abdul Manem Danish. "Maybe it is the nature of these people that needs to be changed."

Child's play, as it turns out, is a serious subject. Despite the unhappy denouement of this tale, it is difficult to fault those who conceived the plan for a kite giveaway in Kabul, for behind this idea lay the realization that establishing the "rule of law" in Afghanistan would require more than merely constructing liberal political and legal structures and training office-holders to operate them. The event, in other words, demonstrated a degree of insight into the connection between liberal government and the everyday habits and customs of a people. But the tale also betrays our tendency to underestimate the strength of customary points of resistance to unfamiliar liberal values and institutions. The kites were redistributed according to the same illiberal mores they were designed to soften. The aid worker's tragicomic remark – complete with an oblique and perhaps unintended reference to the power of habit as second nature – signals a realization that the task of political liberalization may be far more difficult than anyone supposed.

Surveying the events of the last fifteen years, one could produce dozens of similar vignettes, and their illustrative force is only intensified as we view them in the context of broader political trends. Following a remarkable 50 percent increase in the portion of democracies in the world from 1973 to 2000, the year 2018 marked the twelfth consecutive year of a net decline in liberal democratic freedoms worldwide, as measured by Freedom House.[2] Laurence Whitehead reminds us that at the dawn of the current century, global democratization seemed to be proceeding at such a pace that some observers had come to regard "the universalization of liberal democracy as an almost 'natural' state of affairs … as everywhere from Albania to Zimbabwe was assigned a position on a presumably unilinear continuum destined to converge on a predetermined 'end of history'."[3] Such exuberant hopes proved hard to maintain in the face of an Arab Spring turned to Arab Winter and with the return of civil war to Iraq.

---

[2] "Freedom in the World 2013," Freedom House, last modified February 17, 2018, https://freedomhouse.org/sites/default/files/FIW%202013%20Booklet_0.pdf, 12; "Freedom in the World 2018," Freedom House, last modified March 21, 2018, https://freedomhouse.org/sites/default/files/FH_FITW_Report_2018_Final_SinglePage.pdf.

[3] Laurence Whitehead, "The International Politics of Democratization from Portugal (1974) to Iraq (2003)," in *The International Politics of Democratization: Comparative Perspectives*, ed. Nuno Severiano Teixeira (London: Routledge, 2008), 9. See also Francis Fukuyama, *The End of History and the Last Man* (New York: Free Press, 1992).

These trends certainly do not demonstrate that stable constitutional government is unattainable in the Middle East, North Africa, or any other region. But the reality of global democratic stagnation, represented in episodes like our kite story, does serve to raise a set of crucial questions concerning liberal democracy's putative status as the universal regime. What are the preconditions of liberal politics? Should we conceive of liberalism as consisting mainly in a set of institutions and principles that can be installed or applied almost anywhere? Or is liberalism a form of political life that assumes and, in part, consists in a distinctive culture, an "unusual state of mind," in Roger Scruton's phrase?[4] If the latter, how can we reconcile the universal moral claims of liberalism with this reality? Should we expect liberal democracy to prevail at last in all quarters, or should such hopes be tempered by a recognition of its preconditions? Although contemporary events raise these questions afresh, they are as old as liberal theory itself.

This book is written in the conviction that liberal statesmen cannot afford to ignore questions like these, but often do; that contemporary liberal theory has impoverished itself by losing sight of questions of this kind; and that Montesquieu's political philosophy and political science can enrich our reflections concerning this family of questions and teach us to ask them more often and probingly.

At bottom, these questions require us to confront the problem of liberalism's contested universality, and no early liberal theorist was more alive to this problem than was the baron de Montesquieu.[5] In the present

---

[4] Roger Scruton, *The Uses of Pessimism: And the Danger of False Hope* (Oxford University Press, 2010), 189. Emphasis in original.

[5] The term "liberalism" is of nineteenth-century vintage, but in treating Montesquieu as an intellectual founder of classical liberalism, I follow a century of scholarship. Émile Faguet, *La Politique comparée de Montesquieu, Rousseau et Voltaire* (Geneva: Slatkine Reprints, 1981 [1902]), may have been the first to pronounce, "Montesquieu est un liberal" (14). His judgment is shared by Raymond Aron, *Main Currents in Sociological Thought: Montesquieu, Comte, Marx, de Tocqueville, and the Sociologists and the Revolution of 1848*, 2 vols. (New Brunswick, NJ: Transaction Publishers, 1998), 1.1; Isaiah Berlin, "Montesquieu," in *Against the Current*, ed. Henry Hardy (Princeton University Press, 2013), 164-203; Bernard Manin, "Les deux libéralismes: marché ou contre-pouvoirs," *Intervention* 9 (1984), 10-24; Judith N. Shklar, *Montesquieu* (Oxford University Press, 1987); Thomas L. Pangle, *Montesquieu's Philosophy of Liberalism* (University of Chicago Press, 1973); Diana J. Schaub, *Erotic Liberalism* (Lanham, MD: Rowman & Littlefield, 1995); Pierre Manent, *An Intellectual History of Liberalism* (Princeton University Press, 1996); Sharon Krause, *Liberalism with Honor* (Cambridge, MA: Harvard University Press, 2002); Catherine Larrère, "Montesquieu and Liberalism: The Question of Pluralism," in *Montesquieu and His Legacy*, ed. Rebecca E. Kingston (Albany, NY: State University of New York Press, 2008), 279–302; Paul O. Carrese, *Democracy in*

study, I argue that the two principal elements of Montesquieu's thought – his liberal constitutionalism and his critique of political universalism – are mutually reinforcing and complementary parts of a coherent whole. Far from being orthogonal to or in contradiction with his normative commitments, Montesquieu's rejection of universal politics flows from the logic of his liberalism and shares with it the common purpose of securing a stable, moderate politics of liberty. By addressing ourselves to this interpretive task, we may gain insight into the character of liberal political philosophy. A serious encounter with Montesquieu's thought opens to our view the possibility of a liberalism that is, on principle and by design, opposed to universalism in politics and uniquely alert to the relationship of politics and culture. We can best understand Montesquieuian liberalism not merely as an embryonic antecedent of today's liberalism, but rather more aptly as an alternative, half-heard variety of liberal theory that is strong and well-developed at certain points where contemporary liberal theory and statecraft falter. By reorienting our understanding of liberalism and redirecting our attention to modern liberty's distinctive preconditions, a return to Montesquieu's political philosophy leaves us better prepared to confront sensibly the questions we have adumbrated above, and the practical challenges that continue to thrust them into our field of vision.

In this Introduction, we briefly consider the status of these questions in the contemporary theory and practice of politics, identifying several deficiencies in light of which a recovery of Montesquieu's example appears especially fitting. We then turn to the tasks of framing the nested interpretive and theoretical problems of this study and sketching an overview of the book.

IDEAL THEORY AND IDEAL STATECRAFT

No one will accuse late twentieth-century liberal theory of a preoccupation with "facts on the ground." As John Tomasi argues, the "most striking characteristic of academic theorizing" in the wake of Rawls's *Theory of Justice* has been the "willingness of liberal theorists to separate the professional discipline of political philosophy from the more civic

---

Moderation: Montesquieu, Tocqueville, and Sustainable Liberalism (Cambridge University Press, 2016); and many others. For a learned alternative, see Céline Spector, *Montesquieu: Pouvoirs, richesses et sociétés* (Paris: PUF, 2004); Céline Spector, "Was Montesquieu Liberal? *The Spirit of the Laws* in the History of Liberalism," in *French Liberalism from Montesquieu to the Present Day*, ed. Raf Geenens and Helena Rosenblatt (Cambridge University Press, 2012), 57–72.

ideal of political wisdom," understood as "the skill of negotiating the boundaries between theoretical ideals and practical realities."[6] Robert S. Taylor notes that reflections on political transitions or political change have been a special casualty of liberal theory's turn toward the abstract task of identifying "realistically utopian" principles of justice, to the exclusion of feasibility and implementation considerations.[7] Similarly, Douglas Casson observes that as "modern liberalism has come to understand itself as primarily a set of political axioms that can be universally endorsed," we have diminished our capacity to appreciate "the difficulty of fostering stable and just communities at home and abroad."[8] In view of such deficiencies, David Miller suggests the need for a mode of "political philosophy that is sensitive not only to general facts about the human condition but also to facts of a more specific kind, *facts about particular societies*, or types of societies."[9]

In his seminal work, *A Theory of Justice* (1971), John Rawls does indeed comment on the capacities, attitudes, and qualities necessary to sustain liberal democracy; he writes of the need for a sense of justice, mutual trust, and an attitude of friendship among citizens.[10] But as Peter Berkowitz points out, Rawls too readily assumes that well-ordered liberal institutions themselves will produce the qualities necessary for their own stability.[11] With a lick and a promise, Rawls assures us that "when institutions are just (as defined by this conception), those taking part in these arrangements acquire the corresponding sense of justice and desire to do their part in maintaining them."[12] Ideal liberal institutions produce

---

[6] John Tomasi, *Free Market Fairness* (Princeton University Press, 2012), 205.

[7] Robert S. Taylor, "Democratic Transitions and the Progress of Absolutism in Kant's Political Thought," *The Journal of Politics*, 68, no. 3 (2006), 558.

[8] Douglas Casson, *Liberating Judgment: Fanatics, Skeptics, and John Locke's Politics of Probability* (Princeton University Press, 2011), 1, 17–18.

[9] David Miller, *Justice for Earthlings: Essays in Political Philosophy* (Cambridge University Press, 2013), 18. Emphasis added. Miller goes on to note that one of the benefits of such a mode of political philosophy is that, "We will not be tempted to apply the principles in question outside of their proper context. We will not, for example, prescribe that governments everywhere should be constituted democratically, on the grounds that democracy is the only legitimate principle for allocating political authority."

[10] John Rawls, *A Theory of Justice* (Cambridge, MA: Harvard University Press, 1971), ch. 8; esp. 469–79.

[11] Peter Berkowitz, *Virtue and the Making of Modern Liberalism* (Princeton University Press, 1999), 25–6.

[12] Rawls, *Theory of Justice*, 454. Earlier, he explains, "But man's propensity to injustice is not a permanent aspect of community life; it is greater or less depending in large part on social institutions, and in particular on whether these are just or unjust" (245). See John Rawls, *Political Liberalism* (New York: Columbia University Press, 2005), 194–5.

the virtues or qualities necessary for their own maintenance, and a failure in practice to produce those qualities indicates a defect in institutions and the principles they reflect. Rawls assumes that the correct principles of justice, embodied in institutions, "will win the full motivational compliance of all citizens."[13] Thus on his account, even earthy concerns about feasibility and stability lead us back to the tasks of identifying the abstract principles of justice and idealized institutions.

None of this is terribly satisfying. But even if Rawls had not collapsed the question of liberal stability into his search for ideal principles, it would remain the case that his approach to liberal theorizing places the emphasis squarely upon principles of justice. And this emphasis, as much as the defects in his treatment of the origin of liberal capacities and dispositions, seems to account for the theoretical trend that Tomasi and others criticize.

In recognition of the excessively abstract character of Rawlsian liberal theory and in response to the power of Alastair MacIntyre's and Michael Sandel's critical efforts, a number of liberal theorists over the last thirty years have attempted to construct, or to recover from history, an account of the habits of heart and mind upon which liberal democracy depends.[14]

Berkowitz, *Virtue and the Making of Modern Liberalism*, 25–6, and Bonnie Honig, *Political Theory and Displacement of Politics* (Ithaca, NY: Cornell University Press, 1993), 143–4, are critical of this line of thought in *Theory of Justice*. See also David Walsh, *The Growth of the Liberal Soul* (Columbia, MO: University of Missouri Press, 1997), 85.

[13] Tomasi, *Free Market Fairness*, 206.

[14] Alasdair MacIntyre, *After Virtue: A Study in Moral Theory* (South Bend, IN: University of Notre Dame Press, 1981); Michael Sandel, *Liberalism and the Limits of Justice* (Cambridge University Press, 1982). See Rita Koganzon, "Contesting the Empire of Habit: Habituation and Liberty in Lockean Education," *American Political Science Review*, 110, no. 3 (2016), 547–58; Ruth W. Grant, "John Locke on Custom's Power and Reason's Authority," *The Review of Politics*, 74 (2012), 607–29; Casson, *Liberating Judgment*; Krause, *Liberalism with Honor*; Emily R. Gill, *Becoming Free: Autonomy and Diversity in the Liberal Polity* (Lawrence, KS: University of Kansas, 2001); Berkowitz, *Virtue and the Making of Modern Liberalism*; Thomas A. Spragens, *Civil Liberalism: Reflections on Our Democratic Ideals* (Lanham, MD: Rowman & Littlefield, 1999); Nathan Tarcov, *Locke's Education for Liberty* (Lanham, MD: Lexington Books, 1999); Richard Dagger, *Civic Virtues: Rights, Citizenship, and Republican Liberalism* (Oxford University Press, 1997); Ronald Beiner, *What's the Matter with Liberalism?* (Berkeley: University of California Press, 1992); William Galston, *Liberal Purposes: Good, Virtues, and Diversity in the Liberal State* (Cambridge University Press, 1991); Richard Rorty, *Contingency, Irony, and Solidarity* (Cambridge University Press, 1989). Regarding Rorty's inclusion in this list, see William Curtis, *Defending Rorty: Pragmatism and Liberal Virtue* (New York: Cambridge University Press, 2015). Amy Gutmann, *Democratic Education* (Princeton University Press, 1987), focuses mainly on the virtues necessary for democratic deliberation. Stephen Macedo, *Liberal Virtues: Citizenship,*

Most of these efforts have focused on moral and intellectual virtues conducive to the liberal project, while others have considered more broadly the capacities and dispositions that liberal citizens must possess.[15] Each of these studies recognizes that well-ordered liberal institutions, no matter how ideal, cannot themselves produce all of the cultural, moral, and intellectual conditions necessary to their preservation. At times, studies of this kind can partake of an idealism of their own, spinning out lists of impressive "liberal virtues" with no realistic account of their sources and cultivation. But on balance, this turn to liberal culture represents an edifying departure from Rawlsian theory's narrow focus upon abstract principles and formal institutions. The present study travels in the same lane but attempts to go further.

The deficiencies of contemporary liberal theory in the wake of Rawls are, as I have intimated, strangely mirrored in contemporary liberal statecraft. Historian Richard Bourke observes that the "retreat of political philosophy onto the terrain of abstract morals," exemplified in the work of Rawls and Dworkin, "overlapped with the rise of moralism ... in international affairs."[16] It was not John Rawls, but President George W. Bush, who said that "it is the practice of democracy that makes a nation ready for democracy, and every nation can start on this path."[17] He identified democratic institutions as the source of democratic mores, thereby tabling the question of whether Iraq was ready for democracy. In addition to this optimism about the power of formal institutions themselves, President Bush also famously maintained and apparently acted on the view that a natural human nisus toward freedom could supply the

---

Virtue, and Community in Liberal Constitutionalism (Oxford: Clarendon Press, 1990), follows Rawls in holding that "liberal regimes are capable of generating a common ethos" to sustain themselves, despite his rejection of Rawls's view that liberal virtues can remain merely in the public or political sphere (285; 45, 51–73).

[15] For a helpful account of the trajectory of the "virtue liberalism" in contemporary political theory, see Curtis, *Defending Rorty*, 7–21.

[16] Bourke refers explicitly to Bush-era foreign policy. Richard Bourke, "Hume's Call to Action," *The Nation*, April 20, 2016. www.thenation.com/article/humes-call-to-action.

[17] President George W. Bush, "Remarks on the 20th Anniversary of the National Endowment for Democracy, November 6, 2003," in *Public Papers of the Presidents of the United States: George W. Bush, 2003, Book 2, Presidential Documents – July 1 to December 31, 2003* (Washington, DC: Government Publishing Office, 2006), 1471.

qualities necessary to sustain liberal democracy in Iraq, and anywhere else.[18] As he argued in his 2003 speech at Whitehall,

> In our conflict with terror and tyranny, we have an unmatched advantage, a power that cannot be resisted, and that is the appeal of freedom to all mankind... Perhaps the most helpful change we can make is to change our own thinking. In the West, there's been a certain skepticism about the capacity or even the desire of Middle Eastern peoples for self-government. We're told that Islam is somehow inconsistent with a democratic culture. Yet more than half of the world's Muslims are today contributing citizens in democratic societies...
>
> Peoples of the Middle East share a high civilization, a religion of personal responsibility, and a need for freedom as deep as our own. It is not realism to suppose that one-fifth of humanity is unsuited to liberty; it is pessimism and condescension, and we should have none of it.[19]

A year later, in his second inaugural address, President Bush would chastise those who "have questioned the global appeal of liberty." "Eventually, the call of freedom comes to every mind and every soul," he asserted. "Liberty will come to those who love it."[20] In his 2003 address before the US Congress, Prime Minister Tony Blair similarly rejected the "myth that though we love freedom, others don't; that our attachment to freedom is a product of our culture." A universal human love of freedom accounted for the fact that "anywhere, anytime ordinary people are given the chance to choose, the choice is the same: freedom, not tyranny; democracy, not dictatorship." But of course, there is a worm in the rose. As Charles Kesler observes in his critique of this rhetoric, a man's desire for freedom does not guarantee that he will desire the same for his

---

[18] "We believe that liberty is the *design of nature*; we believe that liberty is the direction of history ... And we believe that freedom – the freedom we prize – is not for us alone, it is *the right and the capacity of all mankind*." Emphasis added. Bush, "Remarks on the 20th Anniversary of the National Endowment for Democracy," 1474.

[19] President George W. Bush, "Remarks at Whitehall Palace in London, United Kingdom, November 19, 2003," in *Public Papers of the Presidents of the United States: George W. Bush, 2003, Book 2, Presidential Documents – July 1 to December 31, 2003* (Washington, DC: Government Publishing Office, 2006), 1576–7.

[20] This mode of argument and its detractors have a long history in American political discourse. When, as evidence of the naturalness of democratic republics, Samuel Adams asserted that a "love of liberty" is "interwoven in the soul of man," John Adams shot back, "So it is, according to La Fontaine, in that of a wolf." John Adams to Samuel Adams, October 18, 1790, in *The Works of John Adams*, ed. Charles Francis Adams (Boston: Little, Brown & Co., 1850–56), vol. 6, 417. See also, illustratively, William Jennings Bryan, "Imperialism," in *Speeches of William Jennings Bryan*, ed. William Jennings Bryan (New York, London: Funk & Wagnalls Company, 1909), vol. 2, 24–5.

neighbor; his desire not to be oppressed does not guarantee that he will not oppress.[21]

Taking stock of these practical oversights and theoretical blind spots provides us an occasion to appreciate the distinctive character of Montesquieu's liberal political philosophy. If ever there was a work of "political philosophy that is sensitive ... to facts of a more specific kind, facts about particular societies" (David Miller's tall order), it is Montesquieu's magnum opus, *The Spirit of the Laws* (1748). Montesquieu displays a Herodotean fascination with the mores and manners of virtually every known people on the face of the earth, and he invites theorists and statesmen to attend carefully to the relationship of political institutions to character, custom, and culture: all of this in the context of a robustly liberal project. His political theory lingers over a set of problems commonly (and dangerously) obscured in contemporary liberal theory and statecraft. The aim of the present study is not simply to catalogue the preconditions of liberal government as Montesquieu saw them, although we will certainly consider his approach to such along the way. Rather I seek primarily to explain how Montesquieu develops a liberal constitutionalism that avoids the inclination toward abstract political universalism, a tendency that besets some other strains of liberal theory and entails a neglect of liberalism's "dispositional" preconditions.

No study of Montesquieu's thought can address our contemporary political concerns in a direct or immediate manner. The focal point of this book is not Kabul, Baghdad, or Tripoli, but rather an interpretive difficulty at the heart of *The Spirit of the Laws*, a problem I shall outline later. Yet it is entirely appropriate, as we revisit great works of political philosophy, that we should find the events of our day allow us to see in a text what we had not seen before, to discern connections that had not previously disclosed themselves, and to follow threads we would not otherwise have bothered to trace. If great texts of political philosophy treat perennial questions, questions continually implicit in and arising out of political

---

[21] Charles R. Kesler, "Democracy and the Bush Doctrine," in *Life, Liberty, and the Pursuit of Happiness: Ten Years of the Claremont Review of Books*, eds. Charles R. Kesler and John B. Kienker (Lanham, MD: Rowman & Littlefield, 2012), 171–2. The withdrawal of all American forces from Iraq in 2011 – a decision predicated on our having left behind a putatively "sovereign, stable and self-reliant Iraq" – seemed to betray a similarly deficient understanding of liberal democracy's preconditions. President Barack Obama, "Remarks at Fort Bragg, North Carolina, December 14, 2011," in *Public Papers of the Presidents of the United States: Barack Obama, 2011, Book 2, Presidential Documents – July 1 to December 31, 2011* (Washington, DC: Government Publishing Office, 2015), 1548.

action, we should not be surprised when an encounter with such a text leaves us with a new way of understanding the problems that remain with us. This approach stands at some distance from antiquarian treatments of the history of political thought; it stands equally distant from efforts to inject the details of a current controversy into a text from an earlier time.

Montesquieu is not a participant in a twenty-first-century debate concerning regime change in the Islamic world, but neither was he merely a disputant in an eighteenth-century debate over the *ancien régime*. Although he endeavored to shape the politics of his day, he believed he had written a work of enduring political significance.[22] He even wondered, with a touch of dark irony, whether *Spirit* would prove more useful in a later age than in his own: "I have resolved ... to persuade myself that seven or eight hundred years from now, there will arrive a certain people for whom my ideas will be very useful" (*MP* 1940).

MONTESQUIEU'S POLITICAL PARTICULARISM

The Anglo-American reception of Montesquieu's *The Spirit of the Laws* has long emphasized his constitutionalism as contained especially in his admiring account of English liberty. In the eighteenth century, publishers in London and Edinburgh printed excerpts on the English system of government as free-standing pamphlets – the "essential Montesquieu" for British subjects. Anglophone readers, statesmen, and scholars have tended to see Montesquieu's accounts of the separation of powers, judicial independence, federalism, and limited government as his chief contributions to the science of law and politics.[23] Indeed, it is on the basis of

---

[22] *The Spirit of the Laws* is a work written not only for men of letters, but also for men of political action. Montesquieu modestly notes that *The Spirit of the Laws* "would not be useless in the education of young princes, and would perhaps be worth more to them than vague exhortations to govern well, to be great princes, to make their subjects happy – which is the same thing as exhorting a man who does not know the first propositions of Euclid to resolve some nasty geometry problems" (*MP* 1864). There is significant anecdotal evidence to support the view that Montesquieu hoped that his work would be read in the royal palaces of Europe. See Robert Shackleton, *Montesquieu: A Critical Biography* (Oxford University Press, 1961), 62, 121, 366; Montesquieu à Guasco, March 28, 1748, Nagel 3:1112–14; Montesquieu à Charles-Edouard, March 1748, Nagel 3:1114; Montesquieu à l'abbé Venuti, July 22, 1749, Nagel 3:1247–50; Montesquieu à Guasco, 1753, Nagel 3:1471–2.

[23] See, illustratively, James Madison, Alexander Hamilton, and John Jay, *The Federalist Papers*, ed. Clinton Rossiter (New York: Mentor, 1999); Herbert Storing, ed., *The Complete Anti-Federalist* (University of Chicago Press, 1981), vol. 1, 378; Thomas Jefferson, *Political Writings*, eds. Joyce Appleby and Terence Ball (Cambridge University

these contributions that he has been regarded the father of modern constitutional design – or, more reverently, "the oracle."[24]

On the continent, readers have never neglected Montesquieu's constitutionalism altogether, but many of his most influential legatees concentrated upon another element of his thought: his account of the relationship of law and politics to the mores, manners, customs, history, and "general spirit" of a people. Both Rousseau and Tocqueville drew inspiration from Montesquieu's account of the "relations" of the laws to social and cultural factors, and Hegel believed he had learned from Montesquieu's "immortal work" to judge and justify institutions not merely in the abstract, but on the basis of their coherence with historical circumstances.[25] Later, Émile Durkheim, Louis Althusser, and Raymond Aron would similarly emphasize this crucial element of Montesquieu's political science.[26]

Recent scholarship on *The Spirit of the Laws* and *Persian Letters* has often noted the centrality of this aspect of Montesquieu's thought. Larrère discusses Montesquieu's "critique de l'universel positif"; Dallmyr admires his "anti-Jacobinism"; Schaub highlights Montesquieu's unwillingness to formulate a "universally valid public law"; Kelley comments on his opposition to "abstract universalism"; Berlin notes his skepticism toward "universal solutions"; Lowenthal and Pangle remark upon

---

Press, 1999), 282–4; Kingsley Martin, *French Liberal Thought in the Eighteenth Century* (London: E. Benn., 1929); F.T.H. Fletcher, *Montesquieu and English Politics (1750–1800)* (London: Porcupine Press, 1939); John Plamenatz, *Man and Society: Machiavelli through Rousseau* (New York: McGraw-Hill, 1963); Anne Cohler, *Montesquieu's Comparative Politics and the Spirit of American Constitutionalism* (Lawrence, KS: University Press of Kansas, 1988); Harvey C. Mansfield, *Taming the Prince: The Ambivalence of the Executive Power* (Baltimore: John Hopkins University Press, 1993); Paul O. Carrese, *The Cloaking of Power: Montesquieu, Blackstone, and the Rise of Judicial Activism* (University of Chicago Press, 2003); Lee Ward, "Montesquieu on Federalism and Anglo-Gothic Constitutionalism," *Publius: The Journal of Federalism*, 37, no. 4 (2007), 551–7.

[24] Madison, *Federalist*, No. 47.

[25] Georg W. F. Hegel, "Scientific Ways of Treating Natural Law, Its Place in Moral Philosophy, and Its Relation to the Positive Sciences of Law," in *Natural Law*, trans. T. M. Knox (Philadelphia: University of Pennsylvania Press, 1975), 128–9; Paul N. Franco, *Hegel's Philosophy of Freedom* (New Haven, CT: Yale University Press, 1999), 136; Judith N. Shklar, *Freedom and Independence: A Study of the Political Ideas of Hegel's Phenomenology of Mind* (Cambridge University Press, 1976), ch. 4.

[26] Émile Durkheim, *Montesquieu and Rousseau: Forerunners of Sociology*, trans. Ralph Manheim (Ann Arbor, MI: University of Michigan Press, 1960); Louis Althusser, *Politics and History: Montesquieu, Rousseau, Hegel, and Marx*, trans. Ben Brewster (London: NLB, 1972), part 1; and Aron, *Main Currents in Sociological Thought*, vol. 1, chap. 1.

Montesquieu's opposition to Lockean universalism or Lockean doctrinarism; Ceaser foregrounds Montesquieu's attention to "knowledge of place."[27] Despite differences in nomenclature, each of these scholars refers to the same practical implication of Montesquieu's political sociology. We may call this aspect of Montesquieu's thought *critique of political universalism*, or positively denominated, his *political particularism*. The modifier "political" is an important one, because I mean to draw a bright line between moral universalism and political universalism. Like many early modern liberals, Montesquieu is a moral universalist: he believes that there are foundational moral truths binding upon all peoples in all times.[28] But he is not a political universalist: he denies the possibility of constructing, according to rational or otherwise authoritative principles, a single model of government that is best for all times and all peoples.[29]

---

[27] Catherine Larrère, *Actualité de Montesquieu* (Paris: Presses de Sciences Po, 1999), 34–9; Fred Dallmyr, "Montesquieu's *Persian Letters*: A Timely Classic," in *Montesquieu and His Legacy*, ed. Rebecca E. Kingston (Albany, NY: State University of New York Press, 2008), 239; Schaub, *Erotic Liberalism*, xi; Donald R. Kelley, *The Human Measure: Social Thought in the Western Legal Tradition* (Cambridge, MA: Harvard University Press, 1990), 219–22; Berlin, "Montesquieu," 181, 187; David Lowenthal, "Montesquieu," in *History of Political Philosophy*, eds. Leo Strauss and Joseph Cropsey (University of Chicago Press, 1987), 534; Pangle, *Montesquieu's Philosophy of Liberalism*, 21; James W. Ceaser, *Liberal Democracy and Political Science* (Baltimore: Johns Hopkins University Press, 1992), 61; Paul A. Rahe, *Montesquieu and the Logic of Liberty: War, Religion, Commerce, Climate, Terrain, Technology, Uneasiness of Mind, the Spirit of Political Vigilance, and the Foundations of the Modern Republic* (New Haven, CT: Yale University Press, 2009), 214ff. Dennis Rasmussen and Aurelian Craiutu foreground this element in their discussions of Montesquieu's "moderate" or "pragmatic" liberalism. See Aurelian Craiutu, *A Virtue for Courageous Minds: Moderation in French Political Thought, 1748–1830* (Princeton University Press, 2012), ch. 1; Dennis C. Rasmussen, *The Pragmatic Enlightenment: Recovering the Liberalism of Hume, Smith, Montesquieu, and Voltaire* (Cambridge University Press, 2014), ch. 2.

[28] Denying any universal moral foundations for politics is, of course, one way to avoid political universalism. Liberal "non-foundationalism" or "anti-foundationalists" have made the case for doing just that, and Montesquieu has even been called a non-foundationalist. But Montesquieu was, as I will argue, a moral universalist, and this fact makes his political particularism even more interesting and perhaps more impressive. See Chapter 3.

[29] As we will consider, it is fair to say that Montesquieu's "opposition to despotism indicates his subscription to a kind of universalism." Diana J. Schaub, "Of Believers and Barbarians: Montesquieu's Enlightened Toleration," in *Skepticism and the Origins of Toleration*, ed. Alan Levine (Lanham, MD: Lexington Books, 1999), 238. But here Catherine Larrère's distinction between a *universel positif* and a *universel negative* is instructive: Montesquieu is a critic of the former but not the latter. Larrère, *Actualité de Montesquieu*, 34–9. Species of "positive" political universalism were not difficult to find in Montesquieu's day. For example, the appearance of flexibility in Lockean political

This element of Montesquieu's thought is sometimes reduced to his speculations concerning the political effects of climate: despotism where it's hot, liberty where it's not. But his treatment of climate, eye-catching though it may be, constitutes just one part of his larger discussion of the relationship of laws to various cultural, social, environmental, and economic factors in a country. In his treatment of these various "relations" – which "together form THE SPIRIT OF THE LAWS" – Montesquieu propounds a principle of political sociology: the aptness of a given law depends, in part, on its coherence with the characteristics of the people and place it governs (*EL* 1.1.3). It is therefore "very unlikely that the laws of one nation can suit another." Legislators and state-builders ought to craft political and civil laws that "relate well" to the characteristics of their particular country, he argues.

Montesquieu's political particularism occupies a central place in his philosophical and scientific project. It is enshrined in the very title of his book. Unlike Plato and Cicero before him, he writes not the *Laws* or *On the Laws*, but *On the Spirit of the Laws*. The title contains an allusion with a distinction. The *spirit* of the laws, he explains, is formed by the relations of the laws to the physical and moral aspects of a country (*EL* 1.1.3). On Montesquieu's view, these relations or spirit, and not merely the laws themselves, must constitute the chief concern of statesmen and theorists.

He was certainly not the first legal writer to speak of the *esprit* of law. The usage goes back at least to the old civilian notion of the *mens legum* (commonly translated *esprit des loix*) or *ratio legis*, a concept important to neo-Bartolist legal science in the late seventeenth century.[30] But while these earlier efforts sought to excavate the *esprit* understood as the

thought is belied by juridical arguments pointing definitively toward political forms with popularly elected legislatures. See Chapter 3. Moreover, as Eric Nelson has recently shown, even the broader republican tradition had fallen, after 1650, into the grip of a "republican exclusivism" present in the work of Milton, Harrington, and Sidney, traceable to a particular reading of the Old Testament. See Eric Nelson, *The Hebrew Republic* (Cambridge, MA: Harvard University Press, 2010), ch. 1; *EL* 6.29.19; 2.11.6, p. 166. Consider also Montesquieu, *Réflexions sur la monarchie universelle en Europe* (1734) in VF 2:339–64.

[30] See Donald R. Kelley, "Louis Le Caron Philosophe," in *Philosophy and Humanism: Renaissance Essays in Honor of Paul Oskar Kristeller*, ed. Edward P. Mahoney (Leiden, The Netherlands: Brill, 1976), 30–49, esp. 47; Donald R. Kelley, "'Second Nature': The Idea of Custom in European Law, Society, and Culture," in *The Transmission of Culture in Early Modern Europe*, eds. Anthony Grafton and Ann Blair (Philadelphia: University of Pennsylvania Press, 1990), 150–3; Zachary S. Schiffman, *The Birth of the Past* (Baltimore: Johns Hopkins University Press, 2011), 183–200.

universal and universalizable rational core of Roman law or French law, Montesquieu seeks to unearth the *esprit* understood as relations that confirm the particularity and situated character of all law. Here, as elsewhere, he is compelled to give "new meanings" to old words (*EL* "Author's FW").

The line of argument that leads Montesquieu to these relations commences in the third chapter of Book 1 of *Spirit*. Here, with little fanfare, he raises the question of the best political order: into whose hands should we place the "strength of the whole society" (*EL* 1.1.3)? The question soon takes on a more distinctive tincture: which government is most "in conformity with nature"? Following Algernon Sidney and John Locke, Montesquieu first refutes the argument from paternal power for the rule of one alone.[31] When Sidney and Locke had dispensed with this argument, each turned to his central political principle – consent as the basis of legitimacy.[32] Once Montesquieu has similarly dispensed with the argument for paternal power, he turns to his central political principle. It is not rule by consent. He writes, "It is better to say that the government most in conformity with nature is the one whose particular arrangement best relates to the disposition of the people for whom it is established" (*EL* 1.1.3). In response to his own question, Montesquieu refuses to say whether any particular form of government is "most natural." Here he will offer no rationalistic answer that abstracts from the diversity and complexity of the empirical world. He offers instead what we can only describe as a meta-answer. The naturalness of a particular government can be judged only as we compare its arrangement with the disposition of a particular people.[33]

Both social contract theorists and theorists of paternal power had appealed to the standard of "conformity with nature" in judging regimes. Like Locke and Sidney before him, Montesquieu accepts that the legislator must take his bearings from nature, but he sheds their narrow conceptions of the nature of nature. Locke understood consensual political orders to be in conformity with nature because such orders best reflect

---

[31] Montesquieu was a close reader of both Locke and Sidney, and he distills Sidney's own argument against paternal power. See *EL* 2.11.6 and *LP* 91; Algernon Sidney, *Discourses Concerning Government,* ed. Thomas G. West (Indianapolis: Liberty Fund, 1996), 2.5.

[32] John Locke, *Two Treatises of Civil Government,* ed. Ian Shapiro (New Haven, CT: Yale University Press, 2003), §6–7; Sidney, *Discourses Concerning Government,* 2.

[33] The French *disposition* can refer to disposition in the sense of character or temperament, but it can also refer to arrangement or layout. The term can encompass moral causes (mores, manners, religion) as well as physical causes such as geography and terrain.

the universal moral facts of natural equality and natural freedom. Nature was uniform. But here Montesquieu invokes a different conception of nature: nature is a manifold. A government that is according to nature must strive to reflect moral facts rooted in our common human nature. But crucially, it must also reflect what is distinctively "natural" to each nation in the sense of second nature or disposition – what Jean Bodin, before Montesquieu, had called "the nature of each nation."[34] This view lies at the core of Montesquieu's political particularism.

He does not here deny the existence, in theory, of a common standard for judging regimes. He tells his reader that it is "better to say" that the most natural government is the one that relates well to the disposition of the people (*EL* 1.1.3).[35] It is less dangerous to say this than to answer the question of natural government in a way comparable to Locke or Sidney's response. To propose theories of "natural government" without attending to the diversity of human societies threatens to give license to unwise and, as we will see, effectively illiberal projects of legal and political universalism. Montesquieu will praise a particular kind of politics in *Spirit*; but as the work opens, he declines to follow his predecessors in outlining any universal prescriptions.[36]

Yet the intended effect of Montesquieu's particularism is not simply to dissuade princes and would-be reformers from initiating legal and political change. Rather he aims to help them to discern when change is required, how it should be pursued, and what kind of knowledge is needed to pursue it beneficially. As he opens *The Spirit of the Laws*, he explains how the book will affect his readers' thinking on the subject of political change: "Each nation will find here the reasons for its maxims, and the consequence will naturally be drawn from them that changes can be proposed only by those who are born fortunate enough to fathom by a stroke of genius the whole of a state's constitution" (*EL*, "Pref."). We will find reasons for our maxims. But it seems that our maxims are not fully reasonable in the sense of being perfectly right or good, for in the same breath, Montesquieu speaks of proposing changes.[37] The reasons we will

---

[34] Jean Bodin, *Les Six livres de la République*, ed. Gérard Mairet (Paris: Livre du Poche, [1576] 1993), 4.7.

[35] "Montesquieu does not quite assert it," observes Mansfield. Mansfield, *Taming the Prince*, 220.

[36] This is consistent with Montesquieu's judgment that "the excess even of reason is not always desirable" (*EL* 2.11.6).

[37] Daniel Brewer, *The Enlightenment Past: Reconstructing Eighteenth-Century French Thought* (Cambridge University Press, 2011), 87; Leo Strauss, *Seminar on Montesquieu*

discover are explanations of how particular "moral" and "physical" causes account for or explain the character of particular laws. Diversity in law is not merely the effect of variation in the irrational fancies of men but rather arises, to a significant degree, in regular patterns from the diversity of such causes.[38] Understanding these "reasons" for our laws and their maxims, in this sense, will not lead us to dismiss all proposed changes to our "reasonable" institutions but will rather lead us to recognize that beneficial changes to fundamental laws can only be undertaken by those who can fathom by a "stroke of genius" the relation of the constitution to culture and place (*EL*, "Pref."). As Daniel Brewer rightly notes, "This intrinsic comprehensibility does not function as the acceptance of the status quo; instead it is the condition without which meliorative political intervention cannot be imagined."[39] From *The Spirit of the Laws*, reformers will naturally draw the conclusion that projects of political and legal transformation must be tailored to – and therefore limited by – the particular and distinctive nature, or second nature, of the people whose lot they hope to better.

Montesquieu aims to equip reformers, not merely to warn them. This crucial point becomes clear as we compare the character of his legal and political particularism with what J. G. A. Pocock has called the "theory of presumptive tradition."[40] Theorists of presumptive tradition hold that received customs and traditional institutions must be presumed good or right because they bear the implicit approval of history, of generations. The goodness of a custom can be inferred from its endurance over time. It lasts because it works, and it works because it suits the people and

---

II, spring 1966, ed. Thomas L. Pangle, last accessed April 30, 2018, https://leostrausscen ter.uchicago.edu/course/montesquieu-ii-spring-quarter-1966.

[38] Montesquieu's position contrasts sharply with that of John Locke and other modern natural law thinkers, who held that "the great part of the municipal laws of countries" are but the "the fancies and intricate contrivances of men, following contrary and hidden interests put into words." Locke, *Two Treatises*, 2.12. This explanation for diversity in law, if correct, would clear the way for designs of increasing legal uniformity; Montesquieu aims to show that it is a naïve explanation. See C. P. Courtney, "Montesquieu and Natural Law" in *Montesquieu's Science of Politics: Essays on The Spirit of Laws*, eds. David W. Carrithers, Michael A. Mosher, and Paul A. Rahe (Lanham, MD: Rowman & Littlefield, 2001), 41–68.

[39] Brewer, *The Enlightenment Past*, 87.

[40] Pocock attributes the theory of presumptive tradition to a line of political thinkers that includes Fortescue, Coke, and Burke. J. G. A. Pocock, *The Machiavellian Moment: Florentine Political Thought and the Atlantic Republican Tradition* (Princeton University Press, 2003), 15; J. G. A. Pocock, *Politics, Language, and Time: Essays on Political Thought and History* (University of Chicago Press, 1989), chs. 6 and 7.

circumstances. But why it suits them, we cannot say. Its suitability can "hardly be demonstrated." On this view, we can only say why we presume it to be good (i.e., that is has lasted). For there is no rational or scientific method of "proving that a nation has certain characteristics or that its laws suit those characteristics."[41] Consequently, the theory of presumptive tradition yields a stout conservatism. What is important for our purposes is to recognize that this practical conclusion depends upon the view that reason or science is not capable of accounting for particulars – for example, what is distinctively French, English, or Dutch. But Montesquieu's project consists in explaining the *esprit* of the laws – the mind or rationale of laws. That is, he attempts to provide a rational, scientific account of why particular laws, institutions, and customs exist here but not there. This science has an effect similar to that of presumptive tradition: it diminishes our attraction to "political geometricians" and hasty revolutionaries. But unlike theories of presumptive tradition, the aim of Montesquieu's particularistic science of politics is to discover the kind of knowledge needful for reformers to enact beneficial changes in law and politics, changes suited to a people's distinctive character and circumstances.

LIBERALISM AND THE PROBLEM OF UNIVERSAL POLITICS

Despite Montesquieu's openness to political reform, readers from the eighteenth century to the present have puzzled over the relationship between this political particularism and the other hemisphere of his thought, his normative liberal constitutionalism. Montesquieu famously assails despotic government, defends principled limits on state power, and articulates, for the first time, the modern doctrine of the separation of powers. He argues for religious toleration and the right of free speech; he champions the rights of criminal due process to insure the rule of law; he condemns slavery; he favors the promotion of commerce, both for the material abundance it produces and for its effects upon "destructive" prejudices; he rejects virtue or human perfection as the end of politics, turning instead to a politics of security and liberty. Should we understand Montesquieu's political particularism as an aberration from this robust liberal constitutionalism? Is his liberalism at best an ill-fitting addendum

---

[41] Pocock, *The Machiavellian Moment*, 15.

to his particularistic science of politics? Or do these two great moments of his political philosophy somehow form a coherent whole?

Some of Montesquieu's near-contemporaries judged his rejection of legal and political universalism in politics to be grossly inconsistent with his celebrated moral attacks on despotic government. Such frustration was especially common among the generation of radical thinkers active during the period of the French Revolution, some of whom perceived in Montesquieu's work a neglect of universal justice. The marquis de Condorcet, pseudo-Helvétius, and Antoine Destutt de Tracy – the latter with the backing of Thomas Jefferson – protested the excessive homage Montesquieu seemed to pay to backwards customs and unjust prejudices.[42] According to a letter of pseudo-Helvétius, Montesquieu had "compromis[ed] with prejudice" as an impressionable young man compromises "with certain females, who, although advanced in years, have still some pretensions, and by whom he wishes to be considered polite and well-bred."[43] Against Montesquieu's approach, Condorcet famously asserts the principle of invariability in legislation:

As truth, reason, justice, the rights of man, the interests of property, of liberty, of security, are in all places the same; we cannot discover why all the provinces of a state, or even all states, should not have the same civil and criminal laws, and the same laws relative to commerce. *A good law should be good for all men.* A true proposition is true everywhere. Those laws which appear as if it were necessary they should be different in different countries, or exacted on objects which should not be regulated by general laws, consist for the most part of commercial regulations, or are founded on prejudices and habits which should be extinguished, and one of the best means of doing so, is to cease from giving them the countenance of the laws.[44]

---

[42] Antoine Louis Claude Destutt de Tracy, *A Commentary and Review of Montesquieu's Spirit of Laws, To Which Are Annexed, "Observations on the Thirty-First Book," by the Late M. Condorcet, and Two Letters of Helvétius, On the Merits of the Same Work,* trans. Thomas Jefferson (Philadelphia: William Duane, 1811); James F. Jones, "Montesquieu and Jefferson Revisited: Aspects of a Legacy," *The French Review,* 51, no. 4 (1978), 577–85.

[43] Claude-Adrien Helvétius, "Letters of Helvétius, Addressed to President Montesquieu and M. Saurin, on Perusing the Manuscript of *The Spirit of Laws,*" in Destutt de Tracy, *Commentary,* 285.

[44] Jean Antoine Nicolas de Caritat, marquis de Condorcet, "Observations on the Twenty-Ninth Book of the *Spirit of Laws,* " in Destutt de Tracy, *Commentary,* 274. See also: Jean Antoine Nicolas de Caritat, marquis de Condorcet, "Essay on the Constitution and Functions of the Provincial Assemblies," in *Condorcet, Selected Writings,* ed. Keith Barker (Indianapolis: Bobbs-Merrill, 1976), 86; and J. B. L. Crevier, *Observations sur le livre de l'Esprit des lois* (Desaint et Saillant, 1764), 4. For a similar, later formulation, see William Godwin, *An Enquiry Concerning Political Justice* (London: Robinson, 1793),

The "spirit of the legislator" should be that of justice, not of moderation as Montesquieu had erroneously asserted in *The Spirit of the Laws* (*EL* 6.29.1).[45] And where is Montesquieu's standard for judging the justice of positive laws? "Why has he not laid down some principles which would enable us to discriminate among the laws flowing from a legitimate power, and those which are unjust, and those with are conformable to justice?" asks Condorcet.[46] Destutt de Tracy regrets that Montesquieu has not treated the question of good government "theoretically" nor "establish[ed] *à priori,* the principles of a truly free, legal, and peaceable constitution"; this would have required him to write from position more "elevated and retired" from the empirical world.[47]

These thinkers' collective ire was not merely directed at the theoretical deficiencies of *The Spirit of the Laws*. They also detected that Montesquieu's approach, when applied to France, seemed to support not the radical transformation of the *ancien régime* but rather its reformation along traditional constitutionalist lines. Montesquieu seemed to prescribe a modest regimen of pruning, grafting, and hybridizing. They concluded that he had failed to demonstrate that a commitment to legal and political particularism could be joined with a robust respect for the universal demands of human liberty and political justice. For such thinkers, a commitment to the natural rights of man requires acquiescence in a politics of universalism and rationalism – "politics as the crow flies," in Oakeshott's memorable formulation.[48]

Bemusement at Montesquieu's marriage of liberalism with a critique of political universalism is not an affliction peculiar to the writers of the radical Enlightenment. Indeed the perceived dissonance proved too much for some twentieth-century interpreters to abide: George Sabine concluded that these hemispheres of Montesquieu's *Spirit of the Laws* had "no intrinsic relationship" to one another, and Carl Becker asserted that Montesquieu's work was merely a series of "disconnected essays" on various themes, with its essays on liberty scarcely linked to the essays

---

182: "Truth is in reality single and uniform. There must in the nature of things be one best form of government which all intellects, sufficiently roused from the slumber of savage ignorance, will be irresistibly incited to approve." Cf. David Williams, *Condorcet and Modernity* (Cambridge University Press, 2004), on Condorcet's pragmatism.

[45] This was no minor criticism, for Montesquieu avers that he has written *The Spirit of the Laws* "only to prove" that the spirit of the legislator must be moderation (*EL* 6.29.1).

[46] Condorcet, "Observations," 263.   [47] Destutt de Tracy, *Commentary,* 108.

[48] Michael Oakeshott, "Rationalism in Politics," in *Rationalism in Politics and Other Essays,* ed. Timothy Fuller (Indianapolis: Liberty Fund, 1991).

on political sociology.[49] More recently this approach has been distilled into the claim that there are "two Montesquieus," a pluralistic political sociologist and a prescriptive liberal constitutionalist.[50] Many other scholarly works on Montesquieu have simply not ventured an account of whether and how the two great hemispheres of his political thought cohere.[51]

The notion that Montesquieu's liberalism stands in tension with his political particularism is bolstered by a broader historical narrative, only recently subject to sustained critical scrutiny, that portrays Enlightenment liberalism as essentially universalistic and heedless of the ways in which variety of place, history, and culture must complicate the instantiation of abstract principles. Take as representative Jürgen Habermas's claim that "the project of modernity formulated in the eighteenth century by philosophers of the Enlightenment consisted in their efforts to develop … universal morality and law," or Terry Eagleton's judgment that the "bourgeois ideology" of Enlightenment liberalism has "never really been able to reconcile difference and identity, the particular and the

---

[49] George H. Sabine, *A History of Political Theory*, 3rd edn. (New York: Holt, Rinehart, and Winston, 1961), 552; Carl L. Becker, *The Heavenly City of the Eighteenth-Century Philosophers* (New Haven, CT: Yale University Press, 1932), 113–14.

[50] David William Bates, *States of War: Enlightenment Origins of the Politics* (New York: Columbia University Press, 2012), 134–9.

[51] Isaiah Berlin and Sheldon Wolin gesture toward such an account. In his lecture on Montesquieu, Berlin suggests that Montesquieu's constitutionalism and "anti-uniformism" share a "common libertarian purpose" (Berlin, "Montesquieu," 198-200.). On his view, Montesquieu's constitutionalism is rooted in a rejection of the desire for uniformity ("monism"); this desire for uniformity is the hallmark of both despotism and political universalism. Sheldon Wolin, *The Presence of the Past* (Baltimore: Johns Hopkins University Press, 1989), 100–10, similarly suggests that Montesquieu's political sociology and his liberal constitutionalism are philosophically unified under the banner of respect for diversity and resistance to "Cartesian reason." Unfortunately, neither Berlin nor Wolin develop these highly suggestive points through analysis of the text and argument of *The Spirit of the Laws*. More recently, Céline Spector, *Montesquieu: Liberté, droit et histoire* (Paris: Michalon Éditions, 2010), esp. 275–7, has explored the continuity between the principle of suitability and the principle of political moderation in *Spirit*, arguing that Montesquieu's critiques both of universalism and despotism arise from a deeper rejection of "a political rationality that desires to reduce … plurality to uniformity." Similarly, Carrese's *Democracy in Moderation* foregrounds the principle of moderation as the link between constitutionalism, philosophical balance or blending, and prudent statesmanship in the thought of Montesquieu, Tocqueville, and the American Founders. These efforts to understand the unifying themes of Montesquieu's project are complementary to the suggestions in Wolin and Berlin, as well as to my own approach.

universal."[52] Important studies by Sankar Muthu and Dennis Rasmussen have begun to undermine such common characterizations.[53] But these recent studies notwithstanding, the widespread narrative of a universalistic, rationalistic Enlightenment has seeped into the historiographical groundwater, predisposing us to view Montesquieu's particularistic sensibility as out-of-step with his status as an Enlightenment liberal.

We must also acknowledge that one truly towering figure of the eighteenth century agreed that *Spirit* seems to work at cross-purposes with itself, and his claim can be attributed neither to partisan animus nor to careless reading, for he is the work's author. In his *Pensées*, Montesquieu likens his masterwork to a "big machine" with great gears (*MP* 2092). As one observes "wheels that turn in opposite directions," it does indeed appear that the machine is "going to destroy itself." But "those pieces, which seem at first to be destroying each other, combine together for the proposed purpose." Montesquieu wrote these words in response to the abbé de la Porte's fault-finding commentary, a work that purports to identify various contradictions in the *Spirit*. But I submit that Montesquieu's statement serves not only as a guide to wrestling with specific and relatively minor contradictions but also as an invitation to explore the relationship between two principal elements of his thought that seem to move "in opposite directions." Though few will deny that Montesquieu's liberal constitutionalism and political particularism stand

---

[52] Jürgen Habermas, "Modernity versus Postmodernity," in *Modernity: After Modernity*, ed. Malcolm Waters (London: Routledge, 1999), 11; Terry Eagleton, "Nationalism, Irony, and Commitment," in *Nationalism, Colonialism, and Literature* (Minneapolis, MN: University of Minnesota Press, 1990), 9. John Gray similarly ascribes to Enlightenment liberalism the intention of constructing a "universal civilization" modeled on rational, secular, and cosmopolitan principles. Gray sees *modus vivendi* liberalism as a particularistic alternative, but he declares that "Enlightenment liberalism" offered a prescription for a universal regime. John Gray, *Enlightenment's Wake: Politics and Culture at the Close of the Modern Age* (New York: Routledge, 1995); John Gray, *Two Faces of Liberalism* (New York: New Press, 2000), 2. According to Stephen Toulmin, Enlightenment moral and political philosophy ignored "the particular, concrete, timely, and local details of everyday human affairs." Stephen Toulmin, *Cosmopolis: The Hidden Agenda of Modernity* (New York: Free Press, 1995), 142. See also Brian Barry, *Culture and Equality: An Egalitarian Critique of Multiculturalism* (Cambridge, MA: Harvard University Press, 2002), 11–12; Duncan Ivison, *Postcolonial Liberalism* (Cambridge University Press, 2002), ch. 2; Robert Kagan, *The Return of History and the End of Dreams* (New York: Vintage Books, 2009), 102–5.

[53] Rasmussen, *The Pragmatic Enlightenment*; Sankar Muthu, *Enlightenment against Empire* (Princeton University Press, 2003). The characterization of Enlightenment thought as politically universalistic is not wholly without basis, as, for example, our discussion of Condorcet and pseudo-Helvétius suggests.

as his major contributions to the modern political theory, we lack an extended account of the relationship of these two central teachings.

This book provides such an account. Montesquieu's liberal political philosophy and his critique of universalism in politics form a unified project. The study's interpretative claim is not merely that these two elements coincide in the mind of one influential Enlightenment liberal; this much is obvious. More significantly, I aim to show that Montesquieu's critique of political universalism depends upon several distinctive features of his liberalism and shares with it a common end, the politics of liberty. By its nature, Montesquieu's liberalism invites and even demands a careful consideration of culture, place, and circumstance; it resists the temptation to formulate generalizable political solutions and to apply such solutions mechanically. So far from being an ill-fitting pragmatic amendment or addendum to his politics of liberty, Montesquieu's particularistic approach to political science and statesmanship is essential to it. Here we may aptly appropriate Montesquieu's own words: these "pieces, which seem at first to be destroying each other, combine together for the proposed purpose" (*MP* 2092). While an appreciation of this unity is crucial for understanding *The Spirit of the Laws* and forming a just appraisal of Enlightenment political thought more broadly, this encounter with Montesquieu has, as I have suggested, timely implications for liberal political theory and liberal statecraft stretching beyond the domains of textual interpretation and intellectual history.

OUTLINE OF THE BOOK

The argument of the book proceeds in two movements. I first consider the ancient and modern sources of Montesquieu's particularistic science of law and politics (Chapters 1 and 2). I show how understanding his engagement with classical political science and French legal humanism serves to illuminate the liberal purposes of his particularism in unexpected ways. The book then turns to the substance and structure of Montesquieu's liberalism (Chapters 3–7). I argue that three features of his liberal theory steel it against the appeal of universalism in politics. First, I demonstrate that Montesquieu's regime pluralism is the key feature on the institutional side of his liberal theory that renders his normative thought consonant with his political particularism (Chapter 3). Then, turning to the cultural-psychological side of his political thought, I show how his liberalism avoids two theoretical features that incline some, though not all, species of liberal theory toward an embrace of universalism in politics. These features include a minimalist conception of the liberal self and a formalistic notion of liberty. Not only do we find these features missing from Montesquieu's conceptual apparatus, but we observe in their stead a rich account of liberal culture (Chapters 4–6) and a psychological conception of liberty (Chapter 7) that call his liberalism into partnership with a politics of place. From this analysis emerges a liberalism chary of universalism in politics, open to institutional variety, alive to the preconditions of a humane and moderate politics of liberty, alert to the moral and practical problems that confront liberal reformers and revolutionaries, and reconciled to the facts of contingency and diversity in and across political communities. It is a liberalism worth recovering, as I contend in the Conclusion.

Chapter 1, "Montesquieu and Classical Particularism," argues that Montesquieu appropriates the political particularism of ancient political science and then explicitly turns this sensibility against the classical republic of virtue in service of modern regimes of liberty. Montesquieu draws conspicuously upon Plato, Aristotle, and Cicero – classical republicans, as he understands them – in order to develop his science of the "relations" of laws to moral and physical causes. But he also deftly employs the principles gleaned from ancient political science to dethrone the Ancients' substantive political ideal. Appealing to the insights of classical political particularism, he suggests that the antique republic of virtue is outmoded, unsuited to modern European states, and incompatible with the character of modern peoples. So far from being at odds with his liberalism, Montesquieu's political particularism thus clears away the vestiges of classical republicanism to make way for modern constitutional government. This account of Montesquieu's use of ancient sources brings into focus the liberal purposes of his particularistic art of politics.

With similar effect, Chapter 2, "Montesquieu and Humanist Constitutionalism," argues that while scholars often situate *The Spirit of the Laws* in the theoretical stream originating in Hobbes's *Leviathan* and flowing through Locke's *Second Treatise*, we can better understand Montesquieu's merger of normative liberalism with a particularistic art of politics when we view his work in the context of sixteenth and early seventeenth-century French constitutionalism. I turn to interlocking debates among jurists and legal historians of this period over the status of Roman law and the history of the French constitution. Though a century separates these original controversies from Montesquieu's own work, the stagnancy of French constitutional theory during the seventy-year reign of Louis XIV ensured that they would function as the most important touchstones of a revived French constitutionalism in the eighteenth century. I sketch the remarkable ways in which humanist constitutionalism of this period anticipates Montesquieu's approach. Sixteenth-century humanist constitutionalism defends its case against royal absolutism on the basis of appeals to the peculiarities of time and place – appeals to what is our own, homegrown, and customary. A set of claims about the wisdom and aptness of legal and institutional variety underwrite the constitutionalist or protoconstitutionalist discourse of this time. By contrast, sixteenth-century advocates of absolutism in France depended regularly upon abstract rational and theological argument, universal law (that is, a putatively universal Roman law), and the appeal of legal uniformity. As a jurist and careful student of French legal history, Montesquieu was well acquainted with these debates, and reading *Spirit* against this backdrop, we can better understand why its author saw no theoretical incongruity in his embrace of liberal constitutionalism, on the one hand, and rejection of universal politics, on the other.

The book then turns to Montesquieu's liberal political theory itself. I proceed by exploring three features of Montesquieu's liberalism that incline his thought in the direction of political particularism and allow us to account for the unity of the project.

Chapter 3, "Regime Pluralism," argues that Montesquieu's liberalism is by its nature regime-pluralistic. A descriptive and prescriptive account of free and moderate government emerges in *The Spirit of the Laws*, and the liberty and moderation at the heart of this account are attainable within a wide variety of regime types. The chapter opens with a consideration of the moral foundations of Montesquieu's political thought and demonstrates that these foundations, while genuinely universal, do not guide us toward any particular regime. I then turn to his two books on liberty – Books 11 and 12 – and advance three interdependent lines of argument. First, I show that Montesquieu explicitly presents his conception of liberty as a replacement for regime-specific conceptions of the same. He means to bypass the old and unfruitful quarrel between monarchists and republicans, each acclaiming their regime the exclusive home of liberty. Next, I argue that Montesquieu's account of the free constitution of England does not put other political forms to shame. Rather, the principles of limit, balance, and complexity illustrated in the English example may penetrate a variety of regime types, promoting liberty or at least a "spirit of liberty." Here I am especially keen to challenge both narrowly monarchical and narrowly republican readings of his thought, each of which have been forcefully restated of late. Finally, I show that

Montesquieu's underappreciated second book on liberty indicates the compatibility of liberalized criminal law – a key element of free government – with republics, monarchies, and mixed regimes alike. Book 12's treatment of criminal law intentionally sidelines the contest of regimes and concentrates the reader's attention upon a mode of liberal reform distinct from constitutional renovation. Taken together, these considerations point definitively toward a regime pluralist liberalism, a liberalism wholly consistent with Montesquieu's critique of universal politics.

As the focus shifts from the institutional to the cultural-psychological side of Montesquieu's political thought in Chapters 4–7, I proceed by exploring Montesquieu's replacements for two theoretical features that will, *ceteris paribus*, incline a liberal theory in the direction of political universalism: a minimalist conception of the liberal self and a formalistic conception of liberty. Both features are absent from *The Spirit of the Laws*, and in their place, we find conceptions of the liberal culture (Chapters 4–6) and political liberty (Chapter 7) that, together with his regime pluralism, inoculate Montesquieu's liberalism against the contagion of universal politics. The balance of the study addresses these salutary substitutions in his thought.

Montesquieu's liberalism is not marred by a minimalist account of the "liberal self," a theoretical feature that can skew liberal theory toward political universalism. When it appears, such minimalism may take a variety of forms. In popular political discourse in the United States, as we observed earlier, one periodically encounters the claim that liberal selves come from the hand of Nature. For example, some assert that mankind possesses a natural "love of liberty" sufficient to sustain free institutions.[54] Montesquieu himself suggests that "*l'amour des hommes pour la liberté*" is part of human nature (*EL* 1.5.14), but, tellingly, he floats this idea only in order to assert forthwith that this love of liberty is insufficient to make free and moderate government universal, or even common. Moderate government is a "masterpiece of legislation," requiring both a constitution of tempered and balanced powers and a suitable disposition within a nation. But despotism, he observes, "leaps to view," as it requires only the universal passion of fear to sustain itself. On this account, if any regime is the "default setting" of nature, it is despotic government (*MP* 831, 892).

---

[54] See fns. 20 and 21.

Minimalist accounts of the liberal self also take more sophisticated forms. One well-known version posits rational self-interest as the only characteristic needful for a people in maintaining a liberal constitutional order. This notion appears most famously in the form of Kant's assurance that "the problem of setting up a [constitutional republic] can be solved even by a nation of devils (so long as they possess understanding)."[55] Inasmuch as it suggests that cultural or moral differences are irrelevant to the task of state-building, this view naturally lends itself to universalism in political theory.[56] While Kant refers to the very system of separation of powers that Montesquieu first theorized, the latter never taught that free and moderate government relies merely upon the presence of rational self-interest and a "good organization," as Kant puts it.[57] Liberal political orders can do without the "thick" mores of self-denial that Montesquieu famously attributes to the classical republic, but Montesquieu did not regard liberal government as capable of floating on the mild breeze of rational self-interest alone. Like all regimes, the liberal constitutional orders he champions depend upon congenial habits, mores, manners, maxims of government, patterns in the household, qualities of character, orientations toward action, religious ideas, and feelings. (Montesquieu never tires of multiplying variables.) Talk of the "customs of a free people" comes easily to his lips, and he considers such customs as not only necessary for, but also constitutive of the liberty of a people (*EL* 3.19.25). Over three chapters (Chapters 4–6), I consider the elements of "liberal culture" as Montesquieu understood them.

Chapter 4 serves as an introduction to Montesquieu's notion of liberal culture. Here I attend especially to his broader theoretical insight into the permeability of the boundaries between political and nonpolitical spheres

---

[55] Immanuel Kant, "Perpetual Peace: A Philosophical Sketch," in *Kant's Political Writings*, trans. H. S. Reiss (Cambridge University Press, 1991), 112–13: "It only remains for me to create a good organization for the state, a task which is well within their capability, and to arrange it in such a way that their self-seeking energies are opposed to one another, each thereby neutralizing or eliminating the destructive effects of the rest." Some recent studies have sought to show that Kant's political thought was more sensitive to context than such passages suggest. See Elizabeth Ellis, *Kant's Politics: Provisional Theory for an Uncertain World* (New Haven, CT: Yale University Press, 2005); Jeanine Grenberg, *Kant and the Ethics of Humility* (Cambridge University Press, 2005); and Henry E. Allison, *Kant's Theory of Freedom* (New York: Routledge, 2002).

[56] See Curtis, *Defending Rorty*, 19.

[57] With good reason, Hegel contrasts Montesquieu's approach to law and culture with Kantian universal history as he criticizes the latter in "Scientific Ways of Treating Natural Law, Its Place in Moral Philosophy," 128–9.

of human activity. The patterns of authority, ideas, and moral habits forged in ostensibly "nonpolitical" domains wend their way into the political domain, and the inverse holds true as well. Therefore, liberal political philosophy requires the aid of a liberal political science that seeks to understand the relationship between free institutions and culture.[58] Normative theorizing and practical reform of political institutions must never be divorced from a serious consideration of dispositions of mind and heart by which liberty is sustained. Reserving for Chapters 5 and 6 any discussion of the complex intersection of commerce and religion in the formation and maintenance of liberal culture, Chapter 4 considers the roles of the household, national character forged by physical causes, and "maxims of government" in preparing a nation for political liberty.

Chapter 5, "Religion, Secularism, and Liberal Society," turns to the role of religion in shaping, or obstructing, the formation of mores, manners, and modes of thinking suitable to free and moderate political orders. I argue that Montesquieu's approach to this question balances recognition of the past and present abuses of religion with apprehension regarding the political costs of a future decline in religious belief. Against several prominent interpretations of his thought, this chapter shows that Montesquieu did not welcome commerce as an agent of religion's demise; he did not see the devitalization of European religion as a propitious condition for the growth of political liberty; and he did not regard a narrowly rationalist creed as the only one suitable to free peoples. Rather, on his account, religious faith may serve as a source of moral restraint that frees the state to govern mildly. Properly constituted, the spirit of religion may be advantageously joined to both the spirit of liberty and the spirit of commerce.

Chapter 6, "'The Spirit of Tolerance and Gentleness,'" addresses another dimension of religion's relationship to commerce in the formation of a liberal culture. From the time of his early *Dissertation on the Policy of the Romans in Religion* (1716), until he penned his late *Memoir on the Constitution* (1753), Montesquieu evinced a serious interest in understanding the "spiritual" (i.e., cultural and sentimental) sources of tolerance – or an "*esprit de tolérance* " as he puts it the *Dissertation* (VF 8:92).

---

[58] Consider in this connection Ceaser's case for a political science that comes to the aid of liberal democracy by examining "how existing political cultures in specific cases might be adjusted in the direction of the political culture that best supports the maintenance of the chosen regime," that is, liberal democracy. (Ceasar, *Liberal Democracy and Political Science*, 145).

He understood that a legal guarantee of religious toleration, a fundamental pillar of free government, was a dead letter in the absence of a general pattern of interpersonal tolerance. Three models of tolerant culture caught Montesquieu's analytical eye in the course of his reflections on this problem. These models include what we may call Roman, barbarian, and commercial tolerance. The first two are historical, while the third is a phenomenon "we see every day" (*EL* 4.20.1). By considering Montesquieu's appraisal of the historical models, one is better prepared to understand not only the depth of his long-standing concern with the spirit of tolerance, but also why he came to regard modern commerce as the most promising and suitable means of reviving the spirit of tolerance he had first admiringly observed in his study of Rome.

In this manner, Chapters 4–6 explore the major elements of Montesquieu's treatment of liberal culture, an alternative to minimalist accounts of the liberal self. This theoretical feature inclines his liberalism in the direction of political particularism.

Reflecting on a similarly portentous feature, Chapter 7, "Political Change and the Psychology of Liberty," considers the implications of Montesquieu's psychological account of liberty as an alternative to merely formalistic or institutional conceptions of liberty.[59] Consider, for example, John Locke's formalistic notion: "[F]reedom of men under government is, to have a standing rule to live by, common to every one of that society, and made by the legislative power erected in it."[60] Although Montesquieu, no less than Locke, champions the rule of law, the former would not recognize as complete this narrowly procedural and institutional definition of freedom: it lacks an account of the citizen's state of mind. On Montesquieu's view, liberty is not present *ipso facto* wherever liberal political institutions are set in order. Liberty is not, in other words, simply the condition of men living under the rule of law and a limited government of three distributed powers. Such a conception of

---

[59] The charge of "formalism" often appears in Marxist and postmodern critiques of liberalism. The idea, as Marx himself frames it in "On the Jewish Question," is that liberalism erroneously asserts that man is free when certain formal rules and procedures are followed, without asking whether he is substantively free. See also Wendy Brown, *Edgework: Critical Essays on Knowledge and Politics* (Princeton University Press, 2005), 57–8. While Montesquieu's understanding of freedom stands at some distance from Marx's notion of "human emancipation," it is far less vulnerable to the charge of formalism than other conceptions, for it requires us to consider the experience of actual citizens before judging them free. Knowing whether they live under a regime of rational rules and procedures is not enough to form that judgment, on Montesquieu's account.

[60] Locke, *Two Treatises*, 2.26.

liberty will orient a liberal theory toward political universalism inasmuch as it invites the inference that men can be made "free" simply by installing the proper formal institutions. Instead, in *The Spirit of the Laws*, Montesquieu offers a highly original psychological definition of "political liberty in a citizen": it is "a tranquility of spirit which comes from the opinion each one has of his security" (*EL* 2.11.6). When citizens are prepared to receive and sustain it, free government promotes liberty so understood; it expels the species of fear that dominates men's souls in despotic nations. But when a people is not culturally and socially prepared to receive free political institutions, direct attempts to erect such institutions will likely produce an experience of political disquiet and fear – a "tyranny of opinion" – comparable to the psychological experience of men and women in truly tyrannical states (*EL* 3.19.3). Under these conditions, free institutions are no longer liberal *in effect*, for they fail to yield the tranquility of spirit that constitutes the "liberty of the citizen." This train of reasoning constitutes what can best be described as a liberal critique of political universalism. When Montesquieu warns against untimely institutional reform in nations culturally unprepared for laws of liberty, he speaks from within the moral logic of his liberalism and not on behalf of prudential considerations external to it.

But, as Chapter 7 goes on to show, Montesquieu's anxiety concerning the moral costs of political universalism does not terminate in a quietistic embrace of the status quo. Rather, his liberal and particularistic sensibilities together shape a distinctive approach to political and cultural change in *Spirit*. Montesquieu warns that reformers must refrain from using coercive means to change the nation's culture directly, for such projects transgress the moral limits of state power. This concern flows directly from his liberal conception of the scope of law. Montesquieu therefore sketches the lineaments of an art of political change designed to avoid both resignation to despotism and illiberal cultural legislation. Reformers must seek to change mores and manners indirectly, not through penal legislation. His initial examples of such indirect change in Book 19 are somewhat obscure, but we must understand the subsequent books on commerce (20–22) as an application of this broader counsel. In other words, commerce emerges not merely as a technically efficient means of promoting political liberty, but crucially, as a potential path to liberal culture that does not require resort to illiberal methods of coercive cultural transformation. Only in this context can one understand the true moral and political significance of modern commerce in Montesquieu's thought. This counsel represents the constructive aspect of his particularistic theory of political change, and like the cautionary and critical dimension, it is underwritten by concerns at the center of his liberalism.

Thus Chapters 3–7 demonstrate the unity of Montesquieu's thought by showing how elements of his liberalism permit, demand, and even provide the moral grounding for a particularistic approach to statecraft.

The main task of this book is textual analysis and interpretation. But in the Conclusion, I step back from the interpretive argument and consider its implications for problems in Enlightenment historiography as well as contemporary political theory and practice. As a contribution to the intellectual history of the eighteenth century, this study deepens our understanding of the diversity within Enlightenment thought by allowing us to observe, at high resolution, how Montesquieu's liberalism succeeds in avoiding the will to uniformity in law and politics that is often said to define the Enlightenment project. Of course, liberalism is not only the bequest of the eighteenth century but also a living tradition, and this study of Montesquieu's work serves to highlight key weaknesses in contemporary liberal theory and statecraft. When theorists and practitioners avoid the question of liberalism's "dispositional" preconditions and rely upon formal political institutions and Nature to supply prefabricated liberal selves, they are far from the spirit of Montesquieuian liberalism. While recent efforts in liberal theory to remedy these deficiencies tend in the right direction, Montesquieu's approach represents a more complete and balanced account of the liberal disposition than those lately on offer.

The gravity of these theoretical challenges becomes most palpable as we consider what liberal statecraft stands to gain from a recovery of Montesquieuian liberalism. Resisting any simplistic "applications" of Montesquieu's thought, the Conclusion advances four midrange principles, inspired by this reading of *The Spirit of the Laws*, that may guide practitioners sobered by the global democratic stagnation but unwilling to assume a posture of political resignation in the face of authoritarian retrenchment, civil war, and terror.

I

Montesquieu and Classical Particularism

I admit my taste for the Ancients. That Antiquity enchants me, and I am always led to say with Pliny: 'It is to Athens that you are going. Respect their gods.'

Montesquieu, *MP* 110

Historians of political thought commonly situate Montesquieu in a tradition of protoliberalism that commences with Thomas Hobbes and runs through the work of John Locke and Algernon Sidney. But whatever his debts to this tradition, we cannot count Montesquieu's critique of political universalism among those elements of his thought inspired by his English predecessors, unless that inspiration took the form of instigating a correction. As Diana J. Schaub notes, rendering a judgment shared by others, Montesquieu's political science is "much less doctrinaire, legalistic, and universalistic than that of Hobbes and Locke," each of whom "sought to elaborate a universally valid public law – a constitutional law meant to be applicable to every possible society."[1] Yet it would be a mistake to conclude, on this basis, that Montesquieu's particularism is a political sensibility "without a mother," as he claims of *Spirit* as a whole. Montesquieu does not work without the benefit of muses as he implants the principle of variety into early liberal theory.

His particularism represents a self-conscious and selective recovery of important aspects of classical political science. Montesquieu undertakes this recovery not in order to resurrect the substantive political ideals of the

---

[1] Schaub, *Erotic Liberalism*, xi.

Ancients, but rather as a first step in the overcoming of the classical republican ideal. Drawing upon classical political science, as he understands it, Montesquieu constructs a particularistic framework in which contemporary instantiations of classical republican politics become unthinkable.[2] This critique of the antique republic is a vital element in his case for liberal constitutional government. In this respect, his particularism and liberalism appear as cobelligerents; they "combine together for the purpose proposed" (*MP* 2092). So far from being at odds with his commitment to modern regimes of liberty, Montesquieu's classically inspired political particularism is the most formidable weapon he wields against the classical republican model as he clears space for appropriately modern regimes. Thus, in contrast with earlier efforts and many later efforts, this species of Enlightenment liberalism was midwifed by a profoundly particularistic sensibility with an ancient lineage.

Montesquieu developed and deployed his political particularism in conversation with several ancient sources, including Plato's *Laws*, Aristotle's *Politics*, and Cicero's *On Duties*.[3] While scholars have often noted the affinities between Aristotelian and Montesquieuian political science,[4] extended analyses of the nature of Montesquieu's debts to and departures

---

[2] Here I follow many interpreters who have argued that Montesquieu aims to demonstrate the obsolescence of the classical republic. The innovation of this chapter is to show how he uses a modification of the Ancients' own principles to accomplish this task. On the former point, see illustratively Pangle, *Montesquieu's Philosophy of Liberalism*; Mansfield, *Taming the Prince*, ch. 9; Paul A. Rahe, *Republics Ancient and Modern: Classical Republicanism and the American Revolution* (Chapel Hill, NC: University of North Carolina Press, 1992), 440–4, 582–8; Pierre Manent, *The City of Man*, trans. Marc A. LePain (Princeton University Press, 1998), ch. 1–2; Annelien de Dijn, *French Political Thought from Montesquieu to Tocqueville: Liberty in a Levelled Society?* (Cambridge University Press, 2008), 28ff. Pangle, Mansfield, and Rahe suggest that Montesquieu saw the classical republic as not only anachronistic but also inherently deficient. Other interpreters contend that while Montesquieu viewed the classical republic as outmoded, he wistfully preferred it in the abstract to other regimes. See Robert Shackleton, "La genèse de l'Esprit des lois," *Revue d'histoire littéraire de la France* 52 (1952): 432; and Melvin Richter, "Comparative Political Analysis in Montesquieu and Tocqueville," *Comparative Politics* 1 (1969): 157. For a radically different account of Montesquieu's relationship to the Greek tradition, see Eric Nelson, *The Greek Tradition in Republic Thought* (Cambridge University Press, 2004), chs. 4–5.

[3] This is not to say that Montesquieu's political particularism was shaped exclusively through engagement with classical political science. See Chapter 2.

[4] See Aladair MacIntyre, *A Short History of Ethics: A History of Moral Philosophy from the Homeric to the Twentieth Century* (London: Routledge, 1967), 114; Judith Shklar, "Virtue in a Bad Climate: Good Men and Good Citizens in Montesquieu's *L'Esprit des lois*," in *Enlightenment Studies in Honor of Lester G. Crocker*, eds. Alfred Bingham and Virgil W. Topazio (Oxford: Voltaire Foundation, 1979), 315–28; Simone Goyard-Fabre,

from Aristotle are still lacking. As David W. Carrithers observes, no scholar to date has undertaken a thorough comparison of Aristotle and Montesquieu's political thought.[5] While this chapter makes no such boast, it moves beyond most existing accounts. Similarly, while *The Spirit of the Laws* contains more references to Plato's *Laws* than to any other work of political theory, whether ancient or modern, scholars have afforded little attention to the relationship between Plato's *Laws* and Montesquieu's "*Laws*," as he calls his magnum opus in notes.[6] Finally, while scholars have speculated concerning the nature of Montesquieu's engagement with Cicero's *On Duties* in his unfinished and now mostly

---

Montesquieu: La Nature, les lois, la liberté (Paris: Presses Universitaires France, 1993), 2–12; Bernard Manin, "Montesquieu et la politique moderne," in *Lectures de L'Esprit des lois*, eds. Thierry Hoquet and Céline Spector (Bordeaux: Presses universitaires de Bordeaux, 2004), 171–231; Larrère, "Montesquieu and Liberalism"; Thomas Pangle, *Aristotle's Teaching* (University of Chicago Press, 2013), 273; Carrese, *Democracy in Moderation*, 5–11. David Lowenthal, "Montesquieu and the Classics," in *Ancients and Moderns: Essays on the Tradition of Political Philosophy in Honor of Leo Strauss*, eds. Joseph Cropsey and Leo Strauss (New York: Basic Books, 1964), initially claims that Montesquieu revived the "comprehensive variety and prudent flexibility of Aristotle," but he ultimately concludes that Montesquieu's lopsided preference for modern regimes is responsible for "undermining the prudence he sought to restore to modern teaching" (259, 283). Vickie B. Sullivan, *Montesquieu and the Despotic Ideas of Europe: An Interpretation of the Spirit of the Laws* (University of Chicago Press, 2017), ch. 6, notes several points of confluence but focuses on Montesquieu's critique of Aristotle.

[5] David W. Carrithers, "Introduction: An Appreciation of *The Spirit of Laws* " in *Montesquieu's Science of Politics: Essays on* The Spirit of Laws, eds. David W. Carrithers, Michael A. Mosher, and Paul A. Rahe (Lanham, MD: Rowman & Littlefield, 2001), 34. My argument can be usefully contrasted with that of Carrithers, who contends that the "sociological orientation of Montesquieu's thought is a key aspect of his modernity" (12). He continues, "If [Montesquieu] had one foot in the modern world where his philosophy of law was concerned, however, he had the other foot in the ancient world. Juxtaposed to his sociological perspective on law making was a much more traditional conception of laws as mirroring justice writ large in the universe" (12–13). By contrast, I wish to suggest that Montesquieu owes to his engagement with the Ancients precisely that feature of his thought that Carrithers identifies as a seal of his modernity. See also Andrea Radasanu, "Montesquieu on Moderation, Monarchy and Reform," *History of Political Thought* 31 (2010): 285, who denies that Montesquieu's political science "embodies the spirit of Aristotelian prudence in eighteenth-century France." This chapter provides fresh support for this very view.

[6] For "my *Laws*," see *MP* 153, 205, 252. An exception is the careful treatment in Sullivan, *Montesquieu and the Despotic Ideas of Europe*, ch. 5, which focuses on Montesquieu's critique of Plato. A general discussion of Montesquieu's Platonism appears in Badreddine Kassem, *Décadence et absolutism dans l'oeuvre de Montesquieu* (Geneva: Librarie E. Droz, 1960), 189–203, although Kassem does not explore the points of convergence which I identify as crucial in this chapter. See also Lawrence M. Levin, *The Political Doctrine of Montesquieu's 'Esprit des Lois': Its Classical Background* (New York: Publications of the Institute of French Studies, Columbia University, 1936), 54ff.

lost *Treatise on Duties* (1725; VF 8.437–39, 503–22), I find the more vivid and overlooked imprint of Cicero's ethical theory upon Montesquieu's political science of national character in *The Spirit of the Laws*. Specifically, his reflections upon Cicero's four-personae theory shape his account of the general spirit, an important element of his particularistic theory of politics.

Of course, the differences between Montesquieu's political science and that of the Ancients are manifold, and this chapter does not seek to mute those differences. Even in the task of classifying regimes, Montesquieu's emphasis on each regime's animating passion contrasts sharply with Aristotle's emphasis upon a regime's intelligible claim to rule.[7] More profound still are the differences at the level of moral and metaphysical foundations, as Montesquieu's liberalism entails a rejection of the primacy of virtue for politics and political science. But in considering what he retains from the Ancients – namely, the rudiments of a political particularism – we do not obscure but rather expose to plain view his significant departures from deeper elements of classical political philosophy.

The argument of this chapter proceeds in four parts. First, I offer an account of classical political particularism in the work of Plato and Aristotle. Then, in the subsequent two sections, I show how Montesquieu, operating within this "Platonic-Aristotelian framework," seeks to undermine the classical republican ideal. The first of these sections limns the outline of the relationship between classical and Montesquieuian particularism at a broader thematic level without confining our attention to Montesquieu's explicit references to the Ancients in *The Spirit of the Laws*; the next section considers this same relationship through a more finely grained analysis of specific discussions of Greek political texts in *Spirit*. From there, the chapter turns to Montesquieu's creative appropriation and politicization of Cicero's four-personae theory. As with Plato and Aristotle, so with Cicero, Montesquieu appropriates the particularism of ancient republican thought to expose the obsolescence of ancient republican institutions, making way for the theoretical and historical emergence of his new model. Political particularism is enlisted in the cause of modern liberty.

---

[7] See illustratively Aristotle, *Politics*, 1281a; 1317a40–1317b16. On this point in Aristotle, see Michael Davis, *The Politics of Philosophy: A Commentary on Aristotle's Politics* (Lanham, MD: Rowman & Littlefield, [1947] 1996), 108–9; Melissa Lane, "Claims to Rule: The Case of the Multitude," in *The Cambridge Companion to Aristotle's Politics*, ed. Marguerite Deslauriers (Cambridge, New York: Cambridge University Press, [1956] 2013), 247–52; and Leo Strauss, *What Is Political Philosophy? and Other Studies* (University of Chicago Press, 1959), 83–6.

CLASSICAL POLITICAL PARTICULARISM

At several points in the *Pensées*, one is inclined to mistake Montesquieu for Hobbes or Luther given his harsh words against the Ancients.[8] Plato's dialogues are "a tissue of sophistries," and as for Aristotle, it was "gratuitous for us to have taken up [his] jargon, and I don't know that we have ever gained anything by it" (*MP* 21; 211). Montesquieu complains that there was "no one up until Descartes who did not derive his entire philosophy from the Ancients" (*MP* 50). For too long, scholars have been mere "copyists" of classical writers. These comments, which mostly concern classical metaphysics, are consistent with Montesquieu's declaration concerning his own originality (*EL*, "Pref."; *MP* 105). He had at first selected a line from Cicero's *Laws* as the epigram for *The Spirit of the Laws* – "Law is the right reason of supreme Jupiter." But this line suggested too great an indebtedness to classical natural law theory. Instead, relying on a classical writer to announce his novelty, he lifts his heady epigraph from Ovid: "*Prolem sine matre creatum.*"[9]

Montesquieu was no copyist of the Ancients, but he was more their student than his disparagements of Plato and Aristotle might suggest. Again in his *Pensées*, he writes, "I admit my taste for the Ancients. That Antiquity enchants me, and I am always led to say with Pliny: 'It is to Athens that you are going. Respect their gods'" (*MP* 110). Here he quotes a letter in which Pliny the Younger writes of the Greeks' contributions to political thought and practice: "[Greece] is the land that provided us with justice and gave us laws."[10] Moreover, in the quarrel between the Ancients and the Moderns, Montesquieu announces no general preference for the latter: the quarrel "makes me see that there are good works among the Ancients and the Moderns" (*MP* 111).[11] On balance, Montesquieu's notebooks display his critical affinity for ancient thought generally, and in *The Spirit of the Laws*, we find that this posture extends to classical political science.

---

[8] Hobbes, *Leviathan*, 4.46–7.

[9] "An offspring made without a mother." See Diana J. Schaub's excellent discussion of the epigraph in *Erotic Liberalism*, 150–1.

[10] Pliny, *Letters*, 8.24.

[11] See also *MP* 102, 1315. In *MP* 1424, Montesquieu suggests that the discoveries of the Ancients outnumbered those of the Moderns. Since the decline of the Romans and Greeks, "men have become a cubit shorter" (*MP* 1268). See Christophe Martin, "Une apologétique 'moderne' des Anciens: la querelle dans les *Pensées*," *Revue Montesquieu* 7 (2003–2004): 67–83.

Montesquieu made a careful study of Plato's *Laws*, Aristotle's *Politics*, and Cicero's *On Duties*. In preparation for writing his masterwork, he acquired two French translations of the *Politics*, in addition to the Greek and Latin editions already on hand in his library at La Brède.[12] His notebook on the *Politics* ran at least 100 pages.[13] Evidence for his acquaintance with Plato's *Laws* is no less considerable. In *Spirit*, as we have noted, he cites it more often than any other work of political philosophy, and his notebook on the *Laws* may have been even thicker than the *Politics* notebook: it was at least 175 pages long.[14]

Setting aside our Roman for the moment, I wish to sketch here the elements of a Platonic-Aristotelian approach that substantially shaped both the development and deployment of Montesquieu's political particularism. Like all sketches, this one is a simplification of the real thing. But it is a pardonable simplification, for our goal is not to nuance existing accounts of Platonic or Aristotelian political science, but rather to isolate the elements of classical thought upon which Montesquieu drew most deeply in working out his own concept of the relationship between the "disposition of a people" and the "disposition of the laws," that is, the structure of government (*EL* 1.1.3, 2.12.1). We can identify four principles as the core of a Platonic-Aristotelian understanding of the relationship between circumstances, character, and political orders.[15] First, the regime understood as the authoritative element in the political community gives shape to the character (*êthos*) of the people governed by it. Second, and obversely, a people's character and physical circumstances can also contribute to determining the form of political order that is established and sustained in any given city. The relationship is one of reciprocal causation.[16] Each form of constitution relies upon habits of character and circumstances conducive to its preservation. These two empirical propositions give rise to two practical principles of statesmanship. First, the legislator must adapt his institutions to comport with, though not

---

[12] Shackleton, *Montesquieu*, 265.   [13] Ibid., 265.

[14] These notebooks are now lost. Shackleton, *Montesquieu*, 265. See *MP* 907, where Montesquieu lists Book 3 of the *Laws*, along with the *Politics*, as sources of information on ancient republics.

[15] One possible criticism of this approach is that I have elided the differences between Plato and Aristotle's political thought. Montesquieu himself certainly knew how to tell the difference between the two, and perhaps even how to exaggerate it (*EL* 1.4.8). But as I hope the following discussion will demonstrate, their disagreements notwithstanding, Montesquieu drew upon and appealed to a political particularism present in both Plato and Aristotle's teaching.

[16] See T. H. Irwin, *Aristotle's First Principles* (Oxford University Press, 1989), 456, 622.

simply to reflect, the character and circumstances of the people. In other words, careful consideration of these empirical realities should shape the way in which normative principles find application in law and politics. Second, the legislator must prepare a people's character to support and sustain the political institutions and way of life of the city. Together, these two empirical propositions and two practical principles comprise the core of what we have called *classical political particularism*.

In the *Politics*, Aristotle famously defines the *politeia* as both the arrangement (*taxis*) of offices in a city as well as the way of life (*bios*) of a city.[17] The character or ethos of the people is constitutive of the regime, and the regime in turn shapes the ethos. Aristotle employs causal language to describe this relationship, such as when he explains that the "character [*êthos*] peculiar to each constitution usually safeguards it as well as establishes it initially."[18] A "democratic character" safeguards and establishes a democratic regime; an oligarchic character safeguards and establishes an oligarchic regime. Aristotle states that a people's ethos is a "cause" (*aition*) of the form of government, and it circumscribes the range of suitable choices available to the statesman.[19] The statesman must therefore "introduce the sort of organization [*taxis*] that the people will be easily persuaded to accept and be able to participate in."[20]

Furthermore, Aristotle suggests that a "mismatch" of ethos and constitution often produces a disjunction between provisions of law and de facto civic life. That is, even if a constitution is de jure oligarchic, the de facto politics of the city may be more democratic if the "custom and training" of the people so incline the city. The reverse is also true: "[I]n other places ... the constitution is more democratic in its laws, but is governed in a more oligarchic way as a result of custom and training. This happens especially after there has been a change of constitution."[21] Character developed under one regime may survive a change of formal institutions.[22] Because people's moral character and capacities shape and limit the quality and extent of their participation in the regime, the

---

[17] Aristotle, *Politics*, trans. C. D. C. Reeve (Indianapolis: Hackett Publishing, 1998), 1278b8–10, 1295a40.

[18] Ibid., 1337a14–15; see also 1273a36–39.

[19] Aristotle, *Politics*, 1337a17; see Stephen Salkever, "Aristotle's Social Science" in *Aristotle's Politics: Critical Essays*, eds. Richard Kraut and Steven Skultety (Lanham, MD: Rowman & Littlefield, 2005), 53–4.

[20] Aristotle, *Politics*, 1289a1–2.   [21] Ibid., 1292b11–21.

[22] Terence Irwin, *Aristotle's First Principles* (Oxford, New York: Clarendon Press, 1988), 456.

conduct of politics in two cities could vary widely even if these cities shared an identical constitutional structure or "arrangement." When the statesman confines his inquiry to forms of government in the abstract, without reference to forms of character and even to particular peoples, he has neglected these fundamental political truths.

This aspect of Aristotelian political science finds root not only in common, implicit Greek understandings of the regime,[23] but also in Plato's political thought, especially his *Laws*. This is not to say that we should consider Plato's other explicitly political works – especially the *Republic* – to be at odds with this dimension of Aristotelian political science.[24] Indeed *Rep.* 8 is nothing less than a meditation upon the suggestion that regimes arise not from "oak or rock" but "from the character [*ek tôn êthon*] of the men in the cities."[25] But it is no exaggeration to say that this thesis and its implications preoccupy the interlocutors in the *Laws*. Early in the *Laws*, the Athenian Stranger voices doubts about his own project, suggesting that its realization would require an "opportune circumstance."[26] The interlocutors had been speaking as if they were "molding a city and citizens from wax," but in fact, men willing to tolerate the proposed laws "may not be found." This theme recurs throughout the dialogue: the Athenian Stranger reminds his interlocutors that the laws must suit the circumstances and the people for which they

---

[23] Richard Kraut, *Aristotle: Political Philosophy* (Oxford University Press, 2002), 15.

[24] As Paul A. Rahe notes, "If Montesquieu rivals Aristotle as an analyst of political regimes, it is because he attends to the procedure followed by Plato in the eighth and ninth books of the *Republic* and supplements his strictly institutional analysis with an attention to political psychology which gives his political science a suppleness, a flexibility, a subtlety, and range elsewhere unexcelled in modern times." *Montesquieu and the Logic of Liberty*, 67. I would add that another reason Montesquieu may rival Aristotle as an analyst of political regimes is that he attends to elements of Aristotle's own procedure. See also Malcolm Schofield, *Plato: Political Philosophy* (Oxford University Press, 2006), 32–4.

[25] Plato, *Rep.*, 544d. The translation is mine. This comment is not without irony, for at the close of the previous book, Socrates has proposed sending everyone over the age of ten out of the city, a measure which underscores the impossibility of finding a people fit for the ideal constitution of Kallipolis (541d). This is consistent with the agreement in Book 6 that the philosopher would need to "wipe the slate clean" before entering politics – the slate being the "character of human beings [*êthê anthropon*]" (501a4). See Donald Lutz, *Principles of Constitutional Design* (Cambridge University Press, 2006), 186–7, on how one's method of reading the *Republic* determines how one understands Plato's position on the question of matching a regime to a people. If one reads the *Republic* ironically, Plato appears to be highlighting the folly of failing to accommodate regimes to both human nature and the nature of specific peoples.

[26] Plato, *The Laws of Plato*, ed. Thomas L. Pangle (University of Chicago Press, 1988), 745e–746b.

are intended. Just as the finest sculptor may be limited by his medium, so the prudent founder is limited by the particular character and circumstances of his people. Their regime must be proper to men rather than to "gods or the children of gods."[27] But more than this, the regime must be appropriate for a particular kind of men, in a particular place. The Stranger notes, "Some places differ from one another in their tendency to breed better or worse human beings, and such factors should not be defied when one makes laws."[28] The legislator's efforts are unlikely to succeed if he "defies" the fact of human diversity – if he ventures, that is, to frame laws for a universal human type or blindly assumes that a regime suitable for one people will cause another to flourish. An "intelligent lawgiver" will "inquire as closely as possible" into the particular features of his people and place in an effort to formulate laws that are apt, rather than simply good or just in the abstract.[29]

Both Plato and Aristotle therefore reject the possibility of a universal regime type or law code. Constitutions and laws must vary with character and circumstance. Plato and Aristotle's shared emphasis upon the possibility of improving the ethos through education leads neither to deny the limits and constraints imposed by facts on the ground. On the Platonic-Aristotelian account, the student of politics must be a student of political wholes, and the legislator must adapt his institutions and laws to comport with, though not simply to reflect, the character of the people. In other words, they suggest that careful consideration of this empirical relationship should shape the way in which statesmen seek the good and the right in making and maintaining laws and constitutions.

COMPARATIVE POLITICAL ONTOLOGY

Given the centrality of the regime in classical political science, a pressing question confronts any attempt to link Montesquieu's political particularism to classical political science: What becomes of the classical conception of the regime in *The Spirit of the Laws*? Montesquieu is clearly more concerned with the concept of the regime than are, for example, Hobbes and Locke, whose primary aim is not to compare and educate real regimes but rather to judge them by a pre-political or extra-political standard.

---

[27] Ibid., 739d.
[28] Ibid., 747d. The immediate context is a discussion of the effects of climate on human character. See Aristotle, *Politics*, 1327b19–29.
[29] Plato, *Laws*, 747e.

Montesquieu, by contrast, restores to political science its Aristotelian task of understanding the variety of regimes in the world, the causes of their corruption, and the conditions for their preservation.[30]

In venturing such a comparison, we must take care to appreciate the profound differences that lie just beneath the surface of the formal similarities – differences Montesquieu himself certainly recognized. For if Montesquieu distinguishes regimes by their "principles," understood as the animating passions, Aristotle distinguishes them by their intelligible claims to rule or views of justice.[31] In Part 1 of *Spirit*, Montesquieu presents the contest of regimes largely as a contest among passions or motives (fear, honor, virtue); the task of political science becomes the management and direction of such passions.[32] Aristotelian political science, by contrast, does not merely manage passion, but also adjudicates between competing claims to rule, or opinions about justice, moving from the contest of opinions toward knowledge of the good and just political order. Still a clear recognition of this fundamental distinction between Montesquieuan and Aristotelian political science must not obscure Montesquieu's selective appropriation of other less fundamental elements of classical political thought.

[30] See Pangle, *Aristotle's Teaching*, 167. Montesquieu did not write *The Spirit of the Regimes*. But the focus on laws is not to the exclusion of regimes, and in fact, his analysis of the relationship between the regimes and laws is formally among the most Aristotelian aspects of his project. A central principle of Aristotelian political science holds that regime type ought to shape and will shape the laws, for the laws are no more independent of the regime than any other aspect of city. Aristotle teaches that, "[O]ne should try to see both which laws are best and which are appropriate for each of the constitutions. For laws should be established, and all do establish them, to suit the constitution and not the constitutions to suit the laws" (Aristotle, *Politics*, 1289a11–14). We could aptly describe the third through seventh books of *The Spirit of the Laws* as an elaboration of this basic teaching.

[31] See illustratively, Aristotle, *Politics*, 1281a; Lane, "Claims to Rule: The Case of the Multitude."

[32] One might be inclined to judge this emphasis on the passions a mark of Montesquieu's modernity, although, on this point, his analysis stands within hailing distance of Plato's treatment of regimes in *Rep.* 8 and 9. There Plato distinguishes regimes on the basis of their characteristic desires: love of wisdom, love of honor, love of money (necessary desires), unnecessary desires, and unlawful desires. See Paul Rahe, "Forms of Government: Structure, Principle, Object, and Aim," in *Montesquieu's Science of Politics: Essays on The Spirit of Laws*, eds. David W. Carrithers, Michael A. Mosher, and Paul A. Rahe (Lanham, MD: Rowman & Littlefield, 2001), 70. As in *Rep.* 8, Plato suggests that all desires are present in democracy (559c–561e), so Montesquieu claims that in the free state of England, "all the passions are free," with no one predominant over the others (*EL* 3.19.27).

As we have noted, Aristotle famously offers not one but two definitions of the regime or *politeia*, as both the arrangement (*taxis*) of offices and the way of life (*bios*) of the people.[33] Like Aristotle's regime, Montesquieu's basic political units, the *"espèces de gouvernements,"* have both a structural and, we might say, psychological-cultural dimension. The "nature of each government" corresponds to Aristotle's notion of the arrangement of offices (*EL* 1.2.1), while Montesquieu's notion of the principle (*principe*) corresponds, albeit incompletely, to the classical notion of a regime as the *bios* of the people (*EL* 1.3.1).[34] For Montesquieu, as for Aristotle, the fundamental unit of political life is not a naked structure or institutional scaffolding, but an animate political whole.[35] While Montesquieu typically uses the term constitution to describe only structure or institutional forms, he departs from this practice in a revealing passage in his preface. There he announces that his readers will draw the conclusion that "changes can be proposed only by those who are born fortunate enough to fathom by a stroke of genius the whole of a state's constitution" (*EL*, "Pref."). It is inconsistent with Montesquieu's political science to read the word "constitution" here to mean simply "political structure." For Montesquieu surely does not teach that one can propose changes as soon as one understands the formal structure of a regime. In this instance, "constitution" must refer to the political and cultural whole that Montesquieu will proceed to describe in *The Spirit of the Laws*.

The animating passion or "principle" of a constitution in Montesquieu's political science is undoubtedly less capacious than the Aristotelian notion of the way of life of the people. But this narrower concept is supplemented by Montesquieu's broader notion of the "disposition of the people [*la disposition du peuple*]," which must "relate well" to the "particular disposition [*la disposition particulière*]" of the government or, as he later puts it, the "disposition of the laws [*disposition des lois*]."[36]

---

[33] Aristotle, *Politics*, 1278b8–10, 1295a40.   [34] Cf. Mansfield, *Taming the Prince*, 223.

[35] Simone Goyard-Fabre suggests that Montesquieu's concept of the nature of a government is a "replica" of Aristotle's concept of the *politeia*. *Montesquieu: La Nature, les lois, la liberté*, 7. This is a mistake: the "nature" of a government is its structure, on Montesquieu's account. The classical *politeia* in its fullness comprehends both Montesquieu's nature and principle. As Rahe puts it, Montesquieu's principles put "flesh" on the "constitutional bones" of nature. *Montesquieu and the Logic of Liberty*, 67.

[36] The translation is mine. *EL* 1.1.3, 2.12.1. At 2.12.1, Cohler et al. translate *"la disposition particulière"* as "the particular arrangement" – a reasonable choice in isolation. But in context, this rendering obscures the parallel Montesquieu intends to draw between the *disposition* of the people (i.e., character and circumstances) and the *disposition* of the laws (i.e., institutional structure).

Here again, there is a twofold character to Montesquieu's political ontology. The *disposition* of the people encompasses character, mores, habits, customs, and received examples – elements of the Aristotelian way of life. The *disposition* of the government and laws corresponds to Aristotle's *taxis* of offices. Whether we think narrowly of "nature" and "principle," or more broadly of *la disposition des lois* and *la disposition du peuple*, Montesquieu's constitution shares the twofold nature of the Ancients' regime.

Some might suppose that such formal similarities unravel when we reach the fundamental question of the primacy of the political, a notion central to the classical conception of the regime. For the Ancients, as Leo Strauss and others have argued, the regime is the primary determinant of the form of life of a community.[37] Indeed, the classical *politeia* includes the entire way of life of the society – its habits, customs, and moral beliefs.[38] The form of the regime is determined by who holds authority. This authoritative element – whether the common man, the rich man, the military elite, or suchlike – shapes not only the narrowly "political" decisions of the community, but the community's entire manner of living. Strauss explains, "When the authoritative type is the common man, everything has to justify itself before the tribunal of the common man; everything which cannot be justified before that tribunal becomes, at best, merely tolerated, if not despised or suspect."[39] In this way, we can say that the authoritative element gives distinctive form to the whole. This ancient conception of the regime stands opposed, as Strauss argues, to twentieth-century behavioralism and its successors in political science, which seek to "reduce political life to certain sub-political economic, psychological, or sociological variables."[40]

But if Montesquieu's putatively sociological politics is the forerunner to such reductionism, which treats politics as inevitably downstream from nonpolitical causes, then his social science appears as the antipode of the classical understanding of the relationship between constitution and

---

[37] Leo Strauss, *Natural Right and History* (University of Chicago Press, 1965), 135–40; Strauss, *What Is Political Philosophy?*, 33–5; Leo Strauss, *The City and Man* (Charlottesville, VA: University of Virginia Press, 1964), 45–9.

[38] Steven B. Smith, *Reading Leo Strauss: Politics, Philosophy, Judaism* (University of Chicago Press, 2006), 181–3. See also Pangle, *Aristotle's Teaching*, 95, and Schofield, *Plato*, 32–4.

[39] Strauss, *Natural Right and History*, 137.   [40] Smith, *Reading Leo Strauss*, 181.

character, or politics and "culture" broadly construed.[41] Does not Montesquieu – with his extensive reflections on the political effects of factors such as mores, religion, and climate – reject the "primacy of the political" implied in the ancient conception of the regime? Does he not doubt the capacity of human beings to order their lives together "deliberately, intentionally, and authoritatively?"[42] Ultimately, this objection makes too much of Montesquieu's sociological bent and too little of the Ancients' own understanding of the role of "chance" as legislator, which is to say, their understanding of how what is given limits the choices of the human legislator.[43] Thomas L. Pangle has argued that there is indeed a "de-emphasis of the political" in Montesquieu but that he avoids the complete subordination of the political to the sub-political.[44] In resisting the identification of Montesquieu's political science with modern sociology, Pangle is certainly correct. But it is a mistake to conclude that Montesquieu qualifies the primacy of the political further than had his classical predecessors. For it is only where the legislator lacks political science – Montesquieu's political science – that these physical and cultural factors can be said to determine a people's way of life and politics.

In this respect, his understanding of the effects of character, climate, and other causes is not so alien to the classical approach. In the context of addressing Aristotle's teaching on climate, Leo Strauss explains that on the Platonic-Aristotelian view,

[T]here was very little advance planning in the world – you can say because there was no fully clear political science [or] political philosophy in the world ... Since the influence of political philosophy from Plato's or Aristotle's point of view is very limited, one can say that whole world is governed by chance ... and yet that does not make superfluous a rational consideration, but it also induces us to be not too sanguine about its possible influence.[45]

Like Strauss's Ancients in this passage, Montesquieu attributes laws to nonpolitical causes where there is "no fully clear political science." But this does not mean that he denies the primacy of politics any more than Aristotle or Plato deny it. For as many commentators have suggested,

---

[41] See Durkheim, *Montesquieu and Rousseau*, 1–64. Similar but more nuanced interpretations are contained in Aron, *Main Currents in Sociological Thought*, 1:13–72, and Manent, *The City of Man*, ch. 2.
[42] Pangle, *Montesquieu's Philosophy*, 44. [43] E.g., Plato, *Laws*, 709a.
[44] Pangle, *Montesquieu's Philosophy*, 192.
[45] Leo Strauss, *Seminar on Aristotle, Politics, spring 1960*, ed. Joseph Cropsey. Accessed March 27, 2017. https://leostrausscenter.uchicago.edu/course/aristotle-politics-spring-quarter-1960.

Montesquieu's efforts to identify the causes of legal and political variety across nations ultimately serve a deeper purpose of placing laws, as far as possible, under the control of well-taught human legislators.[46]

Moreover, like Montesquieu, Aristotle recognizes the ways in which the character of the people delimits the range of realizable and sustainable political regimes. T. H. Irwin notes that there is a *"reciprocal* relation between the character of citizens and the nature of the political system" in Aristotle's political science.[47] His confidence in the power of civic education notwithstanding, Aristotle, like Montesquieu, holds that the causal arrow between ethos and constitutional structure runs both ways. This view is clearly in evidence in several texts treated this chapter, such as Aristotle's claim that democratic "customs and training" can lead a city to act democratically even if its constitution is structurally oligarchic, or his assertion that a democratic ethos "establishes" a democratic regime "from the beginning."[48] Commenting on this latter passage, Randall Curren is correct to observe that,

Aristotle would not speak in VIII.1 of a democratic ethos and an oligarchic ethos unless they were in some respects different, and the obvious reason why they would be ... is that he regards the capacity of cities to transform themselves into polities or aristocracies as limited. Cities can only improve themselves by degrees, and only by so much even in the long run, given the nature of their populations and circumstances.[49]

Montesquieu's efforts to understand the political constraints inherent in a people's character and circumstances no more constitute a denial of the primacy of the political than do the efforts of the Athenian Stranger or Aristotle to understand the same. Though differences between Montesquieu and the Ancients abound, on this particular question, there is not much light between them.

Yet just as eagerly as Montesquieu retains the formal elements of classical political particularism, he casts off its moral substance. We may illustrate this point by reference to the passage from *Politics* 8 that

---

[46] David W. Carrithers, "Montesquieu and Tocqueville as Philosophical Historians: Liberty, Determinism, and the Prospects for Freedom," in *Montesquieu and His Legacy*, ed. Rebecca E. Kingston (Albany, NY: State University of New York Press, 2009), 149–77; Ana J. Samuel, "The Design of Montesquieu's *The Spirit of the Laws*: The Triumph of Freedom over Determinism," *American Political Science Review* 103 (2009): 312–13.

[47] Irwin, *Aristotle's First Principles*, 456, 622.

[48] Aristotle, *Politics*, 1292b11–21, 1337a7–20.

[49] Randall Curren, *Aristotle on the Necessity of Public Education* (Lanham, MD: Rowman & Littlefield, 2000), 111–12.

Curren foregrounds. Montesquieu's political science embraces the Aristotelian view that a "character peculiar to each constitution usually safeguards it as well as establishes it initially."[50] But for Aristotle, this formal principle ultimately points toward the highest purpose of both politics and political science: "a *better* character is always the cause of a *better* constitution." Here Montesquieu stops short. Both because he shares Mandeville's view that private vices may prove public virtues, and because he rejects the classical understanding of politics as oriented toward the good life, he cannot follow Aristotle this far (*EL* 3.19.5–11). Montesquieu's political science apprehends the reciprocal, efficient-causal relationship between character and the regime, yet without proceeding to the conclusion that the perfection of character is the goal of the regime and the precondition for the best regime. This break is a telling mark of Montesquieu's modernity and his liberalism. In the next section, as we trace his textual engagement with the Greeks in *Spirit*, we will observe at higher resolution his efforts to retain and deploy for his distinctively liberal purposes the skeleton of classical political particularism, even while shedding its moral substance.

MONTESQUIEU'S "GREEK POLITICAL MEN"

Because his grasp of classical Greek was not strong, Montesquieu relied upon French and Latin editions of Plato and Aristotle.[51] Reading these editions over Montesquieu's shoulder alerts readers to otherwise inaudible resonances between his political science and that of his Greek interlocutors. This proves especially helpful in appreciating the prehistory of Montesquieu's preoccupation with mores (*moeurs*), a concept central to his political particularism. The French term derives from the Latin *mores* (customs); *mores* was the common Latin translation of the Greek êthos (character) from the Hellenistic period through the Renaissance.[52] Significantly, the term was carried into French translations of the *Politics* on which Montesquieu relied. Loys Le Roy renders êthos alternatively as "*meurs* [mores]" and "*coustume* [custom]" in his 1568 edition of the *Politics*.[53] Nicole Oresme repeatedly renders êthos as "*les meurs ou la*

---

[50] Aristotle, *Politics*, 1337a14–17.   [51] Shackleton, *Montesquieu*, 265.

[52] Donald Maletz, "Tocqueville on Mores and the Preservation of Republics," *American Journal of Political Science* 49 (2005): 4.

[53] E.g., Loys Le Roy, *Politiques d'Aristote* (1568), Bk. 8, ch. 1: "Car il fault dresser la police selon chacune republique, ayant chacune ses propres meurs [*êthos*], qui ont accoustrumé de la maintenir & establir du commencement. Comme la democratie les meurs

coustume [mores or customs]" in his 1374 translation.[54] Montesquieu obtained and studied these editions while preparing to write *The Spirit of the Laws*. This suggests that when he discusses the relationship between *moeurs*, *coustumes*, and *lois*, and when he indicates, for instance, that democratic *moeurs* establish and sustain democratic regimes, we should be alive to the possibility that Montesquieu is speaking the language of Aristotle's *Politics* as he received it.

In Part 1 of *Spirit*, with a few interesting exceptions, Montesquieu's republics are Greek.[55] He continually resorts to Greek models in his discussion of republican government, presenting the laws of Lycurgus and Plato as the archetypes of Greek republican government (*EL* 1.4.7). The regime of Plato's *Laws* was the "correction" and the "perfection" of Lycurgan Sparta (*EL* 1.4.6, 1.7.16). Montesquieu even offers that the regime of the *Republic* is realizable, for it is not much different than Sparta. On his reading, Plato's political thought represents the enhancement and completion of Greek (especially Spartan and Cretan) republican politics.

The republican regimes of the Greeks are not simply a subset of republics. They are rather the nearest, purest approximations of republican government as an ideal type. They are "singular institutions [*institutions singulières*]," in contradistinction to "ordinary institutions [*institutions ordinaires*]."[56] Like the "singular man" portrayed in the *Pensées*, singular institutions are "bizarre," peculiar, and inimitable (*MP* 52). Just as an ordinary person could not imitate the "thoughts and actions" of a "singular man" without "betraying and diminishing himself," so an ordinary nation cannot live under singular institutions (*MP* 52). Few peoples could sustain singular republican institutions, and Montesquieu aims to show that modern European peoples are not among these few – a key step in his case for liberal constitutional government.

---

popoulairs, & l'oligarichie oligarchiques: & tousiours la meilleure coustume [*êthos*] est cause de la meilleure republique." The English translation here reads, "In fact, the character peculiar to each constitution usually safeguards it as well as establishes it initially (for example, the democratic character, a democracy; and the oligarchic one, an oligarchy), and a better character is always the cause of a better constitution." Aristotle, *Politics*, 1337a14–17.

[54] Oresme offers a gloss: "For ... as several say, some men are naturally suited for one constitution and others for another." Nicole Oresme, *Politiques d'Aristote* (Philadelphia: American Philosophical Society, [1374] 1970), Bk. 8, ch. 1, 339. Translation is mine.

[55] The exceptions in Part 1 include William Penn's Pennsylvania colony and the Jesuits' Paraguay (*EL* 1.4.6).

[56] See *EL* 1.4.6–7; 2.12.30 n. 84; 4.23.7; 6.29.21.

Of the many "singular institutions" of the Greek republics, none occupy Montesquieu more than their regulations regarding commerce and money. In Part 1, Montesquieu refrains from straightforward criticism of the Greek republican limitations on interstate trade and silver. Indeed, he praises the "wisdom" and "genius" of Lycurgus, Minos, and Plato (*EL* 1.4.7; 3.19.16). Given the right conditions, their institutions "can be good," for restrictions on commerce are necessary to maintain the regimes of virtue they sought. Limits on trade and travel insulate a people from the corrupt mores of foreign peoples (*EL* 4.20.1). Similarly, Montesquieu explains in his own voice that silver and gold tend to

... fatten the fortune of men beyond the limits nature has set for it, to teach men to preserve vainly what has been amassed vainly, to multiply desires infinitely and to supplement nature, which has given us very limited means to excite our passions and to corrupt one another.

(*EL* 1.4.6)

The Ancients were therefore correct in their judgment that money "must be banished" from singular republics (*EL* 1.4.7). While these limits on trade and wealth accumulation are entirely appropriate for protecting the character and constitution of "singular" republics, they have no place in large, modern societies. The "extensive business" of states populated by numerous peoples makes the Greeks' singular institutions unworkable, Montesquieu explains (*EL* 1.4.6). In such circumstances, efforts to "inspire virtue" and to educate a people "as a family" are doomed to fail – as the Greeks themselves first recognized (*EL* 1.4.6).

At every turn, the Greeks' own understanding of the limits of their ideal institutions underwrites Montesquieu's efforts to show that we moderns lie outside those limits. This feature of Montesquieu's strategy is perhaps most striking as he takes up commerce as a subject in its own right. Here we find new reasons to disregard the Greek objections to commerce, reasons that transcend the small republic thesis. He writes,

Commerce has spread knowledge of the mores of all nations everywhere; they have been compared to each other, and good things have resulted from this. One can say that the laws of commerce perfect mores for the same reason that these same laws ruin mores. Commerce corrupts pure mores, and this was the subject of Plato's complaints; it polishes and softens barbarous mores, as we see every day.

(*EL* 1.4.1)

In a book that ultimately aims to effect a dramatic break with the classical devaluation of commerce, Montesquieu denies that he is out of step with Plato. He explicitly ratifies the Platonic-Aristotelian teaching: commerce does indeed ruin pure mores.[57] This alone was the "subject of Plato's complaints." But if a people lacks pure mores, as do the vast majority of peoples, then Plato's theory poses no obstacles. For Plato never taught that commerce is harmful to men who are already ruined. They are not the intended targets of his regulations. Such spoilt men are fortunate to find a legislator in Montesquieu.

Much is afoot in this passage, but it is most important to see that with his invocation of Plato, Montesquieu is carefully hewing to the basic Platonic-Aristotelian principle that no law is suited to every regime, people, or circumstance. He reminds the reader that Plato never proposed universal laws concerning commerce or any other matters: when Plato spoke of the best laws, they were meant for unspoiled men. A given law aims to produce particular effects in a people, assuming a particular *ex ante* disposition. When that disposition is absent, the law is presumably inapt. This particularistic principle allows Montesquieu to cabin "Plato's complaints," banishing them to Sparta and Crete and transforming the classical critique of commerce into a merely contingent or local critique. In this way, the initial premises in the argument for modern liberty are laid upon the foundation of classical political particularism.

Just as Montesquieu appeals to Plato to argue that commerce is neither morally nor politically ruinous for "ordinary" peoples, so he turns to the *Laws* to suggest that other institutions of Magnesia – the city of the *Laws* – are maladapted to commercial societies. In a chapter concerned with civil judges, he turns to Plato's discussion of the effects of maritime commerce: "Plato says that, in a town where there is no maritime commerce, half the number of civil laws are needed, and this is very true. Commerce brings into a country different sorts of peoples, a great number of agreements, kinds of goods, and ways of acquisition" (EL 4.20.18). Montesquieu cites *Laws* 8. There the Athenian Stranger explains that the Magnesians will find sustenance from the land alone; they will not rely upon maritime trade. The absence of maritime commerce "makes things easier" for the lawgiver; the city will need "half as many laws."[58] Why? In the *Laws*, the Stranger explains that without commerce, the lawgiver can "just say good-bye to most of what pertains to shipowning, wholesale trading, retail merchandising, innkeeping, custom duties, mining, loans, compound interest, and tens of thousands of other such things."[59] In

[57]　Cf. Sullivan, *Montesquieu and the Despotic Ideas of Europe*, 155–6.
[58]　Plato, *Laws*, 842c.　　[59]　Ibid., 842d.

other words, a city without maritime commerce needs fewer laws because it has fewer activities to regulate.

Yet before offering this more mundane explanation, the Stranger reasons that the noncommercial city will "need only half as many laws, or even far less than half, and the laws are more fitting for free human beings."[60] The significance of this statement is not lost on Montesquieu. Rather than focusing upon the greater number of activities (shipowning, innkeeping, loans, etc.) in commercial states, his gloss on the passage gives central place to the Stranger's mention of *human types*. Commercial societies require twice as many laws not simply because they are home to more activities, but because they are home to a greater variety of human beings. "Commerce brings into a country different sorts of peoples," Montesquieu explains (*EL* 4.20.18). He understands that the Stranger's chief concern is not the multiplication of activities but rather the multiplication of human types in commercial societies. Maritime commerce introduces into the city a variety of human beings who are not "free" in the Stranger's sense – men with servile minds and corrupt characters for whom the laws of Magnesia are a poor fit. The isolated Magnesians can maintain pure mores and live under laws "fitting" for their homogenous, distinctively "free" character. But commerce spawns cosmopolitan diversity and renders a people unable to sustain the "singular institutions" of the Greeks. Montesquieu invites readers to hear the message from Plato himself: one cannot simply export "singular institutions" to modern nations, filled with diverse human types ("different sorts of people"). In each of these invocations of Plato on commercial society, Montesquieu allows Plato to chasten his latter-day republican disciples, who would aspire to introduce the "singular" republicanism of the Ancients into the heart of modern commercial societies. The classical republic of virtue is inappropriate and unsuitable for peoples such as us: just ask Plato.

This engagement with Plato turns fundamentally on the question of civic education and miseducation, broadly conceived. It is a commonplace to note that Montesquieu follows Machiavelli in breaking with the Ancients' emphasis on character education as he turns to institutional means of harnessing vice for the public good. This account is correct as far it goes. However, Montesquieu retains a role for education of a different sort as a prelude to liberty, and he is aware of his paradoxical affinity with Plato on the subject of politics and education. The discussion

---

[60] Ibid., 842cd.

of "singular" Greek institutions appears in the fourth book of *The Spirit of the Laws*, which proposes to explain how "the laws of education should be relative to the principles of the government" (*EL* 1.4.1). This treatment of education appears early in the work; education is in fact the first substantive matter Montesquieu addresses after outlining his axial notions of nature and principle. Affording this privileged place to the subject of education, Montesquieu suggests that he is, at least formally, tracing the concerns of the Ancients.

The book on education culminates in an "Explanation of a paradox of the Ancients in relation to mores" (*EL* 1.4.8). The paradox finds its boldest expression in Plato's corpus: "Plato is not afraid to say that no change can be made in music which is not a change in the constitution of the state." Though neither Montesquieu nor his modern editors provide a citation, the text he has in mind is in *Rep.* 4, where Socrates warns, "They must beware of change to a strange form of music, taking it to be a danger to the whole. *For never are the ways of music moved without the greatest political laws being moved*, as Damon says, and I am persuaded." Adeimantus adds,

[T]here is no harm, were it not that little by little this spirit of license, finding a home, imperceptibly penetrates into manners [*ta êthê*] and customs; whence, issuing with greater force, it invades contracts between man and man, and from contracts goes on to laws and constitutions, in utter recklessness, ending at last, Socrates, by an overthrow of all rights, private as well as public.[61]

Music modifies the citizens' character or mores (*ta êthê*), and these mores shape the constitution. (Ficino's Latin edition of the *Republic*, on which Montesquieu relied, predictably renders "*ta êthê*" as "*mores*" in this passage.[62]) Montesquieu directs our attention not merely to the Ancients' views on music, but more broadly to the ancient view of the relationship between mores and law, ethos and *politeia*, character and constitution. The ancient teaching on music lies near the heart of classical political particularism.

Montesquieu calls this teaching a paradox because it ascribes political importance to a facet of human life that seems, in itself, thoroughly apolitical. But he explains that Plato was not alone in espousing it:

---

[61] Plato, *Republic*, 424cd.
[62] Plato, *Divini Platonis Opera Omnia quæ Extant*, trans. Marcilio Ficino (Lyon: Apud Franciscum le Preux, 1590), 447.

Aristotle, who seems to have written his *Politics* only in order to oppose his feelings to Plato's, nevertheless agrees with him about the power of music over mores. Theophrastus, Plutarch, and Strabo, all the Ancients, have thought likewise. This is not an opinion proffered without reflection; it is one of the principles of their politics. It is thus that they gave laws; it is thus that they wanted cities to be governed.

(*EL* 1.4.8)

Music shapes politics through mores. That mores influence and sustain regimes is the implicit middle term, a principle more fundamental than the principle concerning music. Having outlined these strange views, Montesquieu announces his intention to explain the rationale behind the Greeks' concern with the politics of music. But his explanation reveals as much about his own science of politics as it does about the politico-musical principles of the Ancients.

He reminds readers that Greeks regarded work for pay as unworthy of free men. Craftsmanship, commerce, and even agriculture degraded human character. Such views put Greek regimes in a "very awkward position": "One did not want the citizens to work in commerce, agriculture, or the arts; nor did one want them to be idle" (*EL* 1.4.8). The solution to this apparent dilemma lay in gymnastics and other activities related to war. But military training, he explains, leads to still another problem. Such activities are "appropriate for making people harsh and savage" and therefore "need to be tempered by others that might soften the mores [*adoucir les moeurs*]." While military exercises arouse men's "roughness, anger, and cruelty," the counterweight of musical education made the soul "feel softness [*la douceur*], pity, tenderness and sweet pleasure," supplying the defect of gymnastics. Directly contradicting the classical view, Montesquieu explains that musical education among the Greeks did not inspire genuine virtues of character or reasonableness but rather counterbalanced the effects of gymnastics and cultivated in the people the passions necessary to sustain their singular political institutions.[63]

But notwithstanding this contradiction of the Ancients on the effects of music, to which we shall return, the chapter serves as a striking marker of Montesquieu's fundamental agreement with the classical understanding

---

[63] As Lowenthal points out, while Socrates consistently associates music with openness to rational, persuasive discourse, he briefly reduces the ends of music to pugnacity in war and gentleness. Montesquieu gloms onto this narrow explanation of the utility of musical education, dropping entirely the connection between music and reasonableness. Lowenthal, "Montesquieu and the Classics," 278.

of the power of character or mores to shape and reshape political forms. He concludes that the Ancients' interest in the political effects of music was not misplaced. Musical education was fully reasonable in the context of Greek republics. While modern legislators will find other means of preparing peoples for modern regimes, the musical education of the Ancients represented an appropriate application of a basic principle that Montesquieu himself endorses: "the character peculiar to each constitution usually safeguards it as well as establishes it initially."[64]

Thus his discussion of the "paradox of the ancients" demonstrates again Montesquieu's serious engagement with classical political particularism. But as we have indicated, it also points to Montesquieu's departure from the substance of ancient political thought, even as he retains the formal elements outlined in this chapter's first section. Montesquieu insists that the principal effect of the musical education of the Ancients was "gentleness" or "softness." Music "softens mores [*adoucir les moeurs*]" and makes the soul "feel softness [*la douceur*]." This same language Montesquieu famously uses later in *Spirit* to describe the effects of commerce upon mores (*EL* 4.20.1). Like the musical education of the Greeks, commerce breeds "gentle mores [*moeurs douces*]"; it "softens barbarous mores [*adoucit les moeurs barbares*]." This commercial gentleness is distinct in kind from the gentleness of soul associated with musical education in Book 4. Commerce cures "destructive prejudices," prejudices that breed harsh, illiberal mores. Montesquieu has in mind a gentleness resembling tolerance, as we will consider in Chapter 6. Commerce exposes a nation to diverse human types and eventually softens a people's response to different ways of life. It prepares a people not for the singular institutions of the Greeks, but for a liberty and political moderation appropriate to modern constitutional regimes (*EL* 2.11.6). Played in a different register, commerce becomes the musical education of the Moderns. As the Greek proscriptions against commercial activity were in fact "laws of education," so modern commerce – the reversal of those proscriptions – educates or forms men for a new kind of politics (*EL* 1.4.6).[65]

---

[64] Aristotle, *Politics*, 1337a14–15.

[65] Some readers may note with interest that the fourth book of the first part of *Spirit* treats civic education, while the first book of the fourth part treats its modern replacement and analogue – commerce – suggesting again the (pseudo-) educative power of commercial activity. I am indebted to Moss Turpan for this observation.

But Montesquieu's use of classical particularism to retire the classical republic is not limited to his discussion of commerce. Other singular institutions of the Greeks, beyond their limitations upon economic activity, appear unsuitable for modern nations. His approach to these other institutions mirrors his approach to the restrictions upon commerce: they were reasonable given the character and circumstances of Greek republics, but they are unsuitable to other forms of political organization. One finds this approach in Montesquieu's discussion of Plato's views on both venality (especially the sale of public offices) and mutual supervision. Citing the *Laws*, Montesquieu turns to his leading Greek republican:

Plato cannot endure such venality. 'It is,' he says, 'as if, on a ship, one made someone a pilot or a sailor for his silver. Is it possible that the rule is good only for guiding a republic and bad in all other life employments?' But Plato is speaking of a republic founded on virtue, and we are speaking of monarchy. Now, in a monarchy, where, if the posts were not sold by a public regulation, the courtiers' indigence and avidity would sell them all the same, chance will produce better subjects than the choice of the prince. Finally, advancing oneself by way of wealth inspires and maintains industry, a thing badly needed in this kind of government.
(*EL* 1.5.19)

Just as in his discussion of commerce, Montesquieu conspicuously avoids a direct collision with Plato. Instead, he marginalizes Plato's views on venality on the basis of his Plato's own political particularism. Plato himself intended to limit his own regulations to a "republic founded on virtue." He would never have pronounced a rule applicable to all regimes, knowing that laws must suit the regime type, just as they suit the character and circumstances of a people. Moreover, because Plato had no generic political recommendations and, like Aristotle, lacked a "clear" and "correct [*juste*] idea of monarchy," he could have entertained no opinions at all on the subject (*EL* 2.11.8–9). The authority of Plato is no argument against modern venality.[66]

The republican practices of censorship and mutual supervision meet with a similar treatment in the same chapter (*EL* 1.5.19). Republics of virtue must have censors, since virtue can be destroyed not only by crimes but also by "slackness in love of the homeland, dangerous examples,

---

[66] In Montesquieu's view, venality was in fact an important source of independence for judges – and so, a source of political liberty – in monarchies like France. See David W. Carrithers, "Introduction: An Appreciation of *The Spirit of Laws*," in *Montesquieu's Science of Politics: Essays on* The Spirit of Laws, eds. David W. Carrithers, Michael A. Mosher, and Paul A. Rahe (Lanham, MD: Rowman & Littlefield Publishers, 2001), 25.

seeds of corruption" and other elements for which laws cannot account (*EL* 2.11.8). But in monarchies, virtue need not be defended so vigorously. Honor suffices to maintain monarchy, and it naturally has "the whole universe as a censor." The office of the censor, at home in republics of virtue, does not befit modern monarchy. And the same is true of civic supervision in other forms. Montesquieu explains that Plato wanted citizens punished if they neglected to alert magistrates when they witnessed wrongdoing, but "[t]his would not be suitable today" (*EL* 2.11.8). Instead, modern states have established the office of public prosecutor to keep watch. The republics of Plato, Lycurgus, and Minos assumed that citizens paid "singular attention" to each other (*EL* 1.3.7), but in the bustle of large, diverse states, legislators lack the luxury of such an assumption. The principles of political particularism allow Montesquieu to reject, as alien to modern politics, the practice of mutual supervision, and thus again to undermine substantive elements of classical republican politics.

This subtle but relentless strategy runs throughout Montesquieu's treatment of ancient republican thought. In contrast with self-styled civic republicans, who would revive the institutions of the Greeks in modern states, Montesquieu follows the Ancients in recognizing that place and character limit the range of suitable options available to the prudent legislator. In this limited sense, he claims the mantle of the Greeks and works as their heir. He effectively breaks with the classical republican ideal, not in spite of, but because of the fact that he operates within the framework of classical political particularism. In this manner, Montesquieu prepares his readers for a species of liberty suitable to large, heterogeneous societies running low on the "painful" virtue of the Greeks (*EL* 1.4.5, 1.5.2).

MONTESQUIEU'S POLITICIZATION OF CICERO'S SECOND PERSONA

But it is not only to the Greeks that Montesquieu turns as he develops the conceptual apparatus of his political particularism across the pages of *Spirit*. In Cicero's ethical theory, Montesquieu similarly found a form of reasoning that would shape his notions of the general spirit and character of a nation and inform his warnings against programs of political transformation that cut against the grain of a people's distinctive character.

Montesquieu's admiration for Cicero was apparently coeval with his interest in moral and political philosophy. Among his earliest writings was a *Discourse on Cicero* (ca. 1717), and as we have noted, he began work on a *Treatise on Duties* modeled upon Cicero's *De officiis* (*On Duties*) (VF 8:125–31, 430–9).[67] In a 1750 letter, Montesquieu recalls, "I devised the plan of writing a work on duties. The treatise on *Duties* (*de Officia*) by Cicero had enchanted me and I took it as a model."[68] Though unfinished, and now mostly lost, he had presented portions of composition before the Bordeaux Academy in 1725. In his *Pensées*, he renders a verdict on the Roman: "Cicero, in my view, is one of the great minds that has ever existed: a soul always beautiful when it was not weak" (*MP* 73).

The surviving fragments of the *Treatise on Duties* do not afford a clear picture of how Cicero's *De officiis* might have shaped Montesquieu's early moral philosophy.[69] But in *The Spirit of the Laws*, one finds echoes of an important element of the moral theory of *De officiis*. In the critical nineteenth book, Montesquieu draws upon the insights of Cicero's four-personae theory to explain and defend his political particularism. The original Ciceronian theory had concerned only individuals, but Montesquieu politicizes this teaching and applies it to nations. Though his engagement with Cicero is more limited and less explicit than his treatment of the Greeks, it ultimately serves to form and reinforce the same particularistic sensibility, and it similarly terminates in a subtle defense of liberal commercial society.

Cicero develops his four-personae theory in Book 1 of *De officiis*. It is a normative theory of moral choice – a "method of finding out our duty" – that directs the chooser to consider his four "roles" or personae as he acts.[70] Each role represents a normative reference point to which the chooser should look as he seeks to act in keeping with seemliness (*decorum*), an aspect of the honorable (*honestum*). These four roles include, first, the role given by our common human nature; second, the role given by my individual nature; third, the role imposed upon me by chance and circumstance; and fourth, the role given by my own decision and will. The first two roles are natural: "We have been dressed by nature for two roles."[71] When I am faced with a moral choice, I must first ask

---

[67] Shackleton, *Montesquieu*, 68–76. In the "Discourse on Cicero," Montesquieu announces that Cicero is the Ancient "whom I would most like to resemble" (VF 8:125).

[68] Montesquieu to Monsignor de Fitz-James, October 8, 1750, in Nagel 3:1327–29.

[69] For an effort to construct such a picture from the fragments, see Paul Dimoff, "Cicéron, Hobbes et Montesquieu," *Annales Universitatis Saraviensis* 1 (1952):19–47.

[70] Cicero, *On Duties*, eds. M. T. Griffin and E. M. Atkins (Cambridge University Press, 1991), Bk. 1, sec. 107.

[71] Ibid.

what actions best comport with my nature as human being, possessed of
rationality and sociability. This role is common to all men. What is good
for me *qua* human being is good for you *qua* human being. But the second
persona differs on this very point. When I consider the second role, I ask
what actions best comport with my individual nature, that is, with my
spirit, character, talents, disposition, and capacities. On Cicero's view,
every moral chooser must consider his individual nature as a normative
point of reference. It is this second role that interests Montesquieu.[72]

   As Cicero unfolds this theory of moral choice, he devotes the greatest
care to explaining the second persona. The first persona holds lexical
priority over the second, but the second nonetheless requires a good deal
more explanation, owing at least in part to its novelty in ancient ethics. As
Christopher Gill notes, the predominant emphasis in ancient ethics was
upon "defining an ideal pattern of human nature," getting straight the
natural duties Cicero connects with the first persona.[73] The four-personae
theory's "stress on the value of retaining one's own, particular characteristics" is therefore striking and, as Cicero recognizes, requires
explication.[74]

   The addition of the second persona represents a complication of the
traditional Stoic ambition of living *naturae congruentes*.[75] For the purposes of moral choice, Cicero suggests that nature is both one and many,
uniformity and variety. To follow nature, I must follow both common
human nature and my individual nature. Cicero explains that "just as
there are enormous bodily differences ... similarly there are still greater
differences in men's spirits [*animis*]."[76] He provides some initial
examples. Some men are naturally jolly, others naturally serious.[77] He
focuses upon dispositional aspects of the second persona and stresses the

---

[72] After his discussion of the two natural roles, Cicero briefly explains the other two
   personae. When faced with a moral choice, I ought to consider the limits that chance
   and circumstances have placed upon my options – the third persona. Finally, I must act in
   a way consistent with the career or life plan I have chosen. This means asking how my
   past decisions constrain the range of choices presently open to me (Cicero, *On Duties*,
   1.115).

[73] Christopher Gill, "Personhood and Personality: The Four-Personae Theory in Cicero, *De
   Officiis* I," in *Oxford Studies in Ancient Philosophy*, ed. Julia Annas (Oxford University
   Press, 1988), vol. 6, 178.

[74] Ibid.

[75] On Cicero's debts to the Stoic Panaetius in his presentation of the four *personae*, see ibid.,
   173–6.

[76] Cicero, *On Duties*, 1.107.   [77] Ibid., 1.108.

moral indifference of these diverse traits: they "do not in the least deserve censure."[78] Each must "hold on to what is his as far as it is not vicious, but is peculiar to him."[79] Even if it means passing up a way of life that is better in the abstract, we must "follow our own nature" and "measure our own by the rule of our own nature." Cicero warns against imitation and emulation: "You cannot preserve [an evenness of life] if you copy someone else's nature and ignore your own."[80] Just as wise actors "do not choose the best plays, but those that are most suited to themselves," so I should be willing to choose a way of life that is fitting for me, whether or not it is best in itself or most admired.[81] When I act otherwise, I "fight against nature" and seek the unattainable.[82]

There is good reason to conclude that this account of the second persona exerted significant influence in the development and articulation of Montesquieu's political particularism. As we have seen, he knew Cicero's *On Duties* well enough to write a treatise modeled on it, and the fruit of his meditation on Cicero's philosophy is discernable as Montesquieu politicizes Cicero's concept of the second persona. In Book 19 of *The Spirit of the Laws,* which contains his most important treatment of regime change, the language and structure of Montesquieu's defense of political particularism strongly indicates the influence of Cicero's approach, as we shall consider. Cicero's theory of individual moral choice furnishes the categories for Montesquieu's counsels concerning political reform. Just as Cicero suggests that each individual must "hold on to what is his" and follow his individual "spirit," Montesquieu suggests that a legislator must not contravene the distinctive spirit or character of his people.[83]

To bring out the affinities between Montesquieu's Book 19 and Cicero's text, it is helpful to consult Philippe Goibaud du Bois's 1714 French translation of *Les Offices.*[84] Montesquieu obtained this edition for his library at La Brède, and while he read Latin, it is reasonable to suppose that he consulted this recent edition with parallel French and

---

[78] Ibid., 1.109.   [79] Ibid., 1.110.   [80] Ibid., 1.111.   [81] Ibid., 1.114.

[82] Ibid., 1.110. "For it is appropriate neither to fight against [particular] nature nor to pursue anything that you cannot attain."

[83] It bears mentioning that Montesquieu's earliest, inchoate formulation of the concept of the "general spirit" appears in "De la politique," which was originally part of the *Traité des devoirs* manuscript. There he speaks of the "*caractere commun*" of a society. See VF 8:505, 515; and ch. 7 below.

[84] Cicero, *Les Offices*, trans. Philippe Goibaud du Bois (Paris: 1714).

Latin text.[85] In this section, I refer occasionally to the Du Bois translation
to highlight the resonances between the language of *Spirit* and *Les
Offices*.

Book 19 of *The Spirit of the Laws* is entitled, "On the Laws in their
relation with the principles forming the general spirit [*esprit général*], the
mores and the manners of a nation." Here Montesquieu insists upon the
need for a fit between political and legal institutions and the *esprit* or
character of the people.[86] Just as Cicero counsels against individuals
following a single, uniformly best plan of life, so Montesquieu counsels
against such a will to uniformity in statecraft. For Cicero, acting in
accordance with one's nature requires acting in accordance with one's
distinctive *animus* or "spirit" (as Du Bois renders it, *esprit*). Montesquieu's discussion of the *esprit général* recalls Cicero's admonition. More
remarkably, Montesquieu offers examples of "general spirits" that mirror
Cicero's examples of "different spirits."

Cicero uses just two simple binaries to illustrate the second persona:
gravity versus gaiety and discretion versus indiscretion. He argues that
though some men are naturally jolly, and others are naturally serious, we
must censure neither type for following their natures. Lucius Crassus was
full of wit, while Gaius Caesar was more reserved. Socrates was "pleasant
and humorous" while Pythagoras was serious (Du Bois: "*serieux* ") and
without any gaiety (Du Bois: "*nulle gayeté dans l'esprit* "). Marcus
Scaurus was exceptionally serious (Du Bois: "*fort grave* ") while Gaius
Laelius was extremely jolly (Du Bois: "*beaucoup ... de gayeté* "). Each of
these characters acted best when he acted in keeping with his natural
disposition – playing the role for which nature had fitted him.

In his discussion of the *esprit général*, Montesquieu unpacks the dis-
tinctly Ciceronian principle that "we do nothing better than what we do
freely and following our natural genius" (*EL* 3.19.5). Four consecutive
chapters serve to illuminate this point using the gaiety-seriousness binary,
now at the national rather than individual level (*EL* 3.19.5–8). He

---

[85] Louis Desgraves and Catherine Volpillhac-Auger, *Catalogue de la bibliothèque de Montesquieu à La Brède* (Naples: Liguori Editore, 1999), 238.

[86] Céline Spector accurately observes that the term "general spirit" is synonymous with
"character" or "genius" as applied to nations in *The Spirit of the Laws* (e.g., *EL* 3.19.5).
Montesquieu draws no meaningful distinctions between the terms. See Céline Spector,
"Spirit, General Spirit," trans. Philip Stewart, in *Dictionnaire Montesquieu*, ed. Catherine
Volpilhac-Auger, http://dictionnaire-montesquieu.ens-lyon.fr. In this connection, it is
worth noting that Du Bois's marginal heading for Cicero's treatment of the second
persona reads, "*Diversité de qualitez & de caracteres*." Cicero, *Les Offices*, 133.

adduces examples reminiscent of those Cicero employs, and his language is redolent of the Du Bois edition. The French have a "sociable humor" and take joy in life: "If one gives a pedantic spirit to a nation naturally full of gaiety [*naturellement gaie*], the state will gain nothing" (*EL* 3.19.5). "May we be left as we are," is the plea of a vivacious French nation. Like the French, the Athenians were also full of gaiety (*gaieté*), in contrast to the "grave, serious [*grave, serieux*]" Spartans (*EL* 3.19.7). Montesquieu suggests that no improvement could have been realized by legislating against the grain in either grave Sparta or gay Athens, but he clearly places the accent upon the need to avoid tampering with national gaiety, a temperament associated with vanity, industriousness, and commerce (*EL* 3.19.8–9).

Though unremarkable in themselves, these examples bear a striking resemblance to Cicero's primary illustration of second persona (gravity/gaiety) in *On Duties*. Moreover, even Cicero's second example of the second persona (discretion/indiscretion) receives a nod when Montesquieu suggests preserving the "often indiscreet" character of the French (*EL* 3.19.5). In this series of chapters, he applies Cicero's concept of the second persona to peoples. The argument, structure, and language of Montesquieu's discussion of the general spirit suggest this connection, and one suspects that the allusions would have appeared even more conspicuous to Montesquieu's contemporaries than they are to today's readers. The former were very likely to be familiar with "Tully's *Offices*," which ranked among the most widely read works on the Continent and in England during the early eighteenth century.[87]

In these Ciceronian chapters of *Spirit*, the discussion of gaiety and gravity leads to a subtle defense of modern commercial society. Montesquieu suggests that gaiety is connected with a sociable temper, and a sociable temper is connected in turn with vanity, the engine of commerce. Legislators and moralists should leave French men and women as they are – gay, vivacious, and vain – as these characteristics give rise to fashion, a "very important subject" (*EL* 3.19.8). Fashion "increases the branches of commerce," a more important subject still. The clear implication is that one benefit of leaving men to their particular natures is that French vanity may fuel French commerce. In this unlikely manner, the Ciceronian concept of the second persona reinforces Montesquieu's defense of the

---

[87] See Andrew R. Dyck, *A Commentary on Cicero, De Officiis* (Ann Arbor, MI: University of Michigan Press, 1996), 39–49.

psychological bases of commercial society.[88] Notably, Cicero's theory requires that each must "hold on to what is his as far as it is not vicious, but is peculiar to him."[89] Montesquieu's counsel, by contrast, culminates in the claim that peoples must be allowed to hold on to what is their own even if it *is* morally vicious (e.g., their vanity). This point he makes explicit two chapters later in a Mandevillean discussion of public virtue and private vice: "I have only wanted to make it understood that ... not all moral vices are political vices, and those who make laws that run counter to the general spirit should not be ignorant of this" (*EL* 3.19.11). Just as Montesquieu had used the Greeks to underscore the incongruity of classical republicanism with modern mores, so he channels Cicero to counsel against "correcting" those very mores. And as with the Greeks' framework, Montesquieu has retained the formal structure of Cicero's theory while shedding much of its moral substance.

This political appropriation of Cicero's second persona relies on an analogy of individual character to national character, an analogy Montesquieu uses explicitly in a passage we have considered earlier: "The legislator is to follow the spirit of the nation when doing so is not contrary to the principles of the government, for we do nothing better than what we do freely and by following our natural genius" (*EL* 3.19.5).[90] The subordinate clause alludes to the everyday experience of following one's "natural genius" in order to support a political application of the same principle.[91] Additionally, as we have seen, Montesquieu's discussion of "singular institutions" in Book 4 tracks closely with his treatment of the "singular man" in the *Pensées* (*MP* 52). Just as few men should attempt to imitate the singular man, so also few nations should seek to imitate the singular institutions of the Greeks (*EL* 1.4.6–7). In short, Montesquieu knew how to analogize collective character to individual character, and his use of Cicero's second persona follows this approach.

---

[88] This seems an especially audacious move when we consider that this is the same Cicero whom Montesquieu, only one book earlier, had quoted as criticizing "men of commerce" for their lack of civic virtue (*EL* 3.18.1).

[89] Cicero, *On Duties*, 1.110.

[90] Commenting on this passage, James W. Ceaser observes, "The *natural* here is given a second meaning, not as a universal, common standard that applies to all individual beings ... but as an inner impulse from which grows something specific to each being." Ceaser, *Liberal Democracy and Political Science* (Baltimore: Johns Hopkins University Press, 1990), 66.

[91] The analogy only goes so far, as Montesquieu is aware. Unlike "natural genius" or Cicero's second persona, the general spirit is formed not only by *natural* attributes but also by laws, habits, and the like.

Finally, we must recall the question that initially motivates *Spirit*'s examination of the relations of the laws: what form of government is most in conformity with nature (*EL* 1.1.3)? Montesquieu's response pluralizes and individuates nature. He states, "It is better to say that the government most in conformity with nature is the one whose particular arrangement best relates to the disposition of the people for whom it is established" (*EL* 1.1.3). For a government to be in conformity with nature, it must do more than merely conform to the requirements of universal human nature. It must also relate well to the *particular* nature of a people, place, and time. Montesquieu thus asserts the manifold nature of nature in contradistinction to, or at least as a supplement to, reigning social contractarian conceptions of nature. This theoretical move mirrors that of Cicero, who complicates the traditional Stoic goal of living *natura*, in accordance with a universal human nature. Cicero brings the idea of a *particular nature* to bear upon moral philosophy, and Montesquieu brings its corollary to bear upon legal and political science.

Cicero's moral theory contributed to the development and articulation of Montesquieu's political particularism, a sensibility he deploys against the classical republican ideal and in service of his new mode. Though Montesquieu understood that Cicero's republicanism was not identical to that of the Greeks, he certainly counted Cicero among the ranks of classical republicans (*EL* 3.18.1). Accruing debts to Athens and Rome alike, Montesquieu follows a pattern of analysis derived from the antique republicans as he mounts a case for the politics of modern liberty.

CONCLUSION

As a magisterial whole, *The Spirit of the Laws* may indeed be "an offspring without a mother." But Montesquieu's encounter with classical political thought played a decisive role in the development of his political particularism, and by tracing this influence, we open to view a new way of seeing the theoretical and rhetorical relationship between his liberal constitutionalism and his political particularism. Previous scholarship has shown that *The Spirit of the Laws* seeks to dethrone the classical republican ideal and to replace it with a more authentically modern regime. But as we have seen, this accomplishment owes something to the Ancients themselves. In Montesquieu's great work, the victory of modern constitutional regimes over the classical republic represents, to a significant degree, the victory of classical particularism over the substantive elements of ancient politics. In a Nietzschean mood, we might even speak of the

self-overcoming of ancient political science. Both rhetorically and theoretically, Montesquieu's classically infused political particularism forms an
integral part of his case for a liberal European future.

This also suggests that one purpose of Montesquieu's *système de
politique* was to show contemporary proponents of classical republicanism that their aspirations ran afoul of their ancient teachers' meta-
principles. For example, Montesquieu likely intended James
Harrington's followers to hear this admonition (*EL* 2.11.6). In his discussion of classical republics, he explicitly addresses "those who want to
make similar institutions" in times present (*EL* 1.4.6). But it is equally
likely that, understanding the enduring appeal of the ancient republic of
virtue,[92] he sought to caution future generations of political men against
allowing the charm of the classical ideal to overwhelm sound political
judgment based upon the realities of the modern disposition – a warning
that would often go unheeded. In *The Spirit of the Laws*, liberal constitutional regimes eclipse the classical republic not only by virtue of their
superior justice, but also by virtue of their superior fit with modern mores
and circumstances, factors that "should not be defied when one makes
laws," as an Athenian once taught.[93]

---

[92] Nannerl O. Keohane, "Virtuous Republics and Glorious Monarchies: Two Models in
Montesquieu's Political Thought," *Political Studies* 20 (1972): 383–96, suggests that he
not only understood the appeal but felt its pull himself. See Chapter 6.
[93] Plato, *Laws*, 747d.

2

Montesquieu and Humanist Constitutionalism

> As God wished to separate us from Italy by a high thrust of mountains, and
> so also he has separated us in almost all things, in mores, laws, nature,
> and humors.
>
> Étienne Pasquier, *Lettres*[1]

At the time of the Revolution in France, one of the most often repeated
complaints against the *ancien régime* was that its laws and jurisdictions were
a confused and irrational decoupage. As Voltaire memorably lamented, a
rider travelling across the Kingdom of France changed laws more often than
he changed horses.[2] By the late eighteenth century, some strains of liberal
political theory had imbibed the principle of legal and institutional uniformity that Voltaire and others championed. Laws so diverse in substance could
not be equally just, and their differences were the products of a benighted
feudal past. This position resulted in the advent of the *Code Napoléon*, and
before that, the replacement of ancient provinces with wholly new administrative *départements*, initially and tellingly drawn by Robert de Hesseln as
perfect eighteen-by-eighteen league squares on a map of France. Among the
difficulties with this plan was that France is not a rectangle, and so De
Hesseln's outermost jurisdictions disappear haplessly into the sea.

But friends of liberty in France were not always enamored of right
angles. When we turn to the state of constitutionalist thought before
Montesquieu's time, and well before the Revolution, we find a strikingly

---

[1] Étienne Pasquier, *Les Lettres* (Paris, 1619), vol. 1, 516.
[2] Voltaire, *Oeuvres complètes de Voltaire* (Paris: Garnier, 1880), tom. 9, 495.

different alignment of political values. More than a hundred years stood between Montesquieu and the French constitutionalists of the sixteenth century, but as we shall see, the most important theoretical touchstones for the revived constitutionalism of the early eighteenth century in France was the *humanist constitutionalism* of the sixteenth century. As Nannerl O. Keohane has observed, French constitutionalism was "stagnant and peripheral throughout much of the seventeenth century."[3] But Montesquieu's own marriage of constitutionalism with a particularistic sensibility is prefigured in the legal and constitutional controversies of sixteenth-century France, particularly in the writings of the legal humanists during the 1560s and 1570s. During this period, constitutionalist arguments regularly invoked the peculiarities of time and place; they appealed to context, to what is homegrown, our own, fitting, and customary – in brief, to the wisdom of legal and institutional diversity.[4] In contrast with the particularism of these humanist constitutionalists, sixteenth-century advocates of royal absolutism often depended upon abstract rational and theological argument, universal law (that is, a universalized Roman law), and the appeal of uniformity.[5] In this context, Montesquieu's liberalism appears in some measure as the culmination of an earlier tradition of constitutionalist thought in France.[6]

[3] Nannerl O. Keohane, *Philosophy and the State in France: The Renaissance to the Enlightenment* (Princeton University Press, 1980), 18. See also Julian H. Franklin, *Jean Bodin and the Rise of Absolutist Theory* (Cambridge University Press, 1973), 105, on the eclipse of constitutionalist theory after the 1590s.

[4] For a classic treatment of this form of constitutional thought beyond the French context, see J. G. A. Pocock, *The Ancient Constitution and the Feudal Law: A Study of English Historical Thought in the Seventeenth Century: A Reissue with a Retrospect* (Cambridge University Press, 1987).

[5] Here I use the term "absolutism" for the view that denies the legitimacy of any limits, checks, or bridles upon the king apart from divine law. In my usage, such a view ascribes to the king "absolute power." But the term *"pouvoir absolue"* is not always used this way in the sixteenth century. For instance, constitutionalist writers will often agree that the king has *"pouvoir absolue"* even while arguing that the king's authority is constitutionally limited in any number of ways (e.g., by precedent, provincial custom, fundamental law, the judgments of parlement). In my usage, such theorists are not "absolutists," despite their willingness to mouth the term *pouvoir absolue*. They are constitutionalists. William Farr Church, *Constitutional Thought in Sixteenth-Century France: A Study in the Evolution of Ideas* (Cambridge, MA: Harvard University Press, 1941), uses the terms in a similar manner.

[6] A number of scholars have briefly noted a connection between Montesquieu's particularism and that of the sixteenth-century legal humanists, and several have observed the connection between legal humanism and constitutionalism. No previous study has considered the way in which Montesquieu's union of particularism and constitutionalism is prefigured in particularistic constitutionalism of legal humanist thought. On the

Both the present chapter and Chapter 1 seek to illuminate the intellectual provenance of Montesquieu's particularism. Our goal is not merely to identify sources but to demonstrate how an understanding of Montesquieu's engagement with these texts and ideas can bring into clearer view the unity of his two animating political sensibilities. In Chapter 1, we observed a writer appropriating a distinct pattern of analysis from the classical world only to turn it against the political ideals of that world; we noted the liberal purposes of Montesquieu's particularism. Similarly, in the present chapter, we consider Montesquieu as heir to a tradition of humanist particularism that set itself against the theory and practice of absolutism. In this way, understanding the antecedents of Montesquieu's particularism prepares us to appreciate the coherence of his project.

HUMANISM, CONSTITUTIONALISM, AND ABSOLUTISM

The Origins of Legal Humanism

Throughout the fifteenth century, to study Roman law was to study the body of commentaries and glosses on the law, in the tradition of the late

---

importance of legal humanist methodology in sixteenth-century French constitutionalism, see especially Quentin Skinner, *The Foundations of Modern Thought* (Cambridge University Press, 1978), vol. 1, 267–75; and Tuck, *Natural Rights Theories*, 38–42. Tuck notes that A. J. Carlyle was perhaps the first modern scholar to take note of the "libertarian," which is to say, constitutionalist character of sixteenth-century legal humanism (39). R. W. Carlyle and A. J. Carlyle, *A History of Medieval Political Theory in the West: Political Theory from 1300 to 1600* (London: W. Blackwood and Sons, 1936), vol. 6, 298–324. On the resemblances between Montesquieu's legal particularism and the historical methods of sixteenth-century legal humanists, see Donald R. Kelley, *Foundations of Modern Historical Scholarship: Language, Law, and History in the French Renaissance* (New York: Columbia University Press, [1931] 1970), 13, 290; Kelley, "Louis Le Caron Philosophe," 48; Adriana McCrea, "Sixteenth- through Eighteenth-Century Philosophy of Law," in *The Philosophy of Law: An Encyclopedia*, ed. Christopher B. Gray (New York: Garland Publishing, 1999), vol. 2, 800; Levy, *Rationalism, Pluralism, and Freedom*, 145–58. A number of scholars have noted Montesquieu's debts to specific legal humanists. On Montesquieu's relationship to François Hotman and Étienne Pasquier, see Édouard Tillet, "*Collectio juris, Oeuvres complètes de Montesquieu*, t. 11 et 12," *Revue Montesquieu* 8 (2005–2006): 220; Robert Launay, "Montesquieu: The Specter of Despotism and the Origins of Comparative Law," in *Rethinking the Masters of Comparative Law*, ed. Annelise Riles (Oxford: Hart Publishing, 2001), 24. Brief appreciations of Pasquier's connection to Montesquieu also appear in Keohane, *Philosophy and the State*, 43–5; Craiutu, *A Virtue for Courageous Minds*, 27; and Isaiah Berlin, *Three Critics of the Enlightenment: Vico, Hamann, Herder* (Princeton University Press, 2000), 158–60.

medieval jurist Bartolus de Saxoferrato.[7] And that body of commentary was voluminous: as one critic of the Bartolist method colorfully observed, when one jurist had glossed a particular word or phrase, scores followed suit, like so many dogs marking a tree. Drawing upon the glosses, the Bartolists engaged mainly in the work of "internal logical analysis" of the *Corpus juris civilis* in order to resolve perceived contradictions in the text. The school operated on the assumption that the Code was a rational body of law, and so apparent contradictions must admit of resolution.[8] This assumption was not as absurd as it first appears, for Bartolist scholarship was not merely antiquarian but practical in its purpose: the Bartolists sought to assist judges who were required to apply Roman law to real cases, and contradictions in the legal corpus hindered this judicial work. In effect, this meant that the Bartolists tended to imbue the *Corpus juris civilis* with coherence and rationality absent in the text.

In 1433, the Italian humanist Lorenzo Valla first called attention to the philological inadequacies of Bartolism.[9] His short treatise attacking Bartolus provoked such uproar among law students at the University of Pavia that he was forced to flee for his life.[10] Valla argued that before rushing to apply the provisions of the *Corpus juris civilis* to contemporary cases, students of Roman law must first take care to discover the original meaning of the words contained in the original Latin texts. Accretions of commentary obscured this meaning. Valla's critique pointed to the need for a new way of studying Roman law that would seek first to recover the original, uncorrupted texts, and then to understand what these texts actually meant in their time. This humanistic approach would require more serious training in classical philology to supplant the barbarous medieval Latin of the Bartolists, as well as a deeper knowledge of the whole of Roman literary, political, social, and legal history.

Valla's call for the development of a humanistic jurisprudence was taken up in earnest by the Milanese jurist and humanist Andrea Alciato, who enjoyed a certain celebrity as he taught Roman law at University of Bourges from 1529–34, and by Guillaume Budé, a French legal scholar

---

[7] Peter Stein, *Roman Law in European History* (New York: Cambridge University Press, [1926] 1999), 71–5.

[8] Julian H. Franklin, *Jean Bodin and the Sixteenth-Century Revolution in the Methodology of Law and History* (New York: Columbia University Press, 1963), 8.

[9] Kelley, *Foundations*, 28–43; Stein, *Roman Law*, 75–6.

[10] Jerry H. Bradley, *Politics and Culture in Renaissance Naples* (Princeton University Press, 1987), 109.

who would emerge as a cofounder of the new humanist school of juris-prudence.[11] Domiciled in Bourges, the school's method became known as the *mos gallicus docendi*, the French way of teaching Roman law, as opposed to the *mos italicus* of the old Bartolists. The *mos gallicus*, or "legal humanism," was marked by two tendencies which, if not exactly contradictory, certainly stood in tension. The first was a reverence for the prize, the uncorrupted text stripped of medieval accretions, a reverence akin to that of both Erasmus and the Protestant humanists for the "recovered" *textus receptus* of the New Testament. Joined with this, however, was a spirit of historical criticism through which humanistic jurists began to see in Roman law not the pristine, rational maxims of wise ancient legislators but a "battered relic" that, even in its presumed original state, was the product of the peculiarities of time and place.[12] It would be decades before the import of this particularistic, and perhaps proto-historicist, sensibility was fully realized in the domain of consti-tutional theory.

Royal Absolutism in Theory and Practice

To trace the path of legal humanism in sixteenth-century France, we must first examine the broader changes afoot in constitutional theory at the time. In the 1520s and 1530s, a swell of absolutist claims arose from the circle of royal legists in the employ of the increasingly absolutist Francis I (r. 1515–47). The legists began to make subtle emendations to the late medieval view of the French constitution, which conceived of the King of France as limited not only by divine law, but also by the authority of an independent clergy, independent *parlements* with judicial as well as quasi-legislative powers, and diverse customary laws impervious to the king's revision or purgation. Claude de Seyssel had captured this traditional view, now under fire, in his *La Grande Monarchie de France* (1519); there he explained that the king has always been limited by *la religion* (ecclesiastical authorities), *la justice* (the parlements), and *la police* (cus-tomary law).[13]

---

[11] Carl Friedrich, "The Humanists," in *The Philosophy of Law in Historical Perspective* (University of Chicago Press, 1963), 208–10; Kelley, *Foundations*, 55.

[12] Skinner, *Foundations*, vol. 1, 207.

[13] Church regards Claude de Seyssel's chief work, published in the first year of Francis's reign, as the classic statement of the traditional view. Church, *Constitutional Thought*, 17. See Claude de Seyssel, *The Monarchy of France*, trans. J. H. Hexter, ed. Donald R. Kelley (New Haven, CT: Yale University Press, [1519] 1981); Rebecca Ard Boone,

Beginning with the unprecedented absolutist tract of the *regalian* Jean Ferrault, *Insignia pecularia christianissimi Francorum regni* (1520), the legists of Francis I began to loosen the traditional bridles described by Seyssel.[14] In doing so, they relied in part on a Roman conception of the French monarch as emperor in his own domain.[15] The analogy of the king of France to the Roman emperor *(princeps)* served as the key pivot point for the use of Roman law to support absolutism in France. Eventually this analogy would be backed by the explicit claim that the ancient kings of France legitimately received the untrammeled authority of the *imperium Romanum* in Gaul.[16] But even before this argument was fully articulated, the analogy had animated absolutist public law doctrine. Many understood Justinian's Code as recognizing the emperor's *merum imperium* – total power including an exclusive right of giving laws – and the legists could by analogy attribute this power to the King of France.[17] Similarly, frequent appeals to the Roman doctrine of *princeps legibus solutus est* ("the ruler is exempt from the laws"), found in the *Digest*, permitted royal legists to argue for the elevation of kingly authority above the customs and fundamental laws of the realm.[18] Applied to France, the Roman principle of *quod principi plaucit habet legis vigorem* ("what

---

War, *Domination, and the Monarchy of France: Claude de Seyssel and the Language of Politics in the Renaissance* (Leiden: Brill, 2007); Keohane, *Philosophy and the State,* 32–42; J. H. Hexter, "Claude de Seyssel and Normal Politics in the Age of Machiavelli," in *Art, Science, and History in the Renaissance,* ed. Charles S. Singleton (Baltimore: John Hopkins Press, 1967), 389–415.

[14] J. W. Allen, *History of Political Thought in the Sixteenth Century* (London: Routledge, 2013), 283; Jacques Poujol, "Jean Ferrault on the King's Privileges," *Studies in the Renaissance* 5 (1958): 15–17.

[15] Franklin, *Jean Bodin and the Sixteenth-Century Revolution,* 41n.15. Keohane also notes that the Roman imperial inheritance was among the most important foundations for absolutist theory in sixteenth-century France. Keohane, *Philosophy and the State in France,* 54. Stephen Murphy goes further: "The Roman tradition is the principal source of absolutist thought in the sixteenth century. With the renewed study of Roman law came a keener perception of what universal authority meant." Murphy, *The Gift of Immortality,* 234. See also Myron Piper Gilmore, *Argument from Roman Law in Political Thought, 1200–1600* (Cambridge, MA: Harvard University Press, 1941), 131–2.

[16] As we will see later in the chapter, this view received its most elaborate expression in the eighteenth-century work of Jean-Baptiste Dubos and its most elaborate refutation in Montesquieu's *Spirit of the Laws.*

[17] Church, *Constitutional Thought,* 55.

[18] Alan Watson, ed., *The Digest of Justinian* (Philadelphia: University of Pennsylvania Press), 1.3.31; Gilmore, *Roman Law,* 131. See Adhémar Esmein, "La Maxime *Princeps legibus est* dans l'ancien droit public français," in ed. Paul Vinogradoff, *Essays in Legal History* (Oxford University Press, 1913), 201–14; Glenn Burgess, *Absolute Monarchy and the Stuart Constitution* (New Haven, CT: Yale University Press, 1996), 97.

pleases the ruler has the force of law") aided jurists in breaking with the traditional medieval understanding of the king as a mere judge, not possessed of the power to make law.[19] In short, "There was a deliberate and well-nigh complete fusion of Roman and French interpretations causing the practical identification of the French king and Roman *princeps*."[20] Naturally, then, absolutists were able to regard any institution that did not accord with the imperial vision of princely power as a product of usurpation.

Crucially, just as the Roman emperor could abolish local customs according to the Code, so also, the legists reasoned, the King of France held authority over the customs of the kingdom.[21] More moderate jurists, such as Chasseneuz,[22] still defended the integrity and independence of custom, holding that royal letters could not override provincial usages. But the avant garde of absolutism began to appeal more strenuously and frequently to Roman law as well as higher law – natural and divine – to back up royal abrogation of customary law. They suggested that the king could nullify local customs that he found to be inconsistent with higher law. Rebuffi argued that the king was bound by custom only when it accorded with natural law and reason as understood, of course, by the king; Tiraqueau asserted that the king was bound by custom only if such custom was supported by divine precept; and Charron protested that the diverse customs of the provinces did not embody true justice and wisdom but were rather arbitrary usages and should be judged according to abstract moral criteria.[23] In short, the absolutists were eager to ground their arguments on universal, natural, and abstract grounds. William Farr Church characterizes the intellectual currents this way:

As the [sixteenth] century progressed, the tendency became more and more to interpret legal problems in terms of natural and divine law rather than the customary law of the land. This increased emphasis upon the upper brackets of the scale ... exercised an unmistakably devitalizing influence upon the older

---

[19] *Digest*, 1.4.1; Justinian, *Justinian's Institutes*, trans. Peter Birks and Grant McLeod (Ithaca, NY: Cornell University Press, 1987), 1.2.6.

[20] Church, *Constitutional Thought*, 9. Skinner adds, "The legists had mainly continued to follow the scholastic approach, treating Roman law as an immediately applicable authority, and arguing that the absolutism of the French monarch should be seen as a direct continuation of the Imperium of the later Roman Empire." Quentin Skinner, *The Foundations of Modern Thought* (Cambridge University Press, 1978), vol. 2, 269. See also Franklin, *Jean Bodin and the Sixteenth-Century Revolution*, 41.

[21] See Church, *Constitutional Thought*, 103.

[22] Franklin, *Jean Bodin and the Rise of Absolutist Theory*, 13.

[23] Church, *Constitutional Thought*, 65, 67, 306.

constitutionalism; for when many of its crucial aspects, such as the essence of customary law and the legal limitations upon the king, were interpreted purely in terms of abstract values, there was certain to occur a change in the qualities ascribed to the legal foundations of the state ... Such a use of universal principles by the legists served as a vital factor in the rise of absolutism.[24]

Though lines separating absolutist from constitutionalist were not perfectly clear, as opponents of royal excess were required to address readers prudently, the appeal of universalism (including the universalization of Roman law) unquestionably served the cause of royal absolutism.

As we will consider in the next section, legal humanism would in time beget a humanist constitutionalism in reaction to this new absolutist theory. But initially, some jurists trained in the methods of legal humanism, and even the early leader of the humanists at the University of Bourges, Guilliame Budé, espoused views consistent with this legist absolutism, grounded in foreign law and higher law.[25] Budé drew the parallel between the Roman emperor and the French king. In his *Annotations on the Pandects*, he comments tellingly on the brocard *"princeps legibus solutus est."*[26] Tying the maxim to Aristotle's discussion of the kingship of a man naturally superior to all others, he argues that such a man is a human Jove, a god among men, no more subject to human or positive law than is God himself. Budé then proceeds to ascribe such authority not only to the *principes Romani*, but also to "our kings ... who have everything in their power [*Reges nostri ... qui omnia in potestate habet*]."[27] While Budé agrees with Rebuffi that the king may voluntarily submit to law in order to maintain popular support, the king is nevertheless without formal obligations save to the divine law.[28] The authority of customary law and fundamental law declined as absolutists recast French public law in a Roman mold.

---

[24] Ibid., 8.

[25] See David M. McNeil, *Guillaume Budé and Humanism in the Reign of Francis I* (Geneva: Droz, 1975), 37–48. See also Tuck, *Natural Rights Theories*, 39. On the connection between early legal humanism and absolutist doctrine in the Parlement of Toulouse, see Allen, *History of Political Thought in the Sixteenth Century*, ch. 3, §1. There is some disagreement about whether Andrea Alciato, a cofounder of the *mos gallicus*, belongs among the absolutists. Compare Tuck, *Natural Rights Theories*, 38–9, with Gilmore, *Roman Law*, 49–56, and Kelley, *Foundations*, 99.

[26] Guillaume Budé, *Annotationes in quator et viginti Pandectarum libros* (Paris: 1535), 90–1.

[27] Ibid., 91.

[28] "Kings should be governed only by divine law," writes Budé in his mirror of princes. Guillaume Budé, "On the Education of the Prince," in *Cambridge Translations of Renaissance Philosophical Texts*, trans. Neil Kenny, ed. Jill Kraye (Cambridge University Press, 1997), vol. 2, 259.

The rise of absolutist theory in the early sixteenth century mirrored practical developments in the exercise of royal power over the same period. Developments especially significant for our purposes are the efforts to codify provincial customs under Louis XII (r. 1498–1515) and Francis I.[29] As we have noted, the early modern kingdom of France, like most of continental Europe, was governed by a patchwork of provincial and local customs. No two domains were governed alike in every point of law. A "prodigious diversity" reigned, as Montesquieu writes (*EL* 6.28.45). Confronted with this diversity, the "spider king," Louis XI (r. 1423–83), first floated the notion of unifying the various customs into a single text for the entire kingdom, but he did little to advance the project.[30] Later, under the reigns of Louis XII and Francis I, efforts got underway to codify and to "correct" the customs of the provinces, with increasing royal control of the codification process.

Few could deny the administrative benefits of clarifying and untangling the customs of the provinces, and all parties recognized that there were many abuses in need of removal.[31] But in time it became clear that the codification process would entail an expansion of the powers of the crown. Before codification, many regarded provincial and local customary law as having independent authority derived from its immemorial usage by the people and their judges. But codification was, as J. G. A. Pocock rightly suggests, an "act of sovereignty, an assertion that the ruler's will and reason were superior even to ancient custom."[32] Codification took place at the behest of the king; the king prescribed the procedures that were to be observed in the depositions when the content of custom was set forth; and only the crown could authorize redactions, as Montesquieu himself points out (*EL* 6.28.45). As the customs were recorded, they were corrected on the basis of abstract criteria of justice and, predictably, Roman legal principles. The final text was published in the name of the king and often with a royal letter attesting to its legality.[33]

[29] See John P. Dawson, "The Codification of the French Customs," *Michigan Law Review* 38 (1940): 765–800.

[30] Dawson, "Codification of the French Customs," 771. Louis XI's father, Charles XII, had undertaken some codification efforts, but with no clear intention to unify the customs into a single text.

[31] Church, *Constitutional Thought*, 35, 311. [32] Pocock, *The Ancient Constitution*, 25.

[33] Dawson, "Codification of the French Customs," 775, 782. The constitutionalist Guy Coquille saw the dangers of this practice and insisted that royal approval of written customs should be seen as a mere administrative technicality, in no way undermining the independent authority of custom. For Coquille, custom was "a manifestation of the

Though there was some variation in this process across the provinces, codification helped to shape a context in which it would be more natural to view custom as subordinate to the king. Because he imparts his authority to it as a legislator, he can in principle abrogate it at any time. The identification of royal ordinances with the authority of custom was therefore increasingly common. In short, while not all early supporters of codification were crypto-absolutists, the movement to codify and to rationalize the customs of France provided new practical foundations for the absolutists' efforts to elevate the king above custom and to undermine the traditional bridle of *la police* articulated by Seyssel.[34]

During the same period, even more significant changes were afoot in the relationship between the crown and the Parlement of Paris, a crucial part of the bridle of *la justice* in Seyssel's account. Following a constitutional crisis concerning ecclesiastical appointments, Francis I made a series of incursions upon the traditional constitutional status of the Parlement of Paris in an attempt to humiliate the *parlementaires* who had resisted him and to prevent future resistance. Francis wished to assert the principle that the crown was the source of all power in the realm, and no organ of government could restrain it. In 1527, he required members of the Parlement of Paris to procure letters of delegation from him annually, a regular reminder of the putatively derivative nature of their power.[35] In principle, the entire parlement could be recommissioned each year, hindering sustained resistance to royal actions.[36] Francis also made several illegal appointments to the Parlement of Paris, which resulted in the body (under new management) acquiescing to the absolutist principle that "authority and power to make a general law belong to him alone."[37] In essence, the crown pressed the parlements to accept a crudely voluntarist and absolutist conception of law: whatever the king willed was law. Whereas they formerly maintained the right to resist the registration of royal acts that were illegal or immoral, they were now forced to agree that they could only resist registration or implementation if they judged that the law "did not embody the king's authentic will" – a flimsy bridle indeed.[38]

This new arrangement mirrored the juridical relationship of the Roman Senate to the emperor, but it was a radical departure from the

ancient and continued authority of the people to establish law over themselves." Church, *Constitutional Thought*, 283.

[34] William Farr Church, "The Decline of French Jurists as Political Theorists," *French Historical Studies* 3 (1967): 23–5.

[35] Lange, *The First French Reformation*, 212.   [36] Ibid., 224.   [37] Ibid., 232.

[38] Ibid., 233.

traditional constitutionalist view of the Parlement of Paris. In his account of the constitution of France, Seyssel had specifically emphasized the superiority of the Parlement of Paris over its Roman counterpart. Under French customary law, he maintained, royal acts "are subject to the judgments of the Parlements, not touching obreption and subreption only, as it is with other princes according to the Roman law, but also with respect to legality and illegality."[39] Unlike the Senate of the Roman Empire, the Parlement of Paris could refuse to enforce a royal ordinance if it judged such an ordinance inconsistent with the fundamental or otherwise long-standing laws of the realm, even if the ordinance contained no hint of fraud ("obreption and subreption"). On Seyssel's understanding, Roman senators under the empire could only block enforcement of an enactment if they judged it fraudulent, that is, if it did not represent the emperor's true will. Less than two decades after Seyssel's account appeared, Francis I would maintain that the Parlement of Paris, like the Roman Senate, was authorized only to judge whether an ordinance represented the king's true will. This assault on the independent power of the Parlement was consistent with and justified by both the Roman template and related claims concerning the divine origin of monarchical power.

Putting Roman Law in Its Place: The Origins of Humanist Constitutionalism

As we have seen, some legal humanists, such as Budé, were complicit in the burgeoning theory and practice of Valois absolutism. Yet on a more profound level, legal humanism had from the first inception begun to sow the seeds of a revived constitutionalism that would emerge in the 1560s in opposition to absolutism. This new constitutionalism would prove to be more radical than the traditional constitutionalism of Seyssel. It would rest on a "new set of theoretical foundations," namely, the humanist's lively awareness of the relationship of law to the particularities of time, place, and mores.[40]

---

[39] Seyssel, *The Monarchy of France*, 55.
[40] Skinner, *Foundations*, vol. 1, 208. Julian H. Franklin suggests that the premises of humanist constitutionalism were present even in the writings of Budé, who was himself an absolutist. Franklin writes, "The philological approach inevitably focused on the relationship of Roman law to the specific circumstances under which it was produced. It is, in fact, the peculiarities of Roman institutions on which Budé lays the greatest

If the legal humanists' immersion in Roman law moved some in the direction of royal absolutism, other elements of the humanist paradigm exerted a more lasting influence in the opposite direction. For as educators and theorists of legal history, the legal humanists nursed a particularistic sensibility more profound than mere preoccupation with Roman legal concepts. Humanism was at bottom a challenge to the ahistorical and decontextualized methodology of its scholastic and Bartolist precursors. At their worst, the Bartolists had ignored the fact that Roman law was a historical artifact; they had treated the language of Roman law as a universal, rational vocabulary. By contrast, the legal humanists would insist upon historical philology as the precondition for grasping the meaning of any classical texts, especially legal texts. This demand was justified by Valla's basic insight that language and meaning are products of consensus and custom, not nature; the temporal distance separating the modern from the ancient world would block our efforts to access directly the meaning of classical texts.[41] Genuine understanding of these texts would come only as the hard-won prize of a new historical philology that could uncover the sense of words and phrases in their particular cultural and political context. As Kelley puts it, Valla insisted on "a return to human 'reality,' for he was convinced that knowledge could be attained only through the examination of particular things."[42] The historico-philological bent of legal humanism suggested that "every age had literally to be understood in its own terms," not through the distorted lens of the present nor from an Archimedian point of natural reason.[43]

This path leads to legal particularism. The philological approach itself was "inevitably focused on the relationship of Roman law to the specific circumstances under which it was produced," as Franklin observes.[44] Laws could no more easily be separated from their cultural milieu than could words. Legal humanist scholarship demonstrated first, the utter dependency of language on time and place, and then correlatively, the dependence of law on circumstances. Laws were no more the product of Reason than were words, nor were they the *ex nihilo* product of the legislator's creative will. Like language, law developed by convention, in history, to suit the needs of the people then living. It was as unlikely that a

---

emphasis. And he frequently attempts to clarify a Roman practice by contrasting it with European counterparts." Franklin, *Jean Bodin and the Sixteenth-Century Revolution*, 23.

[41] Michael Randall, *The Gargantuan Polity: On the Individual and the Community in the French Renaissance* (University of Toronto Press, 2008), 184.

[42] Ibid., 184; Kelley, *Foundations*, 28–33.   [43] Kelley, *Foundations*, 45–6.

[44] Franklin, *Jean Bodin and the Sixteenth-Century Revolution*, 23.

law from the distant past would suit our times as it was that a word from the same distant past had retained its unadulterated meaning. Thus the study of the language of law in its historical context rendered legal humanist scholars acutely alive to the role of time, place, and circumstance in shaping the substance of law.

While legal humanism arose in order to recover the ancient world and bring it nearer to us, the lasting achievement of the school was ironically "to increase the sense of historical distance between themselves and the ancient texts which they made it their business to understand."[45] The legal humanists did not set out to undermine or delegitimize Roman law. But the inevitable effect of their method, as they soon came to understand, was to undermine the notion that Roman law, or any law, could reasonably aspire to universality.[46] From the beginning, legal humanism cultivated a sensibility hostile to the ahistorical assumption that Roman law could be applied to any existing circumstances. This sensibility thus tended to diminish, in the long run, the substantive influence of the Roman law on the constitutional thought of the humanists by demonstrating that the *Corpus juris civilis* belonged to a world long since vanished. "After sixty years of philological corrections, and of logical reworking of the whole," Julian Franklin notes, "it was finally felt that the legislation of Justinian was incomplete and historically particular."[47]

The humanists' sense of the historical particularity and relativity of law was intensified by their insight that the compilation of Roman law contained in the *Corpus juris civilis* reflected not a single historical epoch but rather various periods in Roman history. The humanists accumulated examples of how Roman law had changed to reflect transformations in society and politics, rendering even more improbable its claim to the status of universal law. As Peter Stein writes,

The humanists recognized that the state of Roman law was related to the state of Roman society, and that as that society changed, so did the law. In particular they noted that the law of a particular period was affected by the political situation of the time. Some thought that the study of ancient law might offer answers to their own constitutional problems. But the more they related Roman law to what they discovered about Roman society, the more they realised how different their society was from the society of ancient Rome. That realization led them in turn to question whether it was appropriate to seek to use Roman law as a model for contemporary France at all.[48]

---

[45] Skinner, *Foundations*, vol. 1, 207.   [46] See Schiffman, *The Birth of the Past*, 187.
[47] Franklin, *Jean Bodin and the Sixteenth-Century Revolution*, 79.
[48] Stein, *Roman Law*, 78.

It became difficult indeed to regard a body of law as *ratio scripta* once its content could be accounted the product of social and political flux.

As humanism called into question the immediate applicability of Roman law, legal scholars began to turn with greater interest to their own *lex terrae*, the fundamental and customary laws of France. A vernacular humanism emerged and increasingly occupied many scholars trained in or influenced by classical legal humanism. They had learned that Roman law was maladapted to France and any context other than its own. If humanist scholars aimed to discover useful insights for the reform and refinement of French institutions, their method and energies would be most fruitfully employed in the study of the customs and constitutional history of France. French law and institutions were to be studied on their own terms and in their own historical context without the taint of imaginative Romanizing. While not all scholars turning to vernacular history and jurisprudence were constitutionalists, vernacular humanism inevitably channeled scholarly interests toward the study of the ancient constitution of the Franks, the origin of fiefs, and the history of French customs, an element of Seyssel's *la police*.[49] On balance, this "Gallican turn" contributed to a reinvigorated constitutionalism that had learned to defend limited monarchy not only as the inheritance of the French nation, but also as the political order best suited to the particular history and spirit of the French people.

Hotman's Humanist Constitutionalism

This union of constitutionalism and particularism, which prefigures Montesquieu's own, features in the work of writers at the vanguard of this new genre of French constitutional history, François Hotman (1524–90) and his student, Étienne Pasquier (1529–1615). While the same pattern is present in the work of other humanist writers active during French wars of religion (1562–98) – among them Bernard du Haillan, Pierre Ayrault, Louis Le Roy, and Guy Coquille – Hotman and Pasquier produced the most original and influential contributions to humanist constitutionalism,

---

[49] Customary law was a species of law that aligned perfectly with the paradigmatic conception of law emerging from legal humanist scholarship. The diversity among provincial customs in France testified to the character of law as an outgrowth of local circumstances and character as opposed to the mere product of the legislator's creative will.

and their work captures the diversity of the school.[50] Hotman was a contractarian and favored the Estates General as the source of constitutional renewal, while Pasquier favored strengthening the Parlement of Paris as the historic source of restraint in the French monarchy. Yet these significant differences notwithstanding, both Pasquier and Hotman defend a humanist constitutionalism that places the accent upon historical origins, local fit, and the conformity of law to mores. Present in both are a spirit of relativity and historical sense that recall the original humanist emphasis upon context and anticipate Montesquieu's liberal particularism.

Surveys of sixteenth-century political thought typically place François Hotman at front ranks of the "Huguenot revolutionaries" and "monarchomachs," but he was also a legal humanist and successor to Jacques Cujas in the chair of jurisprudence at the University of Bourges, the hub of legal humanism in Europe. In his influential *Francogallia* (1573), Hotman traces the French monarchy to the ancient institutions of the Gauls and Germans, depicted in Caesar's *De Bello Gallico* and the *Germania* of Tacitus. Before the Roman conquest, he argues, Gaul was divided into several commonwealths, some ruled by nobles, others by elected kings. No ruler in Gaul wielded "unlimited, free and uncontrolled power."[51] Similarly, elected kings led the tribal war bands of Germans, and the "right of the people was supreme" in choosing and cashiering kings.[52] The descendants of these peoples, the Gallo-Romans and Germanic Franks, respectively, cooperated to establish the kingdom of "Francogallia," or France, following the fifth-century Frankish entry into Gaul.[53] Hotman imagines a merger of these two peoples and constitutions with the common election of Childeric as king of the "Francogallic" regime in the mid-fifth century. This political order was but the extension

---

[50] The term *humanist constitutionalism* is my own, but as noted earlier, previous scholars have recognized the importance of legal humanist methodology in sixteenth-century French constitutionalism. See fn. 6.

[51] François Hotman, *Francogallia*, eds. Ralph Giesey and J. H. M. Salmon (Cambridge University Press, 1972), *Francogallia*, 155.

[52] Ibid., 222. The classic study of Hotman's life and thought is Donald R. Kelley, *François Hotman: A Revolutionary's Ordeal* (Princeton University Press, 1973).

[53] Discussion of the ancient Frankish origins of the French state are related to the broader theme of "Gothic constitutionalism," on which see Pocock, *The Ancient Constitution*; James Tully, *Strange Multiplicity: Constitutionalism in an Age of Diversity* (Cambridge University Press, 1995); and Charles Howard McIlwain, *Constitutionalism Ancient and Modern* (Ithaca, NY: Cornell University Press, 1947); Jacob Levy, *Rationalism, Pluralism, and Freedom* (Oxford University Press, 2015), chs. 5–6.

of the immemorially bridled regimes of these two ancient peoples. The king ruled in a mixed regime with warrior-nobles and the assembly of the nation, from which the neglected French institution of the Estates General derives.[54] On Hotman's view, the desuetude of the Estates constituted a profound corruption of the Francogallic regime, and as he makes clear in his dedicatory epistle (judiciously withheld from his censors), the purpose of his history is to call for the restoration of the Estates as the legitimate, representative counterweight to the crown. Hotman moves beyond the traditional constitutionalism of Seyssel, who defended the independence of the Parlement of Paris but never mentioned the Estates General or estates provincial in his treatment of constitutional limits. He regards the parlements as royal innovations introduced to diminish the power of the Estates General, the truly indispensable ballast in the ship of state.[55]

Hotman's radical constitutionalism depends upon an implicit appeal to the authority of custom. The ancient constitution of Francogallia arose organically, like all custom, and it was lost only through the willful interference of enterprising princes, not through any failure to serve or suit the purposes of the people.[56] This implicit regard for custom and particular fit, the foundation of the Francogallia, is on display in Hotman's less well-known *Anti-Tribonian* (1567). A "worthy descendant of Valla's work," the treatise is a culminating contribution to the *mos gallicus* critique of Roman law.[57] Hotman's ostensible target is Tribonian, the unfortunate whom Justinian charged with supervising the compilation of Roman law. Through this attack on Tribonian and the *Corpus juris*, Hotman deals a crippling blow to the view of Roman law as universal, rational, and atemporal. The work shows, first, that the *Corpus juris* does not even contain a faithful account of the laws of Rome at any time in its history. Whereas the Bartolists tended to treat Roman legal texts "as expressions of, or at least approximations of, a single

---

[54] Hotman, *Francogallia*, 205, 219.

[55] Ibid., ch. 29. There was some fluidity in Hotman's views on the relative merits of the Parlement of Paris and the Estates General. See Adrianna E. Bakos, *Images of Kingship in Early Modern France: Louis XI in Political Thought, 1560–1789* (London: Routledge, 1997), 34.

[56] But cf. Zachary S. Schiffman, "Humanism and the Problem of Relativism," in *Humanism in Crisis: The Decline of the French Renaissance*, ed. Philippe Desan (Ann Arbor, MI: University of Michigan Press, 1991), 69–83, esp. 72, on the limits of history as the grounds of Hotman's argument. Hotman appeals sporadically to the views of Plato, Aristotle, and Cicero on the mixed constitution in order buttress his historical defense of the ancient constitution of Francogallia. See especially Hotman, *Francogallia*, ch. 10.

[57] Kelley, *Foundations*, 109.

unchanging code of ideals," Hotman demonstrates that Tribonian's sources were inadequate. The final product was a cut-and-paste job that represented neither the laws of the republic, nor of the empire, nor of Constantinople, but a disorderly collage of all three.[58] More importantly, Hotman shows that, to the extent a scholar can identify the historical provenance of each part of the *Corpus juris*, he can show that these parts fit and reflect the spirit, time, and political regime from which they arose. They are alien to the French situation.

Hotman opens the book with an Aristotelian principle that appears in both Montesquieu's own thought and Chapter 1: "[T]he laws of a country must be accommodated to the state and form of the regime, and not the regime to the laws."[59] The laws are the "diet" of a country and the best diet will vary as forms, "complexions," and "qualities" of social and political life vary.[60] To universalize the law code of one people is as senseless as universalizing the diet of a particular individual. The burden of *Anti-Tribonian* is to show specifically how the Roman diet of laws was suited not to the French body, but to the Roman body at the time of its adoption. A "great and enormous diversity" separates these two bodies, and we should expect a similarly great diversity in their laws.[61]

For Hotman, several striking differences between France and Rome suffice to demonstrate the incompatibility of Roman law and French society. Most conspicuously, the entire *Corpus juris* assumes the existence of a society divided into two classes, the patrician and plebian. Roman law turns upon these two classes as upon "two hinges," but French society has no similar hinges upon which to mount this foreign body of law.[62] Thus Roman law stands "entirely contrary" to the French social

---

[58] Ibid., 88; François Hotman, *Antitribonian* (Paris: 1603; facsimile ed. in *Images et temoins de l'age classique*, no. 9 [Publications de L'Université de Saint-Etienne, 1980]), 22.

[59] Hotman, *Antitribonian*, 6; translations are mine. See Aristotle, *Politics*, 1289a11–14: "One should try to see ... which [laws] are appropriate for each of the constitutions. For laws should be established, and all do establish them, to suit the constitution and not the constitution to suit the laws."

[60] Hotman, *Antitribonian*, 6.

[61] Ibid., 13. On the puzzling and unexpected conclusion to *Antitribonian* (ch. 18), in which Hotman calls for an assembly of jurisconsults to study the laws of all peoples in order to identify the best, see Pocock, *The Ancient Constitution*, 24. Pocock speculates that Hotman may be referring only to legislator's law but not to French customary law, which would not undergo similar evaluation. Other scholars have speculated that Hotman's project would cover private law, but not public law. Still others have suggested that Hotman's conclusion is an anomaly, a paradox, or an oversight. For an additional discussion see Schiffman, *The Birth of the Past*, 187–8.

[62] Hotman, *Antitribonian*, ch. 3; 13.

order.[63] As for political institutions, Hotman emphasizes that Rome was not at any time a monarchy like the regime of France. It was a republic, and afterwards an empire, but these forms bear no resemblance to the French constitution. As Hotman's Aristotelian principle dictates, the laws of such different regimes could not be accommodated to France, for laws follow from and must conform to regime type. Laws of the Roman republic and the French monarchy are mismated.[64] As for laws of the empire, Hotman points out the vast difference among varieties of monarchy. Some monarchies are absolute, while others are "strictly moderated"; some are pacific and small, others belligerent and expansionist.[65] The laws of an absolute monarchy could not be suitably transplanted within the constitutional monarchy of France. Therefore, he concludes, "[I]t follows that the laws of one monarchy are usually almost useless to another monarchy, just as medicines are not appropriate to every person even if they are the same sex, the same age, and of the same country."[66]

Hotman deepens his particularistic analysis by showing in detail that some elements of the Code of Justinian are clearly relics of Rome's republican past – the *"temps de la democratie"* – while others are accommodated to the requisites of the imperial age. Within the Code itself, Hotman finds evidence of the relativity of law to time, regime type, and mores. Some laws in Tribonian's compilation were suitable to Rome in its youth, others to its later grandeur of age. But the Code taken as a whole would have been ill-fitted to Rome herself at any single point in history. As Hotman explains in another colorful analogy: "Not all snacks are appropriate for all horses; even those that would have been appropriate for young horses are not good when they have become old; and therefore the ancients have often said that the laws change often according to the seasons and mutations of the mores and conditions of a people."[67] Hotman understands that the Aristotelian principle entails the view that private and public law must suit the way of life, conditions, and mores of the people. This requirement is more likely to be met when law arises from custom and usage, like the ancient constitution of Francogallia.

---

[63] Ibid., 15.   [64] Ibid., 13.   [65] Ibid., 10.

[66] Ibid., 10–11. Moreover, on a narrower institutional level, Hotman shows that the authority charged with applying the laws, the judiciary, takes radically different forms in Rome and France, suggesting again an incongruity between Rome law and French organs of government (9–10).

[67] Ibid., 12.

A law professor determined to diminish the place of Roman law in French legal education, Hotman laments the squandering of students' time in a tedious examination of offices and laws accommodated to a people of "fashions and humors so different than ours."[68] If your aim is to "prepare a young man to serve the French regime one day, consider which of the two studies he should pursue: that of the Roman and Constantinopolitan magistrates, or that of the officers of the Crown and Justice of the Kingdom, so as to know and understand the right of sovereignty of our kings, the power and authority of the three estates," and other such points of French fundamental law.[69] On Hotman's view, the choice could not be clearer. The study of Roman public law and offices confers little practical value but threatens much political harm as it may multiply the number of public servants who see in the French monarchy a simulacrum of the Roman imperial regime.

Hotman's historical analysis of Roman law was not groundbreaking in every respect, for as I have suggested, its premises had been laid by decades of humanist scholarship. His main contribution in this area was to state more fully and clearly the implications of the humanists' historical-critical method for Roman law. By particularizing, relativizing, and contextualizing Roman law, legal humanism had permanently undermined its claims to universality. The particular suitability of French custom would supplant the universality of Roman law in this new wave of legal humanist scholarship, for the customs of France were not similarly subject to historicizing criticism. As J. G. A. Pocock explains,

Because custom was by its nature unwritten law, the usages of the folk interpreted through the mouths of judges, it could be argued with some plausibility that it could never become obsolete. If this custom no longer suited the needs of the people, it was said, they would by now have thrown it away; that they have not done so proves that, however ancient it may be, it cannot be out of date ... Since the people had retained a given custom through many centuries, it had proved itself apt to meet all the emergencies which had arisen during that period.[70]

Custom, in contrast to Roman law, could thus be regarded as *tam antiqua et tam nova*. Hotman's *Anti-Tribonian* was part of a broader reaction to absolutism that opposed municipal folk-usages to absolutist legislation, as Pocock has shown.

In all this, we see clearly the interdependence of Hotman's particularism, born of legal humanist methodology, and his constitutionalism that

---

[68] Ibid., 18.   [69] Ibid., 17.   [70] Pocock, *The Ancient Constitution*, 15.

rejects the Roman absolutist model in favor of an ancient and native French constitution. By undermining the universal validity of Roman law, humanist constitutionalists attempted to strip the new discourse of absolutism of one of its most important arguments, and they issued an invitation to turn to national, vernacular history as a source of public law.[71] This revived constitutionalism was insufficient to stem the tide of royal absolutism. But it forged or revealed a fundamental link between constitutionalism and political particularism, a feature that would reappear in Montesquieu's work after the relative dormancy of French constitutionalist theory throughout most of the seventeenth century.

Pasquier's Humanist Constitutionalism

Among the humanist constitutionalists of the sixteenth century, Hotman's influence was incomparably great outside France. At home, his significance was matched by that of his student, Étienne Pasquier (1529–1615).[72] A historian and advocate-general at the *Cours de comptes*, Pasquier studied with the great legal humanists of Bourges and Toulouse, and he travelled to Pavia to train under Andrea Alciato.[73] He numbered among the *parlementaires* who, like Seyssel, saw the Parlement of Paris as the key bridle upon royal power. On Pasquier's view, historians could not justly ascribe "*longue ancienneté*" to Hotman's celebrated Estates General, for neither the pre-Roman Gallic assemblies nor the assemblies of the early Franks included the common people, as the Estates did.[74] But notwithstanding their significant institutional disagreements, Pasquier's constitutionalism, like that of Hotman, bears the marks of a strongly particularistic sensibility stemming from their common humanist paradigm.

---

[71] Keohane, *Philosophy and the State*, 54.

[72] Kelley considers Pasquier "the fulfillment of humanist historical thought." Donald R. Kelley, "Legal Humanism and the Sense of History," *Studies in the Renaissance* 13 (1966): 198. Roelker argues that he was a "model for succeeding generations" of *parlementaire* constitutionalists. Nancy Lyman Roelker, *One King, One Faith: The Parlement of Paris and the Religious Reformations of the Sixteenth Century* (Berkeley, CA: University of California Press, 1996), 136. See generally Kelley, *Foundations*, ch. 10.

[73] Kelley, *Foundations*, 123, 272; George Huppert, *The Idea of Perfect History* (Urbana, IL: University of Illinois Press, 1970), 40.

[74] Étienne Pasquier, *Les Oeuvres d'Estienne Pasquier* (Amsterdam, 1723), tom. 1, 85. See Ralph Giesey and J. H. M. Salmon, "Editor's Preface" in Hotman, *Francogallia*, 23–4; and Church, *Constitutional Thought*, 294–5.

Though Pasquier was familiar with Hotman's ideas before they appeared in print, he published his *Recherches de la France* (1560) before Hotman's *Anti-Tribonian* (1567) and *Francogallia* (1573). Like the *Francogallia*, Pasquier's history begins with pre-Roman Gauls. While Hotman would portray the early French constitution as an amalgam of ancient Gallic and Germanic institutions, Pasquier emphasizes the Gallic roots of French government, suggesting that the earliest Frankish kings of Gaul adopted Gallic institutions. Skinner notes that Pasquier was the first legal writer to affirm that, if a given check on the powers of the crown could be shown to have originated in the primitive constitution of France, or to have developed through use over a long period, then "it follows that there must be a right to enforce the same limitation on the powers of the present-day government." Other constitutionalists quickly took up this principle; it grounded the "normative character of the fundamental constitution."[75]

Operating on the basis of this meta-principle, Pasquier extends the historic argument for the authority of the parlements, especially the Parlement of Paris, to counsel and restrain the crown. The parlement was responsible for registering the king's ordinances; without registration the ordinances would not be applied and enforced. While earlier jurists, including even some absolutists, had held that the parlements could refuse to register an ordinance if it was a violation of abstract values such as equity or natural justice, Pasquier "seems literally to have projected into constitutional writing" the principle that the Parlement of Paris had authority to censure the orders of the king if they violated fundamental legal precedent.[76] On his account, the parlementary responsibility for registration of laws is an essential element of the constitutional bridle on royal authority.[77] Only when the royal will passes the tests of both equity and legality can it attain, in judgment of the parlement, "*la civilité*

---

[75] Du Haillan would soon argue, for instance, that the independent power of custom is "so anciently established in this kingdom that any prince ... would be ashamed to break it." Quoted in Skinner, *Foundations*, vol. 1, 272.

[76] Church, *Constitutional Thought*, 143; John J. Hurt, *Louis XIV and the Parlements: The Assertion of Royal Authority* (Manchester University Press, 2002), 2. Like other constitutionalists, Pasquier ascribes a notional "*pouvoir absoluë*" to the crown before insisting that kings have "by an ancient institution wished to reduce their wills" to the civility of law. Pasquier, *Les Oeuvres*, tom. 1, 66. See Skinner, *Foundations*, vol. 1, 271, and fn. 5 on the idea of absolute power in constitutionalist thought.

[77] Pasquier, *Les Oeuvres*, tom. 1, 2.4.

de la loy." While the king's authority is in theory absolute, his will must pass through this "alembic of public order" in order to become law.[78]

In Book 2 of his *Recherches*, Pasquier argues that the constitutional limitation provided by the parlementary check upon the crown accounts for France's status as the only monarchy, erected upon the ruins of the Roman empire, to survive to the present day. He lays bare the roots of this restraint in the ancient history and *moeurs* of the nation. His *Recherches* affords far more attention to the Gauls than to the Franks, but he notes that from of old, the Germanic Franks gave themselves a name meaning "free" in German because they saw "in their spirit" a certain *"liberté & franchise."*[79] The original inhabitants of Gaul likewise had "ancient franchises and liberties" that even Caesar did not extinguish.[80] The germ of the parlements lay in the druidical councils of the ancient Gauls. This germ fortuitously developed over time as the earliest Frankish kings and mayors of the palace in conquered Gaul accommodated themselves to Gallic usages and institutions, eventually leading to the parlements.[81]

Roman law and institutions, by contrast, could never suit the French people so well as institutions of Gallic origin, for the simple reason that Roman institutions arose from entirely allien mores, practices, and environs. Like Hotman, Pasquier believed the effect of Roman law in France had been "profound and, on the whole, pernicious."[82] He shared Hotman's basic view that the *Corpus juris civilis* was a mélange of anachronisms taken from various points in Roman history and was not representative of the Roman law at any given time. More importantly, he concurred in Hotman's judgment that Roman law was unserviceable in France because we share "nothing in common" with Rome at any point in its history.[83] As he asserts in his *Lettres*:

---

[78] Ibid., 66. Numerous constitutionalist writers follow Pasquier in this judgment, and some go further in upholding the authority of the parlement. For example, where Pasquier is silent on the ultimate power of the king to remove members of parlement, Jean Bodin asserts that the king may not remove a judge except for corruption. See Skinner, *Foundations*, vol. 1, 267.

[79] Pasquier, *Les Oeuvres*, tom. 1, 17–18. See also Pasquier, *Lettres*, tom. 1, 6.

[80] Ibid., tom. 1, 8.

[81] Ibid., vol. 1, 2.1–3. See Huppert, *The Idea of History*, 47–51; and Zachary S. Schiffman, "Estienne Pasquier and the Problem of Historical Relativism," *The Sixteenth Century Journal* 18 (1987): 509–10. As Schiffman explains, Pasquier understood that the Parlement of Paris in its modern form was a fourteenth-century development, but he saw it as originating from the earlier assemblies because of their shared function.

[82] Kelley, *Foundations*, 285.

[83] Pasquier, *Les Oeuvres*, tom. 2, 293; quoted in Berlin, *Three Critics*, 197.

It is high time that we rid ourselves of that stupid notion which occupies our minds, by which we trample under foot the true and primitive laws of France and subordinate our judgments to the judgments of the Romans ... As God wished to separate us from Italy by a high thrust of mountains, and so also he has separated us in almost all things, in mores, laws, nature, and humors.[84]

Pasquier's attack on Roman law derives not simply from the national pride evident in this passage, but also from a clearly articulated conception of the isomorphic relationship of law to culture. As he puts it in one especially striking passage, "Any man of good understanding, without seeing a complete historical account of a people, can almost imagine its temper [*humeur*] when he reads its ancient statutes and ordinances, and in a similar manner, can deduce what its laws were when looking at its way of life."[85] So tightly joined are these elements that there is a possibility of inference from laws to mores and mores to laws. Pasquier speaks often of "*la diversité*" among nations, and he essays in many places to account for this diversity along the lines etched in this passage. Crucially, he holds that "diversity of laws arises from the diversity of mores."[86] Laws usually arise *from* mores in the literal sense of actually beginning as mores – the *mos maiorum* or "way of the elders." Only later do they come to be understood as and perhaps recorded as law. On this organic conception, law is both "an expression as well as a means of controlling social behavior."[87] At several points, Pasquier cannot resist the temptation to add another layer of explanation, as he contends that the diversity of regions, air, and temperature produces variation in mores.[88] And betraying a protohistoricist bent, he observes how mores change with "*la diversité des temps*," a recurring phrase in his work.[89] Whatever the origin of mores, their continuity with law is a cornerstone of both Pasquier's particularism and his historical constitutionalism.

He acknowledges that many men, including his French compatriots, believe their laws to be universally reasonable and even derived from the natural law. They are correct in a limited sense, for the diverse positive laws of men tend toward the conservation of society, which is itself a

---

[84] Pasquier, *Lettres*, tom. 1, 515–16. Translation is modified from Kelley, *Foundations*, 288–9. Pasquier oversaw the publication of his own selected correspondence.

[85] Pasquier, *Les Oeuvres*, tom. 1, 4.1.

[86] Ibid., tom. 2, 554. This principle was of sufficient thematic importance that the editors of the 1723 edition of the *Recherches* include it as an entry in the index.

[87] Kelley, *Foundations*, 289.   [88] Pasquier, *Lettres*, tom. 2, 467, 550.

[89] Ibid., tom. 2, 312, 402. Étienne Pasquier, *L'interprétation des Institutes de Justinian* (Paris, 1847), 516.

natural law.[90] Yet in their specifics, the laws of men are based not upon nature but "*la opinion.*"[91] Variation in opinions, mores, and physical circumstances bars the possibility of a universal code of law for all regions, deduced from the natural law. The French believe their Salic law is drawn from nature, observes Pasquier; but the English think the same of their laws of succession. This realization should lead us not to reject our native laws as merely contingent but rather to recognize that our laws, like most, have endured because they promote the conservation of society in a way that accords with our character and circumstances. Pasquier reasons, "Whatever the diversity of the law, it is necessary to live according to those to which one has become accustomed, and to consider that because they are established, we ought to judge them good."[92] Like Hotman, he suggests that politics and law resemble the art of medicine in their adaptive and flexible character. Just as the medical doctor must vary his remedies depending on the "ages" and "humors" of his patients, so the remedy of the laws must vary across regions and peoples.[93] Yet these diverse medical and legal remedies may all conduce to the preservation of the body and the body politic, respectively.

This unmistakable legal particularism informs Pasquier's critique of Roman influence in France. The Romans were not under a monarchy, and "our order and magistrates have nothing in common with theirs."[94] Immersive study of Roman law and political institutions does not "contribute to the edification" of the French, who are "not brought up according to the laws and mores of the Romans."[95] These concerns extend to the influence of both Roman public and private law. In the domain of public law, Pasquier holds that one cannot properly analogize the powers of the French constitution to Roman authorities and offices, whether republican or imperial.[96] As Seyssel had shown, any comparison of the Roman Senate to the Parlement of Paris runs the risk of diminishing the authority of the Parlement, for at no time did the Senate of Rome possess the power to

---

[90] Pasquier, *Lettres*, tom. 2, 460, 465–6.
[91] Ibid., tom. 2, 466. As Keohane characterizes Pasquier's position, "Natural law has nothing to say about what the specific rules for our preservation will be." Keohane, *Philosophy and the State*, 44.
[92] Pasquier, *Lettres*, tom. 2, 467. See *EL*, "Pref."   [93] Pasquier, *Lettres*, tom. 2, 467.
[94] Pasquier, *Lettres*, tom. 1, 690.
[95] Ibid. Translation modified from Kelley, *Foundations*, 288.
[96] See Franklin, *Jean Bodin and the Sixteenth-Century Revolution*, 41–2.

invalidate a new law as inconsistent with precedent.[97] This was true of the Senate even during the height of its power in the Republic. Pasquier protests, "These words senate, senator, consul, tribune ... which are taken from a democracy ... cause us, while speaking French, to Latinize."[98]

Yet even as he insists on this distance between Roman and French public law, Pasquier also seeks to subvert a key absolutist gloss on Roman public law. Commenting upon the oft-cited principle of Ulpian that "whatever pleases the prince has the force of law," he confesses that it is difficult to believe the Roman people ever transferred their full authority to the emperor; surely one of the great Roman historians would have mentioned such an important detail.[99] It is "not necessary to take this saying cruelly," he writes of Ulpian's infamous maxim. In the same spirit, Pasquier's friend and fellow humanist Pierre Ayrault would add, "Not what pleases the prince, but what best and lawfully pleases the prince."[100]

In the domain of private law, Pasquier makes no secret of his distaste for hasty recourse to Roman law to correct or supplement customary law in the *pays de coutume*, northern provinces governed by French customary law rather than civil law. In cases of doubt, obscurity, or omission in the local or provincial law of France, we should not "go begging to Rome," but should look to the customs of the region. Regional customs are more likely to suit us because "customs form in each country little by little, according to the diversity of our mores [*moeurs*], and our mores form according to the diversity of our spirits [*la diversité des nos esprits*]."[101] Peoples closer to us are more likely to resemble us in mores and spirit, but Pasquier's concerns again go beyond the problem of suitability. Roman law introduces a litigious spirit that is alien to the "pure and simple" laws of France,[102] and some Roman private-law concepts are plainly inconsistent with the nature of the French constitution, such as the notion of the *patria potestas* in property law. This concept of absolute paternal power, amenable to abuse by royal absolutists, has "no place among us."[103]

For Pasquier, consigning Roman public law to a remote past and vindicating the bridled monarchy of France were complementary ambitions. Such was the pattern of humanist constitutionalism. The constitutional politics of Pasquier, Hotman, and other legal humanists

---

[97] Seyssel, *The Monarchy of France*, 55.
[98] Pasquier, *Lettres*, tom. 1, 690. Translation modified from Kelley, *Foundations*, 288.
[99] Pasquier, *L'interprétation des Institutes*, 26.
[100] Quoted in Kelley, *Foundations*, 285.   [101] Pasquier, *Lettres*, vol. 1, 522.
[102] Ibid., 537.   [103] Pasquier, *L'interprétation des Institutes*, 59.

originates in the *mos gallicus* vision of each system of law as part of a distinct social, political, and cultural whole. This vision of law would take its most powerful and definitive form in the liberal political science of Montesquieu. The humanists' emphasis on the relationship of laws and mores, their attention to the particularities of time and place, their suspicions about exporting institutions from one nation to another, and their alertness to the dangers of universalism – all these elements of humanist constitutionalism feature prominently on Montesquieu's intellectual landscape. Together they help to account for his own fusion of particularism and constitutionalism.

FROM LEGAL HUMANISM TO *THE SPIRIT OF THE LAWS*

Pasquier, Hotman, and the humanist constitutionalists did not succeed in rolling back the theoretical and practical assault on constitutional limits in France. Their work inspired other historians and jurists to extend such labors into the late sixteenth century; one thinks of Pierre Ayrault, Louis Le Roy, Bernard du Haillan, and Guy Coquille.[104] But the constitutionalist tradition in France suffered a marked decline as the French wars of religion convinced many of the need for consolidation of political power in the crown. Absolutism in France hardened in the seventeenth century, and few developments in constitutionalist theory emerged during the reigns of Louis XIII (r. 1610–43) and the Sun King, Louis XIV (r. 1643–1715).[105] As Keohane observes, the "constitutionalist arguments of the sixteenth-century jurists and historians were somewhat self-consciously reiterated during the abortive rebellions of the mid-seventeenth century." Beyond these restatements, constitutional thought was "rather stagnant and peripheral" in seventeenth-century France.[106] For this reason, sixteenth-century humanist constitutionalism – and its particularistic sensibility – provided the most important intellectual touchstone when French constitutionalist thought revived in the early eighteenth century, first in the writings of Fénelon, Boulainvilliers, and Saint-Simon, and later in work of Montesquieu.

[104] Hotman's *Francogallia* would also influence strains of Gothic constitutionalism and Calvinist resistance theory on other parts of the continent and in England. See Ralph E. Giesey, "The Monarchomach Triumvirs: Hotman, Beza, and Mornay," *Bibliothèque D'Humanisme et Renaissance* 32 (1970): 41–56; Lee Ward, *Politics of Liberty in England and Revolutionary America* (Cambridge University Press, 2010), 55–7.

[105] Keohane, *Philosophy and the State*, 222; Church, *Constitutional Thought*, 302.

[106] Keohane, *Philosophy and the State*, 18.

This chapter ultimately points toward the thematic and structural correspondence of Montesquieu's thought and that of the *mos gallicus* constitutionalists: Montesquieu works as intellectual heir to the humanists' alignment of constitutional politics with legal and political particularism. The striking thematic resonances between Montesquieu's thought and the tradition suggest this connection, and a consideration of his treatment of Roman law and French constitutional history solidly confirms it. In this section, we turn first to Montesquieu's views on Roman law and, second, to his work on the origins of the French monarchy. Each bears the marks of the *mos gallicus*.

While there is considerable evidence that Montesquieu read and knew the writings of the sixteenth-century legal humanists, we should not be surprised if he keeps writers like Pasquier and especially Hotman out of the footnotes. Anti-absolutist work on French history was dangerous business. Hotman was accounted a revolutionary for *Francogallia*, and Henri de Boulainvilliers allowed the publication of his anti-absolutist *History of the Ancient Government of France* only after he was safely on the far side of the grave in 1727. Montesquieu confesses in his *Pensées* that such work requires courage (*MP* 1305). Despite his great subtlety of style, even he decided to publish *Spirit* anonymously and in Geneva, avoiding French censors.[107]

In his library at La Brède, he kept works by Pasquier, Hotman, Budé, Cujas, Alciato, Ayrault, and many others in the tradition; *Spirit* and his *Collectio Juris* contain references to Cujas, Budé, Coquille, and others.[108] Additionally, as I consider in this section, Montesquieu engages at length the work of Boulainvilliers, an important conduit for the transmission of the humanists' genre of constitutional history into the eighteenth century. As a student of law in Paris and at the University of Bordeaux, Montesquieu spent more than two years studying Roman law.[109] His *Collectio Juris* encompasses five notebooks devoted to the subject, and their

---

[107] Shackleton, *Montesquieu*, 240–3; Rahe, *Montesquieu and the Logic of Liberty*, ch. 1.

[108] *EL* 5.26.12, 6.30.16, 6.31.11, 6.31.26, 4.21.29–30, 6.31.34; VF 11.liii–lvii; 4:896. See Desgraves and Volpilhac-Auger, *Catalogue*; Iris Cox, "Montesquieu and the History of Laws," in *Montesquieu's Science of Politics: Essays on* The Spirit of Laws, eds. David W. Carrithers, Michael A. Mosher, and Paul A. Rahe (Lanham, MD: Rowman & Littlefield, 2001), 409–28.

[109] At this time, Montesquieu was training for his future post in the Parlement of Bordeaux, which he would inherit from his uncle. Bordeaux had its own customary law, codified in 1528, but it was part of the *pays de droit écrit* where Roman law was still authoritative in many cases. Charles P. Sherman, *Roman Law in the Modern World* (Boston Book Company, 1917), 230.

contents confirm that he read the whole of the *Corpus juris civilis*.[110] The young law student seems to have emerged from these years impressed with neither the Code of Justinian nor the state of legal scholarship in France. He would later complain, in a remark worthy of Pasquier or Hotman, that Justinian was "not firm enough" for the task of compiling the laws of Rome; Caesar would have produced a better text (*MP* 1512). Writing on the subject of legal scholarship in France, he similarly echoes the old humanist charges against the Bartolists concerning their neglect of the historical origins of laws: "How can one apply a law if one does not know the country for which it was made, and the circumstances in which it was made?" he demands. "Most of those who study jurisprudence follow the course of the Nile, overflow with it, but are ignorant of its source" (*MP* 1827).

Shortly after the conclusion of his legal training, Montesquieu tellingly treats the subject of Roman law in his *Persian Letters*. Here his characters Rica and Usbek rehearse the legal humanists' critique of Roman law. Usbek wonders at "the oddity of the French mind" in having "retained from Roman law an infinite number of things that are useless or worse than useless" (*LP* 76). Rica asks why the French have looked beyond their borders for "everything relating to political and civil government," while looking down their noses at foreigners on matters of style. Rica writes,

> Who can believe that the most ancient and powerful kingdom in Europe has been governed, for more than the last ten centuries, by laws which were not created for it?
> ... They abandoned the ancient laws made by their first kings in the national general assemblies; and the odd thing is that the Roman laws they adopted in their stead were, in part, made and written by emperors who were the contemporaries of their own legislators.
> ... This abundance of laws adopted and, as it were, naturalized, is so vast that it is equally burdensome to justice and to judges. But these volumes of laws are nothing compared with the dreadful army of glossarists, commentators, and compilers; men as weak in their want of judgment as they are powerful by virtue of their huge numbers.
>
> (*LP* 97)

Montesquieu understood that he had given Rica an embellished account: in much of the northern *pays de coutume*, the influence of Roman law was attenuated. But exaggerations notwithstanding, Rica and Usbek's

---

[110] Cox, "Montesquieu and the History of Laws," 420.

views indicate Montesquieu's early affinity for the legal humanist critique of Roman law, an affinity consistent with his nascent particularism.[111]

Legal humanist methodology informs not only the general contours of Montesquieu's political science but also his own analysis of Roman law in *The Spirit of the Laws*. As Édouard Tillet has noted, when Montesquieu treats Roman inheritance law in Book 27, he does not play the Bartolist, relying on internal logical analysis of the *Corpus juris*, but rather deploys the historical methods of legal humanism to locate the origin and to trace the development of law. The account begins with Romulus' founding, not the code. Montesquieu discovers the social and political causes underlying changes in Roman inheritance laws over time.[112] For example, he argues that "when the monarchy was established in Rome, the whole system of inheritances was changed" (*EL* 6.27, only chapter, p. 531). Tillet observes that Montesquieu approaches Roman law "with a certain hostility to the numerous and varied attempts at the universalization of this law" and in keeping with "the relativist current, appearing in the sixteenth century with the humanist school, which in its more radical version (François Hotman and Étienne Pasquier) had denounced the introduction of Roman law in the kingdom of France."[113] While Tillet's mention of relativism may be misleading, Montesquieu's jurisprudential method is clearly in sympathy with the *mos gallicus* tradition.

Within the pages of *Spirit*, Montesquieu explicitly addresses the matter of Roman law in France as he discusses Louis IX's (r. 1226–70) legal reforms in tones reminiscent of both the anti-Romanism and anti-universalism of the *mos gallicus*. He identifies the "internal vice" of the legal compilation known as the *Establishments* of Saint Louis: it was an "amphibious code" mixing "often contradictory" elements, that is, French and Roman law (*EL* 6.28.38). The *Establishments* appear to contain a general code for the whole of France consisting of agglomerated Roman and French material. But Montesquieu explains why this could not possibly have been Louis IX's intention, writing,

---

[111] See Sylvana Tomaselli, "The Spirit of Nations," in *The Cambridge History of Eighteenth-Century Political Thought*, eds. Mark Goldie and Robert Wolker (Cambridge University Press, 2006), 15–19. About this letter Tomaselli remarks, "The oddity of taking on freely and for no apparent reason another people's law could not have been made more explicit" (17).

[112] See Carrese, *The Cloaking of Power*, 85–6.

[113] Tillet, "*Collectio Juris*," 220. The parentheses are Tillet's. See also Launay, "Montesquieu: The Specter of Despotism," 24; and Berlin, *Three Critics*, 160. For a discussion of Roman law in Montesquieu, complementary to my own, see Levy, *Rationalism, Pluralism, and Freedom*, 154–8.

Now, at a time when each town, borough, or village had its own custom, to give a general body of civil laws was to want to reverse in a moment all the particular laws under which men had lived everywhere in the kingdom. To make a general custom of all the particular customs would be rash, even in these times when princes find only obedience everywhere. For, if it is true that one must not alter things when the resulting drawbacks equal the advantages, so much less must one alter them when the advantages are small and the drawbacks immense ...

(EL 6.28.37)

Montesquieu need not elaborate concerning the "immense drawbacks" of legal uniformity. His reader has already learned that unlike moderate government, despotism is *"uniforme partout"* – uniform legally and institutionally *(EL* 1.5.14). Indeed, legal uniformity implies institutional uniformity. By contrast, a complex and varied set of laws and jurisdictions requires multiple loci of power. And once power is plural, the regime begins to incline toward monarchy and away from despotism *(EL* 1.2.4).[114]

It is fitting that Montesquieu's most memorable critique of legal uniformity, in Book 29, follows his historical analysis of Roman inheritance law and French civil law in Books 27 and 28. In a chapter "On ideas of uniformity," Montesquieu warns of the allure of legal uniformity: it sometimes touches great spirits but "invariably strikes small ones" *(EL* 6.29.18). Small spirits see in uniformity "a kind of perfection they recognize because it is impossible not to discover." In contrast to the inconspicuous but superior merits of variety, the superficial "perfection" of uniformity is so obvious that even a small and despotic mind cannot miss it. This judgment follows several chapters, within Book 29, that defend the deeper reasonableness of legal diversity against the shallow rationalism of uniformity; Montesquieu appeals to the character of law as situated within social and political wholes. Like the legal humanists, he adduces examples of the incongruity between Roman laws and French society as he explains, "Roman laws were not made in the same circumstances as ours" *(EL* 6.29.10, 14). The broader precept is that "laws must not be separated from the circumstances in which they were made" *(EL* 6.29.14) – a capsule summary of the legal humanist insight.[115]

---

[114] Jean Bart, "French Law," in *Dictionnaire Montesquieu*, ed. Catherine Volpilhac-Auger, http://dictionnaire-montesquieu.ens-lyon.fr. See also Jean Bart, "Montesquieu et l'unification du droit," in *Le Temps de Montesquieu* (Geneva: Droz, 2002), 136–46.

[115] This is consistent with his announcement, in Book 1, that it is "very unlikely [*un très grand hasard*] that the laws of one nation can suit another" *(EL* 1.1.3). Stein, *Roman Law*, comments, "Most of [Montesquieu's] readers must have drawn the conclusion that

Montesquieu's engagement with the legal humanism of the sixteenth century is similarly manifest in his treatment of French constitutional development and the origin of fiefs.[116] He devotes two often-ignored books of *Spirit* to the history of the French constitution and the rise of feudal government (*EL* 30, 31).[117] In these books, we find Montesquieu working from within the tradition of humanist constitutionalism as he takes up the problem of the "Gothic" constitution and enters a debate about French political origins ignited by Hotman, Pasquier, and others. His proximate point of contact with this debate is a more recent flare-up between the Abbé Dubos and the Comte de Boulainvilliers. In 1734, Dubos had published an arch-royalist narration of French political origins in response to Boulainvilliers's resurrection (with modifications) of constitutional history in the mold of the humanists. As Montesquieu intervenes in the clash between Dubos and Boulainvilliers, we observe clear debts to humanist constitutionalism.

The count and the *abbé* waged a historiographical battle along lines drawn in the sixteenth century. In his *Critical History of the Establishment of the French Monarchy in Gaul*, Dubos develops the very line of argument that constitutionalists had rejected in the 1560s. He contends that the Franks entered Gaul as agents of the Romans, and so the Frankish crown received untrammeled authority from the Roman emperor.[118] This argument was consistent with the habit, common

Roman law reflected the spirit of an ancient society, which was manifestly different from that of contemporary societies" (111).

[116] While this chapter has not emphasized the question of the origins of fiefs, the legal humanists of the sixteenth century labored extensively on the problem; J. G. A. Pocock judges their research in this area to be their most remarkable work. J. G. A. Pocock, "The Origins of Study of the Past: A Comparative Approach," *Comparative Studies in Society and History* 4 (1962): 230.

[117] On these neglected books, see especially Élie Carcassone, *Montesquieu et le problème de la constitution française au XVIIIe siècle* (Paris: Presses Universitaires de France, 1927), ch. 2; Albert Mathiez, "La place de Montesquieu dans l'histoire des doctrines politiques du XVIIIe siècle," *Annales Historiques de la Révolution Française* 7 (1930): 97–112; Iris Cox, *Montesquieu and the History of French Laws* (Oxford: Voltaire Foundation, 1983); Harold Ellis, "Montesquieu's Modern Politics: *The Spirit of the Laws* and the Problem of Modern Monarchy in Old Regime France," *History of Political Thought* 10 (1989): 665–700; Johnson Kent Wright, "A Rhetoric of Aristocratic Reaction? Nobility in *De l'Esprit des Lois*," in *The French Nobility in the Eighteenth Century: Reassessments and New Approaches*, ed. Jay M. Smith (University Park, PA: Pennsylvania State University Press, 2006); Ward, "Montesquieu on Federalism and Anglo-Gothic Constitutionalism"; Levy, *Rationalism, Pluralism, and Freedom*, 145–58.

[118] Jean-Baptiste Dubos, *Histoire critique de l'établissement de la monarchie française* (Paris, [1734]1742), tom. 2, 270, cited in *EL* 6.30.25.

among sixteenth-century absolutists, of running together the King of France and the Roman *princeps*. Dubos's work represented the most sophisticated effort to forge a link between these two offices.

Montesquieu's criticism of the Abbé Dubos is unsparing and extends across several chapters in *Spirit*. "My ideas are perpetually contrary to his," Montesquieu announces (*EL* 30.23; *MP* 795). "[I]f he has found the truth, I have not." Dubos's history reenacts the despotism it seeks to justify: the *abbé* is guilty of exercising "an arbitrary power over the facts" in his account of late fifth- and early sixth-century Gaul (*EL* 6.30.12). He has constructed his system upon a compromised foundation, namely, the fabricated claim that the Frankish king, Clovis, entered Gaul as a Roman officer, at the invitation of Rome, and received *merum imperium* from the Justinian. Starting from this premise, Dubos had concluded that noble privileges in France were illegitimate. Montesquieu demonstrates that Dubos's colossus has "feet of clay," for the Franks under Clovis had in fact entered Gaul as conquerors. They sacked villages and brought with them a society with three orders of persons (noble, middling, and low) as well as a balanced political order (*EL* 6.30.25; *MP* 1826). Frankish power in Gaul derived not from any post-hoc donation of authority from the emperor but rather from the brute fact of conquest.

Dubos had committed such great errors because he had "the Count of Boulainvilliers more in view than his subject" (*EL* 6.30.25). Montesquieu dispraises the count briefly, but his history suffers nothing like the rebuttal Dubos's work receives (*EL* 6.30.10).[119] This is with good reason: Montesquieu agrees with much of Boulainvilliers's approach. He objects to the count's under-evidenced view – shared by neither Pasquier nor Hotman – that the Gauls were enslaved to the noble Franks following the conquest of Gaul. This claim allowed Boulainvilliers to argue that the gradual emancipation of the serfs was a usurpation by the crown designed to degrade the privileges of the nobility. Against Boulainvilliers, Montesquieu shows that there was no universal servitude of Gauls to the Franks after the conquest (*EL* 6.30.5). Montesquieu's view of Franco-Gallic relations was much closer, in fact, to the views of Hotman and Pasquier, who had emphasized the common mores and political cooperation of

---

[119] Montesquieu initially appears to stake out ground between Dubos and Boulainvilliers, but this may be a prudent effort to avoid close association with the latter. Boulainvilliers "is his man," concludes Franklin Ford. Franklin Ford, *Robe and Sword: The Regrouping of the French Aristocracy After Louis XIV* (Cambridge, MA: Harvard University Press, 1962), 242.

the Gauls and Franks. But despite his misgivings about Boulainvilliers's "conspiracy against the third estate," Montesquieu concludes that the count "knew well the great things about our history and our laws" (*EL* 6.30.12).

It is these "great things" that Boulainvilliers shares with the humanist constitutionalism of the sixteenth century and with Montesquieu. The count follows the legal humanists both in upholding the originally limited character of the constitution and "in affirming that institutions and political events are only intelligible in light of their social context."[120] He expresses admiration for Pasquier, and in Hotman, he had found "a model and a method."[121] His history reprises Hotman's thesis in an aristocratic key while retaining its emphasis on a limited Frankish monarchy.[122]

The union of particularism and constitutionalism, present in his humanist forerunners, definitively shapes Boulainvilliers's approach. For Boulainvilliers, as for the humanist constitutionalists, it is "absolutely contrary to the truth and genius [*génie*] of the ancient French" to imagine that their early kings ruled alone.[123] Despotism, by contrast, is "more suitable to the genius of the Persians."[124] He approvingly attributes to Charlemagne the view that the French were "originally a free people, as much by their natural character [*caractère*], as by the primitive right that they had to choose their princes."[125] He maintains that the French monarchy has its roots in ancient Frankish government and that the Franks elected and shared sovereignty with their kings. When the Franks conquered Gaul in the late fifth century under Clovis, they carried with them this balanced political order.[126] The Frankish warriors who had conquered with Clovis were rewarded with fiefs and formed the nobility of the nascent French state, exercising authority over the subjugated Gauls. The Franks participated in government with their king through

---

[120] Olivier Tholozan, *Henri de Boulainvilliers: L'anti-absolutisme aristocratique légitimé par l'histoire* (Marseille: Presses universitaires d'Aix-Marseille, 2015), 1.2.

[121] Harold A. Ellis, *Boulainvilliers and the French Monarchy* (Ithaca, NY: Cornell University Press, 1988), 51n.134; Louis Lemarié, *Les Assemblées franques et les historiens réformateurs du XVIIIe siecle* (Paris: Imprimerie Bonvalot-Jouve, 1906), 73.

[122] Bakos, *Images of Kingship*, 61.

[123] Henri de Boulainvilliers, *Histoire de l'ancien gouvernement de la France* (The Hague and Amsterdam, 1727), tom. 1, 29; 218. In context, Boulainvilliers is referring the "companions" of the king as a source of limit. Compare with *EL* 3.19.5.

[124] Boulainvilliers, *Histoire de l'ancien gouvernement de la France*, tom. 1, "Preface."

[125] Ibid., tom. 1, 217–8; De Dijn, *French Political Thought*, 17.

[126] Boulainvilliers, *Histoire de l'ancien gouvernement de la France*, tom. 1, 26–35.

the general assembly at the Champs de Mar, and Boulainvilliers favors a radical return to this assembly of the nation, now lost through royal usurpation.[127] He likens the lost assembly to the English Parliament, vested with power to tax and to make law; the ancient French assembly of the nation, like the English Parliament and the Diets of Poland and Germany, were legacies from the conquering barbarians of the north.[128] Pace Pasquier, Boulainvilliers does not accept the existing French parlements as legitimate heirs to the ancient assembly.[129] A restored assembly of the nation must be constituted by the Estates General, as Hotman had suggested.[130] Like the constitutionalists of the *mos gallicus*, Boulainvilliers regards limit and restraint as original and essential to the French constitution. The balancing institutions were not usurpations but rather legacies of the primitive constitutional order.

While undercutting Boulainvilliers's "conspiracy against the third estate," Montesquieu accepts and develops the "great things" shared in common by Boulainvilliers and the constitutionalists of the *mos gallicus*. In Books 30 and 31, he accepts the lineaments of their views on the relationship between early French government and the ancient mores of the people, as well as their fundamental historical insight regarding the limited nature of the ancient French crown. Montesquieu's historiographic effort to confute Dubos's errors results in the most carefully evidenced account of the early French state and the rise of feudal government available at the time – an account which, as Iris Cox notes, stands up well against modern historical knowledge.[131] Here Montesquieu

---

[127] Ibid., tom. 1, 210–11. Henri de Boulainvilliers *Lettres sur les anciens parlements de France que l'on nomme Etats-généraux* (London: Wood and Palmer 1753), tom. 1, 37–8. Oliver Thozolan, *Henri de Boulainvilliers: L'anti-absolutisme aristocratique légitimé par l'histoire*. Presses universitaires d'Aix-Marseille, 1999, 2.3.1.3, 2.3.2.2; Ellis, *Boulainvilliers and the French Monarchy*, 162–3.

[128] Boulainvilliers, *Lettres sur les anciens parlements*, tom. 1, 66–7. Thozolan, *Henri de Boulainvilliers*, 2.3.2.2. Compare *EL* 3.17.5 on the northern barbarians.

[129] Boulainvilliers is an advocate for the nobility of the sword, as distinguished from the nobility of the robe. For this reason, he emphasizes the roots of nobility in the warrior companions of Clovis and the early fief-holders of Frankish Gaul. Pasquier, a partisan of the robe nobles and their power in the parlements, associates nobility with wise counsel – e.g., the druidical assemblies of the Gauls – rather than military status. The classic work on the relationship between the sword and robe nobles is Ford's *Robe and Sword*.

[130] Boulainvilliers's *Lettres sur les anciens parlements* is a history of the "*assemblées que l'on nomme en France, Etats-Generaux du Royaume.*" He favors "new measures ... to render them truly useful and advantageous." Boulainvilliers, *Lettres sur les anciens parlements*, tom. 1, 1–2. See Ellis, *Boulainvilliers and the French Monarchy*, 162–8.

[131] Cox, *Montesquieu and the History of French Laws*, 21.

enters into the genre of anti-absolutist constitutional history in the mold of Hotman, Pasquier, and Boulainvilliers.

He likens his task to uncovering the roots of a great oak tree: "to find them, the ground must be dug up" (*EL* 6.30.1). If he is to understand the French regime, he must unearth the mores and laws of the "ancient Germans" before the Frankish conquest of Gaul. Montesquieu shares with Hotman the view that the Franks were descended from tribes broadly denominated "Germans."[132] It is impossible to inquire into the origins of "our political right" without knowing perfectly the "mores of the German peoples" (*EL* 6.30.19). He begins with first-century accounts of the Germans in the Tacitus and Caesar, important sources for Hotman and Pasquier.

In Tacitus and Caesar, Montesquieu finds a race of Germanic princes and their *comites*, forerunners to nobility, who willingly join the prince in his exploits in exchange for horses, weapons, meals, and plunder (*EL* 6.30.3; *MP* 166, 1302). Because these *comites* had no use for agricultural lands, horses and weapons were the first "fiefs." Thus Montesquieu opens his history by identifying the origin of Frankish fiefs, a major historio-graphical concern for legal humanists of the sixteenth century.[133] The early Germanic *comites* competed for honors from their prince; among multiple princes, there was competition for more and braver followers.[134] Montesquieu identifies these ancient princes of Germania as "the seed [*germe*] of the history of the reign of the Merovingians" (*EL* 6.30.4). From the Frankish Merovingian dynasty arose Clovis, the first King of all Franks, who united competing bands of conquering Franks in Gaul (*EL* 3.18.29). Although Montesquieu makes no effort to pinpoint a single founding moment, his analysis leads the reader ineluctably to the conclusion that the early French monarchy was constituted voluntarily by warrior-vassals who shared in deliberations with their prince

---

[132] Hotman, *Francogallia*, ch. 4.

[133] In his account of the development of fiefs, Montesquieu relies on *De Feudis* by Jacques Cujas, Hotman's predecessor at Bourges and a key figure in the *mos gallicus* (*EL* 6.30.16 n. 99, 104, 105; 6.31.11 n. 92). Emphasizing the military character of the fief and its original status as a temporary benefice, Montesquieu is in agreement with Cujas. See Pocock, *The Ancient Constitution*, 70–7.

[134] The discussion of government among pastoral barbarians in *EL* 3.17.14 clearly refers to the ancient Germanic tribes. Montesquieu suggests that their princes gained and retained followers in part through ensuring personal liberty. See also *MP* 699.

(*EL* 6.30.3).[135] Noble privileges were co-original with the Frankish crown. After the fashion of humanist constitutionalists, Montesquieu establishes the immemorially bridled character of the French monarchy and the historical legitimacy of intermediate powers.

When the Franks invaded Gaul, Montesquieu avers, they "preserved their mores, inclinations, and usages" (*EL* 6.30.6; 3.18.30). Crucially, this includes their political system and the usage of the *comites*, who became known as *leudes* or *vassalli* (*EL* 6.30.16). Victorious Frankish companions of the king occupied some of the land of Gaul as revocable fiefs, later to be received in perpetuity (*EL* 6.60.7, 8). The "right of justice" was "of the nature of the fief," and so the lords exercised the judicial function within their domains to the exclusion of the king (*EL* 6.30.20).[136] In conquered Gaul, Frankish (or early French) kings were permitted neither to tax nor to send royal judges into the lands of the lords. The judicial power lay outside royal control (see *EL* 2.11.6, p. 157). Moreover, under the Merovingian and Carolingian dynasties, the lords and bishops often gathered as the "assembl[y] of the nation" to make laws (known as capitularies) and to deliberate about affairs of importance, such as the granting and revocation of fiefs (*EL* 6.28.9, 6.31.1; 3.18.30). Even this latter prerogative was not the king's alone.[137] Ultimately, Montesquieu labors to show that neither the prerogatives of the robe and sword nobles, nor even the rise of feudalism itself, represented usurpations of royal power, much less migration from an original absolutism (e.g., *EL* 6.30.15, 22; 6.31.7–8, 25). His history accords with those of Hotman, Pasquier, and Boulainvilliers: in the early French monarchy, power was combined, tempered, and regulated by institutions of ancient derivation, whether Germanic or Gallic (*EL* 1.5.14).

The effect of Montesquieu's account of early France is not to exalt a pristine, original regime of the fifth century as the measure of political health. Indeed, on his account, the high point of the French regime was

---

[135] As Levy notes, this resistance to identifying a founding moment distinguishes Montesquieu's history from the Gothic contractarianism of some monarchomachs. Levy, *Rationalism, Pluralism, and Freedom*, 158.

[136] Like the *parlementaires*, Montesquieu links nobility with judicial power; but like Boulainvilliers, he traces noble privilege to the Frankish war bands, supporting the antiquity of the sword nobles. As R. R. Palmer suggests, Montesquieu synthesizes the competing constitutional claims of the "old feudal and new parlementary nobility in France." R. R. Palmer, *The Age of the Democratic Revolution* (Princeton University Press, 1969), vol. 2, 56; Ford, *Robe and Sword*, ch. 12, esp. 238–42. See also De Dijn, *French Political Thought*, 23.

[137] In *LP* 125, Montesquieu offers a similar narrative in more condensed and explosive form.

not its earliest form but rather the shape it assumed after most serfs had gained their civil freedom, but before either the desuetude of the Estates or royal predations upon the parlements.[138] In Book 11, he registers his judgment on the constitutional descendants of the "Gothic" polity in France and elsewhere in Europe:

> Here is how the plan for the monarchies that we know was formed. The Germanic nations who conquered the Roman Empire were very free ... The conquerors spread out across the county; they lived in the countryside, rarely in the towns ... [T]he nation had to deliberate on its business as it had done before the conquest; it did so by representatives. Here is the origin of Gothic government among us. It was at first a mixture of aristocracy and monarchy. Its drawback was that the common people were slaves; it was a good government that had within itself the capacity to become better. Giving letters of emancipation became the custom, and soon the civil liberty of the people, the prerogatives of the nobility and of the clergy, and the powers of the kings, were in such concert that there has never been, I believe, a government on earth as well tempered as that of each part of Europe during the time that this government continued to exist; and it is remarkable that the corruption of the government of a conquering people should have formed the best kind of government men have been able to devise.
>
> (*EL* 2.11.8)

The political order in the age of Clovis was a "good government ... with a capacity to become better." It became "better" through "corruption," the liberation of the serfs.[139] This liberation was a "corruption" not in absolute terms but relative only to the regime type (aristocratic-monarchic). Its effect was to introduce into society a new tempering or balancing agent. In his approach to historical development, Montesquieu is closer here to Pasquier than to Hotman and Boulainvilliers. Pasquier had championed the power of the parlements even as he explained that they were late developments. But he regarded them as functionally con-tinuous with a native tradition of constitutional limitation stretching back to pre-Roman Gaul.[140] Similarly, on Montesquieu's view, the liberation of the serfs was not original to the regime, but it amplified the chief virtue of the ancient constitution: political moderation (*EL* 1.5.14).

---

[138] Many serfs were emancipated during the thirteenth century, and the majority were free by the fourteenth. This seems to be the period Montesquieu has in mind. See Wright, "A Rhetoric of Aristocratic Reaction?" 241.

[139] Montesquieu's use of the word "corruption" ironizes Boulainvilliers's horror at the emancipation and ennoblement of serfs. See Ellis, *Boulainvilliers and the French Mon-archy*, 154.

[140] See Schiffman, "Estienne Pasquier," 509–10, on this element of Pasquier's thought.

Unlike Pasquier, Hotman, and Boulainvilliers, Montesquieu remains cagey in his history about which body, if any, is legitimate heir of the ancient balancing institutions. As we have noted, he prudently cuts off Book 31's narrative in the tenth century, sidestepping this most hazardous subject.[141] He never insists on any particular agent of balance as the *sine qua non* of political moderation in France; the purpose of his history is not to ground any narrow doctrine concerning French politics. But he understood the potency of a historical narrative tracing constitutional origins to an ancient, ancestral tradition of political restraint and pluralized power. His history, like that of the *mos gallicus* constitutionalists, shows that the ascription of "power as arbitrary as the sultan" to the King of France "upsets all history" (*EL* 6.30.5). Institutions and practices ensuring political balance, limit, and mediation arise as developments from a germ of political moderation inhering in the usages and mores of "our fathers" (*EL* 1.6.18; 2.10.4; 2.14.14).

Throughout this exercise in constitutional history, we find Montesquieu working with a tradition of French legal and political thought inaugurated in the sixteenth century. It is a tradition that predates the natural rights liberalism of Locke, a tradition in which the value of what is our own and what is particular to us is aligned with respect for liberty, limited government, and mediated authority. Faced with a burgeoning absolutism that rested upon appeals to natural law, divine law, and universalized foreign law, the constitutionalists of the sixteenth century asserted the historical character of law, the reasonableness of legal diversity, the value of "grown" custom, the interdependence of law and mores, and the embeddedness of law within social and political wholes, including the Aristotelian principle that laws are and should be established to suit the regime, and not the regime to suit the laws. In short, the constitutionalism of *mos gallicus* was of a piece with their particularism. This school's most important heir was the baron de Montesquieu. He shares not only the broad outlines of their approach to Roman law and the monarchy's origins, but also the fundamental marriage of political values that defined legal humanism's contribution to the constitutional debates of late sixteenth-century France.

---

[141] Although Montesquieu's history includes a discussion of early participatory assemblies (*EL* 6.28.9, 6.31.1), as a practical matter he seems to view the parlements – not the Estates General – as the likeliest source of constitutional renewal in France (*MP* 589). See Chapter 3 and Wright, "A Rhetoric of Aristocratic Reaction?" 245–51.

There can be little doubt that Montesquieu's liberal constitutionalism also transcends this tradition. Even as he retains and deepens the particularistic sensibility and historical sense of the humanist school, he succeeds in avoiding its near-exclusive reliance on historical arguments to defend constitutional government. Books 30 and 31 complete *The Spirit of the Laws*; they do not provide a foundation for the work. While Montesquieu finds a model of political moderation and liberty in history, he does not ground his normative political theory merely upon the authority of the ancient constitution.[142] His analysis of European constitutional practice and history is overlaid with a new science of constitutional design, and his normative thought rests upon robust yet flexible moral foundations, as we consider next. Still, to understand Montesquieu in the context of humanist constitutionalism is to begin to appreciate why he saw no necessary tension between his particularism and his liberalism, but on the contrary, perceived in the abstract universalism of some Enlightenment thought an impulse inimical to the historic spirit of constitutional government.

---

[142] See Ceaser, *Designing a Polity*, 31–7; C. P. Courtney, *Montesquieu and Burke* (Oxford: Basil Blackwell, 1963), 25; and Chapter 3. See also Schiffman, "Humanism and the Problem of Relativism," on anticipations in Hotman of this movement beyond history.

3

Regime Pluralism

Political liberty concerns moderate monarchies just as it does republics, and is no further from a throne than from a senate. Every man is free who has good grounds to believe that the wrath of one or many will not take away his life or possession of his property.

Montesquieu, *MP* 884

In the foregoing chapters, we have considered how an understanding of Montesquieu's ancient and modern influences allows us to appreciate the consonance of his liberalism and particularism. We now arrive at the elements of Montesquieu's liberalism itself. In the remaining chapters, I aim to show that Montesquieu's political particularism, so far from standing as an ill-fitted codicil to his normative thought, is in fact intricated with the logic of his liberalism. His politics of liberty permit, invite, and even require a statesmanship conducted in light of the "knowledge of place."[1] Later chapters will treat the psychological and cultural elements of Montesquieu's liberal theory; the present chapter turns to its institutional dimension. Here my argument shall be that Montesquieu's approbation of a plurality of decent regimes is an essential feature of his liberal constitutionalism. This *regime pluralism* is among those features of Montesquieu's philosophy of liberty that inoculate it against the contagion of political universalism.

Montesquieu did not set out to construct, at a comfortable remove from the empirical world, a systematic a priori standard for judging

---

[1] Ceaser, *Liberal Democracy and Political Science*, 61.

regimes and institutions. Rousseau was correct in his assertion that the *président à mortier* had failed to develop "principles of political right" akin to the contents of the *Social Contract* or the *Second Treatise*.[2] But Montesquieu's political thought is far from value-neutral, and the normative principles and intimations within his great work betray an unmistakable concern for political right. Normative judgments are diffused throughout his comprehensive science of politics and law, and these judgments have institutional implications. Scholars have widely recognized that despotic government serves as a negative model in Montesquieu's political thought. But readers in the realms of both theory and practice have long disagreed about the nature of the regime or regimes that meet with his approval.

From the earliest reception of *The Spirit of the Laws* to the present, many have concluded that Montesquieu sought to defend monarchy, tempered by a powerful nobility, as the best political form for modern times.[3] The early republican critics of *The Spirit of the Laws* – among them Thomas Jefferson and the Destutt de Tracy – detected in the acclaimed work a dangerous "predilection for monarchy" that was infecting Atlantic political thought and practice.[4] A later incarnation of

---

[2] Jean-Jacques Rousseau, *Emile*, trans. Allan Bloom (New York: Basic Books, 1979), 458.

[3] Some scholars who understand Montesquieu to be an "aristocratic liberal" adhere to this reading. See Carcassone, *Montesquieu et le problème de la constitution*; Loirette, "Montesquieu et la problème de France: Du bon Gouvernment," in *Acts du Congrès Montesquieu* (Bordeaux: Impriméries Delmas, 1956), 219–39; Jean-Jacques Chevallier, "Montesquieu, ou Le Libéralisme aristocratique," *Revue internationale de la philosophie* 9 (1955): 330–4; and Ellis, "Montesquieu's Modern Politics," 665–700. Others who hold to the monarchical reading but without the emphasis upon Montesquieu's aristocratic liberalism include Marc Duconseil, *Machievel et Montesquieu: recherche sur un principe d'autorité* (Paris: Les Éditions Denoël, 1943), 169; Jean Ehrard, *Politique de Montesquieu* (Paris: Armand Colin, 1965), 35; Marcel Prélot, "Montesquieu et les formes de gouvernement," in *La Pensée politique et constitutionelle de Montesquieu: bicentenaire de* L'Esprit des lois, *1748–1948*, 2nd edn., eds. Boris Mirkene-Guezévitch and Henri Puget (Paris: Scientia Verlag Aalen, 1988), 119–32; Michael Oakeshott, *Morality and Politics in Modern Europe,* ed. Shirley Robin Letwin (New Haven, CT: Yale University Press, 1993), 42; De Dijn, *French Political Thought,* ch. 2, esp. 23–8.

[4] Thomas Jefferson, "To Colonel William Duane, September 16, 1810," in *Writings of Thomas Jefferson,* ed. Albert Ellery Bergh (Washington, DC: Thomas Jefferson Memorial Association of the United States, 1907), vol. 11, 413–4. See also Jones, "Montesquieu and Jefferson Revisited," 577–85; Destutt de Tracy, *A Commentary and Review of Montesquieu's* Spirit of Laws; Pseudo-Helvetius, "Letters of Helvetius, Addressed to President Montesquieu and M. Saurin, on Perusing the Manuscript of *The Spirit of Laws* " in Destutt de Tracy, *A Commentary and Review of Montesquieu's* Spirit of Laws, 285–92. See also Gilbert Chinard, *Jefferson et les ideologues* (Baltimore: The Johns Hopkins Press, 1925).

this view arose in the twentieth century, as some scholars suggested that Montesquieu was a "feudal reactionary," the leading spokesman for the "noble reaction" against Bourbon absolutism, and author of a "handbook of aristocratic belief."[5] On this view, his fundamental aim was to bring about a restoration of the power of nobility within the Old Regime. According to a different and more recent statement of the monarchist reading, Montesquieu was in fact an "orthodox monarchist" who favored absolute monarchy and cannot even be numbered among those seeking to reform the Old Regime along constitutionalist lines.[6]

Opposed to the monarchist reading stands what we may call the liberal republican thesis.[7] Scholars of this persuasion argue that Montesquieu's praise of monarchy is belied by subtle criticism of the same throughout *The Spirit of the Laws*. According to this view, Montesquieu saw

---

[5] Wright, "A Rhetoric of Aristocratic Reaction?" 227; Mathiez, "La place de Montesquieu dans l'histoire des doctrines politiques du XVIIIe siècle," 97–112; Althusser, *Politics and History*, 96–106; Ford, *Robe and Sword*, 238–45; Palmer, *The Age of the Democratic Revolution*, vol. 2; Georges Lefebvre, *The Coming of the French Revolution*, trans. R. R. Palmer (Princeton University Press, 2005), 19. This "reactionary" version of the monarchical interpretation of Montesquieu is distinguishable from the aristocratic liberal version, if only in emphasis.

[6] Annelien de Dijn, "Montesquieu's Controversial Context: *The Spirit of the Laws* as a Monarchist Tract," *History of Political Thought* 34 (2013): 66–88. In "Was Montesquieu a Liberal Republican?" *Review of Politics* 76 (2014): 21–41, De Dijn offers a more measured argument, maintaining only that Montesquieu preferred "liberal monarchy" to liberal republicanism.

[7] The leading American voice in this school of interpretation is Thomas L. Pangle, and the view has been reasserted and developed by Diana J. Schaub, Sara MacDonald, and Andrea Radasanu. See Pangle, *Montesquieu's Philosophy of Liberalism*; Schaub, *Erotic Liberalism*, 136; Radasanu, "Montesquieu on Moderation, Monarchy and Reform," 283–307; Sara MacDonald, "Problems with Principles: Montesquieu's Theory of Natural Justice," *History of Political Thought* 24 (2003): 109–30. Schaub states the matter this way: Monarchy is at best "an alluvial delta that can serve as the ground of republicanism" (136). See also Thomas L Pangle, *The Theological Basis of Liberal Modernity in Montesquieu's* Spirit of the Laws (University of Chicago Press, 2010), ch. 3; Judith Shklar, *Montesquieu* (Oxford University Press, 1987), 219. In addition to this liberal republican reading, there are also those who read Montesquieu as a classical republican. See Mark Hulliung, *Montesquieu and the Old Regime* (Berkeley: University of California Press, 1977); with qualifications, Nannerl O. Keohane, "Virtuous Republics and Glorious Monarchies: Two Models in Montesquieu's Political Thought," *Political Studies* 20 (1972): 383–96; and Nelson, *The Greek Tradition*, 165–6. Advocates of both the monarchical reading and the liberal republican reading have shown, in my view, that Montesquieu is no classical republican. See especially Manent, *The City of Man*, 21–34; Ellis, "Montesquieu's Modern Politics"; Pangle, *Montesquieu's Philosophy of Liberalism*, ch. 4; Manin, "Montesquieu et la politique moderne," 171–231. See also Catherine Larrère, "Montesquieu and the Modern Republic," in *Montesquieu and the Spirit of Modernity*, eds. David W. Carrithers and Patrick Coleman (Oxford: Voltaire Foundation, 2002), 235–50.

monarchy as insufficiently hospitable to liberty and security. He therefore heralded and encouraged a gradual but definite transition in Western Europe from monarchy to liberal republican government cast in the English mold.

But neither of these views are satisfactory, for Montesquieu was a regime pluralist. While he admired both the English constitution ("a republic [that] hides under the form of a monarchy") and its precursor, Gothic government, his liberal constitutionalism ultimately includes within its compass a variety of decent regimes (*EL* 1.5.19; 2.11.8; 3.19.27, p. 330). Though a number of scholars have endorsed such a pluralist reading, the literature contains no sustained effort to defend this view and integrate it into a broader account of Montesquieu's liberal political theory.[8]

It is a mistake to imagine that Montesquieu's regime pluralism is explicable merely in terms of his political sociology or his willingness to make concessions in the face of nonideal circumstances. The clearest and deepest support for the pluralist reading emerges from a consideration of the nature of his liberalism itself, which is at its core open to a variety of political forms. In other words, even if Montesquieu were not so prudent and so concerned with matching a regime to a people, his liberalism would nevertheless remain aloof from the conventional contest of regimes. Appreciating the institutional pluralism inherent in his liberalism takes us a long way toward understanding the complementarity of his liberalism and political particularism. A normative vision of free and moderate government emerges in *Spirit*, and the liberty and political moderation at the heart of this vision are attainable within a variety of regime types.

The present chapter develops this argument in four ways. I begin by showing that Montesquieu's liberalism stands upon foundations that are

---

[8] There is a need for a reassessment of the underpinnings of such a pluralist interpretation in light of recent powerful restatements of the liberal republican and monarchist theses, such as De Dijn, "Montesquieu's Controversial Context"; Radasanu, "Montesquieu on Moderation, Monarchy, and Reform"; and Pangle, *Theological Basis*, ch. 3. Studies that treat Montesquieu as a regime pluralist include Manin, "Montesquieu et la politique modern"; Isaiah Berlin, "Montesquieu"; Larrère, *Actualité de Montesquieu*; Sharon Krause, "The Spirit of Separate Powers in Montesquieu," *The Review of Politics* 62 (2000): 231–65; Spector, *Montesquieu: Liberté, droit et histoire*; Larrère, "Montesquieu and Liberalism," 288–9; Rahe, *Montesquieu and the Logic of Liberty*, esp. 281–2, albeit with qualifications (e.g., 314ff.); David Lay Williams, "Political Ontology and Institutional Design in Montesquieu and Rousseau," *American Journal of Political Science* 54 (2010): 525–42; Rasmussen, *Pragmatic Enlightenment*, 92–5; Craiutu, *A Virtue for Courageous Minds*, 40–43.

at once genuinely universal in scope and yet not tethered to any particular political form. His liberalism is compatible with particularism not because the former is shorn of genuinely universal foundations but because of the distinctive character of those universal foundations. Next the chapter turns to Montesquieu's books on liberty – Books 11 and 12 – and advances three interdependent claims. I show that Montesquieu explicitly presents his conception of liberty as a replacement for regime-specific conceptions of the same. He means to bypass the stale quarrel between monarchists and republicans, each acclaiming their regime the unique home of liberty. Then I argue that Montesquieu conceives of the free constitution of England as modeling principles of limit, balance, and complexity that may penetrate a variety of regime types. Finally, turning to Montesquieu's often neglected second book on liberty (*EL* 12), we consider how his treatment of criminal law again sidelines the contest of regimes and concentrates the reader's attention upon a mode of liberal reform distinct from constitutional renovation. He takes care to show that the liberalization of criminal law – a key element of free government – is possible in republics, monarchies, and mixed regimes alike. Montesquieu's is regime pluralist liberalism, and it is therefore wholly consistent with his critique of universal politics.

THE LIMITS OF FOUNDATIONALISM

While Montesquieu's political thought has had its detractors over the years, his reputation has fared relatively well in the last century. Many twentieth-century political theorists, including leading liberal thinkers as well as critics of liberal modernity on both the Left and Right, seem to have discovered something of value in his thought. One thinks of Michael Oakeshott, Isaiah Berlin, Raymond Aron, Hannah Arendt, Judith Shklar, and Sheldon Wolin, each of whom seriously and favorably treated Montesquieu's political theory.[9] Perhaps more than any other major modern

---

[9] Oakeshott, *Morality and Politics in Modern Europe*, 36–43; Michael Oakeshott, *On Human Conduct* (Oxford University Press, 1991), 246–51; Berlin, "Montesquieu"; Aron, *Main Currents in Sociological Thought*, vol. 1, chap. 1; Hannah Arendt, *On Revolution* (New York: Penguin, 1990), 150–2, 188–9; Hannah Arendt, *The Promise of Politics* (New York: Schocken Books, 2005), 63–9; Judith Shklar, "The Liberalism of Fear," in *Liberalism and the Moral Life*, ed. Nancy L. Rosenblum (Cambridge, MA: Harvard University Press, 1989), 21–38; Judith Shklar, *Ordinary Vices* (Cambridge: Belknap, 1985), ch. 1; Wolin, *Presence of the Past*, 100–19; James Wiley, "Sheldon Wolin on Theory and the Political," *Polity* 38 (2006): 211–34.

thinker, Montesquieu appears as a theorist from whom one can borrow an insight or two without becoming committed to an entire system of politics.

That *The Spirit of the Laws* seems to invite promiscuous gleanings indicates something about the nature of the work: Montesquieu's political teachings are rarely if ever explicitly tied to universal and transcendent foundations. He does not develop a demonstrative science of political right; his normative theory certainly does not "proceed according to the model of mathematics," as does John Locke's.[10] This observation led Hannah Arendt to suggest admiringly that Montesquieu was alone among the great modern theorists in his belief that transcendent foundations were unnecessary.[11] Arendt's passing observation is developed in an important recent study by Dennis Rasmussen. Rasmussen's Montesquieu is a "non-foundationalist" or even "anti-foundationalist" thinker – sometimes appearing as a distant ancestor of Richard Rorty – whose political flexibility stems from a disavowal of universal, abstract foundations.[12] Against Arendt and Rasmussen's view, I maintain that Montesquieu's liberalism does indeed stand upon universal foundations. His regime pluralism is made possible not by the absence of such foundations but by their unusual nature, as compared to those of other liberal theorists of the age.[13] But in making this case, my preliminary challenge is to explain why Montesquieu's first principles are so inconspicuous, and why he so rarely connects them to his political prescriptions throughout most of his great work. Does *The Spirit of the Laws* contain the mere "metaphysical residue" of Montesquieu's past experimentation with now-abandoned foundationalist ideas?[14] Or does he have sound reasons for leaving only trace elements of his philosophical foundations? I believe he does.

Montesquieu relegates his first principles to the shadows for at least three reasons. First, he has serious doubts about the efficacy of straightforward, foundational moral argument in politics. As he writes in the opening lines of his unpublished *De la politique*, it is "useless to attack a

---

[10] Grant, *John Locke's Liberalism*, 50.   [11] Arendt, *On Revolution*, 185.

[12] Rasmussen, *Pragmatic Enlightenment*, 82, 96. Cf. Schaub, "Of Believers and Barbarians," 238. Schaub concludes that Montesquieu's "'anti-foundationalism' consists less in his demolition of foundations than in his deliberate neglect of them."

[13] Here James Ceaser's distinction between flexible and rigid foundationalism is instructive. Ceaser, *Designing a Polity*, 17; see also Williams, "Political Ontology and Institutional Design."

[14] See Pierre Martino, "De quelques résidus métaphysiques dans l'*Esprit des lois*," *Revue d'histoire de la philosophie et d'histoire générale de la civilisation* 43 (1946): 235–43.

policy by showing how it is repugnant to morality, reason, justice, as
these kinds of speeches persuade everyone and affect no one."[15] Instead,
he recommends "the circuitous route," a detour, by which the writer
shows the political actor "how little utility" he derives from his immoral
policy. In the *Pensées*, he similarly argues, "It is not by speechifying that
despotism must be attacked, but by making clear that it tyrannizes the
despot himself" (*MP* 1432). The prince must understand that he weakens
himself as he attempts to consolidate power; despotism must be
unmasked as instrumentally irrational. Montesquieu writes, "I will say
to Princes: 'Why do you exhaust yourselves so much to extend your
authority? Is it to increase your power? But the experience of all countries
and all times makes clear that you are weakening it'" (*MP* 1991). This
statement indeed sums up a significant portion of the case against despotism in *Spirit*. Montesquieu aims to show that despotic modes produce an
impotent state and often cycles of revolution. The despot's will "should
produce its effect as infallibly as does one ball thrown against another,"
but thoroughly despotic institutions do not yield consistent obedience.[16]
The quintessence of despotism in *Spirit*, Japan has "powerless" laws (*EL*
1.6.13). The fear that sustains despotic governments eventually "wears
down"; imaginations become "inured" to ever crueler penalties (*EL*
1.6.12). Despotism is a self-defeating proposition. Arguments such as
these, Montesquieu suspects, are generally more effective in making converts to political moderation than are foundationalist moral arguments.
Of course, we have no reason to doubt that Montesquieu believed that his
pragmatic arguments had the additional benefit of being true. To describe
despotism as it is, is to undermine it.

Montesquieu's distrust of direct, systematic appeals to *la morale* stems
from a basic and now familiar psychological insight that shapes much of
his political thought, both in form and substance: self-interest, ambition,
the lust for power, and other human passions can be managed, redirected,
canalized, and offset by competing passions and sentiments; but rarely
will they submit to the voice of reason. In perhaps the most moralistic
chapter of *Spirit*, Montesquieu adopts the persona of a Spanish Jew to
argue against the Inquisition; he offers a moral and theological defense of

---

[15] Montesquieu, "De la Politique," VF 8:511. This work originally comprised chapters
13 and 14 of the *Traité des devoirs*, modeled on Cicero's *De officiis* (VF 8:505).

[16] This "should" must be distinguished from "shall" and "ought." Despotic government, if
it is to endure, should produce reflexive obedience in its subjects. But it eventually loses
the capacity to do so.

toleration. Of this "very humble remonstrance," Montesquieu avers, "I believe it is the most useless [work] that has ever been written. When it is a question of proving such clear things, one is sure not to convince" (*EL* 5.25.13). If a man is not moved by the self-evident cruelty of religious persecution and despotism, icy moral logic will avail little. We should therefore be surprised to find any work comparable in form to the Locke's *Second Treatise* issuing from the study at La Brède.

In addition to these doubts about the efficacy of demonstrative moral argument, Montesquieu also has theoretical reasons for avoiding an explicit discussion of his moral foundations. As we have seen, early in *Spirit* he poses a question that seems to set the stage for a natural law argument concerning the best regime. Which government, he asks, is "most in conformity with nature" (*EL* 1.1.3)? For the modern natural law tradition and the ancient tradition of natural right, to claim that a government is according to nature is to say that it accords with a human universal – constituents of human nature or requirements of human flourishing. Montesquieu himself, as I argue in this chapter, depends upon a number of foundationalist arguments from nature understood in that very sense. But here he refrains from introducing such foundations explicitly. He turns instead to an alternate conception of nature. The government most according to nature is the government that "best relates to the disposition of the people for whom it is established" (*EL* 1.1.3). Nature has become particular. This is not the nature of *homo simplex*, but the nature of particular men, bounded and shaped by place and time. The question is not simply what distinguishes man from nonman but rather what distinguishes this particular human community from another human community. Ceaser characterizes Montesquieu's approach this way: "What is natural is what is unique to each being, with a 'being' in politics now referring not just to an individual person, but also – and especially – to collectivities, such as nations and civilizations."[17] Montesquieu here turns to particular nature not because he lacks a conception of universal nature, but because right political action requires knowledge of both universal and particular nature. Attention to the latter – so prominent in Cicero's ethic, as we saw in Chapter 1 – had waned in the early modern period. By foregrounding particular nature, Montesquieu guards against the misconception that reflection on universal nature is sufficient to determine political action.

---

[17] Ceaser, *Designing a Polity*, 36.

Finally, a third consideration allows us to account for the low profile of the moral foundations in *Spirit*. On Montesquieu's view, deductive or "Cartesian" approaches to normative political theory threaten to sever our contact with concrete models in history that may serve as objects of fruitful philosophical reflection.[18] As he introduces his account of the English free state, Montesquieu serenely assures us that, "Not much trouble need be taken to discover political liberty. If it can be seen where it is, if it has been found, why seek it?" (*EL* 2.11.5). In an earlier draft of this passage, he indicates the nature of the "trouble" he wishes to avoid: "great speculations are not necessary," he writes (VF 3:227). His famous account of the English constitution is an alternative to great speculations. Montesquieu contrasts abstract theoretical seeking with finding in history. He has found political liberty in an actual constitution.[19] When made an object of reflection, the English constitution appears consistent with the moral foundations of Montesquieu's thought, but nothing could be more obvious than that Montesquieu does not reason from his foundations to the English constitution. Caught up in the "trouble" of deductive or speculative political theory, one always runs the risk of missing the concrete examples before one's eyes and seeking instead models both unrealizable and inferior.

Montesquieu reprises this methodological point as he closes his account of the English constitution. He avers that "the excess even of reason is not always desirable" (*EL* 2.11.6, p. 166). The speculative blunders of seventeenth-century political writer James Harrington serve to illustrate his point. He sought in theory when he could have *found* in history.

Harrington ... has also examined the furthest point of liberty to which the constitution of a state can be carried. But of him it can be said that he sought liberty only after misunderstanding it, and that he built Chalcedon with the coast of Byzantium before his eyes.

(*EL* 2.11.6, p. 166)

---

[18] In a similar vein, Paul O. Carrese and Sheldon Wolin write of Montesquieu's rejection of a "Cartesian" approach to political theory. Wolin, *Presence of the Past*, 100–19; Paul O. Carrese, *The Cloaking of Power: Montesquieu, Blackstone, and the Rise of Judicial Activism* (University of Chicago Press, 2003), 102, 116–21.

[19] As is often noted, Montesquieu uses the conditional throughout his chapter on the English constitution, and he suggests at the end that the English may not actually "enjoy" the liberty he has described. But he affirms that this liberty "is established by their laws." *EL* 2.11.6.

Published in 1656 during the Interregnum, Harrington's *Oceana* is a utopian work, but the utopian regime is in fact an idealization of Cromwell's English republic, as Montesquieu knew.²⁰ He later complains that Harrington "saw only the republic of England" (*EL* 6.29.6). Thus the defect is not quite that Harrington fabricates a new theoretical ideal. Rather it is that he explicitly rejects the English constitution, derogating it as a "wrestling match" between crown and nobility, and he models his *Oceana* on the idealization of a regime that never was.²¹ An English republic never actually existed under the de facto military dictatorship of Cromwell; the English "*sought* democracy but *found* it nowhere," writes Montesquieu in Book 3, using the same language of seeking and finding he employs in chapter 5 of Book 11 (*EL*, 1.3.3, emphasis added). If Harrington had proceeded properly, Montesquieu suggests, he would have found liberty in the historic English constitution and its forerunner, the Gothic constitution.²² This is how we must understand Montesquieu's reference to the "coast of Byzantium." In the *Histories* of Herodotus, when Persian general Megabazos learns that Chalcedon was founded seventeen years prior to the founding of Byzantium, he derides Chalcedon's founders for failing to recognize that before their eyes, just across the Bosphorus, lay a site fit for a grander and mightier city – the future location of Byzantium.²³ James Harrington similarly failed to see what was before his eyes: the English regime of liberty, the coast of Byzantium. Such is the theoretical toll exacted by the "excess even of reason" (*EL* 2.11.6, p. 166).²⁴

---

²⁰ See J. G. A. Pocock, "Editor's Introduction," in *James Harrington: The Commonwealth of Oceana and* A System of Politics, ed. J. G. A. Pocock (Cambridge University Press, 1992), vii–xxiii; Nelson, *The Greek Tradition*, 87–8.

²¹ Harrington's idealized English republic relied not on the struggle between crown and nobility that characterized Gothic government but rather on common interests forged through an egalitarian distribution of property. Harrington, *Oceana*, 53. See Nelson, *The Greek Tradition*, 109.

²² See Pierre Manent, *City of Man*, 13–14. Manent concludes: "By his profound play on 'seeking' and 'finding,' Montesquieu constructs for the reader 'before his eyes' neither Byzantium nor Chalcedon, but the modern idea of history" (14).

²³ See Herodotus, *The Histories*, trans. Robin Waterfield (Oxford University Press, 1998), 4:144; Jean Brethe de la Gressaye, "Notes," in *Montesquieu, De L'Esprit des Loix* (Paris, 1950), vol. 1, 350; Harrington, *Oceana*, 161.

²⁴ On "the excess of reason," compare Paul O. Carrese, "The Machiavellian Spirit of Montesquieu's Republic," in *Machiavelli's Liberal Republican Legacy*, ed. Paul A. Rahe (Cambridge University Press, 2006), 128–9, with Rebecca E. Kingston, *Public Passion: Rethinking the Grounds for Political Justice* (Montreal: McGill-Queen's University Press, 2014), 119, and Robert C. Bartlett, *The Idea of Enlightenment: A Post-mortem Study* (University of Toronto Press, 2001), 199–200.

Montesquieu develops this line of thought more vividly still when, two chapters later, he describes the "corruption" of the Gothic constitution as "the best kind of government men have been able to imagine [*pû imaginer*]" (*EL* 2.11.8).[25] Those words ring with irony, for Montesquieu knows that this regime is the undesigned product of a thousand uncoordinated movements and modifications. It owes nothing to the imagination of men.[26] The best actual regime "is a gift of historical accident" rather than theoretical reflection, as James W. Ceaser observes. "Before the best regime came to be, it could not have been known."[27] Once it comes to be and shows its nature through historical experience, reason can both recognize it – finding it without seeking it in the language of chapter 6 – and provide an account of it. Such is the office of normative political theory.

These considerations sufficiently account for the low profile of universal foundations in the text of *The Spirit of the Laws*, and we have no need of auxiliary speculations concerning Montesquieu's inability to purge abandoned ideas from his text.

THE FOUNDATIONS OF REGIME PLURALISM

While Montesquieu's first principles suffuse the text of *Spirit*, his critique of despotism as well as his defense of free and moderate government depend upon an eclectic variety of universal moral foundations. These foundations ground a critique of absolute, arbitrary government, but they do not vindicate any one particular non-despotic regime as the universal model. His regime pluralism and particularistic art of politics are ultimately made possible not by the absence of universal and transcendent foundations but rather by the flexible and indeterminate character of these foundations as Montesquieu construes them.[28] This becomes especially evident as we consider the compatibility of regime pluralism with three

---

[25] The translation is mine. Cohler et al., reads "able to devise."

[26] Montesquieu's words are reminiscent of Machiavelli's reference to the man "*chi ordino*" the French monarchy, which prompted Joseph de Maistre's to remark, "I would like to know him." Pocock, *The Ancient Constitution*, 19; Machiavelli, *Discourses on Livy*, trans. Harvey C. Mansfield and Nathan Tarcov (University of Chicago Press, 1995), 1.16.

[27] James W. Ceaser, "Alexis de Tocqueville and the Two-Founding Thesis," *The Review of Politics* 73 (2011), 232.

[28] For a fine discussion of "transcendent constrained indeterminacy" in Montesquieu and Rousseau, see Williams, "Political Ontology and Institutional Design."

such universal moral foundations present in the normative groundwork of *Spirit*: Montesquieu's theory of the social contract, his conception of law's relationship to "the nature of things," and his account of human nature.[29]

While Lockean and Rousseauian social contract theories require a popular element in all legitimate regimes, Montesquieu emphasizes the wide variety of decent regimes to which a social contract may give rise.[30] In his unfinished *Treatise on Duties* (1725), he explicitly ties the social contract to regime pluralism as he explains the transition from natural clan-based societies, ruled by patriarchs, to conventional political societies founded by social contract:

> Families became divided; the fathers, once dead, left collaterals independent. It was necessary to unite by convention and to do by means of civil laws what natural right had done at the outset ...
> Chance and the imagination of those who entered into conventions established as many different forms of government as there were peoples – all of them good, since they were the will of the contracting parties.[31]

As a foundation of Montesquieu's normative political theory, social contract theory does not yield any single model regime. The moment he locates the origin of the state in a social contract, he underscores its consistency with regime pluralism: social contracts produced "many different forms ... all of them good." The almost reflexive connection between these two thoughts is striking and suggests that social contract

[29] This list is not comprehensive. Focusing on three especially important foundational ideas, we pass over others. Williams, "Political Ontology and Institutional Design," offers a complementary account of the indeterminacy of Montesquieu's conception of justice.

[30] Locke's and Rousseau's regime pluralism is not nearly as capacious as Montesquieu's. Rousseau famously holds that sovereignty remains with the people in their collective capacity. Locke ultimately requires the presence of a popular representative body in modern states because only the people's representatives can legitimately levy taxes. Furthermore, since liberty and life are species of "property," Ruth W. Grant suggests that the requirement of representation for taxation is "a large opening wedge ... toward a requirement for a representative body for many purposes." Grant, *John Locke's Liberalism*, 97n.63. Thomas G. West concurs in "The Political Theory of the Declaration of Independence," in *The American Founding and the Social Compact*, eds. Thomas G. West and R. J. Pestritto (Lanham, MD: Lexington Books, 2003), 128. On Locke's account, any modern regime – indeed, any state dependent on tax revenue – must have a significant democratic element to pass the test of legitimacy.

[31] *MP* 1267. See also *MP* 1318 and *EL* 1.3.8. *Penseés* 1266 and 1267 originally belonged to chapter 5 of the *Treatise on Duties*. Shackleton, *Montesquieu*, 434.

theory interests Montesquieu precisely because it can, properly nuanced, account for the legitimacy of a range of decent regimes.[32]

Without leading him to any determinate conclusions about the ideal ordering of political communities, Montesquieu's social contract theory yields a rejection of despotism. Despotic government is certainly not among the diverse "good" forms that can emerge from a social contract. This judgment appears most prominently in Montesquieu's critique of Hobbes in the *Pensées*.[33] He writes,

> This principle of Hobbes is quite false: that since the people have authorized the prince, the prince's deeds are the people's deeds, and consequently, the people cannot complain about the prince nor demand any account of his actions, because the people cannot complain about the people. Thus, Hobbes has forgotten his principle of natural law: *Pacta esse servanda*. The people have authorized the prince under conditions, they have established him under a convention. He must observe it, and the prince represents the people only as the people have wanted or are reputed to have wanted him to represent them. (Besides, it is false that the delegate has as much power as the one who delegates, and no longer depends upon the latter.)[34]

Contra Hobbes, Montesquieu sees the social contract as limited and conditional. It is not a source of arbitrary power, for the limits of political authority are set by the (inferred) intentions of the contracting parties. Absolute government could never arise from the will of contracting parties.

Montesquieu seems to have contemplated placing in *Spirit* a robust statement of social contract theory along these very lines. "This is good for the *Laws*," he wrote in a note appended to entry 1267 in the *Pensées* (quoted earlier in the chapter). Although he ultimately decided against it, the marks of his enduring contractarian commitments appear at several

---

[32] A number of scholars doubt that Montesquieu was a social contract theorist. See Althusser, *Politics and History*, 22–9; Joseph Dedieu, *Montesquieu* (Paris: F. Alcan, 1913), 168; Ehrard, *Politique de Montesquieu*, 38; Rasmussen, *Pragmatic Enlightenment*, chs. 2 and 5. Some argue that because Montesquieu rejected the asocial state of nature (e.g., at *LP* 91, pp. 125–6), he could not have accepted social contract theory. But a critique of Hobbes's asocial state of nature does not close the door to social contract theory. On Montesquieu's view, natural clan society predates the social contract, but the contract is the source of civil government, as is clear in *MP* 1267 and 1318.

[33] The library at La Brède contained Thomas Hobbes's *Opera philosophica, quae Latine scripsit omnia* (Amsterdam: Apud J. Blaev, 1668) and two French translations of *De cive*. See Simone Goyard-Fabre, *Montesquieu, adversaire de Hobbes* (Paris: Lettres Modernes, 1980).

[34] *MP* 224; see also VF 8.438.

points in the text.³⁵ As Montesquieu opens his chapter on positive laws in the first book of *Spirit*, men are clearly in society, but there are no laws and no state (*EL* 1.1.3). These sociable men lose their natural feeling of weakness in society, and a state of war begins.³⁶ The state of war "brings about the establishment of laws among men" (*EL* 1.1.3). At this point, Montesquieu introduces political right and the political state. "A society could not continue to exist without a government," he reasons, and here he quotes Giovanni Vincenzo Gravina's contractarian definition of the state: a union of all individual strengths and all individual wills (*EL* 1.1.3). He then explains that while paternal power preceded political authority, this proves nothing about the proper constitution of political authority, for "[p]olitical power necessarily includes the union of many families." This political anthropology complements the account in the *Treatise on Duties* of "independent collaterals" who formed governments through "conventions" after the death of fathers.³⁷ Even as he avoids elaborating a full social contractarian account of law and political institutions in *Spirit*, he indicates his basic agreement with the contractarian model.

Contractarian ideas extend beyond these early chapters. Montesquieu later argues that slavery – both civil and political – is "against nature"

---

³⁵ See Mark H. Waddicor, *Montesquieu and the Philosophy of Natural Law* (The Hague: Martinus Nijhoff, 1970).

³⁶ This text leads some scholars to conclude that Montesquieu develops an essentially Hobbesian, asocial account of human nature in *Spirit*. See Michael Zuckert, "Natural Law, Natural Rights, and Classical Liberalism: On Montesquieu's Critique of Hobbes," in *Natural Law and Modern Moral Philosophy*, eds. Ellen Frankel Paul, Fred D. Miller, and Jeffrey Paul (Cambridge University Press, 2001), 236–7, and, less emphatically, Pangle, *Montesquieu's Philosophy of Liberalism*, 32–3. It is true that in Book 1 of *Spirit*, Montesquieu speaks of individuals "before the establishment of societies" (*EL* 1.1.2). But as Dennis Rasmussen has persuasively shown, this concept of asocial man must be purely hypothetical in *Spirit* because two of the natural laws Montesquieu locates within the asocial state of nature entail natural sociability ("natural entreaty" and the "desire for society"). See Rasmussen, *Pragmatic Enlightenment*, 254n.53. Furthermore, as both Rasmussen and Mark Waddicor note, Montesquieu consistently uses conditional language in his account of an asocial state of nature in Book 1, chapter 2, again indicating that he doubts that pre-social human existence was ever a reality. Waddicor, *Montesquieu and the Philosophy of Natural Law*, 48. In the next chapter (1.1.3), when Montesquieu turns to man in society, he abandons the conditional language. See also Victor Goldschmidt, "L'état de nature dans *L'Esprit des Lois*," in *Anthropologie et politique: Les principes du système de Rousseau* (Paris: Vrin, 1974), 189–217.

³⁷ The "independent collaterals" are likely small families, not individuals; they are "independent" because they are free from the authority of the now-deceased clan patriarch. *EL* 1.1.3; *MP* 1267.

because "all men are born equal" (*EL* 3.15.7; 1.8.3). He approvingly quotes Cicero's claim that the city was established "only in order for each one to preserve his goods" (*EL* 5.26.15). In Book 26, he suggests that government arises when "men have renounced their *natural independence* to live under political laws" (Nagel 1.767).[38] Marred by a significant error, the Cambridge translation of this passage has men renouncing "their natural dependence to live under political laws" (*EL* 5.26.15). It is certainly noteworthy that this allusion to social contract theory has been obscured for two decades in the only modern English edition of *Spirit*.

Some may be inclined to view the social contractarian moments in *Spirit* as the "residue" of Montesquieu's past experimentation with and rejection of natural law theory.[39] But given the care of this writer and the pervasiveness of the allusions, the better part of wisdom seems to lie with the view that these passages and others are evidence that Montesquieu never abandoned a contractarian framework.[40] Though submerged in the text for reasons we have considered, his contractarian commitments clearly play a role in his judgments against despotism and in favor of free and moderate politics, without vindicating any single form of government.

Social contract theory constitutes an important moral referent in his normative political thought, but it does not stand alone. Of equal consequence is his theory of "the nature of things." *The Spirit of the Laws* opens with an enigmatic definition of law: "Laws, taken in their broadest meaning, are the necessary relations deriving from the nature of things [*la nature des choses*]" (*EL* 1.1.1). This notion of "the nature of things" plays a significant role in Montesquieu's normative liberalism, particularly in his treatment of criminal law. Readers find a striking example of

[38] The translation is mine. I rely here upon the Nagel edition, the basis of the Cohler, Miller, and Stone edition. No French editions read "dependence."

[39] Martino, "De quelques résidus métaphysiques dans l'*Esprit des lois*." Martino asserts that the hints of natural law thinking in *Spirit* are incompatible with the otherwise non-metaphysical nature of the work.

[40] Waddicor, *Montesquieu and the Philosophy of Natural Law*, ch. 4, esp. 93–9. See also Spector, "Quelle justice," 219–42; Jean-Patrice Courtois, *Inflexions de la rationalité dans L'Esprit des lois – Écriture et pensée sur Montesquieu* (Paris: Presses Universitaires de France, 1999); C. P. Courtney, "Montesquieu and Natural Law," in *Montesquieu's Science of Politics: Essays on* The Spirit of Laws, eds. David W. Carrithers, Michael A. Mosher, and Paul A. Rahe (Lanham, MD: Rowman & Littlefield, 2001); Tzvetan Todorov, "Droit naturel et formes de gouvernement dans *L'Esprit des Lois*," Esprit 75 (1983): 35–48.

this mode of foundationalist reasoning in Montesquieu's discussion of the nature of penalties (*EL* 2.12.4), a crucial element in his defense of the liberty of the citizen. The chapter proposes removing crimes against religion and mores from the domain of criminal law, as we understand it. In a rare explicit appeal to foundations, Montesquieu announces that his argument is "drawn from nature" (*EL* 2.12.4). He begins with the premise that penalties must ensue "not from the legislator's capriciousness" or mere will, but "from the nature of the thing [*la nature de la chose*]" (*EL* 2.12.4). When criminal judgments are drawn from the nature of the thing, this is "the triumph of liberty" (*EL* 2.11.4). A natural class of penalties is implicit in every crime such that when you violate X, you ought to lose the benefits of X. In this way, your penalty follows from "the nature of the thing" you have violated. When you violate religion, you must lose the natural benefits of religion (e.g., incur a sentence of excommunication). When you violate security, you must lose the natural benefits of security (e.g., incur loss of life, freedom, or property). The doctrine in this passage clearly arises from the inaugural principle of *Spirit*: laws are the necessary relations deriving from *la nature des choses* (*EL* 1.1.1). From that highly abstract axiom, a principle so transcendent that it applies to God himself in Book 1, comes the conclusion that to burn a heretic is to commit an act of arbitrary "violence" (*EL* 2.12.4), for there is no logically necessary or natural relation between heresy and the loss of life.[41] Crimes against religion naturally meet with a deprivation of the benefits of religion. Later, in Book 19, Montesquieu reiterates this conception of law, which stands opposed to the Hobbesian voluntaristic notion of law.[42] The law is "not an act of power," and so "every penalty that does not derive from necessity is tyrannical" (*EL* 3.19.14). Here as in

---

[41] While this argument absolutely denies the state a right to persecute religious minorities, it is consistent with a variety of different ways of structuring church-state relations, from total separation to the establishment of religion.

[42] Montesquieu "was clearly opposed to the command theory of law." Carl Joachim Friedrich, *The Philosophy of Law in Historical Perspective*, 107. For an alternative interpretation, see Zuckert, "Montesquieu's Critique of Hobbes," 235–7, echoing David Lowenthal, "Book 1 of Montesquieu's *The Spirit of the Laws*," *American Political Science Review* 53 (1959): 488–91. In Zuckert's judgment, Montesquieu's assertion that positive law "establishes" the "possible relations of justice" or "primitive laws" indicates that he believes these primitive laws are non-binding prior to positive legislation (*EL*, 1.1.1). But Zuckert fails to explain why we should not more naturally understand Montesquieu to mean that the human legislator instantiates ("establishes") eternally binding primitive laws in positive law codes. On this point, see also VF 8:437–38.

Book 1, he means "necessity" in the sense of rational necessity in view of the nature of the offense.

For our purposes, it is important to note that this "triumph of liberty" – a system of penal law grounded on the nature of things – is possible under any constitution, save the despotic, for despotic regimes are lawless by definition (*EL* 2.12.4). Montesquieu does not claim that reflection upon the nature of an offense yields determinate and specific conclusions concerning the proper penalty. Nature cannot tell us whether simple burglary merits a prison term of five years or ten. But such reflection promises more modestly to guide the state away from penalties beyond the scope of law for each class of offenses.

Montesquieu attends not only to the "nature of things," but to human nature. Like the first two foundations we have considered, his conception of human nature is fundamental to both his critique of despotism and his praise of moderate regimes. It has universal implications but remains consistent with his regime pluralism. The phrase *"la nature humaine"* appears exactly six times in Part I of *Spirit*. Each time it serves as the basis for an attack upon despotism: despotism "causes appalling ills to human nature" (*EL* 1.2.4); in view of the evils of despotism, "it seems that human nature would rise up incessantly" against it (*EL* 1.5.14); surveying the severity of despotic governments, "we feel with a kind of sorrow the ills of human nature" (*EL* 1.6.9); despotic princes "trifle with human nature" (*EL* 1.7.9); and human nature "suffers insults" and "affronts" in despotic nations (*EL* 1.8.9, 21). These repeated appeals to human nature are not mere rhetoric. Montesquieu does not offer a fully developed philosophical anthropology, but his treatment of "the constitution of our being" in Book 1 of *Spirit* allows us to reconstruct a convincing picture of his meaning when he depicts despotism as an affront to human nature.

In the third chapter of Book 1, Montesquieu sketches a partial theory of "the laws of nature," which are "so named because they derive uniquely from the constitution of our being" (*EL* 1.1.3). Here he infers three laws of nature from three feelings or sentiments that would be universal to hypothetical pre-social man, and a fourth law of nature from the common human capacity for knowledge. Initially, the natural feelings of inferiority and fear would lead men to refrain from attacking one another; from this would spring the first natural law, to seek peace. The natural feelings of hunger and thirst would lead to the feeling of weakness, inspiring a second natural law: seek nourishment. Signs of mutual fear would lead men to fear less and thus to approach one another. The natural feeling of pleasure in encountering another animal of the same species and the opposite sex would lead to a third natural law – the "natural entreaty [*prière*]" between men and women (*EL* 1.1.3). A fourth natural law, to live in society, would spring from both the general pleasure of encountering other members of the same species and from the bond human beings share as knowing and not merely feeling animals.[43] Here Montesquieu's account of natural law, and so of the "constitution of man," trails off, and he proceeds to a discussion of positive law (*EL* 1.1.3). Can this thin conception of human nature serve as a basis for a moral critique of despotism? Unlike Hobbes and Locke, Montesquieu does not spell out for us how, if at all, his initial sketch of man in the state of nature might ground his normative political conclusions. He often leaves it to his reader to connect premises to conclusions, in keeping with his conviction that "one must not always so exhaust a subject that one leaves nothing for the reader to do" (*EL* 2.11.20).[44]

There is much for the reader to do. Several connections between these natural laws and the deficiencies of despotism present themselves. When Montesquieu introduces the first natural law, the desire for peace, he distinguishes it from the desire for "empire and domination" (*EL* 1.1.2). The desire for domination is not natural to man. Anticipating Rousseau, Montesquieu implies that Hobbes has imported later corruptions into the state of nature. This conception of the first law of nature underwrites Montesquieu's critique of despotism: despotism is an affront to human nature inasmuch as it fails to reflect the original human desire for peace without subjection. Despotic government aims at and delivers a kind of "tranquility," but "this is not peace, it is the silence of the towns that the enemy is ready to occupy" (*EL* 1.5.14, p. 60).

The second and third laws of nature similarly meet with obstruction and perversion in despotic nations. The second consists in the desire to nourish the body, but despotism starves and impoverishes (*EL* 1.5.15, 3.18.3, 4.20.3, 4.23.28). The third law entails the "natural entreaty" of the sexes, but poverty curtails men and women's willingness and ability to form families (*EL* 4.23.28). Moreover, despotic government keeps

---

[43] The natural laws in 1.1.2 do not all derive from man's "animal or sensible" nature, that is, from his "desire for conservation, prior to the development of reason," as Spector argues. Spector, "Quelle justice," 223. Montesquieu clearly links the desire for society to man's capacity for knowledge as an intelligent being.

[44] "To write well, one needs to skip over intermediate ideas – enough not to be boring; not too much, for fear of not being understood. It is these happy deletions that made M. Nicole say that all good books are double" (*MP* 1970). *The Spirit of the Laws* is double.

women "in extreme slavery"; they are removed from public view and many are reserved for one man (*EL* 1.7.9). This is far from the natural entreaty, i.e., willing and affective union, inscribed in the natural law (*EL* 1.1.3). In despotic government one finds unnatural force and slavery in the relations between men and women.

Finally, the fourth natural law is to unite or to live in society. But government is not society, and under despotic government, there is no genuine society. Hidden away in seraglios, women are especially excluded from any simulacrum of true social life. But the deficiency touches all, for all live in relative isolation from one another, and even love within households is threatened (*EL* 1.3.29; 1.5.14, p. 63). In an underappreciated passage on friendship and tyranny in the *Pensées*, Montesquieu anticipates Tocquevillean concerns of social atomization. He explains that in the Roman Republic,

... Citizens were linked to citizens by all sorts of chains: they were bound together with their friends, their enfranchised, their slaves, their children. Today, everything is abolished, right down to paternal power; every man is isolated. It seems that the *natural effect of arbitrary power is to particularize all interests.*

In the meantime, those ties that detached man from himself to attach him to another brought forth great deeds. Without that, everything is vulgar, and there remains only a base interest that is properly speaking merely the animal instinct of all men.

(*MP* 1253, emphasis added)

The degenerating French monarchy had already begun to show evidence of despotism's antisocial influence on its subjects. Human nature is oriented toward sociability, but in France, Montesquieu sees the onset of atomism and social fragmentation. Under the arbitrary power of a prince, fear invades all hearts; one sees "no more trust, honor, love" (*EL* 1.6.5). As we recall, on Montesquieu's account, government is instituted because human society "could not continue to exist" without it (*EL* 1.1.3). But when government becomes despotic or "arbitrary" as Montesquieu puts it in this passage, it dissolves social bonds, blocking the fulfillment of the fourth natural law. Despotism, in sum, thwarts and distorts natural human orientations toward peace, nourishment, the union of the sexes, and sociality. Even relying upon the rather limited picture of human nature in Book 1, chapter 3, we begin to understand much of what Montesquieu means when he insists that despotism inflicts appalling ills upon human nature (*EL* 2.11.4).

But human nature amounts to more than this slim set of four stable desires, important though they are. An intelligent, feeling, and physical being (*EL* 1.1.1), man is born with a complement of radical capacities or potentialities, the development of which depends largely upon his physical and social environs. This is part of what Montesquieu seems to mean when he calls man "that flexible being": human nature is characterized by a significant degree of indeterminacy (*EL* "Pref."; *MP* 1622). It is possible for man to descend to the level of beasts. It may also be possible for man to rise toward the ranks of "intelligences superior to man," but this Montesquieu never enjoins (*EL* 1.1.1).[45] His focus on forestalling descent rather than promoting ascent is a hallmark of his liberalism and a seal of his modernity. Despotism guarantees general human descent. Indeed its perpetuation requires man's descent, for a despot cannot rule elevated souls. Foremost among the radical capacities within human nature is the capacity to acquire knowledge, the "faculty of knowledge" in 1.3. While man in the state of nature may not be possessed of much knowledge, he has the radical capacity to attain it. But despotic government relies upon blocking the development of this faculty in its populace, for "extreme obedience assumes ignorance in the one who obeys" (*EL* 1.4.3; 1.5.13). Though man is by nature an intelligent being (*EL* 1.1.1), his intelligence or rationality atrophies under despotic government as he is habituated to respond only to fear and want.

Similarly, while *The Spirit of the Laws* certainly lacks an account of moral perfection, it portrays the collapse of human character under the influence of despotic power. When he addresses the subject of moral education in despotic states, Montesquieu approvingly cites the view, which he misattributes to Aristotle, that there are no virtues "proper to slaves" (*EL* 1.4.3).[46] Moderate governments may not actively cultivate the life of virtue, but they at least open "a larger space" for the exercise of the virtues that bring "greatness" (*grandeur*) to the "soul" (*l'âme*) than does despotism (*EL* 1.5.12). The despot cannot abide excellence of any kind: "Despotic government constrains the talents of subjects and great men, just as the power of men constrains the talents of women" (*MP* 596). It seeks to purge what is high or exceptional and therefore threatening to his suzerainty, and the nation's permanent state of fear so paralyzes man psychologically that the possibility of higher pursuits is all but completely foreclosed. As we have seen, in detaching men from one

---

[45] On Montesquieu's hostility toward "angelicization," see Lowenthal, "Book 1 of Montesquieu's *The Spirit of the* Laws," 489n.14.

[46] See Aristotle, *Politics*, 1255b22 and 1260a35, on the science a slave might have and the small amount of virtue a slave needs.

another, despotism also suppresses the social source of "great deeds" (*MP* 1253). It ensures that man, whose flexible nature is capable of both elevation and of degradation, descends to the level of the beast. It is in this sense that Montesquieu can claim that despotism becomes "so to speak, naturalized [*naturalisé*]" (*EL* 1.5.14, p. 63; 1.15.7).[47] Despotism's greatest insult to human nature is not merely that it opposes man's principal natural desires, but rather that it finds and exploits within man's flexible nature the capacity to become less than man.

None of this suggests that Montesquieu is a perfectionist liberal. He never boasts that free and moderate government directs man toward the perfection of his nature. A regime need not aim to perfect human nature in order to prove praiseworthy or acceptable on his account. Human laws "enact about the good," not the "best" (*EL* 5.26.2), and on Montesquieu's view, even religious law should not aim at perfection, for "perfection does not concern men or things universally" (*EL* 4.24.7). Even if there were a single highest form of human flourishing (this Montesquieu never avers), no actual form of political organization can direct all men to this end, and efforts to do so invariably eventuate in afflictions of body and soul (*EL* 1.5.2). But while there is no hint of perfectionism in his normative political thought, we have found what we might dub anti-corruptionism. When a political form makes of a man something less than a man, it places itself outside the circle of decent regimes. As Judith Shklar comments, free and moderate government is not a "heaven at the opposite pole of the hell of despotism."[48] There is a studied asymmetry to Montesquieu's normative political thought. The good citizen and the good man may never be the same, but one may at least insist that no regime order itself such that to be a good citizen is to be a good beast.

This aversion to perfectionism does not betoken an ironic indifference to philosophical foundations. We cannot join those who admire Montesquieu as a non-foundationalist thinker, for his liberal politics do indeed draw support from universal and natural moral foundations. This moral universalism, such as it is, begets a political project that stands equally distant from political universalism and political indifferentism. Montesquieu's

---

[47] Montesquieu seems to be aware that he is using the verb *naturaliser* in a novel manner and with significant theoretical import. It was used in the eighteenth century, as now, to refer to the process of gaining citizenship in a foreign nation. See "*naturaliser*" in *Dictionnaire de L'Académie française*, 4th edn. (Paris: Veuve Brunet, 1762). See *EL* 2.11.3; *LP* 97.

[48] Shklar, *Montesquieu*, 86; Shklar, *Ordinary Vices*, 33. See also Spector, *Montesquieu: Liberté, droit et histoire*, 274–275.

moral foundations are real but flexible, plural, and indeterminate with respect to particular regime types. These foundations are consistent with principles of constitutionalism that may find a suitable home in a variety of political orders, as we must now consider in greater detail.

PRINCIPLES OF LIBERTY AND THE CONTEST OF REGIMES

Montesquieu's first book on liberty opens with a rejection of eight definitions of political liberty, among them the venerable old view that liberty consists in wearing a long beard (*EL* 2.11.2). In addition to this hirsute conception, he rejects the view that liberty consists in a right of revolution, he resists the identification of liberty with the presence of electoral institutions or the right to bear arms, and he denies that political liberty merely means freedom from foreign rule. Most significantly, Montesquieu opposes his conception to those that place liberty in any one regime type: "Men have given this name [liberty] to one form of government and have excluded the others. Those who had tasted republican government put it in this government; those who had enjoyed monarchical government placed it in monarchy" (*EL* 2.11.2). The former is the republican, the latter the monarchical view of liberty. Both republican exclusivists and monarchical exclusivists miss the mark, and casting them aside, Montesquieu endeavors to distance the question of political liberty from the contest of regimes.[49] Whatever we might say about the various advantages and disadvantages of the basic forms of political life, we cannot identify political liberty with any single regime type.

Here a comparison with Locke is instructive. Like Montesquieu, Locke resisted, although less explicitly, the view that men are free in virtue of living under a particular type of regime. Locke dedicates only a few pages to the question of political forms.[50] On his view, man's natural freedom and equality are respected only when the requisites of political legitimacy are satisfied. Recognition of these requisites, rather than the establishment of any particular regime, is the source of escape from political slavery. Montesquieu follows Locke inasmuch as he sees liberty as a good independent of any single political form. But unlike Locke, he does not turn to

---

[49] On republican exclusivism, see Nelson, *Hebrew Republic*, ch. 1. For a somewhat different account of the origins of exclusivist republican understandings of freedom, see Quentin Skinner, "A Genealogy of the Modern State," *Proceedings of the British Academy* 162 (2009): 333–40.

[50] John Locke, *Two Treatises of Civil Government*, ed. Peter Laslett (Cambridge University Press, 1970), II, ch. 10.

a theory of political legitimacy when he turns from regime-centric conceptions of liberty. Though his implicit social contractarian commitments tell against the legitimacy of despotism, Montesquieu offers no direct comment on the question of legitimacy in Book 11. It is, for him, neither the most interesting nor the most pressing political question.[51] The degree of liberty in a constitution is determined more by its constitutional structure than by its juridical origin. (Of course, as we will see, mores, manners, and laws are no less important than political institutions in determining the degree of liberty citizens enjoy.) Therefore, Montesquieu will offer an account of the constitutional "principles" on which liberty is actually founded, principles that may be woven into a variety of different constitutions (*EL* 2.11.5).

Once he has cleared the definitional underbrush obscuring the nature of political liberty, our author offers a provisional definition of liberty as "the right to do everything the laws permit," a definition delinked from any of his three types of government (*EL* 2.11.3)."[52] This definition implicates the rule of law as central to liberty, and Montesquieu proceeds apace toward his famous interpretation of the English constitution and its distribution of powers, a feature that secures the rule of law. Here he adds a definition, not of liberty simply, but of "the liberty of the citizen," which consists in a "tranquility of spirit which comes from the opinion each one has of his security" (*EL* 2.11.6).[53] In some measure, this tranquility is secured when, due to the distribution of powers, a citizen need not "fear that the same monarch or senate that makes tyrannical laws will execute them tyrannically" (*EL* 2.11.6).

Many argue on the basis of his treatment of England that Montesquieu commends the "liberal republican" form of the English as a universal model. But before Montesquieu ventures an account of a political system that helps to secure liberty as he defines it, he makes clear that his analytical interest is not in the English constitution itself but in certain principles of liberty exemplified therein. He announces, "We will examine

---

[51] But see Catherine Larrère, "Les typologies des gouvernements chez Montesquieu," in *Etudes sur le XVIIIe siècle*, ed. Jean Ehrard (Clermont-Ferrand: Association des publications de la Faculté des Lettres, 1979), 87–103. Larrère argues that Montesquieu's definition of a state in 2.11.3 is analogous to a conception of legitimacy.

[52] Compare *EL* 5.26.20: "Liberty consists principally in not being forced to do a thing that the law does not order, and one is in this state only because one is governed by civil laws; therefore, we are free because we live under civil laws."

[53] See Chapter 7 for a detailed discussion of the significance of this definition and its relationship to Montesquieu's other definitions of liberty.

the principles on which this nation founds political liberty. If these principles are good, liberty will appear there as in a mirror" (*EL* 2.11.5).
Embodied in the English constitution are principles for dividing and
organizing the ruling element, whatever the composition of that ruling
element may be. They are general principles of liberal constitutional
design applicable to a variety of regimes and circumstances. In this
respect, Montesquieu's use of the English example is akin to
Tocqueville's use of the American case: the latter asks his reader "not to
turn to America in order slavishly to copy the institutions she has fashioned for herself." The Old World must look to America "for instruction
rather than models," for "principles rather than the details of her laws."[54]
This is Montesquieu's approach to the English constitution and its Gothic
forerunner. His liberal political science turns away from both regime-
centric and legitimacy-centric theories of political liberty in order to
examine the fundamental principles upon which liberty may be founded
in aristocratic, democratic, monarchical, and mixed regimes alike. By
design, Montesquieu's categories of free and moderate government cut
across these distinctions among political forms.

LIBERTY AND MODERATION IN THE CONSTITUTION

The Spirit of the Laws contains at least two, and perhaps three, typologies of
political forms. In Books 2 and 3, the author develops his well-known
tripartite typology of republican, monarchical and despotic government.
But by the end of Book 3, he has already begun to speak of "moderate
governments" in opposition to "despotic governments." Finally, in Book 11,
"free states" appear for the first time, a category distinguishable, it seems,
from unfree states. This series of typologies raises several difficult interpretative questions regarding Montesquieu's view of the nature of moderate
government, the connection between moderate government and free states
(e.g., the English regime), and the connection between the three primary
regime types and the standards of liberty and moderation. Confronting these
questions is necessary to understanding Montesquieu's regime pluralist
conception of limited, balanced, and complex government.[55]

---

[54] Alexis de Tocqueville, *Democracy in America*, ed. J. P. Mayer (New York: Harper
Collins, 1988), xiv.

[55] Several scholars have attempted to determine the normative implications of
Montesquieu's classification system, but few have sought to offer clear accounts of the
relationship between both of Montesquieu's typologies and his discussion of "free government" in Book 11. Ehrard argues that the first typology is merely a mask and that the

What is moderate government? What is the meaning of Montesquieu's "second" typology of regimes (moderate–despotic)? Near the close of Book 5, after three ambiguous references to *"gouvernement modéré,"* Montesquieu finally defines the category by means of a sharp contrast with despotism. He writes,

In order to form a moderate government, one must combine powers, regulate them, temper them, make them act; one must give one power a ballast, so to speak, to put it in a position to resist another; this is a masterpiece of legislation that chance rarely produces and prudence is rarely allowed to produce. By contrast, a despotic government leaps to view, so to speak; it is uniform throughout; as only passions are needed to establish it, everyone is good enough for that. (*EL* 1.5.14)

Political power is plural in moderate governments. These powers must be combined, but not united; they must be tempered by one another and by constitutional rules; they must have some ability to resist or balance one another. A moderate regime consists in what Montesquieu calls *"un système,"* a structure he means to distinguish from both an anarchic struggle between unregulated powers, on one hand, and a uniform body of undivided, undifferentiated power, on the other.[56]

On Montesquieu's view, monarchy is the only form of government that is moderate by definition. "Intermediate, subordinate, and dependent powers constitute the nature of monarchical government"; more simply put, "no monarch, no nobility; no nobility, no monarch" (*EL* 2.2.4).[57] Monarchy is the government of one by fixed and established laws. In the absence of intermediate powers, "nothing can be fixed." Fundamental laws assume the existence of both sites of institutional resistance to keep the king within the bounds of the law as well as "mediate channels through which power flows" (*EL* 1.2.4). In monarchies, political power is therefore necessarily plural, though not all powers are equal. The monarch is formally the "source of all political and civil power" (*EL*

---

second typology reveals Montesquieu's true polemical purposes. Jean Ehrard, *L'idee de nature en France a l'aube des lumieres* (Paris: Flammarion, 1970), 292. See also Marcel Prélot, "Montesquieu et les formes de gouvernement," who argues that Montesquieu's definitive regime classification is, in the end, a binary division between "les régimes qui n'ont pas la liberté pour objet" and "les régimes qui ont pour but la liberté" (131). As Carrese notes, Montesquieu "leaves the reader to consider the links between political moderation, a constitution of separate powers, and liberty." Carrese, "The Machiavellian Spirit of Montesquieu's Republic," 134.

[56] See *MP* 831, 892, 918, and 935.

[57] Intermediate powers include parlements, nobles, clergy, estates, towns, and corporations (*EL* 1.2.4).

1.2.4). In political conflicts, he can prevail "by tipping the balance" (*EL* 1.3.10). Though dependent and subordinate, the intermediate powers are capable of a certain kind of resistance: "Just as the sea, which seems to want to cover the whole earth, is checked by the grasses and the smallest bits of gravel on the shore, so monarchs, whose power seems boundless, are checked by the slightest obstacles and submit their natural pride to supplication and prayer" (*EL* 1.2.4). This is delicately stated. Lurking under the "prayer and supplication" of the intermediate ranks – these certainly include parlementary remonstrances – is the confident assertion of ancient constitutional privileges, as we examine in greater detail later in this chapter.[58] Monarchy is by nature a moderate regime.

At first blush it appears republics are also moderate governments on Montesquieu's view. If despotism stands opposite moderate government, then the category of moderate government must, it seems, include the two regimes distinguished from despotism in the first typology. There is some evidence for this view in the text of the *Spirit*.[59] At times Montesquieu seems to indicate that republican government is moderate (*EL* 1.6.2, 1.8.8). But democratic and aristocratic republics are not moderate by definition. Republican government is simply "that in which the people as a body, or a part of the people, have sovereign power" (*EL* 1.2.1). Rule by fixed laws and balancing institutions are not essential to the nature of republican government. Why, then, does Montesquieu seem at times to assimilate republics into the category of moderate government?

Montesquieu tends to move seamlessly between the empirical world and a world of deductively constructed types.[60] As an ideal type, republican government is neither moderate nor immoderate by definition. But empirically, on Montesquieu's view, republican constitutions usually incorporate some balancing or distribution of powers.[61] The consolidation of power in a republic is usually a product of corruption as the people dismiss senates, magistrates, and judges. The result is what Montesquieu

---

[58] See Michael A. Mosher, "Monarchy's Paradox: Honor in the Face of Sovereign Power," in *Montesquieu's Science of Politics: Essays on The Spirit of Laws*, eds. David W. Carrithers, Michael A. Mosher, and Paul A. Rahe (Lanham, MD: Rowman & Littlefield, 2001), 183–92, for an excellent discussion of the historical context of Montesquieu's theory of intermediate powers. See also Carrese, *Cloaking of Power*, 29–34.

[59] See *EL* 1.8.8, 1.5.15, 1.3.10.

[60] See C. P. Courtney, "Montesquieu and Natural Law," 41–68.

[61] Some republics are manifestly immoderate, such as Venice and other Italian aristocracies. "In the Italian republics, where the three powers are united, there is less liberty than in our monarchies" (*EL* 2.11.6, p. 157). See also *MP* 1893; De Dijn, "On Political Liberty," 192.

calls a "despotism of all" (*EL* 1.8.6). Thus the "despotism" of the first typology (republic–monarchy–despotism) is not the despotism of the second typology (moderate–despotic). For the despotism of the first typology consists in the rule of one by will and caprice, whereas despotism in the second typology may include regimes ruled by one, few, or many (*MP* 1893).[62] Thus not all non-despotic governments in the sense of the first typology are non-despotic in the sense of the second typology.

Republics may be either moderate or despotic in the terms of the second typology of regimes, and as we have seen, monarchies are moderate by nature. The project of *Spirit* entails bringing moderation to immoderate regimes and preserving the moderation of already moderate governments. But Montesquieu's normative project does not end here, for Books 11 and 12 take up not moderation but liberty as their grand theme. Montesquieu speaks of "free states" and "laws that form liberty in relation to the constitution" and the citizen (*EL* 2.11.1). What is the relationship between Montesquieu's praise of political moderation and his favorable discussion of the "free state" of England in Books 11 and 12? What is the relationship between free government and moderate government?

Montesquieu initially seems to suggest that monarchy is an inherently "free" political form. Because monarchy is also the only inherently moderate form of government, this would suggest that free government is simply a new name for moderate government. He writes,

Democracy and aristocracy are not free states by their nature. Political liberty is found only in moderate governments. But it is not always in moderate states. It is present only when power is not abused, but it has been eternally observed that any man who has power is led to abuse it; he continues until he finds limits. Who would think it! Even virtue has need of limits.

So that one cannot abuse power, power must check power by the arrangement of things. A constitution can be such that no one will be constrained to do the things the law does not oblige them to do or be kept from doing the things the law permits him to do.

(*EL* 2.11.4)

---

[62] Larrère, "Les typologies des gouvernements chez Montesquieu," 96. See *EL* 1.8.2, where Montesquieu suggests that the despotism of all is usually a stage in the decline of democratic republics into the despotism of one. For a different view, see Anne Cohler, *Montesquieu's Comparative Politics and the Spirit of American Constitutionalism* (Lawrence, KS: University Press of Kansas, 1988), 75–85.

Because Montesquieu insists that democracy and aristocracy are not free "by their nature," he seems to suggest that monarchy is free by its nature.[63] But it is difficult to reconcile this interpretation with Montesquieu's clear assertion that political liberty "is not always in moderate states" (*EL* 2.11.4). Free states clearly form a subset of moderate governments.[64] Like all moderate constitutions, free states are characterized by multiple centers of political power. But for a state to be free, its distribution of power must be of a specific kind. The three powers (the legislative, the executive and the power of judging) must be distributed such that no one organ of government holds more than one power in its entirety.[65] This threefold distribution of powers, as found in the English constitution, is best suited to maintain political liberty defined as a "tranquility of spirit which comes from the opinion each one has of his security," for it frees the citizen from the "fear that the same monarch or senate that makes tyrannical laws will execute them tyrannically" (*EL* 2.11.6). However, even when a monarch wields two of the three powers,

---

[63] Pangle, *Montesquieu's Philosophy of Liberalism*, writes, "Montesquieu carefully refrains from saying that monarchy is 'not free by its nature.' By this silence he implies that monarchy is free by its nature" (113). But Pangle believes Montesquieu later undermines this implication by suggesting, in *EL* 2.11.6, that a truly free regime requires "at least some combination of republican egalitarianism with a more rational balance of power" (114).

[64] On language of the "free state" before Montesquieu, see Skinner, "Genealogy of the Modern State," 333–40. Montesquieu's preference for the term "free state" (as distinguished from free government, free constitution, etc.) deserves notice. He does not treat the concept of the "state" in Part 1 and first introduces it in Book 11. Certainly the choice of a noun other than "government" is indicative of his view that free political forms are not a distinct fourth type of regime, set off against republics and monarchies. But more specifically, in light of the prehistory of the term as Skinner sketches it, Montesquieu's choice of language seems to signal his aim of upending the simple association of the concept of a "free state" with republican government.

[65] Montesquieu prefers the language of "distribution" to "separation," and indeed the idea of distribution better captures his meaning (*EL* 2.11.6). See Albert Postigliola, "Sur quelques interpretations de la 'séparation des pouvoirs' chez Montesquieu," *Studies on Voltaire and the Eighteenth Century* 154 (1976): 1759–75, for the distinction between separation and distribution of powers. See also James Madison, "*Federalist* No. 47" in *The Federalist Papers*, ed. Clinton Rossiter (New York: Mentor, 1999), 235–40, on this point. Charles Eisenmann finds the term "separation of powers" an inapt description of Montesquieu's doctrine because Montesquieu does not advocate complete functional specialization of powers but rather an equilibrium of powers. Charles Eisenmann, "L'Esprit des lois et la séparation des pouvoirs," *Cahiers de philosophie politique* 2–3 (1985): 3–34; and Charles Eisenmann, "La pensée constitutionnelle de Montesquieu," *Cahiers de philosophie politique* (1985): 35–66. On Montesquieu's role in the development of the doctrine of the separation of powers generally, see M. J. C. Vile, *Constitutionalism and the Separation of Powers* (Indianapolis: Liberty Fund, 1998), ch. 4.

as "in most kingdoms of Europe," the government remains moderate (*EL* 2.11.6). When the three powers lie in the hands of a single man or body of men, the state is despotic.

As Montesquieu explains later in Book 11, some modern European monarchies resemble free states. While moderate monarchies do not "have liberty for their direct purpose," they aim at glory, and this glory results in a "spirit of liberty" that can "perhaps contribute as much to happiness as liberty itself" (*EL* 2.11.7).[66] While the distribution of power in continental monarchies differs from that of the English constitution, the distribution in these monarchies "approximates political liberty" (*EL* 2.11.7). Moved by the glory of office, intermediate powers can resist, regulate, and temper the power of the king in a manner analogous to the balancing that occurs between the equal and independent powers within the English constitution. Moderate governments thus at least approach the principles of free states, and free states push to an admirable extreme the balance and complexity present in all moderate governments (*EL* 1.5.14).[67]

In sum, all free governments are moderate governments; not all moderate governments are free governments; and all moderate governments approximate the political liberty found in free governments. Montesquieu does not intend, through his examples of the most well-balanced regime (the "corrupted" Gothic constitution of 2.11.8) and the regime of extreme liberty (the English constitution of 2.11.6), to establish a binary standard whereby all regimes not cast in their mold appear as illiberal. On the

---

[66] On honor as a spring of political agency, and so of liberty, see Krause, *Liberalism with Honor*.

[67] As many scholars have noted, Montesquieu's admiration of the English system is not unqualified. See Ward, "Montesquieu on Federalism and Anglo-Gothic Constitutionalism"; Krause, "The Spirit of Separate Powers in Montesquieu," 231–63; Keith Michael Baker, *Inventing the French Revolution: Essays on French Political Culture in the Eighteenth Century* (Cambridge University Press, 1990), 173–9; Roger Boesche, "Fearing Monarchs and Merchants: Montesquieu's Two Theories of Despotism," *The Western Political Quarterly* 43 (1990): 741–62; Rahe, *Montesquieu and the Logic of Liberty*, esp. 65–85. De Dijn, *French Political Thought*, goes as far as to argue that the English model was "the opposite of monarchy": unlike monarchical liberty, English liberty was "highly fragile" because the English regime lacked intermediary powers (25). But in the relevant passage (*EL* 1.2.4, pp. 18–9), Montesquieu does not say that English liberty is fragile, but rather that if the English lost their liberty at the national level (that is, if the three powers were consolidated), they would become the most enslaved race on earth because they would lack all intermediary powers to mediate the newly consolidated power of the center. This does not imply that England's constitutional liberty is "highly fragile," but only that the English lack what Publius would later call the "double security" of separation of powers and robust subnational sites of power (*Federalist* No. 51).

contrary, he states in his *Pensées*, "I do not at all think that one government ought to make other governments repulsive" (*MP* 934; *EL*, "Pref."). In *Spirit*, he explains that,

The inconvenience is not when the state passes from a moderate government to a moderate government, as from a republic to a monarchy, or from a monarchy to a republic; but when it falls and throws itself from a moderate government to despotism.

(*EL* 1.8.8)

The primary fault line in *Spirit* runs between moderate and despotic government. On this Montesquieu insists. There exists a range of possible regimes within the family of moderate governments, each of them incorporating the principles of liberty.

As we have noted, many scholars arguing for the liberal republic interpretation of Montesquieu's great work maintain that he subtly sets out to exclude monarchy from the circle of liberal regimes. This reading suffers from serious difficulties. When Montesquieu comments explicitly on the contest of regimes – most often in his notebooks – he draws evenhanded comparisons that place republican and monarchical government on equal footing before the canons of liberty.[68] For instance, in an important fragment that was to be part of a treatise called *De la liberté politique* (ca. 1734–5),[69] he writes,

The sole advantage that a free people has over another is the security each individual possesses that a single individual's whim will not take away his property or his life. A subject people who had that security, whether well- or ill-founded, would be as happy as a free people.

This security of one's condition is not greater in England than in France ... Since liberty often generates two factions in a state, the superior faction mercilessly exploits its advantages. A dominant faction is not less terrible than a wrathful prince. How many individuals have we seen lose their lives or their property during the recent disturbances in England! ... Moreover, in free states, the common people are normally insolent ... As for the rest of it, I count for very little the happiness of arguing furiously over affairs of state and never uttering a

---

[68] Radasanu, "Montesquieu on Moderation, Monarchy and Reform," 305, maintains that Montesquieu is "flattering the existing conservative sentiments in favour of monarchy" when he speaks of it approvingly. Compare Rahe, *Montesquieu and the Logic of Liberty*, 214–19.

[69] This lost treatise appears to have been composed *after* Montesquieu drafted the material for his chapter on the English constitution (*EL* 2.11.6). On the dating of *De la liberté politique*, see De Dijn, "On Political Liberty: Montesquieu's Missing Manuscript," *Political Theory* 39 (2011): 187; and Nagel 2: xlv–lxv.

hundred words without pronouncing the word liberty, or the privilege of hating half the citizenry.

(*MP* 32)

Here even the current degenerate French monarchy seems to compare favorably to England, since the English regime has not overcome the problem of majority tyranny. For our present purposes, it is instructive to note that this passage and others like it tell against the view that Montesquieu harbors profoundly anti-monarchical sentiments that go underground in *The Spirit of the Laws*. Elsewhere Montesquieu similarly affirms, "[I]t must be concluded that political liberty concerns moderate monarchies just as it does republics, and is no further from a throne than from a senate. Every man is free who has good grounds to believe that the wrath of one or many will not take away his life or possession of his property" (*MP* 884).[70] Montesquieu identifies liberty with security or the sense of security, as he would in *Spirit*, and on the basis of this identification defends the place of monarchy alongside other decent and moderate regimes.[71] In *Spirit* this sentiment survives in the form of Montesquieu's rejection of both republican and monarchical conceptions of liberty, as we have seen (*EL* 2.11.2).

Still, those inclined to read Montesquieu as a determined critic of monarchy insist that monarchy fails to incorporate the principles necessary for political liberty or its approximation, political moderation. On the liberal republican reading of *Spirit*, Montesquieu means to suggest that monarchy is at best "a moderate government in a very attenuated

---

[70] This entry is also part of Montesquieu's mostly lost manuscript, *De la liberté politique*.

[71] These passages leave the impression that Montesquieu had no preference between the English regime and traditional French constitutional monarchy. But in *Spirit*, his preference for the English regime is clearer. See also the *Notes sur Angleterre*, where Montesquieu writes, "At present, England is the freest country in the world; I don't except any republic. I say free, because the prince lacks the power to inflict any wrong imaginable upon anybody at all, since his power is controlled and limited by statute. But, if the lower house were to become master, its power would be unlimited and dangerous." Montesquieu, "Notes on England" in Iain Stewart, "Montesquieu in England: his 'Notes on England,' with Commentary and Translation," *Oxford University Comparative Law Forum* 6 (2002). See fn. 74 on the dispatches of the Comte de Brogle, French Ambassador to England. During Montesquieu's visit to England, De Brogle reportedly asked Montesquieu to stop lavishing such high praise upon the English constitution in the company of the Queen and at the French Embassy.

sense,"[72] for it is not a regime in which one power is "put it in a position to resist another" (*EL* 1.5.14). It lacks a "rational balance of power."[73] This interpretation of Montesquieu's views on monarchy depends upon a particular understanding of his account of monarchy's nature. As we have seen earlier, he maintains that "intermediate, subordinate, and dependent powers" constitute the nature of monarchy (*EL* 1.2.4). He emphasizes this string of modifiers by repetition in the very next line: "I have said intermediate, subordinate, and dependent powers; indeed, in a monarchy, the prince is the source of all political and civil power [*la source de tout pouvoir politique et civil*]" (*EL* 1.2.4).[74] Radasanu suggests that if we consider this account of monarchy alongside *Spirit*'s description of free and moderate government, it becomes evident that Montesquieu intends to indicate that monarchy is neither moderate nor free, despite his flattering statements to the contrary. If the power of intermediate bodies is derived from the crown in a monarchy, how could such a state satisfy the requirements of moderate government? How could a power check its source?[75]

This objection assumes that there can be no meaningful checks and balances within a hierarchy. It is one thing to expect three powers to resist *one another* if they share a *common* source, as in the US Constitution. But it is a different matter to expect a power to resist its source. But before examining Montesquieu's account of monarchy in greater detail, we might first turn to an unlikely place – the American regime framed by students of Montesquieu's constitutionalism – to consider how a power might be understood to check its source. Specifically, Madison's argument for the Senate in *Federalist* No. 63 suggests a way to remove the apparent paradox. He writes,

---

[72] Radasanu, "Montesquieu on Moderation, Monarchy and Reform," 286.

[73] Pangle, *Montesquieu's Philosophy of Liberalism*, 114.

[74] The earlier versions of 1.2.4 refer only to "intermediate powers." Montesquieu clarifies by adding "subordinate" and/or "dependent" at three different points in the text. VF 3:23.

[75] Radasanu writes, "[I]n moderate governments there ought to be more than one source of power such that one power is strong enough to check another." But Montesquieu never says that there must be more than one source of power in a moderate state. Later in the chapter, I show why we should take Montesquieu at his word when he suggests that power can check power even in a state where there is only one ultimate source of power. By way of further contrast with my view, see MacDonald, Althusser, and de Dijn, all of whom suggest that checks and balances are not at work in monarchy. MacDonald, "Problems with Principles," 120; Althusser, *Politics and History*, 97; De Dijn, *French Political Thought*, 25.

I shall not scruple to add, that such [a Senate] may be sometimes necessary as a defense to the people against their own temporary errors and delusions. As the cool and deliberate sense of the community ought, in all governments, and actually will, in all free governments, ultimately prevail over the views of its rulers; so there are particular moments in public affairs when the people ... may call for measures which they themselves will afterwards be the most ready to lament and condemn. In these critical moments, how salutary will be the interference of some temperate and respectable body of citizens, in order to check the misguided career, and to suspend the blow meditated by the people against themselves, until reason, justice, and truth can regain their authority over the public mind?[76]

In the US Constitution, the people are (to appropriate Montesquieu's language) the "source of all power civil and political" (*EL* 1.2.4). All organs of the American republic derive their powers "directly or indirectly from the great body of the people,"[77] and, as Madison insists in *Federalist* No. 63, the will of the people can "ultimately prevail" over its elected ministers, just as the king in Montesquieu's monarchy can "prevail by tipping the balance" (*EL* 1.3.10). The power of the Senate is, like the *pouvoirs intermédiaires* in a monarchy, formally "subordinate" to and "dependent" upon the people. And yet on Madison's view, the Senate is able to check and suspend the will of the people. Madison understood that neither "some power altogether independent of the people" nor a "will independent of the society itself" would be strictly necessary to check the will of the sovereign people.[78] Similarly, while the will of Montesquieu's despot produces "its effect as infallibly as does one ball thrown against another," the will of the monarch does not follow a similar course, due in no small part to the intervening influence of the *pouvoirs intermédiaires*, subordinate and dependent though they remain (*EL* 1.3.10). One can think of Madison's Senate as an analogue of monarchy's intermediate powers – a power able to check its source. In this way, the American example serves to clarify what is for many commentators an ambiguity or contradiction in *Spirit*.

Even as he acknowledges their formal subordination and dependence, Montesquieu freely uses the language of "checking" or "stopping" to describe the work of intermediate powers in monarchical government (*EL* 1.2.4, p. 18). The same language describes the operation of the free government generally and the English constitution in particular (*EL* 2.11.4; 2.11.6, p. 160, 162). Montesquieu recognizes that the power of

[76] James Madison, "*Federalist* No. 63," in *The Federalist*, 352.
[77] James Madison, "*Federalist* No. 39," in *The Federalist*, 209.
[78] James Madison, "*Federalist* No. 51," in *The Federalist*, 293.

the intermediate bodies may appear negligible when compared to the monarch, who wields "*la soveraine puissance* " (*EL* 1.3.2).[79] But monarchs, "whose power seems so boundless [*paraît sans bornes*], are checked by the slightest obstacles" (*EL* 1.2.4). Montesquieu acknowledges that the monarch's power appears to be without limit, both empirically and perhaps within the deductively constructed type of Part 1. But whatever *la soveraine puissance* might entail, it does not consist in boundless or limitless power ("*puissance sans bornes*").[80] Despite appearances, the subordinate, dependent, and intermediate powers can restrain royal authority.

In the *Pensées*, Montesquieu explains why one can expect the intermediate powers to restrain the monarch despite the formally contingent and limited nature of their authority. He writes, "Even though the Parlements of France do not have much authority, this does not keep them from doing good. Neither the ministry nor the prince wants to be disapproved by them, because they are respected. Kings are like the Ocean, whose impetuosity is often curbed, sometimes by the grasses, sometimes by the stones" (*MP* 589). Even the weakened parlements of France, having suffered royal encroachments since at least the sixteenth century, retain some ability to "do good." It is worth noting here that Montesquieu does not attribute the ability of the parlements to the good will, self-restraint, or virtue of the prince. It is the prince's very "impetuosity" they curb.[81] This passage illuminates Montesquieu's cryptic remark in Book 2, chapter 4, where he explains that the monarch's royal council is ill-suited to serve as a "depository of the laws." A council of royal ministers "does not sufficiently have the people's trust: therefore, it is not in a position to

---

[79] Montesquieu never ascribes "*puissance absolue* " or "*pouvoir absolu* " to the monarch. This is particularly striking in light of his certain acquaintance with Bodin's definition of sovereignty: "*La souveraineté est la puissance absoluë et perpetuelle ...*" (*Republique*, Bk. 1, ch. 11). Mosher, "Monarchy's Paradox," argues that if we "assume the words mean what they say" in 1.2.4 ("the prince is source of all power civil and political"), then we must conclude that Montesquieu has ascribed Bodinian sovereignty to the king (175). "Bodin and Montesquieu are in agreement," he writes (179). But it is remarkable indeed that Montesquieu never employs the key terms in the Bodinian definition of sovereignty. This suggests that he considers "*puissance absolue* " to be an inapt characterization of monarchical sovereignty. Montesquieu continues to employ "*puissance arbitraire* " as an unqualified term of opprobrium (*EL* 1.2.4). The monarch may be the source of all civil and political power, but this does not mean that either the power itself or its mode of application is unlimited.

[80] Montesquieu uses *borner* and *limiter* similarly, if not interchangeably, in Book 11 (*EL* 2.11.6, p. 162; 2.11.11).

[81] Cf. Radasanu, "Montesquieu on Moderation, Monarchy and Reform," 295.

enlighten them in difficult times or to return them to obedience" (*EL* 1.2.4). The depository of the laws – for Montesquieu, it was the parlements – enlightens the people by speaking against the innovations and abuses of the king during "difficult times." Despite the derivative character of their authority and two centuries of degradation, the Parlement of Paris and those of the provinces are "respected," Montesquieu maintains in *pensée* #589. They enjoy the respect of the people, whom they "enlighten" when royal malfeasance arises. Parlementary remonstrances serve as a signal to the people that the king is violating the fundamental laws of the state. A parlement's subsequent approval of the king's actions, following negotiations, may "return [the people] to obedience" (*EL* 1.2.4). This mention of returning the people to obedience clearly suggests that a parlement's efforts to enlighten the people to royal abuses may produce, *in extremis*, popular resistance to the king's ordinances. In this light, the checking power of the parlements begins to appear far from negligible.[82]

As Montesquieu makes clear in his *Pensées* and intimates in *Spirit*, by the eighteenth century, the French crown had substantially eroded its constitutional limits. The "public law" of his day was only the "feeble and wretched remnants of our laws, which arbitrary power has been able to hide up to now, but which it will never be able to annihilate except with its own demise" (*MP* 1183). While royal authority had not completely overflowed its banks, the strength of traditional French constitutional limits was failing. Montesquieu points to the death of Charles VII (r. 1422–1461) in 1461 as the "last day of French liberty" (*MP* 1302). As we saw briefly in Chapter 2, Louis XI (r. 1461–1483) "abolished the towns' privileges, made the Nobility anxious, eliminated offices or reduced their

---

[82] Montesquieu here implies that if the king were to dissolve the parlements, the people could not be "returned to obedience." In other words, the king needed the support of the parlements to prevent revolution. The events leading up to the French Revolution support Montesquieu's understanding of the role of the parlements. The decisions of Louis XV and Maupeou to purge the provincial parlements and replace the Parlement of Paris hastened progress toward the Revolution, and Louis XVI's restoration of the parlements in 1774 was not sufficient to forestall it. See James B. Collins, *The State in Early Modern France* (Cambridge University Press, 1995), 253–4. See also Bruce Chauveau-Maulini, "La notion de monarchie tempérée dans les remonstrances des parlements au XVIIe siècle: Montesquieu et l'idéologie de robe," in *Annales* (Paris: Institute Michel Villey, 2006): 197–242. On the Montesquieuian character of parlementary remonstrances leading up to the Revolution, see Jacob Levy, "Montesquieu's Constitutional Legacies," in *Montesquieu and His Legacy*, ed. Rebecca E. Kingston (Albany, NY: State Univeristy of New York Press, 2009), 125–7. See also Nagel 3: 1465–69.

prerogatives" (*MP* 1302). He attacked the intermediate powers. Therefore, in seeking the best examples of the kind of monarchy Montesquieu has in mind, we must look not to seventeenth- and eighteenth-century practices of an increasingly consolidated French monarchy, but rather to the constitutional practices prior to the fifteenth century. Here we can see, in concrete terms, how Montesquieu understood the tempering and balancing work of intermediate ranks within monarchy.

"The king cannot do everything he is able to do," he writes epigrammatically (*MP* 1225). His meaning is laid bare in the practices of the traditional French monarchy, and one need look no further than the work of the Parlement of Paris. As a "depository of the laws," theirs was the decision whether to register an edict or ordinance of the king as a law of France, and registration by provincial parlements was likewise necessary for the royal act to be binding in each province. As we have seen in Chapter 2, registration was not automatic. In theory, Parlement could, and in practice it often did, refuse registration on several grounds. Montesquieu, *président à mortier* of the Parlement of Bordeaux, explains this practice more elegantly than any modern historian:

It is the Parlement that knows all the laws made by all the monarchs, that has learned their sequence, that has known their spirit. It knows whether a new law perfects or corrupts the immense volume of other laws, and it says: things are thus, it is from there that you must begin; otherwise, you ruin the whole work. It says to the Prince, you are a legislator, but you are not all the legislators; you do indeed have all the laws executed, but you have not made all the laws. They were before you, they are with you, they will be after you.

(*MP* 2266)

Montesquieu's remarkable gloss on registration suggests that Parlement speaks for the authority of bygone kings as a check against the innovations of the living. In this sense, the Parlement declares that the current prince is "not all the legislators." Its task was to ensure that the king's acts were consistent with the spirit of the whole body of French law. When the Parlement issued a remonstrance refusing to register a royal edict, ordinance, or decree, negotiations with the crown and fresh deliberations of the king in his Council might commence.[83] If the parties reached no satisfactory agreement, the king could either relent or force registration of the act

---

[83] Roland E. Mousnier, *The Institutions of France under the Absolute Monarchy, 1598–1879: The Organs of State and Society*, trans. Arthur Goldhammer (University of Chicago Press, 1984), 259-260; Franklin, *Jean Bodin and the Rise of Absolutist Theory*, 5.

through a *lit de justice*, in which he personally appeared to preside over the court and register the act.

But the *lit de justice* had major drawbacks. The members of the Parlement, in their capacity as judges, could allow the forcibly registered law to fall into disuse. They could and often did openly protest the use of the *lit de justice*, both by marking forcibly registered laws as "*de mandato expresso*" and by drawing attention to the overuse of this nuclear option.[84] Most importantly, many *parlementaires* held that forcibly registered acts would perish with the king. They could never attain the status of perpetual laws of the realm and were instead mere personal orders of the king to be obeyed for a season.[85] In addition, Montesquieu subtly suggests that the threat of parlementary disapproval was made more serious still by their ability to "enlighten the people" if the king pursued a determined course of abuses (*EL* 1.2.4).[86] Even when Parlement was legally understood as an instrument of royal administration, it provided what can only be described as a check upon the crown. Though imbued with *la soveraine puissance*, the king did not enjoy *puissance sans bornes*. He could not do everything he was able to do.

On Montesquieu's account, these traditional constitutional arrangements were corrupted in time. The parlements, together with other intermediate powers within the French monarchy, gradually lost their prerogatives and functional independence during the sixteenth and seventeenth centuries.[87] But this example of corruption did not suggest to Montesquieu that monarchy was an unacceptable or insufficiently moderate regime.[88] Monarchy is no more prone to degenerate into "the despotism of one" than is democracy to degenerate into the "despotism

---

[84] Church, *Constitutional Thought*, 136, 148; 152–5; Franklin, *Jean Bodin and the Rise of Absolutist Theory*, 5.

[85] Albert N. Hamscher, *The Parlement of Paris After the Fronde* (University of Pittsburgh Press, 1976), 85–6; Nicholas Henshall, *The Myth of Absolutism: Change and Continuity in Early European Monarchy* (London: Longman Group, 1992), 135–7; Church, *Constitutional Thought*, 148.

[86] On revolution, see *MP* 1253, p. 483.   [87] See Chapter 2.

[88] Defenders of the liberal republican thesis often suggest that Montesquieu believes monarchy to be especially unstable and fragile. See illustratively Schaub, *Erotic Liberalism*, 136. By contrast, as we have seen, critics of the liberal republican thesis have suggested that English liberty is, on Montesquieu's view, highly fragile, for England lacks intermediate powers. De Dijn, *French Political Thought*, 25; Ward, "Montesquieu on Federalism." Vulnerability to decay is unique neither to the English republic nor to monarchy. Montesquieu shows that all political orders are more fragile than the ordinary observer supposes.

of the people" (*MP* 1893; *EL* 1.8.6). Even the English constitution will perish, Montesquieu predicts at the close of 2.11.6: "Since all human things have an end, the state of which we are speaking will lose its liberty ... when legislative power is more corrupt than executive power." No prophet of perpetual progress, behind and before him Montesquieu sees the "constant ebb and flow of empire and liberty" in human history (*MP* 100). This does not mean human prudence cannot act to preserve, but its work will always be temporary (*MP* 1917). To predict the eventual decline of a regime is not to condemn its architecture but simply to indicate its participation in the nature of all human things.[89] Advocates of the liberal republican thesis may be correct when they suggest that Montesquieu believes the English regime is likely to endure longer than any traditional European monarchy.[90] The "last sigh of liberty will be heaved by an Englishman," he once reassured an English correspondent in 1749.[91] But the example of the traditional French monarchy's decline, even when compared with the longer life of the English regime, is for Montesquieu no reason to place monarchy outside the circle of decent regimes. The monarchy of France – at its apex the most well-tempered regime ever known – was a moderate constitution from the sixth century through the fifteenth century (*EL* 2.11.8). Nine hundred years was not a bad run.[92]

---

[89] On Montesquieu's philosophy of history and historical pessimism, see David W. Carrithers, "Montesquieu and Tocqueville as Philosophical Historians: Liberty, Determinism, and the Prospects for Freedom," in *Montesquieu and His Legacy*, ed. Rebecca E. Kingston (Albany, NY: State University of New York Press, 2009), 149–78; Henry Vyerberg, *Historical Pessimism in the French Enlightenment* (Cambridge, MA: Harvard University Press, 1958), esp. ch. 18; Gilbert Chinard, "Montesquieu's Historical Pessimism," in *Studies in the History of Culture: The Disciplines of the Humanities*, ed. Gilbert Chinard (Menasha, WI: George Banta, 1942), 161–72.

[90] Radasanu, "Montesquieu on Moderation, Monarchy and Reform," 292. In his fragmentary history of France, Montesquieu writes the following, after commenting upon the eighth-century reign of Pepin the Short: "Through this very system ... it was inevitable that the Crown engulf everything in the end, for it had a right to everything, and it had to happen that everything would end up being swallowed up by it like the rivers in the Ocean" (*MP* 1302). Of course, this inevitable process took almost nine centuries to unfold, and even still Montesquieu seems to hold out hope of forestalling it. The attribute of impermanence does not condemn a regime. See Sharon R. Krause, "The Uncertain Inevitability of Decline in Montesquieu," *Political Theory* 30 (2002): 702–27.

[91] Montesquieu to William Domville, 22 July 1749, in Nagel 3:1244–5. See Donald Desserud, "Commerce and Political Participation in Montesquieu's Letter to Domville," *History of European Ideas* 25 (1999): 135–51.

[92] See *MP* 100. It is not clear that Montesquieu thinks the decline is irreversible.

Monarchy can prove a sufficiently long-lived, balanced constitution. Its moderation does not depend upon the virtue of kings, but rather upon the self-assertion of the intermediate powers and the king's desire to preserve his reign. We therefore cannot accept the view that Montesquieu reprobates all political forms save the republic of England. Such a view makes a regime monist of a regime pluralist.

LIBERTY AND MODERATION IN THE LAWS

Montesquieu's liberalism is not confined to reflections on the questions of constitutional structure that we have considered earlier in the chapter. This is nowhere more evident than in *Spirit*'s second book on liberty, Book 12. While Book 11 considers the constitutional forms conducive to political liberty, its sequel affords equal attention to the civil laws that "favor" liberty (*EL* 2.12.1). An account of political liberty limited to constitutional forms is incomplete because "it can happen that the constitution is free and that the citizen is not" (*EL* 2.12.1). More importantly, "The citizen can be free and the constitution not. In these instances, the constitution will be free by right and not in fact; the citizen will be free in fact and not by right" (*EL* 2.12.1). These seeming paradoxes rest upon Montesquieu's distinction between "the liberty of the citizen" and "the liberty of the constitution." The conceptual distinction is a device Montesquieu employs to resist the view that constitutional structure alone determines the degree of liberty that a citizen will enjoy. In a sense, the distinction represents a depoliticization of the concept of political liberty, for it now appears that political liberty is as much a function of law and culture as it is of political institutions in the narrow sense. (The major questions of liberal culture, or the "mores of a free people," we reserve to Chapters 4–6 (*EL* 3.19.25).)

Montesquieu holds that even if a citizen does not live under a fully free constitution, with three powers distributed, that citizen may yet enjoy a modicum of liberty due to the presence of liberal criminal law, which is not tethered to a particular regime type. Similarly, though he lives in a state with a free constitution, a citizen may not enjoy liberty (security and tranquility of spirit) due to the absence of a liberal approach to criminal justice. This turn in the argument opens up even greater space for Montesquieu's regime pluralism, for the legal protections he outlines may find a home in monarchies, republics, and mixed regimes alike. He shows that legal reformers can work within a range of existing constitutional structures to cultivate and secure liberty.[93] Indeed this practical posture is evident in the original title of Book 12: "The relation of the laws with liberty in the different governments, and what they can do in order to favor the spirit of liberty" (VF 3:291).

The first substantive chapter commences with a striking superlative: knowledge of "the surest rules one can observe in criminal judgments" is "of more concern to mankind than anything else in the world" (*EL* 2.12.2). It is more important than even knowledge of constitutional design, the subject of Book 11, because criminal judgments are the locus of contact between public power and private persons.[94] Only here does the state touch individuals and threaten them with loss. Montesquieu continues in this emphatic tone: "Liberty can be founded only on the practice of this knowledge" (*EL* 2.12.2). Such knowledge must include the rules that delineate what counts as an act worthy of criminal penalties, how a citizen is tried for a crime, and how to determine appropriate penalties. If Book 11's treatment of the "liberty of the constitution" is an argument for limits, complexity, and balance in the distribution of power, Book 12's account of "liberty of the citizen" is ultimately an argument for limits, complexity, and balance in the judicial application of power.

These "sure rules" of criminal justice include rules governing the decriminalization of nonpublic acts, as we have seen in our discussion of Montesquieu's foundations. Such decriminalization is suitable for republics, monarchies, and mixed regimes alike. "Crimes concerning religion" must

---

[93] Carrese argues that Montesquieu envisages a gradualist, imperceptible process of reform in criminal law and procedure, led by judges: "The judging power is eminently more suited to such a strategy than are the powers more animated by passion and more inclined toward grand plans." *Cloaking of Power*, 18, 42–3. See David W. Carrithers, "Montesquieu and the Liberal Philosophy of Jurisprudence," in *Montesquieu's Science of Politics: Essays on* The Spirit of Laws, eds. David W. Carrithers, Michael A. Mosher, and Paul A. Rahe, (Lanham, MD: Rowman & Littlefield, 2001), 291–334, for an excellent contextualist account of Montesquieu's reform agenda. Carrithers shows that while Montesquieu's approach to the reform of punishments and decriminalization was quite radical, his approach to criminal procedure does not represent a clean break with the French Criminal Ordinance of 1670, under which he operated for ten years while assigned as a judge to the criminal section of Bordeaux Parlement. See also David W. Carrithers, "Montesquieu's Philosophy of Punishment," *History of Political Thought* 19 (1998): 213–40; Craiutu, *A Virtue for Courageous Minds*, 43–6.

[94] After speaking of the judicial power in *EL* 2.11.6, Montesquieu writes, "The two other powers may be given instead to magistrates or to permanent bodies because they are exercised upon no individuals, the one being only the general will of the state, and the other, the execution of that general will."

meet with only religious punishments (e.g., excommunication). For crimes against "public or individual continence," Montesquieu suggests that fines may be appropriate, though most of the penalties he names are, in Mill's language, only "the spontaneous consequences of the faults themselves" – shame, infamy, and social isolation (*EL* 2.11.4, 6).[95]

Crimes against public tranquility and public security merit the application of heightened penalties, but all within natural limits. In the former case, penalties must be sufficient to restore the public peace. In the latter, the state is permitted to act in a truly retributive fashion. Here Montesquieu cautions against the use of capital punishment for robbery; it is "more natural" to reserve capital punishment for crimes against the life of another. Likewise, he rejects physical penalties and imprisonment for debtors (*EL* 2.12.21). Within this framework, penalties for thoughts, speech, and writings have no place (*EL* 2.12.11–13). Legal penalties are themselves external, and so they must punish "only external actions." Speech is an action of sorts, but it "frequently has no meaning in itself." Its meaning depends so completely on tone and context that it is impossible to judge in court. When freedom of speech is absent, not even a "shadow" of liberty remains (*EL* 2.11.12).

As important as these rules limiting the definition and punishment of crime may be, Montesquieu concentrates especially on the problem of criminal procedure. He recommends rules of criminal procedure designed to promote liberty understood as security and "one's opinion of one's security," each of them applicable to a variety of political regimes (*EL* 2.11.1). To curb private citizens' wont to abuse one another through false accusations in court, enact penalties for perjury. Employ a public prosecutor or enact severe penalties for frivolous private indictments. Require at least three witnesses to convict; do not admit testimony from slaves, children, or anonymous accusers; and do not employ extrajudicial commissions to try particular offenders (*EL* 2.12.2, 20, 3, 15, 6, 24, 22; 1.6.8). By this point in the text, Montesquieu has also endorsed the right to petition for a writ of habeas corpus and rejected the use of torture in investigations (*EL* 2.11.6, p. 159; 1.6.17). These are among the "best possible laws" concerning criminal judgments; in states with laws such as these, "a man against whom a proceeding has been brought and who was to be hung the next day would be freer than is the pasha in Turkey" (*EL* 2.11.2). In the domain of criminal justice, liberty means that the integrity

---

[95] J. S. Mill, *On Liberty and Other Writings*, ed. Stefan Collini (Cambridge University Press, 2003), 78.

of my life and limb does not depend upon the caprice of another, just as in the domain of constitutional structure, liberty requires that the right use of power not depend upon the self-restraint of any public officeholder.

This unfolding account never suggests that liberal criminal law is the unique province of any particular political form; none of the first seventeen chapter titles name a regime type.[96] Only when Montesquieu begins to note the particular threats to liberty in each form of government do we find distinctions among the requirements of liberal criminal procedure in each regime. Chapters 18–21 address laws for criminal judgments in republics, while chapters 22–28 treat monarchies. Even here, the aim is not to condemn either regime as inhospitable to liberty but to propose suitable remedies for their native infirmities. For instance, both republican and monarchical modes of accusation can threaten liberty: the absence of a public prosecutor in many republics imperils liberty, while the frequent use of anonymous accusers and domestic spies in monarchies can pose a similar threat to one's "tranquility of spirit" (*EL* 1.6.8; 2.12.19-20, 23–24). Both regimes may adopt liberal criminal laws, avoid the pitfalls peculiar to their natures, and thus secure the "liberty of the citizen" in greater measure.

This is not the first time in *Spirit* that the *président à mortier* takes up the subject of criminal law. In Book 12 Montesquieu examines criminal laws in relation to political liberty, but Book 6 had examined criminal laws in relation to the three forms of government. In this earlier treatment, he finds elements of liberal criminal law in monarchies and republics alike (e.g., *EL* 1.5.1, 2, 9). After describing the absence of due process in despotism, Montesquieu writes,

> But in moderate states, where the head of even the lowest citizen is esteemed, his honor and good are removed from him only after long examination; he is deprived of his life only when the homeland itself attacks it; and when the homeland attacks his life, it gives him every possible means of defending it . . .
> One can see that there must be at least as many formalities in republics as in monarchies. In both governments, formalities increase in proportion to the importance given to the honor, fortune, life, and liberty of the citizens.
>
> (*EL* 1.6.2)

Like the procedural requirements for laws of liberty in Book 12, these judicial formalities of moderate government serve as barriers between

---

[96] See also Carrese, *Cloaking of Power*, 37, 41. Carrese finds in Books 11 and 12 "praise . . . for a balance between monarchical and republican judging," a judgment complementary to my interpretation here.

state power and the accused. And here we find that criminal laws in republics are not by nature more liberal than the criminal laws of monarchical governments. Contrary to the view that republican political forms suffice to preserve liberty, Montesquieu insists that republics require "at least as many" judicial formalities as monarchies (*EL* 1.6.2). Popular institutions do not guarantee the innocent individual against loss, and Montesquieu suggests that republics may in fact require more formalities than monarchies.[97] But moderate and liberal criminal procedure lies within reach of republics and monarchies alike.

In Book 12's treatment of criminal law, Montesquieu circumvents the contest of regimes; this poses a challenge to both liberal republican and monarchical readings of his work. The discussion of criminal law concentrates the reader's attention on a mode of reform distinct from constitutional renovation. Montesquieu acknowledges as much in the opening lines of the book: "[A]s in most states liberty is more hampered, countered, or beaten down than is required by their constitutions, it is well to speak of the particular laws that, in each constitution, can aid or run counter to the principle of liberty of which each government can admit [*peut être susceptible*]" (*EL* 2.12.1).[98] Each form, save despotism, is "susceptible" to a non-negligible principle of liberty. Liberalization does not always require constitutional change, and it certainly requires more than constitutional change. Monarchies or republics that lack liberal criminal protections can achieve meaningful advances in liberty by incorporating these protections without alterations in constitutional structure. Montesquieu emphasizes this point by assigning equal billing to constitutional design (Book 11) and criminal law (Book 12) in his discussion of liberty. Indeed, it is in part because criminal law stands on all fours with constitutional design that Montesquieu's liberalism admits of a robust regime pluralism.

Several lines of argument converge upon the conclusion that regime pluralism is built into the structure of Montesquieu's liberal theory. We

---

[97] Vickie B. Sullivan, "Against the Despotism of a Republic: Montesquieu's Correction of Machiavelli in the Name of the Security of the Individual," *History of Political Thought* 27 (2006): 263–89, shows that Montesquieu's liberal approach to criminal procedure and punishment is a crucial element in his critique of Machiavelli's harsh form of republicanism.

[98] Unlike the other forms, despotism can only admit of what Montesquieu calls, with some irony, "*un peu de liberté.*" See *EL* 2.12.29–30. But it is indicative of Montesquieu's political sensibility that he endeavors to show that even within the universe of despotic governments, some are better than others.

have seen that his foundations, his rejection of regime-centric conceptions of liberty, his theory of constitutional design, and his approach to liberal criminal law all point away from the traditional contest of regimes and toward a set of political norms that transcends this contest.

Limit, balance, and complexity are the axial principles of Montesquieuian liberalism in its formal institutional dimension. These principles guide not the composition of power (rule by one, few, or many) but the distribution of the three powers and application of judicial power. Power may be rightly distributed and rightly applied in any regime save the despotic, for despotic power alone is, by definition, unitary, lawless, and unmediated. Montesquieu depicts these principles incarnate in a real constitution. They are not the deliverances of a deductive science of constitutional design; we have no reason to doubt his claim to have found them in a historical regime rather than through great speculations. This fact alone suggests the limits of abstract political theorizing, and Montesquieu surely intends for us to draw just such an inference. Montesquieu's liberal constitutionalism is in this sense a theory of political practice, a rational account of what is done, a theoretical redescription and defense of a system that emerges from the dark forests of Germany (*EL* 2.11.6, pp. 165–6). But this should not lead us to conclude that Montesquieu offers the English constitution as a blueprint meant to "make ... repulsive" all regimes that do not follow its particular manner of distributing, limiting, and mediating power (*MP* 934). As we have seen, it is less a blueprint and more an architectural pattern book from which we are to learn an old grammar of constitutionalism, long developing in practice if not in theory – a grammar now codified and made explicit. The political and legal reformer, or founder, must apply this grammar in ways suitable to the regime and place that is his own. Montesquieu's liberal constitutionalism is regime pluralist at its core, and for this reason, it is especially amenable to a particularistic art of politics.

4

Understanding Liberal Culture

If, by chance, a prince had taken it into his head in those days to talk about unlimited authority and despotic power, he would have made his whole army laugh, and he would have been viewed as insane.

Montesquieu, *MP 699*

When in Pegu, a Venetian named Balbi was brought to the king. When the latter learned that there was no king in Venice, he laughed so much that he began to cough and could scarcely talk to his courtiers.

Montesquieu, *EL* 3.19.2

If a clever student of political thought were asked to identify the central elements of classical republican theory, he would arrive, in short order, at the republican emphasis upon civic virtue as a precondition of healthy political life and institutions. A distinctive conception of political culture lies at the center of classical republican thought. But if the same student were asked to identify the two or three most important elements of liberal political theory, he would likely mention nothing at all about liberal culture. He might speak of pre-political rights, consent, and limited government, but talk of culture, character, and mores would come slowly to his lips. Liberal political theorists have not wholly neglected the question of liberal government's cultural prerequisites, but often this question lies at the periphery of liberal theory.

Two sound explanations are forthcoming. First, some have held that liberal government assumes no particular qualities of heart and mind in its citizens apart from universal natural passions and capacities, such as rational self-interest. We find such minimalist conceptions of the liberal self in a surprisingly wide cross-section of liberal thought and discourse, from Kant's claim that "the problem of setting up a [constitutional republic] can be solved even by a nation of devils (so long as they possess understanding)"; to Samuel Adams's suggestion that a universal human "love of liberty ... interwoven in the soul of man" makes republicanism a natural form of rule; to President George W. Bush's assertion that the "call of freedom" reaches "every mind and every soul."[1] Pushed to an extreme, this minimalist conception of the liberal self yields the conclusion that liberal formal institutions – the subject of our preceding chapter – require no particular cultural or psychological bases and are therefore uniquely universalizable. A second, more sophisticated approach to the problem of liberal culture, found in the work of John Rawls and some of his followers, acknowledges that liberal institutions require distinctive habits of head and heart, but asserts that these habits will emerge as the product of life under just liberal institutions themselves. This approach, no less than the first, in effect diminishes the importance of developing a rich account of liberal culture; it justifies a disproportionate concern with the articulation of abstract principles and the identification of institutions that embody these principles.

Montesquieu's liberalism eschews minimalist conceptions of the liberal self and narrowly institutional accounts of the origins of liberal culture. Near the center of his field of vision lie the "mores, manners, and received examples" that "give rise" to liberty and the "customs ... of a free people" that are "a part of their liberty" (*EL* 2.12.1, 3.19.27). While Montesquieu famously notes that ancient civic republics made greater demands upon citizens than do modern regimes, he resists the conclusion that a theory of liberal politics is complete without an account of the cultural prerequisites and constituents of liberty. Every political order, on his view, must draw support from suitable cultural resources, and liberal government is no exception.[2] Both liberal political philosophy and the

---

[1] Kant, "Perpetual Peace," 112–13; Adams, "John Adams to Samuel Adams, 18 October 1790," vol. 6, 416; Bush, "Remarks at Whitehall Palace in London," 1576–7. See also, illustratively, Bryan, "Imperialism," 24–5.

[2] Montesquieu's mores, manners, maxims of government, received examples, etc., are all part of what is intended by those who use the catchall language of "culture" today. At times Montesquieu himself refers to these things summarily as "customs" (*EL* 3.19.27). In other words, he sees a common thread uniting these "moral causes." So long as our analysis makes clear the distinctions between these elements of culture, the use of a shorthand term like "culture" is tolerable. This usage is consistent with Raymond Aron's

work of practical reform therefore requires the aid of a liberal political science that discerns the relationship between free institutions and culture, including the dispositions of mind and heart by which liberty is sustained.[3]

Crucially, on Montesquieu's account, liberal culture is not merely a "cause" of free formal institutions, which in turn make a people free; liberal culture is also itself directly constitutive of liberty. Montesquieu means exactly what he says when he asserts that the "customs of a free people" are "*part* of their liberty," just as the "customs of a slave people are a *part* of their servitude" (*EL* 3.19.25; emphasis added). For example, liberal mores of tolerance enable the maintenance of free institutions, but they do more as well. Such mores are themselves *part* of the liberty of a free people; the prevalence of tolerant mores, in itself, promotes a "tranquility of spirit" in which consists liberty. The same is true of other liberal mores, manners, and received examples. Liberal culture, then, has a dual significance for Montesquieu: it is at once a foundation for free formal institutions and a source of liberty in its own right.

Our aim in Chapters 3–7 is to consider how three features of Montesquieu's liberalism incline his thought in the direction of political particularism and allow us to account for the unity of his project. In Chapter 3, we considered how in its institutional dimension, Montesquieu's liberalism is not tethered to any single political form and is therefore essentially compatible with his critique of universal politics. Turning to the cultural dimension of his liberalism, the present chapter is the first of three in a series that considers the implications of Montesquieu's rejection of the minimalist conception of the liberal self and seeks to reconstruct his alternative to this conception – a rich account of the culture of liberty. The problem of liberal culture lies near the heart of our broader line of inquiry, for Montesquieu's critique of universal politics

---

judgment that "what Montesquieu called the general spirit of a nation is what the American anthropologists call the 'culture' of a nation." Aron, *Main Currents in Sociological Thought*, 1:41. For a learned case against speaking of culture in this way, see Mark Blitz, "How to Think about Politics and Culture," *Political Science Reviewer* 25 (1996): 5–21.

[3] It is a mistake to speak of an "opposition" in Montesquieu's analysis between "a world of tradition, of unreflective and unwritten *moeurs* " and "the modern world of written law." Elena Russo, "Virtuous Economies: Modernity and Noble Expenditure from Montesquieu to Caillois," in *Postmodernism and the Enlightenment: New Perspectives in Eighteenth-Century French Intellectual History*, ed. Daniel Gordon (London: Routledge, 2001), 70. The liberal order Montesquieu champions is not a society without need of "mores and manners"; it is rather a society built upon mores suited to its distinctive requirements.

derives its force not only from his regime pluralism, but also from his conviction that free and moderate government does not flow spontaneously from untended human nature. Despotic government "leaps to view"; "everyone is good enough for that" (*EL* 1.5.14; *MP* 831, 892). It is not so for liberal government.

Montesquieu's approach to the problem of politics and culture resembles certain elements of classical political science, as I have argued in Chapter 1. But for many, it will also call to mind the "political culture school" within contemporary political science. An alternative to rationalist theories of politics, this approach emphasizes the effects of political culture ("a people's predominant beliefs, attitudes, values, ideals, sentiments, and evaluations about the political system of their country and the role of the self in that system") upon political outcomes (e.g., regime change, political stability, democratic consolidation).[4] Like Montesquieu, the political culture school would predict that when formal political institutions are changed without corresponding changes in the political culture, the institutional changes are likely to be short-lived. In such instances, the political culture school would expect that "the long-run effects of attempted revolutionary transformation will diverge considerably from revolutionary intentions and resemble more the pre-Revolutionary condition of society."[5] The effects might include "political extremism, ritual conformity, retreatism, rebellion, intransigence, regression or other unintended outcomes."[6] These are some of the ill effects of failing to take political culture seriously, and as we will see, Montesquieu addresses several of them.

But Montesquieu's cultural concerns go beyond the narrow bounds of political culture. When he speaks of "*la manière de penser*," "*les exemples des choses passées*," "*les moeurs*," "*les manières*," or "*la disposition du peuple*," he is not simply referring "to beliefs, attitudes, values, ideals ... about the political system."[7] These elements of culture are not always about politics in a direct sense, but they are nonetheless of deep

---

[4] Larry Diamond, *Developing Democracy: Toward Consolidation* (Baltimore: Johns Hopkins University, 1999), 163. Almond's initial formulation defined political culture as the "particular pattern of orientations to political action." Gabriel Almond, "Comparative Political Systems," *The Journal of Politics* 18 (1956): 396.

[5] Harry Eckstein, "A Culturalist Theory of Political Change," *American Political Science Review* 82 (1988): 800.

[6] Herbert H. Werlin, "Political Change and Political Culture," *American Political Science Review* 84 (1990): 249.

[7] Diamond, *Developing Democracy*, 163.

political import. They contribute to what Eckstein has called "the distinctive, variable set of ways in which societies normatively regulate social behavior" or what Inglehart calls "a system of basic common values that help shape the behavior of the people in a given society."[8] Montesquieu addresses the relationship of politics to culture in this broader sense.

Today, culturalist theories of politics are often said to suffer from three serious defects. First, some charge that culture and political culture are impossibly difficult to define. For this reason, testing cultural explanations is said to be a fool's errand. Some critics even suggest that the ambiguity of the concept of culture provides cover for intellectual laziness: when we cannot explain a particular political outcome, we conclude that culture must be the culprit without articulating a compelling causal logic.[9] Second, culturalist theories are said to obscure the importance of politics, or genuinely political explanations for political outcomes.[10] Third, many argue that culturalist theories of politics cannot adequately explain political change.[11] If culture is assumed to be relatively stable or "glacial," then political continuity is the expected state of affairs.[12] Contemporary theorists of political culture have attempted to respond to these objections, and our purposes do not require a rehearsal of their responses. But what is worthy of note here is that Montesquieu's approach to politics and culture suffers from none of these defects.

First, Montesquieu does not ascribe causal power to culture or custom without specifying what element of culture he intends to identify, whether

---

[8] Eckstein, "A Culturalist Theory of Political Change," 803; Jim Granato, Ronald Inglehart and David Leblang, "The Effect of Cultural Values on Economic Development: Theory, Hypotheses, and Some Empirical Tests," *American Journal of Political Science* 40 (1966): 608. See also Gabriel Almond and Sidney Verba, *The Civic Culture: Political Attitudes and Democracy in Five Nations* (New York: Sage, 1963), 13. For a useful summary of the debate concerning terminology of political culture, see Consuelo Cruz, *Political Culture and Institutional Development in Costa Rica and Nicaragua: World Making in the Tropics* (Cambridge University Press, 1999), 4–5, 27ff.

[9] On the putative lack of conceptual clarity in the political culture school, see James Johnson, "Conceptual Problems as Obstacles to Progress in Political Science: Four Decades of Political Culture Research," *Journal of Theoretical Politics* 15 (2003): 87–115; Ronald P. Formisano, "The Concept of Political Culture," *The Journal of Interdisciplinary History* 31 (2001): 393–426; Werlin, "Political Change," 96ff.

[10] See especially Robert W. Jackman and Ross A. Miller, "A Renaissance of Political Culture?" *American Journal of Political Science* 40 (1996): 632–59; Robert W. Jackman and Ross A. Miller, "The Poverty of Political Culture," *American Journal of Political Science* 40 (1996): 697–716.

[11] Ronald Rogowski, *Rational Legitimacy: A Theory of Political Support* (Princeton University Press, 1974).

[12] Cruz, *Political Culture*, 21.

mores, manners, received examples, religion, or the like. Second, he does not discount the importance of political and legal causes in explaining both political outcomes themselves as well as the formation of mores and customs. Like the Ancients, he repeatedly highlights the relationship of reciprocal causality that obtains between political institutions and culture. Montesquieu's method shares much in common with more integrative approaches to the study of political change that recognize culture as one of several important forces in political life.[13] Third, Montesquieu's political science manages to incorporate cultural variables without denying the possibility of political transformation. His recognition of the salience of cultural variables does not leave him unable to account for political change. Rather, it suggests to him the propitious preconditions for beneficial political change. His approach leaves considerable room for both political agency and cultural change as a forerunner to political change, as we shall consider in detail in Chapter 7.

Just as his concern with liberal culture anticipates developments in the political culture school, so too Montesquieu's approach is in sympathy with developments in the study of liberal virtues, capacities, and dispositions within contemporary political theory. In response to both the failure of Rawlsian liberalism to address these matters convincingly and the power of MacIntyre's and Sandel's critical efforts, a number liberal theorists in the last twenty years have attempted to recover a theory of liberal virtue and cultivation.[14] Rather than merely articulating the abstract principles that good liberal citizens must accept, these scholars have attempted to describe the capacities that many or most citizens must possess in a healthy liberal polity. The aims of *The Spirit of the Laws* do not lie far from this project, but the approaches can be distinguished in at least two important ways. First, Montesquieu does not confine his account of liberal culture to a discussion of moral and intellectual virtues (e.g., respect, tolerance, good judgment, reciprocity). As he asks what is necessary to achieve the liberal citizen, he casts a wide analytical net that takes in sentiments, mores, manners, maxims, and beliefs. His interests extend to almost every domain of human life. In this respect, his account suggests that forming a people fit for liberal government requires more

---

[13] Doug McAdam, Sidney Tarrow, and Charles Tilly, "Toward an Integrated Perspective on Social Movements and Revolution" in *Comparative Politics: Rationality, Culture, and Structure*, eds. Mark Irving Lichbach and Alan S. Zuckerman (Cambridge University Press, 1997), 142–73.

[14] See "Introduction," fn. 14.

than the cultivation of so-called liberal virtues. But it also requires less. The elements of liberal culture that emerge in *Spirit* are not as lofty as some of the rarified qualities – such as the "virtues of public reasonableness" – sometimes invoked in contemporary theoretical treatments of this question.[15]

Second, Montesquieu affords nearly as much attention to the task of understanding the creation of "the customs of a free people" as he affords to the task of explaining their political effects and importance (*EL* 3.19.27). Throughout *The Spirit of the Laws*, the recurring pattern of analysis is first to consider the causes or determinants of cultural variable X, and then to consider the political effects of cultural variable X. For instance, Montesquieu seeks to understand the political effects of the relations between the sexes: what are the political effects of polygamy, the enclosure of women, and patriarchal social orders? But before answering this question, he analyzes the causes as effects. What are the causes of polygamy, the enclosure of women, and patriarchy? This is why *Spirit* often appears to be a study in the formation of culture. I shall attempt to reflect something of the scope of Montesquieu's social scientific ambitions in what follows.

As an introduction to Montesquieu's approach to the problem of liberal culture, the present chapter attends especially to his broader theoretical insight into the permeability of the boundaries between political and nonpolitical spheres of human activity. Unlike many liberal theorists, Montesquieu has a rich "theory of interface," a well-developed conception of the connection between our political and nonpolitical selves, our public and nonpublic identities.[16] The patterns of authority, ideas, and moral habits forged in ostensibly nonpolitical domains wend their way into the political domain, and the inverse holds true as well.

Because of the complexity and scope of the material, I reserve for Chapters 5 and 6 our discussion of the intersection of international commerce and religion in the formation and maintenance of liberal culture. If Chapters 5 and 6 consider supranational sources of liberal culture, our focus here is subnational sources of liberal culture, including the role of the household, character forged by physical causes, and "maxims of government." Before taking up each of these elements in their turn, the first section will consider how a history of free and moderate political institutions contributes to the formation of liberal culture,

---

[15] See Macedo, *Liberal Virtues;* Spragens, *Civic Liberalism*, ch. 8.
[16] Tomasi, *Liberalism beyond Justice*, 39.

reversing the causal arrow. This section has the character of a preemptive qualification: politics is not simply "downstream" from culture in Montesquieu's account. Having considered Montesquieu's conception of liberal political culture in this chapter and the two that follow, we shall find ourselves in a better position to understand his approach to the even thornier question of liberal political transitions (Chapter 7), and with that, to appreciate more fully the relationship between his normative liberalism and his political particularism.

INSTITUTIONS AS A SOURCE OF POLITICAL CULTURE

If one has faith in the power of law and politics to reeducate citizens in a stroke, then one need not consider subpolitical sources of liberal culture. On this view, one could expect liberal institutions to impart the national character necessary for their own survival. Such a view is fully compatible with political universalism. Montesquieu's approach is more balanced. While legal and political institutions alone cannot produce the customs requisite for their own maintenance and health, it is nonetheless true that patterns of the political and legal spheres invariably "spill over" into and influence other spheres of life.[17] Montesquieu sees in politics and law a real though finite power to influence customs, mores, and manners, even as he also develops a rich account of the cultural constraints upon political change. He has a sociology, but it is a political sociology that never denies the formative or educative power of law and politics.[18]

In many instances, Montesquieu identifies "cultural" factors that both shape and are shaped by political institutions, and so by political history. As we saw in Chapter 1, an especially important such relationship of

[17] Elster's definition of the "spillover effect" in Tocqueville's social thought applies to Montesquieu as well: "The spillover effect says that if a person follows a certain pattern of behavior P in one sphere of his life, X, he will also follow P in sphere Y." Elster, *Tocqueville*, 13.

[18] See *MP* 1876. That his method was not pristinely sociological was the subject of Durkheim's complaint. Durkheim believed that Montesquieu had constructed a "defective science" because he had had not realized that the "nature of society," "circumstance," and mores determined the shape of laws and institutions with "something like a physical necessity." By denying that a relationship of necessity obtained between sociological causes and political outcomes, Montesquieu had left too much space for reflection and choice in politics, especially in the person of "the legislator." He was too eager to investigate the role of "final causes" in the political world. As this critique makes clear, Montesquieu's view that political and legal institutions could shape culture preserved the place of political agency and human purpose in his political science. Durkheim, *Montesquieu and Rousseau*, 49–53.

reciprocal causality obtains between the "nature" and "principle" of a constitution. Every government possesses a nature – that is, a structure or arrangement of formal political institutions (*EL* 1.3.1). Each of the three basic forms of government also has a "principle" or animating passion that gives life to the structure and makes it act like the thing it is (*EL* 1.3.1). These principles are clearly an element of political culture, as we have come to use the term. Now if Montesquieu believed that politics is entirely downstream from culture, we would expect him to teach that nature is merely an effect of principle. But in fact, he conceives of neither as holding general causal priority over the other.

Principles "derive naturally" from the nature of each government, but this indicates a logical rather than causal relationship (*EL* 1.3.2). These principles or passions are deductively necessary for a government of this or that form to function.[19] Similarly, though Montesquieu writes that the principle of each government has a supreme influence on the laws (*EL* 1.1.3), he does not suggest that principle determines the nature of the government. Changes in a government's principle trigger changes in its nature, as when a democratic republic loses virtue and thus its nature begins to become more despotic, monarchical, or aristocratic (*EL* 1.8.2). But principle is not the unique motor of history, for even when a change in principle sparks this process of corruption, the principle itself is transformed by subsequent changes in the nature of the regime. Louis Althusser ably captures the dynamism of Montesquieu's thinking on this point:

> If these two terms [principle and nature] are in harmony (Republican Rome and virtuous Romans), the totality of the State is peaceful, men live in a history without crises. If the two terms are in contradiction (Republican Rome and Romans who have abandoned virtue), crisis breaks out. The principle is no longer what is *wanted* by the nature of the government. Whence a chain reaction: the form of the government tries blindly to reduce the contradiction, it changes, and its change drags the principle along with it, until, with the help of circumstances, a new harmony emerges (imperial-domestic Rome and Romans living in fear), or a catastrophe which is the end of this breathless chase (barbarian conquest) ... It is not clear which of these two terms [nature and principle] linked together in the fate of the totality is the preponderant one.[20]

---

[19] On the deductive character of Montesquieu's theory of nature and principle, see Courtney, "Montesquieu and Natural Law"; *EL*, "Pref.," xliii.

[20] Althusser, *Politics and History*, 50–1.

Montesquieu never identifies any single first cause in his science of politics.[21] The nature, laws, and principal passions of a nation have a relationship of reciprocal causality and constraint.

When Montesquieu turns in earnest to the task of elaborating the
relationship of the principles to various kinds of law – laws concerning
education (Book 4), "the laws given by the legislator" (Book 5), criminal
law (Book 6), and luxury and women (Book 7) – he demonstrates that
many laws "follow from" and "conform to" the principle of the nation.
The animating passion of the nation shapes these laws; they flow from the
principle "as from their source" (*EL* 1.1.3). Some of these laws are political
laws, constitutive of the regime itself. However, the laws and political
forms produced by the principle have a life of their own and exert influence
upon the principle. The principle "receives new force from the laws" that it
helped to shape, and this "tightens all the springs of the government" (*EL*
1.5.1). Montesquieu imagines a kind of perpetual reverberation between
the character of the people and the institutions of the state. As in physical
motion, so in political motion: "an action is always followed by a reaction"
(*EL* 1.5.1). The principle influences laws and institutions, but the laws and
institutions leave their stamp upon the principle, customs, and way of life,
which shape the institutions in turn, and so on.

In his *Considerations on the Causes of the Greatness of the Romans
and their Decline*, Montesquieu characterizes the relationship this way:
"At the birth of societies, the leaders of republics create the institutions;
thereafter, it is the institutions that form the leaders of republics."[22] Of
course, not all institutions are created products of human agency. In the
rise of political institutions, chance typically plays a greater part than
human prudence (*EL* 1.5.14).[23] But whether products of chance or intelligence, institutions invariably play a role in forming a people's character.
In this chapter of the *Considerations*, Montesquieu proceeds to explain
that the office of consul tended to form particularly ambitious leaders
owing to the office's short one-year terms. But even beyond their influence
upon leaders, political institutions impart to the populace "a certain
orientation, a certain disposition" (*MP* 603). This is true of despotic
and moderate governments alike.

Montesquieu devotes a lengthy chapter to the cultural and psychological
consequences of liberal politics in particular – what we might call the
political sources of liberal culture. While the first twenty-six chapters of

[21] Tocqueville's first cause is the social state. Tocqueville, *Democracy in America*, 50.
[22] Montesquieu, *Considerations*, 169.   [23] Plato, *Laws*, 709a-c.

Book 19 take up the question of how culture constrains and determines political horizons, the final chapter reverses the causal arrow and addresses, "How laws can contribute to forming the mores, manners, and character of a nation" (*EL* 3.19.27). Though the title suggests that a rather general account will follow, Montesquieu focuses narrowly on the effects of the English constitution upon English cultural life.[24] He announces,

> The customs of a slave people are part of their servitude; those of a free people are a part of their liberty.
> I have spoken in Book 11 of a free people, and I have given the principles of their constitution; let us see the effects that had to follow *the character that was formed from it*, and the *manners that result from it.*
>
> (*EL* 3.19.27)[25]

Laws of liberty neither effect nor follow from the supersession of custom by Reason; rather, the principles of this free constitution help to forge customs of a particular kind, the "customs of a free people." These customs are a "part of their liberty" both because the customs themselves are liberating and because they serve as informal foundations of liberal institutions. Taken on their own, not all customs of a free people are morally or aesthetically impressive, but they tend to bolster the free institutions that contribute to their formation.[26]

In this twenty-seventh chapter, Montesquieu opts for breadth over depth in his account of these customs. The chapter's purpose is not to analyze fully the various elements of liberal culture but rather to demonstrate the possibility of such an analysis. So, for instance, we find just two lines on poets: the individualism and independence instilled by liberal institutions produce an "original bluntness of invention" in poetic works.

---

[24] Throughout the chapter, Montesquieu speaks in the subjunctive mood ("they *would* be"; "they *would* have") to make it clear that his analysis is in some measure deductive and therefore generalizable.

[25] Here Montesquieu alludes to a memorable passage in the *Agricola* of Tacitus, although without a footnote. Tacitus, *Agricola* (Oxford University Press, 2009), §21. Tacitus writes of how, under Agricola's governorship of Britain, the Romans gave the sons of leading Britons a Roman education, dressing them in togas and teaching them Latin. The Britons also acquired a taste for eloquence, warm baths, and elegant banquets. Tacitus gravely comments the new customs were in fact "part of their servitude." The introduction of Roman customs was not merely a foundation for formal or legal subordination to Rome; it was, Tacitus suggests, constitutive of the servitude of the Britons.

[26] For a different view, see Rahe, "Forms of Government," 88ff; Paul A. Rahe, *Soft Despotism, Democracy's Drift: Montesquieu, Rousseau, Tocqueville, and the Modern Prospect* (New Haven, CT: Yale University Press, 2009), 32–62; Rahe, *Montesquieu and the Logic of Liberty*, 99–102. Rahe sees worries regarding soft despotism embedded in Montesquieu's account of English political culture.

We read one sentence on historians: partisanship engendered by liberal constitutionalism leads historians to lie in favor of their party. There is a single observation about comedy under free governments: liberal citizens feel their own vices more vividly, so satirical writings are downright scathing. In free states, philosophers and scientists tend to think alone; again, a single sentence suffices to cover the subject. One cannot help but recall the second volume of Tocqueville's *Democracy in America*, which devotes many chapters to a similar mode of analysis under Montesquieu's inspiration.[27] Montesquieu's brief treatment serves as only an opening of doors; he means to demonstrate the power of political liberty to shape culture in unanticipated ways. These elements of liberal culture in turn strengthen liberty's foothold in England.

Montesquieu also considers how participation in and life under liberal institutions shape a people's character and habits of heart. The signal liberal institution of separation of powers would lead to a constant struggle between the legislative and executive powers. Inevitably taking sides in the struggle, the people would develop a kind of low-grade, habitual suspicion, uneasiness, and attentiveness. But unlike the agitated spirit of the people in an ancient democracy, the suspicions of citizens in representative governments are moderate as they can be regulated and calmed by the elected representatives. This civic vigilance, produced by liberal political institutions, helps to sustain those institutions, as citizens watchfully keep government within its limits and cast their weight against the power they judge to have overstepped its bounds. As C. P. Courtney observes, "Montesquieu shows that the institutions of England tend to reinforce the spirit of liberty which produced them."[28]

Montesquieu's understanding of the effects of political institutions upon the hearts and minds of citizens is equally evident in his treatment of despotism: "The customs of a slave people are a part of their servitude" (*EL* 3.19.27). Despotic governments indiscriminately assign cruel and severe penalties to all crimes, and as a result, men are soon moved only by the threat of severe suffering. The nature of a slave is acquired through life as a slave. The slave in form becomes a slave in fact.[29] Despotism's harshness weakens the subtler bridles of the human spirit – love of honor,

---

[27] Tocqueville's analysis shows greater alertness to the possibility that a form of politics may create cultural features that, in turn, undermine that form of politics. See Tocqueville, *Democracy in America*, vol. 2, part 1.

[28] Courtney, *Montesquieu and Burke*, 95.

[29] Frederick Douglass, *The Narrative Life of Frederick Douglass* (Cambridge, MA: Harvard University Press, 2009), 78.

fear of shame, hope of reward, and "maxims of philosophy, morality, and religion" (*EL* 1.6.13). The character and customs of a slave people become so corrupt that the rulers feel themselves under compulsion to govern with increasing brutality.[30] "If you see other countries in which men are restrained only by cruel punishments," Montesquieu explains, "reckon again that this arises largely from the violence of the government, which has employed these punishments for slight transgressions" (*EL* 1.6.12). Men become "accustomed to despotism" and "accustomed to harshness" as their form of government impresses itself upon customs and character (*EL* 1.6.12, 1.6.9). In short, despotic institutions transform men into the kinds of beings that despotic laws presume men to be. This is why "a subjugated nation can only have another oppressor," while a "free nation" – free in character and custom – "can have a liberator" (*EL* 3.19.27).[31] Despotic politics yields despotic culture, and so the nation doubles down on its servitude.

In neither his analysis of despotism nor his analysis of moderate government does Montesquieu treat political institutions as mere derivatives of culture. Though he devotes more attention to the political effects of culture, he knows how to turn the causal arrow. Political institutions are not epiphenomenal emanations of subpolitical forces, and mores and manners are not for Montesquieu what modes of production were for Marx. Politics has a life of its own. Montesquieu's lively sense of the power of the subpolitical to constrain viable choices is joined with an equally strong sense of the considerable though not boundless power of political institutions to form and deform men over time. Indeed it is this very power that makes despotic institutions capable of inspiring horror. Despotism is an obscenity not merely because despotic government is unjust and cruel, but also because it remakes man, inscribing its form of rule in a way of life.[32] But by the same token, free institutions foster customs and habits that serve, in limited measure, to brace these institutions in turn.

---

[30] At times Montesquieu suggests that the government in a despotic state is itself victim to the logic of despotism: "I beg you to observe with what industry the Muscovite government seeks to escape the despotism which weighs on the government even more than it does on the peoples" (*EL* 1.5.14).

[31] "Revolutions formed by liberty are but a confirmation of liberty" (*EL* 3.19.27). But see Chapter 7.

[32] Montesquieu warns that European mores are not sufficiently strong to resist erosion by despotic government: "Most European peoples are still governed by mores. But if, by a long abuse of power or by a great conquest, despotism became established at a certain time, neither mores nor climate would hold firm ... " (*EL* 1.8.8).

HEARTH AND COURT, HOUSEHOLD AND CITY

Montesquieu's understanding of the reciprocally causal relationship of "culture" and "politics" perhaps is most vividly on display as he traces the subterranean passages between the domestic and political spheres. Customs governing the organization of the household and the status of women are, on his view, among the most politically consequential elements of culture. He devotes two of the thirty-one books that comprise *The Spirit of the Laws* primarily to the relationship of women to men, society, and the state. This may seem unremarkable, but when compared to other leading early modern political theorists, Montesquieu appears keenly and even uniquely interested in understanding politics in light of "the natural bifurcation of humankind into sexes."[33] His concern with the political implications of sexual difference, which pervades *Persian Letters*, appears on the pages of *Spirit*. In Book 6 on "sumptuary laws, luxury and the condition of women" and Book 16 on "domestic slavery," as well as in a handful of other key sections of the work, Montesquieu clearly aims to account for and draw out the implications of what he believes to be an empirical verity: political freedom is, generally speaking, coincident with the social and domestic liberty of women, and political servitude is generally coincident with the subordination and strict confinement of women. The domestic is political, and the political domestic.

In Book 16, the third in a series of four books treating the effects of climate, Montesquieu attempts to explain the subordination of women as, in part, an effect of climate. As noted earlier in the chapter, Montesquieu insists upon treating every cause of variation in political institutions as an effect as well. Climate, he speculates, affects the nubile age, and variation in the nubile age partly accounts for variation in the condition of women and the social (in)equality of the sexes (*EL* 3.16.2). Even if Montesquieu's theory of nubility is dubious, his reflections on the political importance of "domestic government" do not appear so fanciful.[34]

He sketches three connections between a nation's politics and the condition of its women. First, he suggests in both *Persian Letters* and

[33] Schaub, *Erotic Liberalism*, xi.
[34] See especially M. Steven Fish, "Islam and Authoritarianism," *World Politics* 55 (2002): 4–37, who argues that the treatment of girls and women in Islamic nations explains why these nations are "democratic underachievers." For a different view, see Daniela Donno and Bruce Russett, "Islam, Authoritarianism, and Female Empowerment: What Are the Linkages?" *World Politics* 56, no. 4 (2004): 582–607.

Spirit that the liberty of women to interact socially and to maintain relationships with others outside the household results in the liberation of vanity. Men and women alike now desire to impress and allure. Vanity produces new needs – or rather, new desires for unnecessary goods. Each person "is a spectacle for another," and each hopes to please the spectator (*EL* 3.19.8). A thousand unnecessary arts are required to satisfy these wishes. One thinks of the inestimable number of artisans, merchants, and traders that make possible, and are made possible by, a single night of festivities at Versailles: "A woman takes it into her head that she should appear at a gathering in a certain dress, and from that moment fifty artisans can sleep no more nor find leisure to drink and eat" (*LP* 106; *EL* 3.19.8). Vanity thus serves as an engine of commerce. Greater communication between the sexes produces greater "communication between peoples" – interstate commerce (*EL* 1.6.11, 3.19.8). Montesquieu sees political good in this promotion of commerce, as we consider both in the next section and again, from other vantages, in Chapters 6 and 7. The emancipation of women from "domestic servitude" promotes liberty *in part* through opening new avenues for commercial activity.

But this teaching on the utility of feminine vanity, treated ably in previous scholarship, does not comprise the whole of Montesquieu's teaching on the relationship between the domestic and political spheres.[35] Two additional ties unite these spheres, and neither has received significant attention from scholars. This is no doubt because Montesquieu's account of the first link is most explicit and prominent. But the others are no less interesting, and they are perhaps even more illustrative of the common thread running throughout Montesquieu's analysis of the cultural preconditions of liberal government.

There exists, on his view, a resonance between the domestic sphere and the political sphere that the legislator ignores at great cost. We learn in our home life certain lessons about the nature of authority, peace, and submission. We learn these lessons not didactically but through experience of the mundane. The patterns of authority established in the domestic sphere leave their stamp upon us; they "stamp spirits" and "impress all hearts," to appropriate his language from a related context (*EL* 3.19.17, 19). These patterns shape the way in which we conduct ourselves in the political sphere. The reverse also holds true. In our role as citizens and subjects, we are habituated, often unwittingly, to distinctive modes of

---

[35] On this point, see esp. Schaub, *Erotic Liberalism*.

human relation.[36] We develop habitual ways of understanding peace, cooperation, order, and conflict. These lessons from the political realm have a way of seeping back into the domestic sphere. In short, our political lives and our domestic lives are not essentially distinct.

Commenting specifically upon life in despotic nations, Montesquieu writes, "Each man follows the spirit of the government and brings to his home what he sees established outside of it" (*EL* 1.7.9).[37] In despotic states, this will mean the enslavement and enclosure of women. Subjects of despotic states keep their wives away from society for fear that they will simply be noticed, in itself a dangerous thing under despotic regimes. "A government that has not the time to examine the conduct of its subjects is suspicious of it simply because it appears and makes itself felt" (*EL* 3.16.9). The enclosure of women is part of the important business of laying low. Additionally, in despotic regimes, men see established outside the home a species of power that keeps order through severity and fear; this despotic form of rule every man "brings to his home," where he too rules harshly. Montesquieu explains, "In a government in which one requires tranquility above all and in which extreme subordination is called peace, women must be enclosed" (*EL* 3.16.9). No peace without subjection – this maxim of despotic government comes to dominate around the hearth.[38] In the household, despotism's habits and patterns of authority become perhaps more deeply embedded and engrained than they are within the political sphere itself. The staying power of despotism flows in no small measure from its ability to infect the everyday rhythms of domestic life.

The causal arrow also runs in the other direction. Shaped by life under a despotic state, the habits and patterns of authority in the domestic sphere reinforce those of the political sphere and thereby constrain potential for political reform, moderation, or liberalization. The selves formed at home in despotic states are poorly suited for participation in and maintenance of more moderate regimes. Montesquieu argues,

In a republic, the condition of the citizens is limited, equal, gentle, and moderate; the effects of public liberty are felt throughout. Empire over women would not be as well exercised; and, when climate required this empire, the government of one

---

[36] See Tomasi, *Liberalism beyond Justice*, 26–39.

[37] Here is a clear example of the "spillover effect" in Montesquieu's social science. Tocqueville uses similar language to describe the same type of phenomenon. See Elster, *Tocqueville*, 14.

[38] Tocqueville, *Democracy in America*, 291.

alone was the most suitable. This is one of the reasons it has always been difficult to establish popular government in the East.

(EL 3.16.9)

When a man wields absolute power over his wife (or wives), when he governs her harshly and by means of fear, and when he orders his home on the assumption that peace requires subordination, such a man is unlikely to be a good democratic citizen. The same is true of citizenship in any moderate government. While the condition of citizens in a trad-itional monarchy may not be equal, it is similarly "limited," "gentle," and "moderate" and therefore at odds with the patterns of authority estab-lished around the despotic hearth. Montesquieu does not provide an elaborate analysis of how such a domestic sphere can impede ascent from despotism; this is an "intermediate idea" over which he skips, allowing the reader to work it out (*MP* 1970). He seems to believe that most men are incapable of living divided lives. They will inevitably harmonize their domestic and political lives. The mores and habits forged in the domestic sphere are recalcitrant and can forestall changes in the political sphere. In short, as Tocqueville would later say of the domestic and political spheres, "These things hold together."[39]

Finally, there is a third way Montesquieu invites us to understand the mutual permeation of domestic and political departments of life. The enclosure of women and the separation of the sexes, in despotic regimes, deprive men of the salutary influence of feminine company and the conta-gion of what we may call the feminine virtues. Montesquieu suggests that this deprivation is politically consequential. The physical weakness of women "gives them more gentleness and moderation, which, rather than the harsh and ferocious virtues, can make for a good government" (*EL* 1.7.17). For this reason, he argues, government by women is not "against nature" (*EL* 1.7.17). This claim is intriguing in its own right, but for our purposes, it is notable that while men may be inclined to "harsh and ferocious virtues" by nature, the feminine virtues do not come naturally to them. Yet when men and women are permitted to keep company socially, a kind of ethical cross-fertilization may take place. Montesquieu suggests that men's characters may become more gentle in nations that "allow communication between people," especially between men and women (*EL* 3.16.11). He describes commerce, that other source of *la douceur*, as the communication between peoples. Communication between

---

[39] Ibid., 589.

the sexes, like communication among the nations, softens our characters, and gentle mores form of part of Montesquieu's vision of liberal society.[40] Just as communication among nations through commerce makes their customs and habits more alike, as Constant would later point out,[41] so the communication between the sexes tends to render men and women more alike (*EL* 3.19.12). Montesquieu suggests that on balance, communication between the sexes leads to gentler men, rulers, and citizens.[42]

There is no deterministic relationship between the domestic and political spheres, but neither are they independent of one another. Dynamic relations of reciprocal causality unite these two spheres; experience in each shapes the character of the other. Humans are "flexible beings," but perhaps not so flexible that they can live according to different patterns of authority in public and private life (*EL*, "Pref."). This is central to Montesquieu's theory of the interface between culture and politics. On his account, political actors cannot afford to ignore the relationship between the domestic and political spheres. Liberal reformers and statesman, in particular, will take heed of the domestic constraints upon the establishment and maintenance of liberal politics.

CLIMATE, TERRAIN, AND "THE CHARACTER OF THE SPIRIT"

The treatment of environmental causes in *The Spirit of the Laws* boasts less *prima facie* plausibility than the treatment of relations between the sexes. We are all climate skeptics when it comes to Montesquieu's theory of climate. But if we isolate the account of human character and its relation to political action contained within Montesquieu's discussions of climate and terrain, we find a theory less easily dismissed as a product of eighteenth-century natural science.

Montesquieu conducted the first and, we may hope, the last political science experiment involving a sheep's tongue. He bisected the tongue and froze half. Under microscopic observation, papillae on the frozen half appeared "considerably diminished" and had "slipped beneath their sheaths" (*EL* 3.14.2). The principal investigator then let the frozen half

---

[40] See *EL* 4.20.1–2, and Chapters 6–7.
[41] Benjamin Constant, "The Liberty of the Ancients Compared with That of the Moderns," in *Political Writings*, trans. Biancamaria Fontana (Cambridge University Press, 1988), 325.
[42] See also John Stuart Mill, "On the Subjection of Women," in *Basic Writings of John Stuart Mill: On* Liberty, The Subjection of Women *and* Utilitarianism (New York: Modern Library, 2010), 211–12.

thaw and watched as the papillae began to enlarge and the smaller, secondary papillae began to reappear. Because these papillae are the principal receptors of taste sensation, Montesquieu believed this confirmed his hypothesis (developed in advance of the ovine experiment) that cold air makes sensations less vivid (*EL* 3.14.2). Cold air also acts upon the circulatory and digestive systems, making blood circulate at a more rapid pace and causing men to draw the thickest juices from their food. These physiological effects lead to marked differences between men's characters and passions.

Men in colder climates are stronger physically, he believed, and therefore more courageous, more confident, more frank, less suspicious, less vengeful, and less sensitive to pleasure and pain (*EL* 3.14.2–6). Hot climates produce men driven by the desire for pleasure and the fear of pain. Their physical weakness leads to enervation of the spirit, passivity, laziness, a deficit of effort, and a lack of "noble enterprise" (*EL* 3.14.2–3). Heat "inclines men to rest," while cooler climes lead men to action (*EL* 3.14.5). Northern peoples are marked by impatience; they are unwilling to play the patient, to be acted upon (*EL* 3.17.3). As Montesquieu's treatment of climate unfolds, it becomes clear that this is the fundamental distinction he wishes to make.

Modern science does not support Montesquieu's physiology of fibers and juices.[43] But history has not delivered all wisdom through thinkers fully acquainted with twenty-first-century biology. If we dispense with the claim that climate makes men active or passive, what remains is the proposition that these dispositions – toward action or passivity – have political implications. To say that hot air makes men passive and lazy may not be edifying; but less fantastic is the view that a human being oriented toward action is more likely to demand and preserve political liberty than is a passive character.[44] Montesquieu supposes that peoples oriented toward daring action are more difficult to subjugate, whether by a tyrant

---

[43] His speculations are not, however, a vehicle for "scientific racism." For such criticisms, see for example, Ivan Hannaford, *Race: The History of an Idea in the West* (Washington, D.C.: Woodrow Wilson Center Press, 1999); and Paul B. Miller, *Elusive Origins: The Enlightenment in the Modern Caribbean Historical Imagination* (Charlottesville, VA: University of Virginia Press, 2010), 11. Montesquieu's theory of climate has no racial basis at all. He thought that if an English child were raised in a hot climate, she too would acquire the vices of that climate (*EL* 3.15.3, 8).

[44] See John Stuart Mill, "Considerations on Representative Government" in *On Liberty and Other Essays*, ed. John Gray (Oxford University Press, 1998), ch. 4. Mill draws imperialist implications from this claim; Montesquieu does not.

or a conqueror, because they are relatively unafraid of death, inclined to vigilance, and not easily discouraged by the hardships one encounters in resisting rulers' concentration of power. Such peoples do not prize peaceful order enough to accept it when offered by a despot.

On Montesquieu's account, a people's orientation toward action is also a product of their country's terrain, another important "physical cause" treated in *Spirit*. Unlike the argument concerning climate, Montesquieu's analysis of the effects of terrain is not physiological. It is grounded in a theory of habituation. He asks what qualities of character are more likely to develop among a people for whom a subsistence living is obtained only with difficulty. Inhabitants of fertile countries are inclined toward passiveness, laziness, and softness because there a subsistence living is easily maintained; nature seems to spoil by her plenty.[45] Residents of barren countries, however, are inclined toward "*l'industrie et l'activité*" (*EL* 4.21.3). They are accustomed to exertion and inured to work (*EL* 3.18.4). Such peoples do not allow nature to act upon them; rather they act upon nature. They adopt, in Hegelian terms, a negative attitude toward nature: their preservation is by no means a gift of nature but the hard-won product of work. In the south, "nature gives," while in the north, "liberty procures" (*EL* 4.21.3; 3.18.4). Southern peoples survive by nature, northern peoples by art.

A political consequence of this difference comes into clear view as we recall that despotism, while *contra naturam* from the perspective of human nature, seems to come from the hand of nature (*EL* 1.5.14). Montesquieu invites the inference that northern peoples become habitually disinclined to passivity in political matters because they are compelled to act upon nature to secure their daily bread. This, it seems, is one of the reasons why Scandinavia (from whence Montesquieu believed the Goths originally came) is the "source of European liberty," and why northern Europe is "the manufactory of the instruments which break the chains forged in the south" (*EL* 3.17.5). By contrast, southern peoples, habituated to relate passively to nature, accept despotic rule as it "leaps to view" (*EL* 1.5.14). Implicit in this line of thought is the view

---

[45] Tocqueville follows Montesquieu closely on the question of terrain. In the opening chapter of *Democracy in America*, on "The Physical Configuration of North America," Tocqueville contrasts the nature's brilliant plenty in the West Indies with nature's gray austerity in rocky New England. He pushes Montesquieu's line of thought a step further, speculating that the cheerful beauty of fertile countries leads men into such a state of comfort that they feel no need to employ their intelligence to prepare for the future. It is enough for the senses to enjoy the present. See Tocqueville, *Democracy in America*, 26–7.

that a people's habitual modes of relating to forces in the natural world will influence the way it understands and responds to power in the domain of politics.

This orientation toward nature is shaped by the experience of natural needs. Montesquieu argues that northern peoples are more likely to demand liberty because they have more natural needs than southern peoples. They require better housing, clothing, agricultural equipment, and the like; northern peoples have "many needs and few of the comforts of life" (*EL* 4.21.3). In the north, nature is stingy when allotting resources but lavish in its imposition of needs. But this multiplication of needs is politically advantageous, for it induces northerners to demand, unreflectively, the liberty they require to produce and accumulate the goods they need. "The northern peoples need liberty, which procures for them more of the means of satisfying all the needs nature has given them" (*EL* 4.21.3). Southern peoples, by contrast, often require less complex coordination, less accumulation of capital, and less supplementation from foreign sources (international commerce) to satisfy their relatively limited needs.[46] As southern Europeans can "easily do without wealth, they can do even better without liberty" (*EL* 4.21.3). But coordination, accumulation, and trade are more necessary for northern peoples with their many needs. They must therefore have a lower tolerance for extractive despots than southern peoples. Liberty understood as security is the precondition for the vigorous life of action and industry required to sustain resource-poor nations.

Even if we reject Montesquieu's argument concerning the physical causes of character, his hypothesis regarding the relationship of national character to political institutions remains. We are left, specifically, with his claims that a people habituated to and therefore naturally oriented toward a life of action are inclined to resist despotism with greater energy and resolve; and that an impatient posture toward the natural world, an acquired unwillingness to be acted upon by one's environment, carries over into the political world. None of these traits guarantee the

---

[46] Montesquieu does not counsel acquiescence in the mores encouraged by hot climates. The wise legislator (whether secular or religious) must resist the inclination to passivity. He warns against what we might call the enculturation of nature in such cases, that is, against cultural institutions that simply reflect, and so reinforce, the deficiencies of an unfavorable climate. See *EL* 3.17.1–3. Only among "savages" do "nature and climate" dominate "almost alone" (*EL* 3.19.4). An insightful treatment of this problem appears in Melvin Richter, "An Introduction to Montesquieu's 'An Essay on the Causes That May Affect Men's Minds and Characters,'" *Political Theory* 4 (1976): 132–8.

achievement of a free and moderate politics, but their absence is a formidable impediment to transitions from despotism to mild government. It could not be otherwise, on Montesquieu's view, for the boundaries between the political and ostensibly nonpolitical departments of human activity are thoroughly permeable. The defense of liberal institutions therefore requires an account of the form of life those institutions presuppose.

COMMERCIAL MOBILITY, POLITICAL SCIENCE, AND THE MAXIMS OF GOVERNMENT

Though we have thus far confined our attention to character, habits, and mores, Montesquieu never suggests that political institutions rely exclusively on support from the unreflective movements of the heart. The head also has a role to play, for "maxims of government" and a people's "way of thinking" may incline a nation toward monarchy or republicanism, political liberty, or despotism (*EL* 3.19.3–4). For example, Montesquieu states that the most "forceful" causes shaping the "general spirit" of Rome were both Roman mores and Roman "maxims of government," the old saws or commonplace political wisdom that often guide rulers (*EL* 3.19.4). In this section, we consider the maxims of government conducive to liberal politics and, in particular, how Montesquieu's own political and economic science aims at the inculcation of new ways of thinking about statecraft – new "maxims of government" – that may bolster political moderation and forestall despotic drift.

Scholars often note that Montesquieu's condensed discussion of the effects of commerce upon mores served as the chief modern source of the *doux commerce* thesis, the view (simply stated) that commercial activity softens the mores of a people, making them more peaceful or civilized.[47] Given its complex relationship to religion, we reserve Montesquieu's discussion of commercial mores to Chapters 5 and 6. This section focuses

[47] Albert O. Hirschman, *The Passions and the Interests: Political Arguments for Capitalism before Its Triumph* (Princeton University Press, 1977), 70–81; Albert O. Hirschman, "The Concept of Interest: From Euphemism to Tautology" in *Rival Views of Market Society and Other Recent Essays*, ed. Albert O. Hirschman (New York: Viking Penguin, 1986), 35–55; J. G. A. Pocock, *Commerce, Virtue, and History: Essays on Political Thought and History, Chiefly in the Eighteenth Century* (Cambridge University Press, 1985), 103–56; Helena Rosenblatt, *Rousseau and Geneva: From the First Discourse to the Social Contract, 1789–1762* (New York: Cambridge University Press, 1997), ch. 2.

upon his discussion of the relationship of commercial mobility to maxims of government.[48]

On Montesquieu's view, the revolutions in modern commerce have created an entirely new system of political economy in Europe and thus a new structure of incentives for political rulers. Happily, these changes now make it instrumentally irrational for rulers to plunder the goods of their citizens; consistent protection of property rights and mild government now pays. But few in Europe have grasped the full import of these changes. The work of articulating the nature of these changes, and propagating the new maxims they imply, falls to the liberal political scientist. This is in essence the task of enlightening the self-interest of rulers, of pushing each to consider his true interests. The liberalization of "maxims of government" precedes political liberalization.

In his second book on commerce, Montesquieu turns to an empirical change in modern commerce that will, when fully digested, require all regimes to amend their maxims of government: the mobility of assets and persons has increased dramatically, and this new mobility shifts the balance of prosperity further in the direction of moderate political regimes and away from despotism. Montesquieu first sketches this connection between mobility and liberty in his discussion of barbarian peoples, and his analysis of modern commercial liberty is in this respect an extension of his analysis of barbarian liberty.

Like his Goths, many savage and barbarian peoples have enjoyed and presently enjoy "a great liberty" (*EL* 3.18.11). Because nonagricultural peoples are errants and vagabonds, without any necessary attachment to the land, their leaders are unable to take their liberty from them (*EL* 3.18.14). Their property is moveable, so they are moveable. If any leader attempted to accumulate absolute authority among such a people, his subjects would slip through his fingers like sand, for they could simply "go and seek [liberty] with another leader or withdraw into the woods to live there with their family" (*EL* 3.18.14). Among them a despotic king would become, virtually overnight, a king without a kingdom. Despotic government proves nearly impossible to establish in these circumstances, and for this reason, it becomes scarcely imaginable in such societies. Speaking of the Goths in the *Pensées*, Montesquieu writes, "[I]f, by chance, a prince had taken it into his head in those days to talk about

---

[48] David W. Carrithers, "Introduction" in *The Spirit of the Laws: A Compendium of the First English Edition* (Berkeley: University of California Press, 1977), 28–30.

unlimited authority and despotic power, he would have made his whole army laugh, and he would have been viewed as insane" (*MP* 699).[49] The Goths' circumstances made absolute power unthinkable. When citizens have access to a low-cost option of flight or exit, absolute government becomes quite literally a joke.

For a few barbarian peoples, however, flight is not possible. Montesquieu explains that the Tartars, a pastoral people, live on an "immense plain" with "no towns, no forests ... few marshes" (*EL* 3.18.19). They therefore enjoy "no place of retreat or defense" ("*aucune espèce de retraite ni de defense*") (*EL* 3.18.19). Absolute authority easily spreads across the vast East European plain because it is unimpeded by forests, rivers, or mountains, which sometimes serve to check political authority. Consequently, the Tartars do not enjoy barbarian liberty, and indeed they are "in political slavery." Without a viable *espèce de retraite*, there is no credible threat of exit. But for most herdsmen and hunters, the basic liberty to get up and go secures liberty of a higher order: "Among these peoples [who do not cultivate the land], the liberty of the man is so great that it necessarily brings with it the liberty of the citizen" (*EL* 3.18.19). The establishment agricultural civilization slowly erodes the barbarian foundations of liberty. Agrarian peoples are tied to the land, and the establishment of permanent settlements only further constrains a people's practicable freedom of movement. They can no longer, like dissatisfied barbarians, "withdraw into the woods to live there with their family" (*EL* 3.18.14). Thus in Europe, the physical basis of barbarian liberty disappears even as the institutional legacy of the Germanic barbarians – the "Gothic" constitution – endures, at least for a time.

In this context, we can appreciate Montesquieu's understanding of commercial mobility as a new source of support for free and moderate politics. Modern commercial peoples possess moveable wealth.[50] Because their goods are "further from the sovereign's reach," the peoples themselves are "more independent" politically (*MP* 45). Commerce opens a way of returning to an approximation of barbarian liberty because it re-establishes the freedom of movement that had blocked the possibility of despotic rule in barbarian society. This represents a kind of return to nature by means of the artifice of commerce, particularly in its modern

---

[49] See also Montesquieu, "Réflexions sur la Monarchie Universelle en Europe," in VF 2:349.

[50] See *EL* 4.20.23 and *MP* 45 on commercial wealth existing in a "single [cosmopolitan] state."

incarnation. On Montesquieu's account, commerce renders us at once more civilized and more like the barbarians, or better, it becomes possible to combine the comforts of civilization with the barbarian good of liberty.

Modern commerce provides a liberty of movement far more extensive than the liberty secured by pre-modern commerce. The goods of traders and merchants have always been further from the sovereign's reach than is the vast acreage of farmers, but still a determined tyrant could extract the wealth of pre-modern commercial peoples. As Montesquieu explains in the crucial twentieth chapter of Book 21, the princes of Europe effectively plundered the wealth of Jewish merchants in the Middle Ages. Under England's King John, "A Jew who had seven teeth pulled out, one each day, gave ten thousand silver marks on the eighth" (*EL* 4.21.20). The wealth of commercial men has always been easier to hide than real estate, but the right methods could unearth even hidden silver.

In Montesquieu's account, the great turning point in the history of commerce comes with the invention of letters of exchange (*lettres de change*). The letter or bill of exchange is a financial instrument, developed in Genoa and Florence during the late Middle Ages and early Renaissance. Prior to its advent, merchants and traders saved and sent their wealth exclusively in the form of specie or goods. If a Florentine merchant wanted to acquire goods from Barcelona, he would send the requisite sum of gold or silver and would receive his goods in return. With the development of accounting in the fourteenth century, the same Florentine merchant could pay for the goods in Barcelona by simply crediting the account of the Spanish merchant in Florence, without any transfer of specie. It was in this context that bills of exchange developed to allow a third party to draw upon the Spanish merchant's account in Florence. The early bills of exchange worked like so: the Spanish merchant could purchase goods from a merchant in Genoa, and in lieu of payment in bullion, he could provide the Genoese seller with a notarized letter (eventually a simple formulaic "bill") in which he recognized receipt of the merchandise and promised payment from his account in Florence, where he had a credit balance. The Genoese trader could then present this bill of exchange at the Florentine firm and receive payment in gold or simply a credit to his own account. The bills could also be bought and sold. Forerunners to accounting devices such as bank checks, they allowed a merchants and traders to keep vast wealth outside their home country and to transfer great sums quickly when circumstances demanded it. While commercial peoples had always possessed a form of property more mobile than that of agricultural peoples, the invention of these instruments gave wings to wealth.[51] "Pregnant with thousands flits the *scrap* unseen," writes Pope.[52]

The new devices provided merchants and traders with unprecedented access to secure "*éspeces de retrait*" for their property (*EL* 3.18.14). Montesquieu explains,

> The Jews, proscribed by each country in turn, found the means for saving their effects. In that way, they managed to fix their refuges [*retraites*] forever; a prince who wanted very much to be rid of them would not, for all that, be in a humor to rid himself of their silver.
>
> They invented letters of exchange, and in this way commerce was able to avoid violence and maintain itself everywhere, for the richest trader had only invisible goods, which could be sent everywhere and leave no trace anywhere.
>
> (*EL* 4.20.20)

Here, Montesquieu uses the same language of "*retraites*" he had used to describe barbarian liberty. Just as a despotic king of barbarians will soon make himself a king without a kingdom, so a despotic king of commercial peoples will soon make himself a king without an economy. Men can no longer retreat into the woods to live with their families, but sovereigns now face the greater threat of wealth disappearing across borders to hide upon foreign ledgers, virtual *espèces de retraite* (*EL* 3.18.19). Naturally, as wealth becomes more mobile, merchants themselves also become more mobile, as they need not carry sacks of bullion with them when they choose to flee one nation for another. The bill of exchange is transforming asset mobility and personal mobility in Europe, returning the continent to a state of affairs analogous to that of the ancient German forests.[53]

The implications of this change in incentives for political rulers are slowly beginning to affect the maxims of government in Europe, and Montesquieu's own ambition is clearly to amplify and hasten this impact by making the new incentive structure plain. He famously announces that acts once thought to be *coups d'autorité* are beginning to be seen as

---

[51] Richard A. Goldthwaite, *The Economy of Renaissance Florence* (Baltimore: Johns Hopkins University Press, 2009), 210–14; Mark C. Taylor, *Confidence Games: Money and Markets in a World without Redemption* (University of Chicago Press, 2004), 75–6; Pierre Force, *Self-Interest before Adam Smith: A Genealogy of Economic Science* (Cambridge University Press, 2003), 151.

[52] Alexander Pope, *An Essay on Man: Moral Essays and Satires* (London: Cassell & Company, 1906), 80.

[53] In light of this potential for commerce to create a virtual "*espèce de retraite*" (*EL* 3.18.19), the reader of *Spirit* may need to reconsider Montesquieu's earlier, grim predictions regarding the impossibility of a "government of laws" in regions lacking natural barriers to movement – e.g., the great plains of Asia (*EL* 3.17.6).

maladroit; what were once called *coups d'État* are beginning to appear as "only imprudences" (*EL* 4.21.20). When its causes are well understood, the flight of capital from despotic princes reveals that "only the goodness of government brings prosperity" (*EL* 4.20.21).[54] While Montesquieu believes it has long been true that free and moderate governments tend to prosper, a clear analysis of the revolutions in modern commerce confirm this truth with unprecedented clarity. Europe has "begun to be cured of Machiavellianism" and "will continue to be cured of it," as assets become more mobile and even indecent rulers learn the political meaning of asset mobility.[55]

"Happily," Montesquieu concludes, "men are in a situation such that, though their passions inspire in them the thought of being wicked, they nevertheless have an interest in not being so" (*EL* 4.21.20). The liberal political scientist aids rulers in seeing their enlightened self-interest, thus reshaping the political shorthand or maxims of the realm. This is not simply a story of rational actors adjusting their preferences in response to new material conditions. Montesquieu makes clear that the important empirical changes he is explaining are only dimly understood, and European maxims of government have only just begun to adapt in response to them. It is the task of liberal political and economic science to explain the material changes and to suggest, and even to promulgate, new maxims of

---

[54] Montesquieu would not need to look far for evidence of the effects of these revolutions in commerce. The persecution of the Huguenots and the Revocation of the Edict of Nantes in 1685 led to the flight of at least two hundred thousand citizens, many from the area around Bordeaux, bearing away tens of millions of *livres* in the form of bills of exchange, letters of credit, and specie. Warren Scoville, *The Persecution of Huguenots and French Economic Development 1680–1720* (Berkeley: University of California Press, 2006), 102–7, 291–302.

[55] Taking this line of analysis a step further, later political and economic theorists in France would suggest that that these new financial instruments forced princes to grant political participatory rights to citizens. For instance, the Marquis de Mirabeau, an acquaintance of Montesquieu, observed, "In whatever place [the trader] may live, he will always enjoy the immunity which is inherent in the scattered and unknown character of his property ... It would be useless for the authorities to try to force [a trader] to fulfill the duties of a subject: they are obliged... to make it worth his while to contribute voluntarily to the public revenue." Hirschman, *The Passions and the Interests*, 95. According to this view, modern commerce not only moderates princes, as Montesquieu saw; it also democratizes governments. Several contemporary scholars have argued that monarchs across Europe were forced to grant powers to representative assemblies to coax wealthy citizens with highly mobile assets to acquiesce in taxation. See especially Robert H. Bates and Da-Hsiang Donald Lien, "A Note on Taxation, Development, and Representative Government," *Politics & Society* 14 (1985): 53–70; and Michael L. Ross, "Does Taxation Lead to Representation?" *British Journal of Political Science* 34 (2004): 229–49.

government on the basis of the new material conditions. In other words, changes in political-economic incentives yield changes in political behavior only when they are assimilated into the maxims of political elites, and one role of the political scientist is to facilitate this change in understanding or perception, to act as a legislator of new maxims (*EL* 6.29.19). In the *Pensées*, as we saw earlier in this section, Montesquieu describes the role this way: "I will say to Princes: 'Why do you exhaust yourselves so much to extend your authority? ... [T]he experience of all countries and all times makes clear that you are weakening it'" (*MP* 1991). Montesquieuian political science seeks not only describes the preconditions of liberal politics but to hasten their development. Properly interpreted and distilled into maxims of government, the changes wrought by revolutions in modern commerce leave us likelier to laugh, with the Goths, at the self-defeating character of despotism (*MP* 699).[56]

As we have seen in this chapter, free and moderate institutions are more sustainable among a people with a history of moderate rule, possessed of an orientation toward action, open to some measure of sexual equality, and led by elites who believe the pursuit of absolute power is averse to their long-term interests. In the next two chapters, turning from subnational to the supranational sources of liberal culture, we consider the role of religious piety and commercial mores in the maintenance of a milieu suitable to political moderation and liberty. Throughout Montesquieu's analysis, a core insight recurs: the boundaries between domains of human activity are crossed regularly from both directions. Our experience in each shapes the character of the other. Every regime both produces (to a limited extent) and depends upon a constellation of maxims, passions, customs, and mores, many of them ostensibly private and nonpolitical in nature. Liberal regimes are no exception. Though free governments extend toleration to diverse ways of life, and though, as we saw in Chapter 3, they may be justified on the basis of universal moral foundations, such governments nonetheless rely upon a particular disposition and frame of mind for their maintenance and health. "The *ethos* peculiar to each constitution usually safeguards it as well as establishes it initially": on Montesquieu's view, this Aristotelian principle holds for liberal regimes as well.[57]

---

[56] Note then the significant role of barbarian society in Montesquieu's political thought. The liberal regime develops from the ancient Gothic regime and the liberty of the citizen requires a place of retreat analogous to that of the Germanic tribesmen.

[57] Aristotle, *Politics*, 1337a13–15; see Chapter 1.

   This account of liberal culture does not leave one with the impression that a free and moderate politics is possible only among individuals graced with the highest "liberal virtues." But neither does Montesquieu suggest that the preconditions of political liberty are so thin, so rooted in first nature, or so readily manufactured, as to be inconsequential. In contradistinction to many other voices in the liberal tradition, he abjures a minimalist conception of the liberal self and develops in its place a complex account of the reciprocally causal and mutually constitutive relationship in which liberal politics and culture stand. This theoretical substitution, perhaps more than any other feature of Montesquieu's thought, gives his liberalism with its distinctive character, and it plays a crucial role in harmonizing his liberal and particularist sensibilities.

5

Religion, Secularism, and Liberal Society

Any serious attempt to understand the problem of liberal culture must address the question of religion's relationship to political liberty. Is the decline of traditional religion a necessary precursor to the full flowering of modern liberty? Is emancipation from religious duty the precondition for political emancipation? If not, which varieties of religious belief, practice, and organization may be compatible with, or even necessary for, the maintenance of free and moderate political regimes? In our present age, characterized by unresolved doubts about the liberal prospect in the face of religious fundamentalism, the force of these questions is not lost on us. But the questions are as old as liberalism itself.

A prevailing narrative in recent scholarship has held that Montesquieu regards revealed religion – and specifically, Christianity – as an obstacle to political and cultural liberation.[1] He therefore commends the promotion

---

[1] Recent exponents of this reading include Pangle, *Theological Basis*; Clifford Orwin, "'For Which Human Nature Can Never Be Too Grateful': Montesquieu as the Heir of Christianity," in *Recovering Reason: Essays in Honor of Thomas L. Pangle*, ed. Timothy Burns (Lanham, MD: Lexington Books, 2010); Robert C. Bartlett, "On the Politics of Faith and Reason: The Project of Enlightenment in Pierre Bayle and Montesquieu," *The Journal of Politics* 63 (2001): 1–28; Bartlett, *The Idea of Enlightenment*; Schaub, "Of Believers and Barbarians: Montesquieu's Enlightened Toleration," 197–224; Schaub, *Erotic Liberalism*. See also Shklar, *Ordinary Vices*, 98; Judith Shklar, *Montesquieu* (Oxford and New York: Oxford University Press, 1987), 84; Serguey Zanin, "Rousseau, Montesquieu et la 'religion civile,'" in *Montesquieu, L'État et la Religion*, ed. Jean Ehrard (Sofia, BG: Éditions Iztok-Zapad, 2007), 186–212, esp. 209–10. One of Montesquieu's contemporary ecclesiastical critics also suggested that he had failed to appreciate the practical benefits of religion to society, though his charge is somewhat vague. Montesquieu, "Suite des Nouvelles Ecclesiastiques, 16 Octobre 1749," in VF 7:26–7. The primary ecclesiastical charges during the four-year *querrelle de l'Esprit des lois* concerned Montesquieu's allegedly

---

of commerce, on this interpretation, as the chief way to "attack" religion and "to remove the concern for it from the human soul."[2] As commerce trains all human eyes upon the comforts of this life, genuine religious belief is attenuated, and "God's voice gradually ceases to be heard by human beings."[3] According to this narrative, Montesquieu heralded and encouraged these developments because he believed that free government could breathe easily only in the atmosphere of "liberal rationalism," and he saw commerce as the gentlest and most effective means of producing such a condition.[4] Montesquieu's project cannot succeed unless he can show the way to a "destruction or emasculating transformation of Christianity."[5]

There are two serious problems with this narrative. First, it ignores or downplays Montesquieu's view that religion – including revealed religion – can and does confer considerable political benefits in Europe, even

---

Spinozistic conception of God; his views on moral matters such as polygamy, suicide, celibacy, divorce, and abortion; his views on religious toleration; and his naturalistic account of the causes and conditions of religious belief. Neither Montesquieu's reviser at the Vatican nor the Faculty of Theology at the University of Paris charged that Montesquieu had underestimated the political utility of revealed religion. See "Rapport de Mgr. Bottari" and "Project de censure de la Sorbonne" in VF 7:190–7 and 7:237–44. See also Charles-Jacques Beyer, "Montesquieu et la censure religieuse de *L'Esprit des lois*," *Revue des sciences humaines* 70 (1953): 105–31.

[2] Bartlett, "On the Politics of Faith and Reason," 18; Pangle, *Theological Basis*, 108. See also Orwin, "For Which Human Nature," 277; Schaub, "Of Believers and Barbarians," 231; Bartlett, *The Idea of Enlightenment*, 31–2; Strauss, *Seminar on Montesquieu II*, 1966.

[3] Pangle, *Theological Basis*, 103.

[4] In effect, the prevailing narrative associates Montesquieu with the traditional understanding of the Enlightenment as uniformly "anti-Christian, anti-church and at the point of sliding into irreligion and proto-atheism." Knud Haakonssen, "Enlightened Dissent: An Introduction," in *Enlightenment and Religion: Rational Dissent in Eighteenth-Century Britain* (New York: Cambridge University Press, 1996), 1. Haakonssen dissents from this traditional view. A leading example of the traditional understanding is found in Peter Gay, *The Enlightenment: The Rise of Modern Paganism* (New York: W. W. Norton & Company, 1966). In the last several decades, this view has been challenged on many fronts, and the result has been an increasingly multiform understanding of Enlightenment views on religion. See, for example, Mark Curran, *Atheism, Religion and Enlightenment in Pre-Revolutionary Europe* (London: Royal Historical Society, 2012); S. J. Barnett, *The Enlightenment and Religion: The Myths of Modernity* (Manchester, UK: Manchester University Press, 2004); J. G. A. Pocock, *Barbarism and Religion*, 2 vols. (Cambridge University Press, 1999); Haakonssen, *Enlightenment and Religion*; B. W. Young, *Religion and Enlightenment in Eighteenth-Century England: Theological Debate from Locke to Burke* (Oxford: Clarendon Press, 1998). Considered as a piece of Enlightenment historiography, the present chapter belongs to this revisionist current.

[5] Pangle, *Montesquieu's Philosophy of Liberalism*, 3, 248.

in politically free and moderate states. Religion is not useful merely as a means of taming despots at the margins (this the prevailing narrative sometimes acknowledges), but also as a means of shaping the character of citizens in healthy regimes. The second error, related to the first, lies in a misconstrual of the relationship between commerce and religion in Montesquieu's political thought. This error stems mainly from a popular misreading of Montesquieu's chapter on the use of penal laws in religious matters. Often considered the "most important section of his treatment of religion,"[6] the twelfth chapter of Book 25 is commonly portrayed as Montesquieu's manual in miniature for enlightened statesmen, in which the author furtively invites them to attack religion by the comforts of life, i.e., by encouraging commerce. If this interpretation is sound, then the prevailing narrative is correct. But the interpretation is misguided. Montesquieu's aim in this chapter is to convince a religiously intolerant audience that incentives for conversion are more effective than violent persecution at producing religious conformity. The chapter is not designed to encourage the growth of commerce as an engine of secularization.

Here I offer a balanced alternative to the prevailing narrative.[7] I grant that Montesquieu sees threats to political liberty in some elements of both

---

[6] Bartlett, "On the Politics of Faith and Reason," 18. See also Pangle, *Theological Basis*, 102, and Schaub, "Of Believers and Barbarians," 231.

[7] Several scholars endorse the view that Montesquieu saw significant political advantages in certain forms of religious belief and institutions, but none offer a comprehensive rejoinder to the prevailing line of interpretation. Most of these studies either register dissenting views in passing or focus narrowly on the power of the institutional church in tempering the power of despotic princes rather than the role of religion in shaping citizens of moderate or free regimes. See Rebecca E. Kingston, "Montesquieu on Religion and the Question of Toleration," in *Montesquieu's Science of Politics: Essays on* The Spirit of Laws, eds. David W. Carrithers, Michael A. Mosher, and Paul A. Rahe (Lanham, MD: Rowman & Littlefield, 2001), 375–408; and Sergio Cotta, "La funzione della religione secondo Montesquieu," *Rivista internazionale di filosofia del diritto* 43 (1966): 582–603, on the role of the institutional church as a check upon the power of princes. Lorenzo Bianchi, "La funzione della religione in Europa e nei paesi orientali secondo Montesquieu," in *L'Europe de Montesquieu: Actes du Colloque de Gêne*, (Oxford: Voltaire Foundation, 1995), 375–87, argues that Islam moderates princes in the East just as Christianity tempers monarchy in the West. On Montesquieu's return to a more traditional, "pre-Bayle" account of civil religion, see Ronald Beiner, *Civil Religion: A Dialogue in the History of Political Philosophy* (New York: Cambridge University Press, 2011), 189-198; and Lorenzo Bianchi, "'L'auteur a loué Bayle, en l'appelant un grand homme:' Bayle dans la *Défense de L'Esprit des lois*," in *Montesquieu, oeuvre ouverte? (1748–1755): Actes du colloque de Bordeaux*, ed. Catherine Larrère (Naples and Oxford: Liguori and Voltaire Foundation, 2005), 103–14. Rasmussen, *Pragmatic Enlightenment*, 174-8; Rahe, *Montesquieu and the Logic of Liberty*, 174; and James W. Ceaser, "Alexis de Tocqueville and the Two-Founding

Protestantism and Catholicism. His treatment of religion is therefore partly critical and corrective. He certainly does not view European Christianity as a comprehensive or unalloyed political good. But crucially, I argue that Montesquieu sees equal cause for concern on the opposite bank, in the philosophic assault on religion that he finds, for instance, in the works of Bayle and Bolingbroke. The prevailing narrative downplays or ignores Montesquieu's exertions on this front. He does not welcome the eradication or enervation of religious belief in Europe. Instead he sees significant political advantages in traditional religion, and not merely natural religion or the "religion of reason," as Thomas L. Pangle and others suggest.[8] Specifically, he holds that the doctrine of the afterlife gives force to religious laws that in turn allow the civil laws to be less repressive (*EL* 4.24.14). On his view, a robust sense of religious obligation can contribute to the formation of citizens fit for free and moderate government. The gentleness of commercial mores does not nullify the advantages of religious piety in citizens. Indeed, Montesquieu may have seen in religious piety a means of mitigating the shortsighted spirit of calculation engendered by commercial life, a spirit which if unchecked threatens to put a price on "all human activities," "all moral virtues," and perhaps on political liberty itself (*EL* 4.20.2; *MP* 810).

Far from confirming the conventional understanding of the Enlightenment as a movement that pitted religion against political liberty, Montesquieu's approach to the question actually anticipates Tocqueville's view that the spirit of liberty and the spirit of religion may be compatible. He emerges not as the tutor of those later thinkers – Tocqueville called them "the dirty democrats of our day"[9] – who would set the cause of liberty against the cause of religion, but rather as a forerunner to liberals like Tocqueville and Guizot, who regarded moderate religious conviction as constitutive of a healthy liberal political culture. In short, Montesquieu

---

Thesis," *Review of Politics* 73 (2011): 237, each endorse the view that Montesquieu saw ongoing political benefits in Christianity. See also Lorenzo Bianchi, "Histoire et nature: la religion dans l'Esprit des Lois," in *Le Temps de Montesquieu: Actes du colloque international de Genève (28–31 October 1998)*, eds. Michel Porret and Catherine Volphillhac-Auger (Geneva: Librarie Droz, 2002), 289–304.

[8] Pangle, *Theological Basis*, 87, 103, 108; Zanin, "Rousseau, Montesquieu et la 'religion civile.'"

[9] Tocqueville, "To Eugène Stoffels, on his Love of Freedom and New Kind of Liberalism, July 24, 1836," in *The Tocqueville Reader*, eds. Oliver Zunz and Alan S. Kahan (Oxford: Wiley-Blackwell Publishers, 2002), 152.

addresses not only the past and present dangers of religion but also the possible future dangers of irreligion.

The argument of the chapter unfolds in three parts. First, I call into question the view that Montesquieu offers a blueprint for luring men away from traditional religious faith by means of modern commerce. Next, I argue that far from wishing to do so, he actually believes that religious piety produces significant social goods, even within politically free, commercial states. Finally, I offer an account of the shape that Montesquieu suggests religion must take if it is to support a liberal politics. On Montesquieu's account, the liberal self is not a "given," supplied by nature or by institutions themselves, but rather the product of enculturation in which particular forms of religious belief and practice continue to play a part.

ATTACKING RELIGION BY COMMERCE?

According to the prevailing scholarly narrative, Montesquieu proposes to eradicate or disable traditional religion through the encouragement of commerce. At the center of this interpretation is Montesquieu's chapter "On penal laws" (*EL* 5.25.12). For several leading scholars, this passage serves as the key to understanding Montesquieu's political and cultural program. The chapter has been described as the most important passage on religion in *The Spirit of the Laws*, a "remarkably forthright" statement whereby the author shows his hand to careful readers.[10] In it, Montesquieu counsels that the "more certain way" to attack religion is "by favor, by comforts of life, by the hope of fortune" rather than by fear of penalties (*EL* 5.25.12). Here, some suppose, Montesquieu recommends detaching souls from Christianity by encouraging commercial prosperity.[11] Commerce will serve as an "engine of religious liberation."[12] Almost all scholars sympathetic to the prevailing narrative lean heavily

---

[10] Pangle, *Theological Basis*, 102; Bartlett, "On the Politics of Faith and Reason," 18; Schaub, "Of Believers and Barbarians," 231.

[11] Pangle, *Theological Basis*, 103; Schaub, "Of Believers and Barbarians," 231; Orwin, "For Which Human Nature," 277; Bartlett, *The Idea of Enlightenment*, 31–2; Strauss, *Seminar on Montesquieu II*, 1966. Quoting this passage, Bartlett asserts: "If Montesquieu refused to go quite as far as Bayle in toying with the possibility of a simply atheistic politics, this refusal stems only from his greater moderation or prudence, not from a disagreement over principle" (38).

[12] Pangle, *Theological Basis*, 99.

upon this chapter, finding in it solid evidence that Montesquieu intended to "let loose the dogs of commerce" upon religion.[13]

But this interpretation is mistaken. Montesquieu speaks here not of commerce but rather of a system of incentives for religious conversion, such as the one employed occasionally by Louis XIV in the 1670s. Montesquieu introduces this "more certain way to attack religion" in order to persuade his audience of the instrumental irrationality of violent coercion in religious matters (*EL* 5.25.12). Skeptical about the power of explicit moral argument in political life, he turns to the more effective "*raisonnement pragmatiste*" to make the case against state-sponsored religious violence.[14] In short, his aim in this putatively crucial chapter is not to recommend an assault on religion by means of commerce but rather to convince his readers to swear off persecution. This alternative interpretation of "On penal laws" finds solid footing as we consider the place of chapter 12 in Book 25's argument, the text of the chapter itself, and the historical context of the whole (*EL* 5.25.12).

First, we turn to the function of chapter 12 ("On penal laws") in its immediate context, Book 25 of *The Spirit of the Laws*. Chapter 12 forms a crucial part of a broader case Montesquieu is prosecuting against religious violence in Book 25. This book is devoted entirely to the twin questions of religious attachment and detachment. Chapters 1–8 explore the causes and conditions of religious attachment: What makes men hold fast to a particular religion? Chapters 9–15 take up the question of detachment: What makes men abandon their religion? The question of changing religions is important from the point of view of one concerned with liberty, because it bears directly upon the problems of religious coercion and toleration. Indeed, the themes of coercion and toleration shape the entire discussion of detachment in chapters 9–15.

By this point in *Spirit*, Montesquieu has already recorded his support for religious freedom. He offers a natural law argument for toleration in Book 12, where he maintains that punishment should be determined by the nature of the offense in question (e.g., religious penalties for religious crimes) (*EL* 2.12.4). Later, in chapters 9–12 of Book 25, Montesquieu returns to the question of toleration, but he does not reproduce this natural law argument. Instead, he first attacks religious intolerance through indirect and, he thinks, considerably more pragmatic means. Montesquieu reserves his direct moral appeals for later (*EL* 5.25.13)

[13] Orwin, "For Which Human Nature," 277.
[14] Ehrard, *Politique de Montesquieu*, 191.

and opts instead for two alternatives: first, he aims to lead the opponents of toleration into viewing the question from the perspective of the perse-cuted. Second, he pursues what he elsewhere calls the "circuitous route" whereby a writer shows the political actor "how little utility" he derives from his immoral policy.[15] Here, the task is to demonstrate not that despotic policies are unjust but that they are instrumentally irrational.

In 5.25.9, Montesquieu counsels that "when the laws of the state have believed they should allow many religions," the state should also require sects to tolerate one another. In effect, Montesquieu urges that official state toleration must be joined with state enforcement of private toleration, lest civil war break out among sects. We note here that Montesquieu does not speak of a universal moral imperative to tolerate multiple sects; he warns only that *if* a state tolerates multiple sects, then it should, for the sake of its own preservation, enforce civil peace among the sectarians. This kind of case for toleration exemplifies the "circuitous" mode of political argument. In the next chapter, Montesquieu appears to strike an intolerant note when he announces that it will be a "very good law" not to allow the establishment of a new religion in a state, since proselytizing religions are invariably intoler-ant (*EL* 5.25.10). But, he hastens to add, there is a "*principe fondamental*" for political laws in religious matters: "When one is master of the state's accepting a new religion, or not accepting it, it must not be established; when it is established, it must be tolerated" (*EL* 5.25.10). The state may use its power over immigration to keep out foreign gods (*EL* 5.25.14–15).

These sections (5.25.9–10) attracted censure from Montesquieu's ecclesiastical critics. Clerics singled out chapter 10 as particularly scan-dalous (VF 7:13–14, 36, 238). But the precise nature of their criticism underscores the subtlety of Montesquieu's method in these chapters. In essence, they argued that when Montesquieu declared it "very good" to exclude new religions, it was as if he had "whisper[ed] into the ear of the King of Cochinchina," telling him to expel Christian missionaries.[16] The chapter stirred them to protest persecution; it forced them to take the place of the persecuted and to consider the question from this point of view. Without resort to direct moral argument, but rather through an appeal to interest and self-love, Montesquieu attacks religious intoler-ance. At the same time, he endorses toleration of heretics, including

---

[15] Montesquieu announces that it is "useless to attack a policy by showing how it is repugnant to morality, reason, justice, as these kinds of speeches persuade everyone and affect no one." Montesquieu, "De la politique," in VF 8:511.

[16] Montesquieu, *Défense de l'Esprit des lois*, in VF 7:95.

Huguenots. The Huguenots were already "established" in France and therefore "must be tolerated" according to the *principe fondamental*. In this way, Montesquieu creates a conflict in the minds of his devout readers: his ecclesiastical critics must reconcile their own demands for toleration of Christian missionaries abroad with their dismay at his extension of toleration to "established" heretics at home.

In this context, we can begin to appreciate the aims of the next two chapters, chapter 11 ("On changing religion") and the crucial chapter 12. In each, Montesquieu starts from the low but solid assumption that the prince wishes to change or destroy some religion in his state, and he offers instrumental counsel: if you want to do it, here's how. But he aims to use this advisory posture to persuade his audience to limit or forgo the use of coercion in religion. Chapter 11 addresses the pace of state-directed religious change, and chapter 12 addresses the means of this change. The audience, one imagines, might include princes and elites unmoved by both Montesquieu's natural law argument for toleration in Book 12 and his implicit invitation to trade places with the persecuted in 5.25.10. In chapter 11, Montesquieu warns that the prince is "greatly exposed" to danger when he seeks to destroy or change religion in a stroke, because such cultural changes require a great deal of time (*EL* 5.25.11). Courting popular unrest, the ruler undermines faith in the old religion and his own government without securing genuine devotion to the new religion. The people quickly come to regard this new imposition as the meanest act of tyranny. This message, Montesquieu clearly believes, is more useful than direct moral suasion in preventing mass persecution.

Montesquieu continues this line of argument in "On penal laws," the chapter that plays a decisive role in the prevailing narrative. Here he insists that the use of force in religious matters is futile and even counterproductive. Specifically, Montesquieu aims to convince his readers that penal law is a means poorly adapted to the end of religious conformity. State persecution inspires fear of civil penalties, but this fear is "canceled out" in the persecuted party by fear of God. Moreover, rather than effecting a detachment from religion, these penal laws actually tend to augment religious devotion because they animate the very passions that reinforce the human spirit's attachment to religion, passions such as fear of death and hope for the martyr's crown. For this reason, Montesquieu concludes, "Penal laws have never had any effect other than destruction" (*EL* 5.25.12).

But invitations to convert succeed for the same reason penalties fail: to detach a soul from religion, one must stir up those elements of the human soul that can compete with and drown out the "motives of attachment" to its religion. Penalties for nonconformity remind men of death, and fear of death reinforces attachment to their religion rather than weakening it. Invitations are the "more certain way" to detach a soul from its present object of devotion:

> Penal laws must be avoided in the matter of religion. They impress fear, it is true, but as religion also has its penal laws which inspire fear, the one is canceled out by the other . . .
>
> Religion has such great threats, it has such great promises, that when they are present to our spirits, no matter what the magistrate does to constrain us to abandon it, it seems that we are left with nothing when religion is taken away, and nothing is taken from us when religion is left to us.
>
> Therefore, one does not succeed in detaching the soul from religion by filling it with this great object, by bringing it closer to the moment when it should find religion of greater importance; a more certain way to attack religion is by favor, by comforts of life, by the hope of fortune, not by what reminds one of it, but by what makes one forget it; not by what makes one indignant, but by what leads one to indifference when other passions act on our souls and when those that religion inspires are silent. General rule: in the matter of changing religion, invitations are stronger than penalties.
>
> (EL 5.25.12)

State-directed programs of religious change with any hope of success must employ thoroughly terrestrial promises rather than morbid threats that turn men's thoughts to the afterlife.

According to the prevailing narrative, Montesquieu here means to advocate the promotion of commercial prosperity as a generalized means of undermining religious devotion. This allusion to commerce appears so obvious to some commentators that they hardly argue for it. Pangle quotes this "most important single passage on religion" as he closes his section on "Commerce as the Engine of Religious Liberation," and he offers a single sentence of analysis: "As the 'commodities of life' become secure, Montesquieu confidently asserts, God's voice gradually ceases to be heard by human beings."[17] Orwin similarly concludes, "Few will doubt that commerce is the intended distraction."[18]

I doubt it. This interpretation fails to make sense of the text itself, and it ignores the critically relevant historical context. The text offers a fairly

[17] Pangle, *Theological Basis*, 103. In 5.25.12, Pangle translates "*commodités*" as "commodities." But Montesquieu's "*commodités*" does not necessarily have the narrowly commercial ring of the modern English cognate. See his references to "*commodités de la vie*" in EL 1.5.17; 1.5.18; 3.19.11; and 4.21.3. "Comforts of life," as in the edition by Cohler et al., is preferable.

[18] Orwin, "For Which Human Nature," 277.

straightforward distinction between reward and punishment. Rather than punish those failing to abandon their sect, the prince should reward those who willingly acquiesce in his preference. He should extend the comforts of life as recompense to all men willing to leave the disfavored sect. Rather than offering men the hope of a martyr's crown, he should set before them the hope of fortune. This is a program of conditional rewards, a cash-for-conversions scheme. Montesquieu does not prefer such a religious policy to all others. But he recommends it because he believes that appealing to the prince on the basis of utility is the most effective way to shape his conduct, and he considers conversion incentives to be far less cruel than the auto-da-fé or dragonnade. The text does not suggest that commerce itself reliably weakens religious devotion or Christian belief.

Previous scholarship has failed to recognize that in arguing for the use of inducements over punishments in religious policy, Montesquieu is entering into a debate familiar to his contemporaries. They would have understood that his counsel to attack religion by favor was not an exercise in originality. It is worthwhile to establish the historical and intellectual context of Montesquieu's position. The "more certain way" of attacking a sect by favor was employed at several points in the seventeenth century, especially under the reign of Louis XIV as part of the "godly wonders of de-Calvinisation."[19] In 1675, the King appointed Paul Pellisson, a Huguenot convert to Catholicism, to oversee an institution charged with providing pecuniary rewards to converts from Calvinism. The enterprise was quickly dubbed the *Caisse des Conversions*, or Fund for Conversions.[20] Pierre Bayle condemned it as a "fair for souls," while Archbishop Fénelon celebrated the devout Pellisson's commitment to dispensing the favors of the prince for the good of the Church.[21] Some justified the scheme on the grounds that certain converts – especially ministers – would lose their livelihoods upon conversion. Most converts could expect a few livres from the fund, but public recantations by ministers, noblemen, and rich bourgeois might fetch more than a hundred.[22] The payments could also take the form of pensions, moratoria on debts, or tax rebates. Pellisson

[19] Bertrand Van Ruymbek, *New Babylon to Eden: The Huguenots and the Migration to Colonial South Carolina* (Columbia, SC: University of South Carolina Press, 2006), 20.

[20] W. J. Stankiewicz, *Politics and Religion in Seventeenth-Century France* (Berkeley: University of California Press, 1960), 190–3; Van Ruymbek, *New Babylon to Eden*, 14–15.

[21] Élizabeth Labrousse, "Calvinism in France, 1598–1685," in *International Calvinism*, ed. Menna Prestwich (Oxford: Clarendon, 1986), 307.

[22] Emmanuel-Orentin Douen, "Le Fondateur de la Caisse des Conversions," *Bulletin de la Société de l'histoire du protestantisme francais* 30 (1853):145–60.

regularly sent Versailles meticulous records with names of converts at so many livres a head.[23]

The fund paid ten thousand converts between 1675 and 1678.[24] But the crown grew impatient, and the General Assembly of the Clergy pushed for old-fashioned penal methods. Soon the dragonnades ensued. In 1685, the new wave of violent persecution was made official policy with the promulgation of the Edict of Fontainebleau, and the Huguenot exodus commenced. The Regency of Philippe d'Orléans allowed for a lull in persecutions. But during his adult life, Montesquieu witnessed the revival of persecutions under the severe 1724 anti-heresy law of the Duc de Bourbon. Protestant preachers were to receive death, their accomplices were to receive life in the galleys, and their women were to be shaved and imprisoned.[25] One imagines this made an impression on Montesquieu and his Huguenot wife.[26]

As an alternative to violent persecution, Pellisson's fund would have represented the most recent example of the "more certain way," but it was not the only such example. Before the institution of the fund, it was common in seventeenth-century France for the crown to grant pensions and favors to prominent former Huguenots who had recrossed the Tiber.[27] Lucrative career advancement was open to Huguenot artisans and professionals willing to convert. Beyond the French realm, Ignatius of Loyola had advised the Catholic Hapsburgs of Austria to remunerate converts, and the practice was not unknown among Jesuit missionaries. In his *Dictionnaire historique et critique* (1697), Pierre Bayle denounces the use of monetary incentives by Pope Gregory I, who cut taxes for Jews willing to convert. The connection to Pellisson's fund was obvious.[28] "I

---

[23] Walter C. Utt and Brian E. Strayer, *The Bellicose Dove: Claude Brousson and Protestant Resistance to Louis XIV* (Brighton, UK: Sussex Academic Press, 2003), 14.

[24] Van Ruymbek, *New Babylon*, 15.

[25] Marisa Linton, "Citizenship and Religion Toleration in France," in *Toleration in Enlightenment Europe*, eds. Ole Peter Grell and Roy Porter (Cambridge University Press, 2000), 160.

[26] Because of these family ties, aggrieved Protestants occasionally asked Montesquieu to intercede with the royal administration on their behalf. His great-grandfather, the founder of the family of Secondat de Montesquieu, was also a Huguenot. See Geoffrey Adams, *The Huguenots and French Opinion, 1685–1787: The Enlightenment Debate on Toleration* (Waterloo, ON: Wilfrid Laurier University Press, 1991), ch. 5; Shackleton, *Montesquieu*, 1.

[27] Raymond A. Mentzer, Jr., *Blood and Belief: Family Survival and Confessional Identity among the Provincial Huguenot Nobility* (West Lafayette, IN: Purdue University Press, 1994), 136.

[28] Labrousse, "Calvinism in France," 307.

shall observe," Bayle writes, "that the expression 'traffickers in the word of God' [2 Cor., 2:17] would apply *par excellence* " to those who use inducements.[29]

The practice of inducements came clothed with theological and psychological justifications, as Montesquieu would have known. Indeed, his own account of the "more certain way" resembles some of these arguments. Pellisson and others contended on putatively Augustinian grounds that when a man does not perceive the truth, it is because his unruly passions are obscuring his moral vision. "By manipulating greed in favor of the true religion, it was claimed that his previous leanings were neutralized so that his impartiality thus recovered might enable him to recognize the truth."[30] The scheme could effectively silence unlawful passions (which attached the heretic to his heresy) and thereby provide an opportunity, an "open door," for him to come to faith.[31] Of course, not everyone accepted the view that the rewards were more effective than punishments. In his widely read *Political Testament*, Cardinal Richelieu, prime minister under Louis XIII, had staked out a clear position in favor of the stick as a "surer means" of obtaining obedience.[32] In Book 25, Montesquieu takes sides in this long-standing debate, though his purposes are very much his own.

Previous scholarship has failed to consider Montesquieu's "more certain way" in relation to this broader debate. But in light of this context, the arc of Book 25 as an argument for toleration, and the text of chapter 12, it seems plain that Montesquieu is not advocating the promotion of commerce as an anti-religious therapy. He commends to would-be persecutors a Pellissonsque system of rewards – invitations to renounce – as a substitute for threats of fire and faggot. The prevailing narrative holds that Montesquieu favors the encouragement of commerce in order to destroy traditional religious belief, and the keystone of this view is 5.25.12. But this chapter cannot bear the weight of such an interpretation.

---

[29] Pierre Bayle, *Political Writings*, ed. Sally L. Jenkinson (Cambridge University Press, 2000), 71, 73. Montesquieu owned Bayle's *Dictionnaire historique et critique* as well as Pellisson's *Reflexions sur les differends de la religion*. See Desgraves and Volphilhac-Auger, *Catalogue*, 304, 86.

[30] Labrousse, "Calvinism in France," 307.   [31] Utt and Strayer, *The Bellicose Dove*, 14.

[32] Montesquieu knew the *Testament* well and refers to it four times in *Sprit*. Cardinal Richelieu, *The Political Testament*, trans. Henry Bertram Hill (Madison, WI: University of Wisconsin Press, 1961), 84–5.

THE UTILITY OF PIETY

All scholarly treatments of Montesquieu's approach to religion and politics acknowledge his view that religious traditions and religious institutions often check despotic governments. Religious authorities may act as intermediary powers, much like the parlements and local governments, limiting the power of the prince by circumscribing his jurisdiction (*EL* 1.2.4). Because religious laws are generally believed to apply to prince and subject alike, they may also serve to limit the scope of despotic power (*EL* 1.3.10).

Scholarship on Montesquieu's political thought often reduces the political advantages of religion – if they receive mention at all – to this ability to rein in despotism at the margins. Commenting on passages in which Montesquieu seems to speak favorably concerning religion, Pangle asserts that "what all this amounts to" is merely a claim that Christianity is opposed to *pure* despotism.[33] Aside from this, it is simply "a massive political factor which ... cannot much help us."[34] In fact, Schaub and Pangle suggest that Christianity is preternaturally compatible with despotism on Montesquieu's view. It was born in a Middle Eastern climate and under a despotic government, and its native character is therefore inclined toward despotism.[35] Christianity promises merely to hold the regime a few degrees away from the harshest form of political rule. Likewise, on Orwin's account, the ongoing utility of religion seems to be limited to its institutional role as a bulwark against pure despotism in some regimes.[36]

Montesquieu speaks often of the political benefits of religion in despotic governments and in "monarchies ... tending to despotism" (*EL* 1.2.4). But a single-minded focus upon this function leaves one with the

---

[33] Pangle, *Theological Basis*, 103. See *MP* 1993.

[34] Pangle, *Montesquieu's Philosophy of Liberalism*, 250.

[35] Schaub, "Of Believers and Barbarians," 242; Pangle, *Theological Basis*, 105. This view is mistaken. Montesquieu saw Christianity as European, and for that reason he believed missionary efforts to take Christianity to the climates of Asia were likely to fail. Climate has "prescribed limits to the Christian religion" (*EL* 4.24.26). Unlike most religions, Christianity is, according to Montesquieu, ill-suited to its native climate.

[36] Orwin, "For Which Human Nature," 271. Bianchi, "La funzione della religione secondo Montesquieu," and Kingston, "Montesquieu on Religion and the Question of Toleration," also emphasize the church as an institutional check on political power. Cf. Marc Régaldo, *Montesquieu et la Religion* (Bordeaux: Académie Montesquieu, 1998), 84, who explicitly notes that Montesquieu does not limit the social utility of religion to its power to restrain princes.

impression that religion is of no use in maintaining relatively healthy states, those with more than a few degrees separating them from despotism. In particular, this approach leads to the conclusion that "free states" have little or nothing to gain from the presence of belief in revealed religions. Such a view is consistent with the prevailing narrative's account of the effects of commerce on religion: Montesquieu can welcome the devotional enfeeblement wrought by commerce because religion offers little political good and much harm in a free state. Christianity may have exerted eighteen centuries of generally salutary influence upon European mores, but commerce now promises to soften mores without the inconveniences and baggage of traditional religion (e.g., intolerance, passivity, intellectual conformity, otherworldliness, and prohibitions upon usury).[37]

While this interpretation possesses an admirable elegance, it is not what Montesquieu taught. Instead, he believed that religious faith in the supernatural – and not merely "natural religion" or "the religion of reason" – could produce a complementary source of mores and habits conducive to the preservation of genuinely free and moderate states. In this section, I will defend the attribution of such a view to Montesquieu, and I will offer an account of what, on Montesquieu's view, are the sources of religion's utility in modern regimes of liberty.

We begin at an unlikely place in Montesquieu's corpus. Scholarly treatments of his religious thought almost invariably overlook his revealing 1751–4 correspondence with William Warburton, Bishop of Gloucester.[38] Warburton was a prolific writer and controversialist, a staunch partisan of the established church. He was also a theorist of civil religion who vigorously defended the political utility of religious belief and institutions. In 1752, Montesquieu wrote two brief letters to Warburton – one expressing gratitude for a gift and another commenting on his rift with Bolingbroke, a subject Warburton had apparently raised in a

---

[37] See Guillaume Barrera, *Les Lois du monde: Enquête sur le dessein politique de Montesquieu* (Paris: Gallimard, 2009), 258, whose view on this last point is identical to that of the prevailing narrative.

[38] Two of Montesquieu's 1752 letters to Warburton and part of his 1754 letter are missing from existing editions of the *Oeuvres complètes*. The complete 1754 letter, along with the other two omitted letters from 1752, can be found in William Warburton, *A Selection from the Unpublished Papers of the Right Reverend William Warburton*, ed. Francis Kilvert (London: John Bowyer Nichols & Son, 1841), 234–8. The complete 1754 letter appears in translation in John Selby Watson, *The Life of William Warburton* (London: Longman, Green, Longman, Roberts, & Green, 1863), 424–5. Robert Shackleton, "Montesquieu's correspondence: additions and corrections," in *French Studies* 12 (1958): 338–42, confirms their authenticity.

now lost letter.[39] A year and a half later, Montesquieu wrote to his friend Charles Yorke to request Warburton's current address, so impressed was he with the cleric's "beautiful works."[40] Montesquieu seems to have recently read Warburton's *Julian* and *The Divine Legation of Moses*.[41] He avers that he would have written Warburton a hundred times if only he had the right address.[42] In February of 1754, the bishop wrote Montesquieu, enclosing an advance copy of his forthcoming critique of Bolingbroke's philosophy and a new edition of *Divine Legation*.[43]

A multivolume edition of Lord Bolingbroke's posthumous works had recently appeared in England, and the tomes contained attacks upon Moses, the prophets, Jews, Christians, revelation, natural religion, and the clergy. (By some lights, his most damnable blasphemy was to brand Montesquieu a dishonor to French genius.[44]) Warburton believed that Bolingbroke's philosophical project represented nothing less than an "attempt to overthrow" religion. He quickly composed the two-volume *A View of Lord Bolingbroke's Philosophy* to respond to the posthumously published works. In addition to disputing some of Bolingbroke's substantive claims against religion, Warburton took special care to assail him for his failure to consider the political and social injury he would cause by attacking religion.

In his 1754 package for Montesquieu, Warburton enclosed a substantial letter further detailing his disdain for Bolingbroke's work. He again emphasized the social harm wrought by Bolingbroke and his ilk:

I ... can not but lament the mischief a licentious book of this kind does to society: for, though Truth may be a gainer by the solider answer given to them ... yet, in the meantime, the public suffers. The people are corrupted who have only talents to see what is plausible, not what is true (which lies somewhat deeper). Besides, in such a time as this, the general dissolution of manners, which makes them read licentious books which flatter their passions, with eagerness, gives them a contrary prejudice to the answer.[45]

---

[39] Montesquieu to William Warburton, 7 Juil. 1752, in *Unpublished Papers of Warburton*, 235–6.
[40] Montesquieu to Charles Yorke, 4 Déc. 1753, in Nagel 3:1482.
[41] Yorke to Montesquieu, 11 Avril 1750, in Nagel 3:1300; Montesquieu to Yorke, 4 Juil. 1752, in Nagel 3:1432.
[42] Montesquieu to Yorke, 4 Juil. 1752, in Nagel 3:1432–3.
[43] Warburton to Montesquieu, 9 Févr. 1754, in Nagel 3:1490–1.
[44] Watson, *The Life of William Warburton*, 418–9.
[45] Warburton to Montesquieu, 9 Févr. 1754, in Nagel 3:1490–1.

To this letter Montesquieu penned a telling reply that suggests deep sympathy with Warburton's concerns about Bolingbroke's militant irreligion.

Lord Bolingbroke, Montesquieu writes, has provided Warburton a "perpetual subject of triumph" inasmuch as his wholesale assault on religion is easily answerable.[46] By criticizing all religion, Bolingbroke has recklessly left men "no curb at all" – a "very dangerous" proposition. After addressing Bolingbroke's treatment of natural religion, Montesquieu asks,

What can be the motive now for attacking revealed religion in England, where it has been so effectually purged of all destructive prejudices, as that it can do no hurt, but on the contrary produce an infinite deal of good [*une infinité de biens*]?

I will readily allow that a man in Spain or Portugal, whom the ruling powers would burn, or who fears that he may be burnt, because he does not believe in certain articles of revealed religion, has just reason to attack it, because such an attack may in some sort be considered as provided for his own personal defense. But the case is otherwise in England; every man there who attacks revealed religion, does so without any interest, and even supposing that he were right at bottom, if he should succeed in destroying it, he would destroy an infinity of practical good, to establish a truth purely speculative.[47]

England, the exemplary free state of *Spirit*, continues to derive numberless practical goods from revealed religion. Even if the speculative truth lay on Bolingbroke's side, these social and political benefits would easily tip the balance in favor of silence (*EL* 4.24.1).[48]

After this remarkable statement about revealed religion in England, Montesquieu concludes with a word concerning Warburton's *Divine Legation of Moses*. In a paragraph missing from all editions of the *Oeuvres complètes* and *Correspondance*, Montesquieu declares that he was pleased to find that Warburton had extended his *Divine Legation* and informs him of a French translation now underway: "I should be glad if [the volumes] do not come into the hands of some of our translators,

---

[46] Montesquieu to Warburton, Mai 1754, in Nagel 3:1508–10. On Montesquieu's complex intellectual and personal relationship to Bolingbroke, see Rex A. Barrel, *Bolingbroke and France* (Lanham, MD: University Press of America, 1988), 72–82.

[47] Montesquieu to Warburton, Mai 1754, in Nagel 3:1509–10; Montesquieu, *Complete Works of M. de Montesquieu*, vol. 4, letter XLII (London : 1777), 106. The letter's date is speculative.

[48] If Montesquieu's Jansenist accusers were correct in charging him with Spinozistic and otherwise unorthodox religious views, we may speculate that he himself lived by this maxim. From the point of view of "one who writes about politics," the falseness of a religion does not constitute a reason for seeking its destruction.

who disfigure everything they touch and convert gold into iron."[49] Since this book was also among the "beautiful works" Montesquieu had praised in his letter to Yorke, we might ask what vein of gold he discerned there.

Warburton's thesis in *Divine Legation* is that the doctrine of a future state is necessary for maintaining social order.[50] The grand theme of the work is the political utility of religion. In fact, critics wondered aloud whether Warburton thought there was any difference between one religion and another, beyond relative political utility.[51] In light of this, Montesquieu's movement in his letter from religion in England to a discussion of *Divine Legation* seems a smooth transition. He questions Bolingbroke's attack on religion in a nation where it confers infinite practical benefits, and then he turns immediately to praise Warburton's book on the social utility of belief in the afterlife. Revealed religion's practical benefits for English social life are tied, at least in part, to religious laws reinforced by doctrines of an afterlife. Montesquieu and Warburton do not refer narrowly to religion's capacity to curb the passions or check the power of a prince. They share a concern over the loss of popular moral restraints, the "general dissolution of manners," that would follow the demise of revealed religion in the free state of England.[52]

Why does Montesquieu so value religion's capacity for social restraint in England? Is this concern with English religion in some way connected to his understanding of English liberty? Any law-and-order man would welcome social restraint for the sake of civic peace, but one suspects that this does not exhaust Montesquieu's aims. And indeed, it does not. In *The Spirit of the Laws*, he takes up this theme of religion's power as a social restraint. Little time had elapsed from the 1748 publication of *Spirit* to Montesquieu's 1751-4 exchange with Warburton, and Montesquieu's views had not changed. In his first book on religion (Book 24), we find that he favors religious social restraint because he believes that when religious laws effectively repress antisocial vices, the severity of civil penalties may be diminished. "[T]he less repressive religion is," he reasons, "the more the civil laws should repress" (*EL* 5.34.14). For example, because religion in Japan proposes no heaven or hell, "the laws,

---

[49] This missing paragraph can be found in Warburton, *Unpublished Papers of Warburton,* 238. See also Watson, *The Life of William Warburton,* 425; Robert Shackleton, "Montesquieu's correspondence," 341-2. Translation is mine.

[50] William Warburton, *The Divine Legation of Moses* (London, 1846).

[51] Watson, *The Life of William Warburton,* 216.

[52] Warburton to Montesquieu, 9 Feb. 1754, in Nagel 3:1490-1.

in order to supplement [religion], have been made with extraordinary severity and have been executed with an extraordinary punctiliousness" (*EL* 4.24.14). In this connection, one must recall that milder, less repressive criminal laws are essential to the "liberty of the citizen" on Montesquieu's account (*EL* 2.12.1, 2, 4). Here in Book 24, his argument suggests that when vice is repressed through religious piety, free and moderate government can be itself: it can repress less. Social order is not simply the product of free and moderate government but is, to some extent, a precondition for the gentleness and mildness that characterize free and moderate government (*EL* 2.12.4–6; 1.6.2, 9, 12, 13). By contrast, societies with "no curb at all" must increase the severity and cruelty of civil penalties. This principle, which Lorenzo Bianchi aptly calls "a general rule of equilibrium" between these two elements (law and religion), is central to Montesquieu's science of moderate government.[53]

Montesquieu employs this rule of equilibrium to explain the harshness of Japanese government, nearly an archetype of despotism in *The Spirit of the Laws*.[54] He ties the severity of its laws to the impotence of its religion. Here only fear of penal cruelty motivates obedience. At the other end of this spectrum is England, whose mild civil penalties seem to require or assume the restraints of religion: "There is no nation that needs religion more than the English. Whoever is not afraid of being hanged has to be afraid of being damned," Montesquieu writes in the *Pensées* (*MP* 591). In societies devoid of such sources of restraint, the hangman tends to pick up the clergyman's slack. English religion helps to make English penal moderation possible. Just as in his exchange with Warburton, Montesquieu makes clear in the *Pensées* that the general rule of equilibrium applies to England.[55] Even in the free, commercial state of England, religious social restraint has not outlasted its usefulness. *La douceur du commerce* seems not to suffice for forming characters fit for political liberty.

---

[53] Bianchi, "Histoire et Nature," 300.

[54] Montesquieu avers, *"Au Japon les loix les plus cruelles les plus vigilantes qu'il y ait dans l'univers,"* in VF 7:791. See also Montesquieu, *Considerations*, ch. 22, 210.

[55] At a few places in his notebooks, Montesquieu suggests that the English are irreligious, but in each instance he is referring not to the great mass of the Englishmen but to elites – members of Parliament, learned men and regulars at the French embassy in London where he spent much time during his visit. Montesquieu, *"Notes sur l'Angleterre,"* in Nagel 3:292. See also *MP* 854 and 1052. According to the description of English life in Book 19, free men ordinarily gravitate toward either a single dominant religion or a multiplicity of sects (*EL* 3.19.27).

In fact, religious piety may actually mitigate some of the unwelcome elements of commercial mores. Montesquieu believed vibrant commercial activity was on balance a great political good, and this we explore carefully in Chapter 6. But commerce is not an unalloyed good from the point of view of one concerned with the formation of a people fit for free government. Even commercial mores have a dark side. "This spirit of commerce makes everything a matter of calculation," Montesquieu observes in the *Pensées*.[56] The commercial spirit is opposed both to injustice and to "those moral virtues that make it so that one does not always discuss one's own interests alone and that one can neglect them for those of others" (*EL* 4.20.2). These reflections on the ambivalent character of commercial mores represent more than an exercise in moral nostalgia. Along with real benefits, Montesquieu sees social and political risks in the spirit of commerce and calculation. The same commercial activities that breed just habits also tend to convince us that everything has its price. "[T]here is traffic [or trade] in all human activities and all moral virtues; the smallest things, those required by humanity, are done or given for money" (*EL* 4.20.2). Montesquieu adverts to the political dimension of this concern most clearly in the *Notes sur l'Angleterre*: "The English are no longer worthy of their liberty. They sell it to the King; and if the King gave it back to them, they would sell it to him again."[57] Ultimately, in the English case, Montesquieu concluded that this traffic in liberty would not doom the regime.[58] But it represents at least a potential threat to free government, as the spirit of commercial calculation inclines a people to put a price on their liberties.

Does Montesquieu offer a remedy for this problem? In Book 20, he states that there is traffic in all human activities in countries where the people are "affected *only* by the spirit of commerce" (*EL* 4.20.2). In a footnote, we read simply, "Holland." Here the spirit of commerce reigns alone. But the implication is that in some nations, other "spirits" or moral influences may temper the spirit of commerce, perhaps precisely in such a way as to mitigate, without eliminating, its unwelcome effects while preserving its benefits. One thinks here of Montesquieu's comments regarding the genius of the English in combining religion, commerce, and liberty. In a line that would later catch Max Weber's attention, he

---

[56] Montesquieu, *MP* 810.
[57] Montesquieu, "*Notes sur Angleterre*," in Nagel 3:288. The reference is to the civil list. See Stewart, "Montesquieu in England, 2002.
[58] See "Letter to Domville" in Montesquieu, *MP* 1960.

opines, "This is the people in the world who have best known how to take advantage of each of these three great things at the same time: religion, commerce, and liberty" *(EL* 4.20.7).[59] "These three things," he writes in an earlier draft of this chapter, "are extremely linked in the spirit of this nation" (VF 3:504). Does religion in England check and moderate the spirit of commerce? Perhaps among the infinite benefits of English religion is its tendency to temper the spirit of calculation by pointing toward higher considerations, thereby discouraging men from putting a price upon "all human activities" – including politics *(EL* 4.20.2).

JUDGING SHADOWS

Not every religion is compatible with liberal culture. Religion in England delivers infinite practical benefits because it has been cured of "destructive prejudices." It has shaken off all destructive prejudices, though not all prejudices simply. What remains is not the "religion of reason" or a Comtean *religion de l'humanité,* but religious faith, including a doctrine of life after death.[60] Indeed, in Book 24 of *Spirit,* where Montesquieu provides a sweeping account of the relative social utility of various doctrines and practices, one does not find a plan for recasting traditional religion in the narrow mold of Enlightenment rationalism. Rather, one finds Montesquieu subtly commending important emendations to religious practice and belief, while leaving much of the main tradition intact. He certainly does not insist that dogma and practice conform to the canons of reason, but rather that they be measured against the more modest canons of political utility. In this section, I will offer an account of this process as it unfolds in *The Spirit of the Laws* in order to clarify

---

[59] See Melvin Richter, *The Political Theory of Montesquieu* (Cambridge University Press, 1977), 100; Rahe *Montesquieu and the Logic of Liberty,* 231. Of this line, the Vatican's reviser declared, "[N]othing can be said more contrary to the Catholic faith." "Rapport de Mgr. Bottari," in VF 7:195. Other ecclesiastical critics agreed that Montesquieu surreptitiously favored Protestantism on account of its putative political benefits. See *"Suite des Nouvelles Ecclesiastiques,* 16 Octobre 1749," in VF 7:34. This interpretation of his work is not without merit. Consider, for example, *EL* 4.24.5 on the link between Protestantism and republicanism, as well as Usbek's praise of Protestantism's "infinite advantages" in *LP* 112–13, 22–3, 33, 115, 117.

[60] Contra Pangle, *Theological Basis,* 87, 103, 108. Here my view complements that of Céline Spector, "Le fait religieux dans *L'Esprit des lois,*" in *Montesquieu, L'État et la Religion,* ed. Jean Ehrard (Sofia, BG: Éditions Iztok-Zapad, 2007), 77. See also Sanford Kessler, "Religion and Liberalism in Montesquieu's *Persian Letters,*" *Polity* 15 (1983): 392.

what it means for religion to shed its destructive prejudices. In doing so, I hope to dissolve preemptively the objection that a religion cured of "destructive prejudices" is not really religion but Enlightenment rationalism by another name. At the same time, I aim to show what renders a religion compatible with the requirements of free and moderate regimes, on Montesquieu's view.

In the first two chapters of Book 24, Montesquieu argues that political men must judge religions on the basis of political utility alone. He suggests that for atheists like Pierre Bayle, this would require openness to the possibility that even if all religions are false, some or most are more politically serviceable than irreligion. For Christian thinkers, this would mean openness to the possibility that Christianity is not the singular or comprehensive political good and that non-Christian religions may be politically beneficial. "Just as one can judge among shadows those that are the least dark," so one can judge, among false religions and superstitions, the most politically advantageous (*EL* 4.24.1).

This approach clearly entails a distinction between the study of religion from the theological versus the political point of view. The latter is concerned not with theological truth but rather with the effectual truth about religion. In the words of Montesquieu's letter to Warburton, the political man seeks to discover the truth about the "practical good" (and harm) wrought by religion, whereas the theological study of religion seeks to discover "purely speculative truth." After the publication of *Spirit*, Montesquieu's Jansenist critics would allege that only an irreligious writer could embrace a method that treats "all religions, even the true one, as *une affaire de politique* " (VF 7:37). But in the *Défense de l'Esprit des lois*, Montesquieu would defend his separation of theology from political science, accusing his critics of "confound[ing] the various sciences" and imposing the standards and aims of theology upon a work of political science (VF 7:108).[61] Ironically, while the Jansenists may have been right to see this approach as suggestive of a certain disdain for theology, Montesquieu also deploys it against the "speculative" atheism of Bayle and Bolingbroke. Each had failed to treat religion from a strictly political point of view.

---

[61] Montesquieu may have been disingenuous when he suggested, in the *Défense*, that his political analysis of religion did not at least imply unorthodox theological views (e.g., his naturalistic account of religious belief). But this does not obscure the fact that there is, in principle, no contradiction in seeing religion as both false and politically indispensable.

Having established the autonomy of political science in the opening of Book 24, Montesquieu turns to a comparison of Christianity and Islam. He argues that Christianity's ethic of gentleness, the prohibition on polygamy, and the Christian prince's lack of timidity explain why moderate government is "better suited to" Christianity than it is to Islam (*EL* 4.24.3).[62] The cumulative effect of Montesquieu's account is to support the conventional view of his time that associated Islam with despotism and Christianity with humane government.[63] Not content with mere theory, Montesquieu offers a case study to provide empirical support for his claim. With its vast scale and hot climate, one would expect Ethiopia to be ruled despotically, as its neighbors are. Yet the Ethiopian government is not despotic. Why? "[T]he Christian religion has kept despotism from being established there and has carried the mores and laws of Europe to the middle of Africa," he explains. Holding constant other important variables (size, climate, terrain), Montesquieu suggests that Ethiopia's Christianity infuses its politics with a mildness alien to its Islamic neighbors.[64]

Following this discussion of Ethiopia, Christianity wins praise for its gift of "a certain political right in government and a certain right of nations in war, for which human nature can never be sufficiently grateful" (*EL* 4.24.3). Leaders are generally less harsh toward their people than in times past, and conquerors are less rapacious. As the chapter closes, Montesquieu seems to have offered a rather conventional account of the political superiority of Christianity over Islam. He returns to the theme in the next chapter. There, he notes that Christianity "softens the mores of men," unlike Islam, which "continues to act on men with the destructive spirit that founded it" (*EL* 4.24.4). A historical anecdote follows. We would expect it to be drawn either from the annals of Islamic politics or the history of Christian Europe. But oddly and, as we will see, portentously, Montesquieu closes these reflections with an illustration from ancient (pre-Christian and pre-Islamic) history:

---

[62] In *Spirit*, Montesquieu explains that Christian princes are "less timid and consequently less cruel." But in an earlier draft, Christian princes are "less bold and consequently less cruel" (VF 4:653). Timidity seems to have overcome Montesquieu.

[63] See Hichem Djaït, *Europe and Islam*, trans. Peter Heinegg (Berkeley: University of California Press, 1985), 11–29.

[64] See Montesquieu, "Quatrieme recueil: Voyage d'Ethiopie," in VF 16:360, where Montesquieu wonders, "*La religion chretiene fait en Ethiopie une espece de mélange des moeurs d'Europe avec les moeurs d'Asie et d'Afrique que donneroit le climat du pais?*"

The history of Sabaco, one of [Egypt's] pastoral kings, is remarkable. The god of Thebes appeared to him in a dream and ordered him to put to death all the princes of Egypt. He judged that the gods were no longer pleased for him to reign because they ordered him to do things so contrary to their usual will, and he withdrew into Ethiopia.

(*EL* 4.24.4)

The account is from the *Bibliotheca historica* of Diodorus Siculus. On its face, the point of this story is that a good king would never obey a religious command that contravened his understanding of basic decency and justice. How exactly does this tale advance Montesquieu's foregoing argument concerning Islam and Christianity? The apparent connection seems to be that ancient pagan spirituality sometimes encouraged cruelty just as Mohammedan religion sometimes encourages cruelty. But this seems a rather strained illustration, especially for an author in possession of a seemingly limitless fund of apt historical anecdotes.

Montesquieu closes this story of Sabaco's abdication by remarking that Sabaco "withdrew into Ethiopia." When we turn to the account of Diodorus (Montesquieu directs the reader there in a note), we learn that Egypt's King Sabaco was actually Ethiopian by birth. In his retelling of the story, Montesquieu makes a point of alerting the reader to this seemingly insignificant detail. Of course, Ethiopia has played an important role in his case for the political superiority of Christianity. "Ethiopian exceptionalism" provided empirical support for his argument about the political advantages of Christianity. And the two concurrent references (in chapters 3 and 4) are the only instances of the word "Ethiopia" in *Spirit* (cf. *EL* 5.26.7). Is the second mention of Ethiopia tied in any meaningful way to the first? In the passage Montesquieu cites, Diodorus provides additional details about Sabaco, Egypt's Ethiopian king. This mild king surpassed his Egyptian predecessors in "piety and uprightness," replacing the frequent use of capital punishment with more moderate penalties of forced labor.[65] If one credits Diodorus' later account of the Ethiopians (in Book 3 of the *Bibliotheca*), it seems that Sabaco merely acted in keeping with the ways of his people, whose kings were extremely mild toward their subjects.

Perhaps we can chalk up to coincidence Montesquieu's offhand, second mention of Ethiopia. But is it possible that Montesquieu recounts the story of Sabaco's dream and return to Ethiopia to remind his readers

---

[65] Diodorus Siculus, *The Library of History*, trans. Charles H. Oldfather (Cambridge, MA: Loeb Classical Library, 1933–1967), 3:5.

of the *pre-Christian* state of political life in Ethiopia as described by
Diodorus? If so, the implications would be unmistakable. This allusion
to the mildness and political moderation of pre-Christian Ethiopia (" ...
and he withdrew into Ethiopia") would be nothing less than an acknow-
ledgement that Ethiopian monarchy is not the fruit of Christianity alone.

When we turn to the *Pensées*, this hunch is solidly confirmed. In entries
1796-8, Montesquieu contemplates the nature of Ethiopian political
mores. Entry 1796 is entitled, "Character of the Laws in Certain Climes."
Here Montesquieu is working through the empirical puzzle presented by
Ethiopia's moderate government and blazing hot climate. Ethiopia has
"more mildness" in government than any other African country.[66] In
search of an explanation, he turns to ancient history and notes that two
Ethiopian kings of Egypt – Sabaco and Amasis before him – abolished the
death penalty in Egypt. This must have been the practice in Ethiopia itself,
he speculates. Montesquieu quotes Diodorus' account of the mild Ethiopian king who clipped off the noses of thieves to avoid imposing a capital
penalty for theft. These brief reflections on the mildness of the Ethiopian
kings of Egypt culminate in the following conclusion:

MILDNESS OF PUNISHMENTS IN ETHIOPIA. Mildness of punishments.
Hanging or beheading. Sometimes loss of property, with prohibition against
offering them anything to drink or eat, which makes them wander like beasts.
The Emperor often extends grace. He is just; he believes that the exact justice
meted out in this realm, and its administration, bring forth innocence in mores ...
Notice, then, that in Ethiopia, the mildness of mores has been from all time.[67]

Ethiopia's enigmatic moderation has pre-Christian roots, and the earlier
account of Ethiopian exceptionalism in *Spirit* now appears incomplete.
Montesquieu seems to have placed the story of Sabaco at the end of
4.24.4 to call attention to the fact that "in Ethiopia, the mildness of mores
has been from all time (emphasis added)." When we return to 4.24.3 with
this in mind, we notice the limited character of Montesquieu's claims. He
never ascribes to Christianity the full credit for Ethiopia's political moderation. Rather, he more modestly observes that, "the Christian religion
has kept despotism from being established there" (*EL* 4.24.3). Perhaps
Ethiopian Christianity has kept despotism out by reinforcing existing
mores. Christianity did not cause political moderation but rather helped
to preserve it. Montesquieu seems to wish to temper the conventional

---

[66] Montesquieu, *MP* 1796.
[67] Ibid., 1798. Montesquieu wrote entries 1796–8 during the preparation of *The Spirit of
the Laws*.

tendency to ascribe supreme political good to Christianity. On his view, it is superior to Islam from a political point of view. But the reader is to surmise that Christianity may not have been sufficiently potent to sustain moderate politics in Ethiopia if not for the people's immemorially mild character. I do not suggest that by his allusion to Sabaco, Montesquieu means to contradict the argument of chapter 3. But he does wish to qualify his valorization of Christianity and to suggest the limits of his case for its political superiority.

In the ensuing chapters, he turns away from the consideration of whole religions to discuss the political and social benefits of specific religious dogmas and practices. His primary concern in chapters 6–23 is to understand how these dogmas and practices shape a people, fitting them for various forms of political rule. First, Montesquieu seeks to undermine extravagant practical doctrines that stand at cross-purposes with basic natural duties, the performance of which is required to sustain political societies. Related to this first aim is a second, namely, to undermine religious dogmas and practices that habituate a people to passivity as opposed to action. Finally, Montesquieu attempts to identify dogmas and practices that most reliably incline a people toward morally decent living. His commitment to liberty and political moderation guides his analysis from the beginning, as he isolates features he considers needful for citizens of free and moderate regimes.

In chapters 6–9, Montesquieu attacks what he calls laws of perfection. His proximate targets are both Pierre Bayle *and* the monastic or ascetic spirit. Here again we see, with particular vividness, that Montesquieu's exertions are on two fronts, against both excessive criticism of religion as well as religious practices inconsistent with political health. Bayle was wrong to suggest that a "state formed by true Christians" could not continue to exist (*EL* 4.24.6). On Montesquieu's account, Bayle's error was to ignore the distinction between the precepts of religion and their counsels.[68] Bayle elided the distinction between counsels and precepts and so assumed that a state formed by true Christians would follow all the counsels. But when "the legislator, instead of giving laws, has given counsels, it is because he has seen that his counsels, if they were ordained like laws, would be contrary to the spirit of the laws" (*EL* 4.24.6). Montesquieu is not merely criticizing Bayle; he is criticizing the ascetic spirit that blurs the distinction between counsels of perfection and

---

[68] See Aquinas, *The Summa Theologiae*, II-II, q. 184, a. 4. Cf. Pangle, *Theological Basis*, 105–6; Schaub, "Of Believers and Barbarians," 235–6.

precepts of the gospel. The latter can be followed as laws by the great mass of people, but the observance of the former must be left to "those who love perfection" (*EL* 4.24.7).

Montesquieu opposes treating counsels of perfection as if they were laws. Often, these counsels of perfection require men to act against natural inclinations that help sustain the political community – namely, the inclinations to procreate and to defend the body. A more straightforward statement of this concern is found in chapter 7 of Book 26, entitled, "That one must not decide by the precepts of religion when those of natural law are in question." This chapter describes how the Abyssinians fast for fifty days at a time annually, and the Turks reliably attack the languishing devout on the fiftieth day.[69] Both the multiplication of religious laws and the transformation of counsels into laws threaten to run up against our obligations under the natural law. Moreover, since violating laws of perfection comes so naturally to us, an "infinity" of auxiliary laws must be imposed to keep the faithful from breaking the laws of perfection (*EL* 4.24.7). Thus even when laws of perfection do not conflict with natural law obligations, these auxiliary regulations "tire the society" and distract from simpler and more basic duties.[70]

Next Montesquieu turns to the problem of excessive passivity in religions. The positive counterexample is the Stoic sect, which he glibly incorporates into his treatment of religion (*EL* 4.24.10). Montesquieu

---

[69] St. Basil the Great, St. Jerome, and St. Francis de Sales (whose popular works Montesquieu owned) also criticized excessive fasting as a hindrance to labor and service. See Francis de Sales, *Introduction to the Devout Life* (New York: Vintage Books, 2002), ch. 23; and M. D. Peterson, "Fasting: Eastern Christian," in *Encyclopedia of Monasticism* (Chicago: Fitzroy Dearborn Publishers, 2000), vol. 1, 469.

[70] Montesquieu identifies the Peguans, the Essenes, and the Stoics as "religious" groups that best exemplify this emphasis on the basic duties of life rather than more demanding works of devotion (*EL* 4.24.8–10). In the original and bolder version of his discussion of the Essenes, Montesquieu contrasts them with "our monks," who tend to aim too high (*VF* 4: 659). A more elaborate critique of excessively demanding religious regulations appears in *LP* 27, 44, 75, 81. In the eighty-first letter, Usbek remarks that if he could only heed the mere voice of justice in his mind, he would be the "best of men." Natural reason, apart from revealed religion, would suffice to show him his duties. However, Usbek notes that "justice raises her voice, but she has difficulty making herself heard amid the tumult of the passions." Even if Montesquieu agreed with Usbek's assertion that obedience to the mind's "dictates of justice" would suffice to make us the best of men, this tells us little about what is necessary to produce such obedience in the great mass of men. Schaub aptly concludes that, on Montesquieu's view, "[T]he content of natural equity, simple though it is, remains abstruse and, even when promulgated, too abstract to oblige ordinary men." Schaub, "Of Believers and Barbarians," 238. See also Lowenthal, "Book I of Montesquieu's *The Spirit of the Laws*," 489n.14.

admires the sociability and orientation toward action inspired by Stoic philosophy. The Stoics were "born for society," and they believed that "their destiny was to work for it." The common thread running through Montesquieu's earlier critique of laws of perfection and his praise of the Stoics is his conviction that religious laws must not run counter to man's natural ends. This is evident in the next chapter, where he criticizes overly contemplative religions: "Men, being made to preserve, feed and clothe themselves, and to do all the things done in society, religion should not give them an overly contemplative life" (*EL* 4.24.11). (The manuscript originally had men "being made for action" (VF 4:659).) Like religious laws of perfection, overly contemplative religions are at cross-purposes with the natural ends of man and society. The Mohammedan practice of praying five times daily leads Muslims to become "speculative by habit." A speculative people turns its eyes away from "all that belongs to this world" (*EL* 4.24.11). For this reason, in chapter 12, Montesquieu insists that penances should come in the form of works rather than prayers. His fear is that excessively speculative habits will inevitably lead to political detachment, indifference, and passivity as opposed to the impatient vigilance necessary for a free people.[71] Clearly, Montesquieu's critique of Mohammedanism touches elements of Christianity.

Just as Montesquieu's opposition to overly contemplative religious inclinations and excessively demanding religious rules stems from his concern with supporting free and moderate government, so his interest in religion as a bridle upon men derives from his aversion to despotism. As we recall, all things being equal, religions capable of curbing men's passions are preferable because they free the state to repress less (*EL* 4.24.14). Following his discussion of contemplative religion in chapters 10–12, Montesquieu proceeds to consider the sources of religion's power to restrain. He criticizes a wide range of dogmas and practices that he regards as corrosive of religion's moral force. After voicing support for active penances in 4.24.12, he argues that while a religion may teach that all crimes are expiable, it must make men feel that an entire life of injustice may not be expiable (*EL* 4.24.13). Men must sense that grace has some limit. Religions must not teach the "dogma of the necessity of human actions" nor the "Mohammedan dogma of predestination;" men must believe themselves to be responsible agents (*EL* 4.24.14; *MP* 1945).

---

[71] Montesquieu once encouraged Bible translator Jacob Vernet to keep the language of his translation "male and vigorous," like Michelangelo's *David*. Quoted in Adams, *The Huguenots and French Opinion*, 72.

Religions also must not teach that simple amoral rituals, such as dying on the banks of the Ganges, can expunge penalties in the next life. Religious dogmas ought not to engender in men an absolute assurance that they will enjoy eternal rewards, for this compromises the power of religious laws. Hope of blessedness must be balanced by fear of damnation. Taken together, these views suggest that a politically useful religion will preserve a place for human responsibility and fear of punishment in the afterlife. Such features enhance a religion's capacity to restrain.

To be sure, Montesquieu's critical analysis reaches a number of doctrines, practices, and attitudes associated with the Christian tradition. But one can hardly say that a religion approximating the requirements of social utility as he outlines them must simply be a "religion of reason" or a "natural religion." That he makes utility rather than theological orthodoxy his standard is beyond dispute. But the result is not a narrowly rationalist creed; Montesquieu does not aim at the "inanition of irrational religious belief."[72] Major elements of traditional religious faith may remain even after religion's "destructive prejudices" are removed. This is consistent with what we have seen in Montesquieu's exchange with Warburton.

All of this raises an important final question. While Montesquieu did not believe the rationalization of European religion was necessary to make religion useful, he nonetheless thought certain changes desirable, as I have suggested earlier. What was the plan for effectuating these changes or reinforcing the reforms already in place? Insight into Montesquieu's thinking emerges from one of his more cryptic criticisms of Lord Bolingbroke in the letter to Warburton. Bolingbroke's work is full of energy, Montesquieu observes, but this polemical philosopher errs in always employing his energy "against things" rather than "to depict things [*a peindre les choses*]."[73] Montesquieu's opposition of critique to depiction is striking. What would it mean to depict things as a substitute for employing oneself against them? I believe we see in Montesquieu's own treatment of religion an example of this approach. Rather than attacking the elements of Catholicism and Protestantism that are inconsistent with the requirements of social utility, he depicts Christianity as consistent with these requirements, often by his very silences.[74] It is

---

[72] Pangle, *Theological Basis*, 108.

[73] Montesquieu to Warburton, Mai 1754, in Nagel 3:1509.

[74] Rasmussen, *The Pragmatic Enlightenment*, 176–7, sees Montesquieu as engaged in "subtle, unobtrusive acts of reinterpretation" throughout his depiction of Christianity.

Mohammedanism (not Jansenism or Calvinism) that tempts men toward fatalism (*EL* 4.24.14). It is the religion of Foë (not monastic Christianity) that makes men excessively passive (*EL* 4.24.11). It is the Hindus (not Catholics) who impose morally dangerous restrictions regarding indifferent things (*EL* 4.24.14). Christianity always makes the right distinctions between counsels and precepts; it teaches gentleness rather than severity; its doctrine of bodily resurrection is just the right medicine (*EL* 4.24.6, 3, 9). Instead of attacking religion in order to destroy it, one must depict it as the thing one wishes it to be in order to amend it and to fortify its reforms. In his depiction of religion in Book 24, Montesquieu seeks to accomplish what bare-knuckled critique, in the pugnacious mode of Bolingbroke, could not achieve.

CONCLUSION

Among the ranks of the eighteenth-century *philosophes*, there were no doubt many who championed "the dream of the radical Enlightenment" understood as "the progress of trade and the regress of positive religion."[75] Montesquieu was not among them. He was not especially impatient of the human condition and did not long for a world in which "God's voice gradually ceases to be heard by human beings."[76] While he understood and condemned the past and ongoing abuses of religion in Europe, he also looked ahead to the potential political costs of silencing revealed religion. He therefore did not encourage the elimination of traditional religious piety. He did not welcome commerce as an engine of secularization, and more fundamentally, he did not see widespread irreligion as a propitious condition for political liberty and moderation. Even in the commercial, free state of England, Montesquieu counted popular religious faith – and not merely "the religion of reason" – an important element of liberal culture, as it was a source of moral restraint that freed the state to govern mildly.

But this account does not exhaust Montesquieu's treatment of the relationship between religion and commerce in the formation of liberal culture. Although commerce is not the solvent of religion, Montesquieu does observe in modern commercial activity a salutary tendency to weaken the springs of religious intolerance without directly modifying religious doctrine and practice. The "*esprit de tolérance*" is an essential

[75] Strauss, *Seminar on Montesquieu II*, 1966.   [76] Pangle, *Theological Basis*, 103.

element of liberal culture on Montesquieu's view, for formal legal requirements of toleration are ultimately a dead letter without a foundation in
tolerant mores (VF 8:92). In the cultivation of such a tolerant spirit, and
not in the elimination of revealed religion, Montesquieu locates the great
contribution of modern commerce to the formation of a religious climate
conducive to human liberty. To this prospect of commercial tolerance we
must now turn.

6

"The Spirit of Tolerance and Gentleness"

Historians of early modern Europe now commonly distinguish tolerance from toleration. Toleration often designates government policies of religious liberty, while tolerance "refers to interpersonal attitudes or social practices exercised informally on a day-to-day level."[1] The effort to separate the two concepts stems from the observation that the growth of religious freedom in early modern Europe cannot be attributed solely to government policies but must also be understood as dependent upon the shifting attitudes and ways of thought among a people. In a similar vein, within the discipline of political theory, Andrew R. Murphy has encouraged the maintenance of a distinction between toleration as a set of legal and political practices, and tolerance as a set of attitudes.[2] Among other benefits, this distinction provides a language to express the simple – and Montesquieuian – observation that in the absence of mores of tolerance, formal legal regimes of toleration may fail us.

Few early modern theorists of toleration (in the foregoing sense) were more intensely concerned with the problem of locating sources of

---

[1] Scott Sowerby, "Tolerance and Toleration in Early Modern England," in *A Lively Experiment*, eds. Chris Beneke and Christopher S. Grenda (Lanham, MD: Rowman & Littlefield, 2015), 53; Stuart B. Schwartz, *All Can Be Saved: Religious Tolerance and Salvation in the Iberian Atlantic World* (New Haven, CT: Yale University Press, 2008), 6; Christopher Grasso, "The Boundaries of Toleration and Tolerance: Religious Infidelity in the Early American Republic," in *The First Prejudice: Religious Tolerance and Intolerance in Early America*, eds. Chris Beneke and Christopher S. Grenda (Philadelphia: University of Pennsylvania Press, 2011), 287.

[2] Andrew R. Murphy, "Tolerance, Toleration, and the Liberal Tradition," *Polity* 29 (1997): 595–602.

tolerance (also in the foregoing sense) than was Montesquieu.[3] He addresses both species of *tolerantia*, but he is more deeply engaged in understanding the cultural and sentimental sources of interpersonal tolerance – an element of a liberal culture – than in fashioning new philosophical arguments against state persecution.

As we have seen, *The Spirit of the Laws* certainly advances a subtle case for state policies of toleration – now pragmatic, now theoretical, now sentimental. Montesquieu endorses and reframes the basic elements of Locke's theory of toleration, and he is equally at ease reprising the *politique* case against state-sponsored persecution (*EL* 2.12.4, 5.25.9). But he understood the fragility of a regime of legal toleration not supported by mores of tolerance, and he was not sanguine about the promise of intellectual argument to strike deep roots in the soil of national consciousness. "When it is a question of proving such clear things," he laments, "one is sure not to convince" (*EL* 5.25.14). Though he did not despair of changing men, it would require means deeper and subtler than "convincing."[4] It is difficult, as he theorizes in Book 19, to "stamp spirits" with "something intellectual" (*EL* 3.19.17). But spirits must be stamped. Thus Montesquieu's sights were not mainly trained on formulating new philosophical arguments for toleration, but rather on uncovering the "spiritual" (i.e., cultural and sentimental) sources of tolerance.

From at least the time he read his *Dissertation on the Policy of the Romans in Religion* (1716) before the Bordeaux Academy, until he penned his late *Mémoire sur le silence à imposer sur la Constitution* (1753–4), Montesquieu evinced an interest in this practical problem of forming a culture of tolerance, or an *"esprit de tolérance"* as he puts it the *Dissertation* (VF 8:92). Three models of tolerant culture caught Montesquieu's analytical eye his reflections on this problem. These models include what we may call Roman, barbarian, and commercial tolerance. The first two are historical, while the third is a phenomenon

---

[3] Of course, this particular linguistic distinction was not available to Montesquieu in French. But he certainly understood the distinction conceptually. See Antonio Carlos Dos Santos, "L'intolérance dans la Querelle de *L'Esprit des lois*," in *Montesquieu, Oeuvre ouverte? (1748–1755): Actes du colloque de Bordeaux, 6–8 décembre 2001*, ed. Catherine Larrère (Napoli: Liguori Editore, 2005), 136–7; Rainer Forst, *Toleration in Conflict: Past and Present* (Cambridge University Press, 2013), 269–74.

[4] See Sylvana Tomaselli, "Intolerance, the Virtue of Princes and Radicals," in *Toleration in Enlightenment Europe*, eds. Ole Peter Grell and Roy Porter (Cambridge University Press, 2000), who suggests that Montesquieu indulged "very limited expectations of human nature becoming more tolerant" (94).

"we see every day" (*EL* 4.20.1). By considering Montesquieu's appraisal of the historical models, we are better prepared to understand not only the depth of his long-standing concern with finding sources of a spirit of tolerance, but also why he finally came to regard modern commerce as the most promising and suitable means of reviving the spirit of tolerance he had first admiringly observed in his study of Rome. This spirit of tolerance, so crucial to liberal culture, appears not as a universal feature of human nature, but rather as a historical achievement, if initially an accidental one.

ROMAN TOLERANCE

As an early modern proponent of religious toleration, Pierre Bayle could not help but note with relish the conspicuous absence of religious wars in the classical world prior to the rise of Christianity. This observation armed Bayle with an empirical refutation of writers who argued that the extension of religious liberty guaranteed perpetual religious war. As Bayle explains, "I don't remember [that] I have ever read of a Religious War among the Pagans ... [A]s for Wars undertaken with a design of compelling one Nation to the Religion of another, I find not the least mention of any such in the Heathen Authors."[5] He concludes that intolerance rather than religious diversity must be the cause of religious war, "the Source of Confusion and Squabble."[6] Three decades after Bayle's work, Montesquieu would turn to the ancient Roman example, similarly struck by the glaring contrast between antique Rome and Christian Europe on this point.[7] Montesquieu's aim was not simply to establish the compatibility of toleration and civic peace, but also to understand the sources of the tolerant mores among the Romans, perhaps as a model for modern Europe.

A twenty-seven-year-old Montesquieu takes up this question in his *Dissertation on the Policy of the Romans in Religion* (1716), his first address to the Academy of Bordeaux.[8] The mere fact that this, his first

---

[5] Pierre Bayle, *A Philosophical Commentary on These Words of the Gospel, Luke 14.23, 'Compel Them to Come In, That My House May Be Full'*, eds. John Kilcullen and Chandran Kukathas (Indianapolis: Liberty Fund, 2005), 57.

[6] Bayle, *Philosophical Commentary*, 57.

[7] For a discussion of Bayle's influence on Montesquieu, see Robert Shackleton, "Bayle and Montesquieu," in *Pierre Bayle, le philosophe de Rotterdam*, ed. P. Dibon (Amsterdam: Elsevier, 1959), 142–9.

[8] The work was published posthumously in 1796.

serious political essay, treats the relationship of religion to politics – and specifically, the sources of tolerance – signals the significance of this concern in Montesquieu's nascent political thought. As several scholars have noted, the work's main argument bears the marks of Machiavelli's influence.[9] The principal purpose of Roman religion, Montesquieu contends, was political; its popular form was an illusion manufactured by Rome's early kings and perfected in use by its ruling elites. The intended effect was to amaze the people, to make them marvel and fear, and so to obey. The ridiculous character of the religion, exemplified in going to war based on the appetite of chickens, had the happy consequence of only increasing the wonder of the credulous many while making the people's religion unbelievable to the wiser elites. Unconstrained by sincere belief in the people's religion, the elites remained free to use its rites for maximal political advantage.

Having fashioned this Machiavellian framework, Montesquieu turns to a question absent from Machiavelli's analysis of Rome – Roman religious toleration and its theological underpinnings. Drawing on the work of Cambridge Platonist Ralph Cudworth, he notes that while Roman elites did not believe in the gods of the pantheon, they were not atheists. Rather they were believers in a "supreme deity" in whom the people's gods were a "mere participation" (VF 8:91).[10] On their view, it is not true, strictly speaking, that a divine being called Venus gave good fortune; but to worship Venus is merely to worship the supreme deity "as she is susceptible to every creation" (VF 8:92). Likewise, it is not true that the sun is a divine being. But to worship the Unconquered Sun is to worship the supreme deity as he animates plant life. Indeed God participates in "everything worldly": "he is Ceres on earth, and Neptune on the waters" (VF 8:91). Montesquieu's account of this view suggests that Roman theism, or pantheism, represented an amalgam of Platonic and Stoic theologies. On the Platonic version – Montesquieu refers to it as the "dogma of the world's soul" – God is the soul of the universe. In the Stoic account, God is identified with the immanent rational principle of the universe that structures all inert matter.[11] The practical effect of this

---

[9] Peter Gay, *The Enlightenment*, 285; Paul A. Rahe, "Introduction" in *Machiavelli's Liberal Republican Legacy*, ed. Paul A. Rahe (Cambridge University Press, 2006), xxvi.

[10] Here Montesquieu may be relying on Bayle's discussion of Cudworth in his *Continuation des pensées diverses* (H. Uytwerf, 1722), §21. See VF 8:92, n. 32.

[11] See Catherine Larrère, "Montesquieu et le stoïcisme," in *Stoïcisme antique et droit naturel moderne*, ed. Jean Terrel (Bordeaux: Presses Universitaires de Bordeaux, 2003), 59–84.

theology is to allow the patricians to respect, not without some condescension, the piety of the many while recognizing the superstitious character of their practices.

It appears at first that this pantheism was the preserve of the elites, but then Montesquieu adds that this doctrine was "almost universally received" in the pagan world (VF 8:92). No doubt he means to suggest that while the doctrine was received in sophisticated philosophical form by elites, it came down to the many in pedestrian and inarticulate forms that allowed pagan worshippers to see the divine in all things and therefore to remain open and even congenial toward diverse cults of worship. "As each part of the universe was seen as a living member in which this soul was widespread, it seemed one was permitted to adore all of the parties equally."[12] In his search for the sources of Roman tolerance, Montesquieu has come ashore: "Here was born the spirit of tolerance and gentleness [*esprit de tolérance & de douceur*] that ruled in the pagan world."[13] This spirit of tolerance is not begrudging, nor is it merely prudential.[14] It arises fundamentally from an acceptance of nearly every cult as a site of divine worship. Despite the significant differences in religious understanding between plebeian and patrician that occupy Montesquieu in the early sections of the *Dissertation*, this "spirit of tolerance" is common to both classes.

The Roman spirit of tolerance was so robust that it operated not only within the existing empire but also in territories freshly conquered. Triumphant Roman armies did not purge foreign gods and cults but rather submitted to the gods of conquered peoples (VF 8:97). Romans granted foreign gods legal residency, as Montesquieu puts it, identifying these deities with gods already ensconced in the Roman pantheon: Zeus is Jupiter, and so on. Thus the Romans neither waged religious wars nor suffered intestine religious conflicts. Montesquieu's analysis invites readers to consider the remarkable fact that, for all the blood the Romans shed in the four corners of the earth, they achieved a robust pattern of toleration, grounded neither upon ethical argument nor upon a *modus vivendi* compromise, but rather upon the mores and beliefs of the populace.

---

[12] VF 8:92.

[13] VF 8:92. Here we should note the virtual identification of *la douceur* with *la tolérance*, an important point when we arrive at Montesquieu's treatment of *doux commerce* later in the chapter.

[14] Montesquieu speaks not simply of tolerance but of the *esprit* of tolerance, employing a term that of course becomes important to his later social thought. The *esprit* of tolerance, unlike the mere practice of toleration, is a feature of the character or habits of the people.

Before Montesquieu, Bayle had cited Egyptian religion as the one exception to this hypothesis of pagan tolerance. Montesquieu similarly notes that an early exception to Roman tolerance was Roman persecution of Egyptian religion. The Romans forbade Egyptian cults, and the Senate ordered the temples of Isis and Serapis destroyed. Indeed, as Montesquieu reports in an earlier draft of the *Dissertation*, the Roman consul Aemilius Paullus personally took an axe to the Egyptian temples.[15] But paradoxically, he maintains that Roman hostility toward these cults was not an aberration from, but rather the fruit of, the Romans' tolerant *esprit*. What they abhorred in Egyptian religion was in fact its intolerant spirit: "[I]t wanted to rule alone, and to base itself upon the ruins of others; such that the spirit of gentleness and peace that ruled among the Romans was the veritable cause of the war they relentlessly waged" (VF 8:93). When the Romans encountered Jews and Christians, they concluded that these Near Eastern cults were branches of Egyptian religion and so treated them with similar roughness.[16] Montesquieu implies that the reason the Romans confused Christianity and Judaism with the Egyptian religion was that each shared the exclusivist character of Egyptian religion (VF 8:93–94).[17] These religions' common goal of exclusive and total loyalty accounted for the Roman persecution of all three.[18] Each was incompatible with the "dogma of the world's soul" and thus threatened to poison the wellspring of Roman tolerance.

Montesquieu's early reflections on the Roman spirit of tolerance have led some to suppose that he believed the Roman model "should become a model for modern societies seeking to free themselves from the yoke of

[15] VF 8:93. Montesquieu cites the account in the *Memorable Deeds* of Valerius Maximus: "The Senate decided that the temples of Isis and Serapis should be demolished, but none of the workers dared to touch the temples. The consul Lucius Aemilius Paullus took off his official striped toga, grabbed an axe, and smashed the doors of that temple." Valerius Maximus, *Memorable Deeds*, trans. Henry John Walker (Indianapolis: Hackett Publishing Company, 2004), 1.3.4.

[16] In the same chapter of the *Memorable Deeds* that recounts the story of Lucius Aemilius and the Egyptian temples, Valerius Maximus writes that the Jews "had tried to pass their religion on to the Romans" (Ibid., 1.3.3).

[17] Cf. Montesquieu, *Considerations*, 148–9.

[18] In *The Spirit of the Laws*, Montesquieu asserts that, "there are scarcely any but intolerant religions that are greatly zealous to establish themselves elsewhere, for a religion that can tolerate others scarcely thinks of its propagation" (EL 5.25.10). Here Montesquieu reasons much like his Romans.

Christianity."[19] This is a reasonable inference regarding Montesquieu's thinking on the subject in 1716. But there is good reason to conclude that just as Montesquieu came to regard Roman Erastianism as inapt for modern states, so he came to see that Rome could not provide a blueprint for the task of cultivating mores of tolerance in modern Europe.[20]

Thirty-five years after he delivered his *Dissertation*, a mature Montesquieu would argue in his *Mémoire* that religious liberty in Europe could never be established on the basis of what he calls "*tolérance interieure,*" a species of tolerance that mirrors the Roman model (VF 9:529).[21] In the *Mémoire*, written in the context of continued persecutions of the Jansenists in France and in response to controversy over the papal bull *Unigenitus* (1713), the reader learns that great evils have arisen from our tendency to confound the "very distinct ideas" of internal and external tolerance (VF 9:529). Montesquieu's "external tolerance" is roughly equivalent to what we have earlier called toleration – the practice of permitting and protecting diverse forms of religious observance. But internal tolerance is a "kind of approbation," an inner acceptance and approval of the sect in question (VF 9:530). As Montesquieu explains,

> Everyone knows that the Roman Catholic religion does not in any way allow for internal toleration. It does not admit of any internal sect; according to its own principles, it is the only vehicle of salvation so it is unable to tolerate any competing internal sect where salvation would be deemed impossible.
>
> (VF 9:530)

To tolerate internally is to affirm that the sect is a genuine locus of the divine worship; it is to tolerate the sect not only in the public domain, but also to

---

[19] Guy G. Stroumsa, *A New Science: The Discovery of Religion in the Age of Reason* (Cambridge, MA: Harvard University Press, 2010), 155. Oscar Kenshur, *Dilemmas of Enlightenment* (Berkeley: University of California Press, 1993) contrasts "Montesquieu's valorization of Roman religious politics" with Hume's valorization of Dutch and English toleration. But as this chapter shows, the Dutch and English model of tolerance replaces the Roman model in Montesquieu's later work.

[20] As Rebecca E. Kingston argues, Montesquieu concluded that while the Erastianism of the Roman polity was an admirable bulwark against clericalism, it would threaten the balance of power in the French monarchy and other continental monarchies, as independent ecclesiastical institutions provided a check upon the crown. Rebecca E. Kingston, "Religion," in *Dictionnaire Montesquieu*, ed. Catherine Volpilhac-Auger, http://diction naire-montesquieu.ens-lyon.fr.

[21] Larrère recognizes the same parallel between "internal toleration" in the *Mémoire* and Roman tolerance in the *Dissertation*. On this basis and with the benefit of hindsight, she concludes that one should not regard the *Dissertation* as a "militant call or polemic in favor of natural religion" in the eighteenth century. Larrère, "Montesquieu et le stoïcisme," 69–70.

approve of the sect in the tribunal of one's conscience. Roman tolerance consisted in just such affirmation or approval. In context, Montesquieu is writing of the dispute over Jansenism in France, and so he speaks of Roman Catholicism, but the observation extends to all mainstream forms of Christianity: one cannot give inner approbation to other religions. By contrast, external tolerance – the practice of permitting multiple sects – does not demand interior approval. If the ideas of external and internal tolerance can be kept distinct, the Christian prince can tolerate Jansenists and others without being suspected of tolerating them internally. Montesquieu puts words in the mouths of the Christian prince who grasps this distinction: "'My conscience tells me not to approve in my heart those who think differently from me; but my conscience also tells me that there are circumstances when it is my duty to tolerate them externally'" (VF 9:531).[22] A Christian prince may grant external toleration; he may protect minority sects; but this practice cannot normally derive from inner approval as it had among the Romans.

In the absence of internal tolerance, what might motivate a Christian magistrate to extend external toleration to a sect? Montesquieu alludes to his *politique* argument (*EL* 5.25.9), reminding the reader that *"le salut de l'état est la supreme loi"* – a Roman maxim to replace the Romans' internal toleration (VF 9:531).[23] But it is a poor replacement, for while the general aims of civic peace and political stability may move rulers to grant official toleration, those aims may not similarly motivate a private man to tolerate his neighbor. Surveying the argument of the *Mémoire*, Larrère concludes that with the Stoic or Roman basis of toleration unavailable to modern Christians, Montesquieu simply resigns himself to the hard reality that modern toleration must necessarily be "imposed by political power."[24] But a broader view of Montesquieu's writings on

---

[22] Montesquieu explains that when a Catholic ruler practices external toleration, it is as if he were saying, "'I have been granted power by God to maintain peace in my state; to prevent assassinations, murders, rapes; to ensure that my subjects do not destroy one another; to ensure they live peacefully: it is necessary then that my laws be such, in particular circumstances, that they do not diverge from this objective. My conscience tells me not to approve in my heart those who think differently from me; but my conscience also tells me that there are circumstances when it is my duty to tolerate them externally." VF 9:530–1.

[23] See Cicero, *De legibus*, 3.3.8.

[24] Larrère, "Montesquieu et le stoïcisme," 69–70. By contrast, Dos Santos notes Montesquieu cannot be fully satisfied with external toleration by the state in the absence of a "personal motivation" among the people to tolerate their neighbors. Though Montesquieu fails to identify the source of such personal motivation in the *Mémoire*, he

toleration shows that he understood well the limitations of the *politique* approach and that, characteristic of his insistence on the importance of mores, he never looked to state power alone to secure a general pattern of interpersonal tolerance. His recognition of the unsuitability of the Roman model does not keep him from looking elsewhere for sources of an *esprit de tolérance* more reliable than the black letter of law and the gray on gray of philosophy.

BARBARIAN TOLERANCE

Montesquieu's reflections on Roman tolerance left him convinced that religious diversity was not a sufficient condition for religious war; it alerted him to the possibility of civic peace amidst religious diversity through a spirit of tolerance. Five years after he delivered his *Dissertation*, he reasserts this possibility through Usbek in *Persian Letters* (*LP* 83), where we learn that religious conflict is caused not by the multiplicity of sects but rather by the "*esprit d'intolérance*," a spirit Usbek ties to Egyptian, Jewish, Christian, and Muslim religions.[25] But *Persian Letters* does not go beyond this affirmation to identify the sources of the spirit of tolerance. Only later, in *The Spirit of the Laws*, does Montesquieu identify alternatives to the Roman culture of tolerance.

Conspicuously absent in *Spirit* is any mention of Roman tolerance. Instead we find two new models of tolerant culture: the barbarian and the commercial. Montesquieu considers the case of barbarian tolerance in his analysis of the "motives of attachment" to religion (*EL* 5.25.2).[26] It is impossible to regard this analysis of religious attachment as a piece of disinterested sociology of religion, for as we saw in the last chapter, it culminates in Montesquieu's memorable call to disavow violent methods of detaching men from religion; such methods are impractical, cruel, and unchristian (*EL* 5.25.12–13). We soon realize that in the course of examining motives for attachment to religion, Montesquieu is also

---

nevertheless understands the need to cultivate "*la tolérance individuelle, particularisée, pour que la tolérance collective puisse exister.*" Dos Santos, "L'intolérance dans la Querelle," 136–7.

[25] In fact, a multiplicity of religions is on balance advantageous to the state as religious competition puts every man "on his guard, fearful of doing something that would dishonor his own side and expose it to the unpardonable scorn and criticisms of the adversary" (*LP* 83).

[26] See Schaub, "Of Believers and Barbarians," 228, on "Tartar tolerance."

considering motives for tolerance and intolerance – the very question that occupied him in his youthful address to the Academy many years earlier.

The relevant discussion, found in Book 25 of *Spirit*, commences with the unremarkable observation that not all religions possess the same power to engender deep devotion in men. Some religions, such as idolatrous ones, may gain many adherents but are nevertheless unable to sink deep roots into the human heart. These religions will be a mile wide but an inch deep, for "we are exceedingly drawn to idolatry, and nevertheless we are not strongly attached to idolatrous religions" (*EL* 5.25.2). Montesquieu deploys a naturalistic method to explain such variation in attachment across different religions. He argues that the intensity of our attachment to various religions "depends largely on how they fit into men's way of thinking and feeling" (*EL* 5.25.2). Montesquieu is aware that religion itself can decisively shape a man's "way of thinking and feeling." Moreover, he understands that a religion's ability to take root will also depend upon regime type, law, and custom. But here he uncharacteristically brackets those causes and examines only the natural pathways by which religion may penetrate the human heart.

Religion does not typically enter through the front door: Montesquieu invokes no natural religious impulse or *sensus dei* to explain religious attachment. Rather, religion enters the human heart through the mundane and even low points of our nature. To engage the affections and fidelity of men, religions must appeal not only to our hope – the only elevated motive Montesquieu mentions – but also to our vanity, our self-satisfaction, our susceptibility to flattery, our penchant for the tactile, and our fears (*EL* 5.25.2–3). As Montesquieu catalogs each of these motives, it becomes clear that he is at the same time sketching a natural history of religious belief.

The early religions are those of nomadic hunters, herders, and raiders. Their simple religions lack temples, elaborate ceremony, lavish externals, and permanent priesthoods. But with the advent of agriculture, men begin to dwell in fixed places and erect houses for themselves and their gods. As temples arise, agricultural peoples become more attached to their religion, as they now have a fixed site "where they can worship [their god] and go to seek him in their fears and their hopes" (*EL* 5.25.3). Men are "exceedingly drawn to hope and fear," and temples provide a focal point for both passions. With the advent of temples, religious practices and ceremonies become more onerous, growing in number and complexity. This deepens religious attachment further still, for men are "attached to things that continually occupy them," and they "love in religion everything that presumes an effort" (*EL* 5.25.2, 4). Predictably, a priesthood arises to supervise increasingly complex religious practices of a more advanced civilization; "peoples without priests are usually barbarians" (5.25.4). Men warm to their sect further still as they feel "flattered" by the increasing magnificence in the "externals of worship" that a priesthood makes possible. The trend is clear: all else being equal, religion in more advanced civilizations gains a stronger hold upon the affections of men.

Montesquieu also suggests that the development of civilization generally leads away from idolatry and toward more spiritual conceptions of the divinity. "We regard idolatry as the religion of coarse peoples," he observes (5.25.2). Paradoxically, on his account, men are most easily drawn to idolatrous religions, but they are most attached to non-idolatrous, spiritual religions. As a physical being (*EL* 1.1.1), man finds attractive the sensory experience of god available in idolatrous religion; but spiritual religion attaches him more permanently because it appeals to his vanity, a passion with roots apparently deeper than our merely sensory passions. Adherents of spiritual religions congratulate themselves on their intelligence in worshipping an invisible deity (*EL* 5.25.2), and so vanity fuels fidelity to the sect.

In the midst of this complex discussion of both the natural history of religion and the causes of religious attachment, Montesquieu broaches once again the problem of the *esprit de tolérance*. Although Genghis Khan is an unlikely poster boy for religious toleration, Montesquieu reminds the reader of the spirit of tolerance that prevailed in the religiously diverse Tatar-Mongol empire under Khan. In a passage reminiscent of the *Dissertation*'s account of the Roman consul who takes an axe to an Egyptian temple, Montesquieu recounts how Khan once entered a mosque and cast the Koran under his horses' hooves (*EL* 5.25.4, n.5). He explains,

Genghis Khan showed ... great scorn for mosques. This prince interrogated Mohammedans; he approved all their dogmas, except the one on the necessity of going to Mecca; he could not understand that one could not worship god everywhere. As the Tartars did not live in houses, they did not know of temples.

Peoples who have no temples have little attachment to their religion: this is why the Tartars have always been so tolerant, why the barbarian peoples who conquered the Roman empire did not hesitate for a moment to embrace Christianity, why the savages of America are so little attached to their own religion, and why, since our missionaries have had them build churches, they have so much zeal for ours.

(*EL* 5.25.4)

Like Montesquieu's Roman consul confronting the cult of Isis, Khan was hostile to Islam not because he was intolerant, but because he detested the exclusivism represented by the mosque and the Hajj. Montesquieu explains that like Khan, the Tartar people were always tolerant because they were little attached to their own religion due to the absence of divine sanctuaries and, we infer, the trappings of civilized religion that accompanies sanctuaries. This species of tolerance is not peculiar to the Tartars but extends, Montesquieu insists, to other barbarian peoples with simple, shrine-less religions. He suggests that barbarian peoples lack a necessary (though not sufficient) condition for intolerance: a strong attachment to one's own religion. Without such an attachment, he explains, one is in fact more likely to embrace a novel religion than to persecute it. Thus in a classically Montesquieuian note of irony, it appears that more civilized religions are more "barbaric" than barbarian religions in their treatment of religious minorities.[27]

In a footnote, we learn that the barbarian spirit of tolerance is also found among the contemporary Japanese, whom Montesquieu believed to be descended from the Tartars (*EL* 5.25.3, n.7).[28] He finds in Japan another example of a nation in which diverse sects tolerate one another, further supporting his view that religious uniformity is not a precondition for civic peace. The Japanese retain the tolerant spirit of their barbarian forebears because, as we saw in the previous chapter, their leading sects have no doctrines of the afterlife and so they are scarcely attached to their cults (*EL* 5.24.14). While the Japanese persecute Christians, Montesquieu explains, they do so neither on religious grounds, nor out of any particular zeal for homegrown sects. They persecute because they fear Christianity "as a change in government" (*EL* 5.25.15) and because the exclusivism of Christianity runs afoul of their otherwise tolerant pluralism (*MP* 374). As Montesquieu notes in the *Pensées*, the brutal treatment of Christians in Japan is exceptional: among the seventy other sects in the nation, there is absolutely no conflict and "dispute for preeminence" (*MP* 374). In fine, the Japanese abhor in Christianity precisely the same fault the Romans found in the cult of Isis and Genghis Khan detected in Islam: the exclusive character of these religions threatens the fragile spirit of tolerance. Japanese hostility to Christianity counts as further evidence of the link between religious apathy and barbarian tolerance.

---

[27] In his "remonstrance" against religious persecution, he writes, "We must warn you of one thing; it is that, if someone in the future ever dares to say that the peoples of Europe had a police in the century in which we live, you will be cited to prove that they were barbarians" (*EL* 5.25.13).

[28] The same may be true of "all eastern peoples": "All the eastern peoples, except the Mohammedans, believe all religions are indistinguishable" (*EL* 5.25.15).

Montesquieu's reflections on the barbarian culture of tolerance might in turn seem to suggest that he looks to religious apathy as a promising source of the spirit of tolerance in modern Europe. But this is the wrong conclusion to draw from Montesquieu's account of barbarian tolerance. To understand why, we need look no further than his other comments on Japanese religion, which I have treated in Chapter 5. Its tradition of religious toleration notwithstanding, Japanese government represents for Montesquieu the epitome of despotic severity, and he insists that there is a causal link between the weakness of men's attachment to Japanese religion and the despotism of the state.[29] He explains Japanese state and society with reference to his "general rule of equilibrium," which holds that "the less repressive religion is, the more the civil laws should repress," i.e., despotically (*EL* 5.24.14).[30] Because religious sects in Japan lack sufficient potency to regulate mores, "the laws, in order to supplement [religion], have been made with extraordinary severity and have been executed with an extraordinary punctiliousness" (*EL* 5.24.14). By contrast, the mildness of free and moderate government is made possible in part by religion's regulation of mores.[31]

Like Roman tolerance, barbarian tolerance demonstrates the crucial point that religious diversity does not guarantee religious strife and civic unrest. But this curious feature of the Tartar empire and despotic Japan does not emerge as Montesquieu's solution to the problem of forging a culture of interpersonal tolerance in modern Europe. A different source of tolerant mores was needed, one that neither undermined other elements of liberal statecraft; nor required the elimination or visionary refashioning of Christianity; nor proved so ill-suited for addressing the challenge of exclusivist religions. For such a source, Montesquieu would turn from the pages of history to a phenomenon that "we see every day" (*EL* 4.20.1).

COMMERCIAL TOLERANCE

Montesquieu's Romans and barbarians were not, in his estimation, commercial peoples. The tolerant Romans "regarded commerce and the arts

---

[29] "Au Japon les loix les plus cruelles les plus vigilantes qu'il y ait dans l'univers." VF 7:791.

[30] Bianchi, "Histoire et Nature," 300.

[31] Rebecca E. Kingston makes a complementary argument concerning Montesquieu's rejection of religious skepticism as a basis for toleration. She argues that apathy born of religious skepticism "was a questionable basis for toleration as he felt it was a stance which weakened the force of religion, particularly in its ability to provide a check on political power." Kingston, "Religion."

as the occupation of slaves," the tolerant Tartars lived by plunder rather than exchange, and the tolerant Japanese spurned trade with foreigners.[32] But as early as 1721, Montesquieu had begun to note an additional example of tolerant mores, and this one appeared before his own eyes. In *Persian Letters*, Usbek observes in that,

> Jews in Europe have never before experienced such peace as they now enjoy. Christians are beginning to abandon that spirit of intolerance which formerly inspired them; the Spanish regret having banished the Jews, and the French regret having persecuted Christians whose beliefs differed slightly from those of their monarch. They have realized that zeal for the advancement of religion is different from the love one should bear it, and that in order to love it, and observe its precepts, there is no need to hate and persecute those who do not do so.
>
> (*LP* 58)

Usbek provides no explanation for this movement away from the *esprit d'intolérance*, and Montesquieu had perhaps not yet drawn the conclusion that commerce lay behind it.

But by the time he authored *The Spirit of the Laws*, he had come to identify the commercial activity prevailing in much of Western Europe as the chief cause of this softening. Though scholars have not widely recognized the connection between Montesquieu's valorization of *la commerce douce* and his concern for religious toleration, the evidence for the connection is incontrovertible. As we have already seen, as early as 1716, Montesquieu explicitly identifies the *esprit de douceur* with the *esprit de tolérance* (VF 8:92). While he never mentions religion by name in his memorable discussion of the moral effects of commerce in Book 20, chapters 1–2, it is unthinkable that Montesquieu or his contemporary readers could have missed the centrality of religious conflict and tolerance in this discussion. When he asserts that commerce "cures destructive prejudices" through "softening" mores, there can be little doubt that the prejudices he has in mind here are chiefly religious prejudices, for, as he has just stated in Book 18, "the prejudices of superstition are superior to all the other prejudices" (*EL* 3.18.18). While many scholars have emphasized the relevance of Montesquieu's remarks to the problem of national or cultural prejudice, at the center of his concerns in Book 20.1–2 lie the destructive prejudices of superstition – that is, sentiments of religious intolerance.[33]

---

[32] Montesquieu, *Considerations*, 98–9.

[33] Most commentators make no mention of religion in their treatment of 4.20.1–2, but there are exceptions: Sharon A. Stanley, *French Enlightenment and the Emergence of Modern Cynicism* (Cambridge University Press, 2014), 110, 113; Céline Spector, "Was

Montesquieu came to believe that modern commercial activity had promise as a spring of tolerance, not merely through the incentives it created for political rulers (taken up in Chapter 4), but also through the habits of heart it could engender in the commercial public. That Montesquieu would have explored such a causal link is not surprising given his empirical frame of mind: after all, he knew well that the two most religiously tolerant European nations in the mid-eighteenth century, England and Holland, were also host to the two most robustly commercial cultures. Indeed, the spirit of commerce reigns alone in Holland (*EL* 4.20.2), and the English "have best known how to take advantage of each of these three great things at the same time: religion, commerce, and liberty" (*EL* 4.20.7).

A close reading of Montesquieu's crucial account of commerce in Book 20 suggests that it produces tolerant mores in two distinct and coincident ways: the first is highly reflective and interpersonal, outlined in chapter 1 of Book 20 of *Spirit*; the second is entirely unreflective and habitual, outlined in chapter 2 of the same book. We may call these processes *reflective commercial tolerance* and *unreflective commercial tolerance*.

In his description of commercial mores, Montesquieu announces an "almost general rule" that modern commerce produces gentleness (*la douceur*) and soft mores.[34] "Dragged by a torrent," he offers this highly condensed account:

Commerce cures destructive prejudices, and it is an almost general rule that everywhere there are gentle mores, there is commerce and that everywhere there is commerce, there are gentle mores.

Montesquieu Liberal? *The Spirit of the Laws* in the History of Liberalism," in *French Liberalism from Montesquieu to the Present Day*, ed. Helena Rosenblatt (Cambridge University Press, 2012), 67; Andrea Radasanu, "Polishing Barbarous Mores: Montesquieu on Liberalism and Civic Education" in *Civic Education and the Future*, eds. Elizabeth Kaufer Busch and Jonathan W. White (Lanham, MD: Lexington Books, 2013), 59; Alan Levine, "The Idea of Commerce in Enlightenment Political Thought," in *Rediscovering Political Economy*, eds. Joseph Postell and Bradley C. S. Watson (Lanham, MD: Lexington Books, 2011), 63; Pangle, *Theological Basis*, 101.

[34] Destructive prejudice and ferocious mores are supplanted by *la douceur*, a quality of character Montesquieu frequently mentions in *Spirit*. He associates this gentleness or softness with moderate government, moderation, and even fairness. Indeed, perhaps no other term is used as often to describe the tone and practices of moderate and free government (*EL* 1.5.15; 1.6.9; 1.7.17; 2.10.9; 3.15.16; 4.22.25; 4.24.15; cf. 1.8.10). So when in Book 20 Montesquieu finally announces that commerce produces "*des moeurs douces*," the reader is prepared to see the association between commercial gentleness and moderate politics. On the concept of *doux commerce* generally, see Hirschman, *Passions and Interests*, 70–81; Pocock, *Commerce, Virtue, and History*, 103–56.

Therefore, one should be not surprised if our mores are less fierce than they were formerly. Commerce has spread knowledge of the mores of all nations everywhere; they have been compared to each other, and good things have resulted from this.

One can say that the laws of commerce perfect mores for the same reason that these same laws ruin mores. Commerce corrupts pure mores, and this was the subject of Plato's complaints; it polishes and softens barbarous mores, as we see every day.

(EL 4.20.1)

Through international trade, nations have come to know the mores of their trading partners. Naturally, as commerce has diffused knowledge of foreign mores, mores have been "compared to each other"; in modern commercial activity one tends in passing to compare one's own beliefs and way of life to those of other peoples.[35] The notable effect of these comparisons has been not an upsurge in feelings of superiority but rather "great goods [*grands biens*]" (EL 4.20.1). The "great goods" these constant comparisons produce are in fact "our mores," which have become "less fierce."

One suspects that it is the incidental character of these comparisons that accounts for their potency. The merchant ventures out to make a fortune. He has no high-minded designs of meaningful cross-cultural exchange, no self-conscious plans of cultural hegemony, and certainly no intention of making advances in the study of cultural anthropology. But as he conducts business both with his fellow countrymen of different creeds and with foreign peoples, he observes differences and compares what he sees to his own beliefs, mores, and manners. At the same time, this trader notices his trading partners' responses to his odd ways. Montesquieu's use of the passive voice – "[mores] have been compared" – comprehends both sides of this experience: I have compared my ways to theirs, and they have compared their ways to mine. "The history of commerce is that of a communication among peoples," and regular

---

[35] Here it is worth recalling that traders were among Montesquieu's most important sources for information about foreign peoples. For instance, he drew substantially upon the travel writings of diamond merchant Jean-Baptiste Tavernier and Huguenot jeweler Jean Chardin, who, as Montesquieu writes, "befriended prominent Persians, knew the provinces as well as the capital, and always tried to get behind appearances." Quoted in David Young, "Montesquieu's View of Despotism and His Own Use of Travel Literature," *Review of Politics* 40 (1978): 395.

communication makes such comparisons inevitable (*EL* 4.21.5).[36] But Montesquieu does not offer an elaborate account of how comparison across cultures produces *la douceur*.[37] How exactly does the activity of comparison mellow ferocious mores? Inclined to make us think rather than to make us read, Montesquieu leaves it to us to discern why this activity of comparison softens mores, "as we see every day" (*EL* 2.11.20; 4.20.1).[38] We must therefore try to understand what Montesquieu might have said if he had had the luxury "to glide on a tranquil river" rather than being "dragged by torrent," as he characterizes his composition of these chapters on commerce (*EL* 4.20.1).

The concept of "comparison" runs deep in Montesquieu's philosophy, a point underappreciated in scholarly treatments of his views on commercial society. The activity of comparing takes on an almost metaphysical significance in his "Essay on the Causes that May Affect Men's Minds and Characters" (1736–43). There he announces that the "principal faculty of the soul is to compare."[39] Good sense is nothing other than the "just comparison of things" (*MP* 1682), and in the "Essay," such just comparison appears as the aim of education. Education begins by expanding our stock of ideas (VF 9:247–52). The addition of these ideas produces in us new modes of feeling (*"manières de sentir "*) (VF 9:249). Having provided us with a fund of ideas and sentiments, a good

---

[36] Cf. Rousseau, "Discourse on the Origin and Foundations of Inequality among Mankind," in *The Social Contract and the First and Second Discourses*, ed. Susan Dunn (New Haven, CT: Yale University Press, 2002), 118.

[37] Montesquieu's mention of the comparison of mores is one of the most quoted and least explored passages in *The Spirit of the Laws*. Even the recent major studies by Pangle (2010) and Rahe (2009), which devote substantial attention to the role of commerce in *Spirit*, offer no explanation of the process Montesquieu describes in 4.20.1. Christopher J. Kelly argues that Montesquieu reasons as follows: "People who compare morals, it seems, will have a preference for gentler over harsher ... Looking beneath the luster of virtue, Montesquieu finds harsh repression or self-repression. Those who, under the influence of commerce or Montesquieu's account of it, compare morals, are led to make the simple choice between pain and gentleness." Christopher J. Kelly, "Rousseau and the Illustrious Montesquieu," in *The Challenge of Rousseau*, eds. Eve Grace and Christopher J. Kelly (Cambridge University Press, 2012), 24. See also Marc Belissa, "Montesquieu, *L'Esprit des Lois* et le droit des gens," in *Le Temps de Montesquieu: Actes du colloque international de Genève (28–31 octobre 1998)*, eds. Michel Porret and Catherine Volpilhac-Auger (Geneva: Librarie Droz, 2002), 171–84.

[38] See *MP* 1970.

[39] Richter, "Essay on the Causes," 149; VF 9:249. Again, he reiterates, "[O]ur capacity to compare ... is the preeminent faculty of the soul." Richter, "Essay on the Causes," 150; VF 9:252. Montesquieu may have been influenced here by Locke's prominent treatment of comparison in his *Essay Concerning Human Understanding* (XI.4–5, XV).

education must generate a "harmony among these ideas, modes of feeling, and things as they really are" through the activity of deliberate and judicious comparison.[40] But our misfortune is that the "force of impressions" made by things typically depends more upon "circumstances than upon the merit of the thing which has struck us."[41] We are disproportionately impressed both with those ideas and sentiments we have received first, as well as those we have received through sensory experience. As a result, most men do not "receive ideas in just proportion."[42] With this sterile language of proportion, force, and impressions, Montesquieu ultimately seeks to explain not only the meaning of education, but also the meaning of prejudice. These ideas received in unjust proportion can be nothing other than prejudices: they arise as we prejudge things without the benefit of conscious and deliberate comparison in the soul. Disproportionate impression, or prejudice, "spoils our capacity to compare, which is," Montesquieu reiterates, "the preeminent faculty of the soul."[43]

Though somewhat cryptic and incomplete, this account of comparison displays the centrality of the faculty of comparison in Montesquieu's moral psychology and hints at its potential as a cure for the problem of prejudice. Following our discussion in the "Essay," Montesquieu portentously notes that, "Travel also adds greatly to the scope of the mind: one leaves the circle of the prejudices of his own country and is scarcely likely to take on the prejudices of foreign countries."[44] This mention of the power of travel and communication anticipates the discussion of commercial comparison in *Spirit* and recalls the role of travel in *Persian Letters*.

Persian Letters affords us insight into Montesquieu's understanding of the practical effects of comparing mores.[45] As the reader overhears two Persian travelers' observations concerning "our" odd ways, he discovers

---

[40] Richter, "Essay on the Causes," 149; VF 9:249.
[41] Richter, "Essay on the Causes," 149, 151; VF 9:249.
[42] Richter, "Essay on the Causes," 150; VF 9:252.   [43] Ibid.
[44] Richter, "Essay on the Causes," 156; VF 9:260.
[45] Of course, the impact of a book like *Persian Letters* on a serious reader may be deeper and more profound than the effect of "commercial comparison" on the average trader. Fred Dallmyr, "Montesquieu's *Persian Letters*: A Timely Classic," in *Montesquieu and His Legacy*, ed. Rebecca E. Kingston (Albany, NY: State University of New York Press, 2008), 252, describes the pedagogical strategy of that work: "What is particularly noteworthy here is that cosmopolitan and interfaith tolerance in his case were linked with a deep appreciation of cultural and religious traditions and hence not predicated on an abstract rationalism or universalism aloof from the past and prone to reduce tolerance to mere neutral indifference."

that French mores, manners, and religion may seem at least as odd and incomprehensible to the foreign observer as Persian ways appear to him. The Persians' comparative reflections engender an experience of self-suspicion in the reader. As he witnesses the Persians' initial, comic misunderstanding of Western ways, he is led to ask whether Persian ways appear comically odd or hideous to him on account of his want of an internal perspective on them and not because of any defect inherent either in them or in the mind of the Persian. As Montesquieu himself explains in a preface to the 1754 edition of *Persian Letters*, the travellers are initially confounded by the oddity of European ways, but "the longer [Usbek and Rica] stay in Europe, the customs of this part of the world come to seem less marvelous and less bizarre to them."[46] In this way, prolonged contact and comparison may soften our judgments under the right circumstances.

The letters of Usbek also expose a second route, closely related to the first, by which the activity of comparison leads to a softening toward difference. By the time he writes his fifth letter from Paris, Usbek believes he has discovered striking similarities between Parisian ways and Persian ways. As he closely examines the Christian religion of the French, he comes to believe he has discerned in it "the seeds of our dogma": "I see Muhammadanism everywhere, although I do not find Muhammad there" (*LP* 33). He later notes that "no matter what religion one follows, observance of law, love of one's fellow men, and filial devotion are always the principal results of religion" (*LP* 44). This suggests that on Montesquieu's view, the activity of comparison leads one to form the opinion that one's own ways are surprisingly similar to the ways of others that had seemed, at a distance, to be comprehensively "bizarre," as Montesquieu put it. Of course, whether there truly is such a common core present in all religions is beside the point; indeed, it is difficult to believe that Montesquieu could agree with Usbek's judgment that all religions inspire love of fellow men and observance of law. True or not, this judgment engenders softness in the observer who believes he has hit upon an underlying "irreducible core" of common principles or values.[47] Here is a second pathway running from the activity of comparison to *la douceur*.

---

[46] Montesquieu, "Quelques Réflexions sur les *Lettres Persanes*" in *Oeuvres complètes de Montesquieu* (Paris: Firmin Didot Frères, 1845), 1.

[47] Tzvetan Todorov highlights this effect, although he does not seem to appreciate the improbability that Montesquieu believes such a common core actually exists, at least as Usbek describes it. Tzvetan Todorov, *On Human Diversity: Nationalism, Racism, and Exoticism in French Thought* (Cambridge, MA: Harvard University Press, 1993), 360.

It requires little imagination to see how the reader's experience in *Persian Letters* might be replicated in commercial activity. Among foreigners and countrymen of different confessions, commercial man discovers likeness in the midst of radical difference. He may, like Usbek, casually theorize the existence of a common core of values present in his religion and those of his trading partners. He may likewise sense that even if they share nothing else, they share natural needs and a small but potent set of universal human passions – hope of gain, fear of death, love of home. This further softens the harshness of his judgments.

The commercial man observes the responses of others to his ways and engages in such comparative reflections himself. Montesquieu cannot expect that such a man will attain a deep and genuine understanding of alien beliefs and ways of life. That is asking too much; no ethnographer, he remains a spice trader. But he perceives that his confidence in and commitment to his own beliefs and way of life are matched by the confidence and commitment of his trading partners. He sees how limited are the horizons of his foreign partners' understanding, and he gradually draws the inference that his own horizons may be similarly circumscribed. He may not come to view the content of his own beliefs and mores as entirely conventional, but he will come to see the fact that he *holds* those beliefs, and his ability to discern their worth and meaning, as largely contingent upon his circumstances.[48]

This constitutes a kind of self-knowledge or self-remembrance. Prejudices cause one to be "unaware of oneself"; they lead a man to "forget himself" (*EL*, "Pref."; 1.1.1). Therefore the cure for destructive prejudices fittingly involves a regimen of self-knowledge or self-remembrance. In his preface, Montesquieu avers that he would be the happiest of mortals if he could "make it so that men were able to cure themselves of their prejudices" (*EL*, "Pref."). There is no further discussion of "curing" prejudices until the books on commerce, and there we come to understand why Montesquieu had initially spoken of men curing themselves (*EL* 4.20.1). For through commercial activity, they are enabled to do just that. In Book I, Montesquieu portrays philosophers as the agents responsible for curing human self-forgetfulness: "Such a being could at any moment forget himself; philosophers have reminded him of himself by the laws of morality" (*EL* 1.1.1). But as we have seen, Montesquieu is not especially sanguine about the prospect of such philosophic reminders moving men

---

[48] See Levine, "The Idea of Commerce," 64.

toward self-remembrance: "When it is a question of proving such clear things, one is sure not to convince" (*EL* 5.25.13). Other philosophers have attempted to remind men of themselves through the "laws of morality," but this philosopher shows men how they have begun to remind *themselves* of themselves – that is, how they have begun to "cure themselves" through comparison in commerce (*EL*, "Pref.").[49] The activity of comparing mores thus appears as a form of sub-philosophic reflection, or an imperfect substitute for philosophic reflection.[50] Happily, this activity may be potent enough to cure men of "destructive prejudices," but it is unable to produce the full-fledged *homme d'esprit* that a fine education aims to cultivate, per the "Essay on the Causes" (*EL* 4.20.1; VF 9:252).[51] It certainly cannot cure men of all prejudices. We "see every day" how reflections of this inferior variety are producing within commercial peoples a stronger sense of common humanity, a greater sympathy for peoples with dissimilar beliefs and mores, and so a new kind of softness, gentleness, and spirit of tolerance.

Commerce destroys destructive prejudices by spreading "knowledge" – thus far a classic Enlightenment formulation (*EL* 4.20.1). But paradoxically, the prescribed tonic is "knowledge of mores," that is, knowledge of prejudices.[52] Here we see something of the distinctiveness in Montesquieuian enlightenment. Our prejudices only appear as prejudices when we come to see them as analogous to the prejudices of others. Here Montesquieu looks to commercial enlightenment to deliver what proponents of philosophical and scientific enlightenment promise. We may call the result reflective commercial tolerance.

---

[49] As Paul A. Rahe writes, "[T]he 'knowledge' produced by enlightenment is indistinguishable in its effects from the cosmopolitan spirit inspired by commerce." Rahe, *Montesquieu and the Logic of Liberty*, 198.

[50] See Chapter 1 on commerce as the modern analogue of ancient Greek musical education. Just as musical education was an imperfect but serviceable substitute for philosophic education on the classical view, so commerce appears in *Spirit* as an imperfect but useful means of curing men of their prejudices in the absence of genuine philosophical enlightenment.

[51] Thus reflective commercial tolerance does not involve "stamping spirits" with "something intellectual," in the sense of philosophical arguments or principles (*EL* 3.19.17). It merely reshapes the manner in which we hold or regard our beliefs. Moreover, comparison across cultures does not lead to truly comprehensive self-knowledge, as the example of Usbek illustrates in *Persian Letters*. Despite the softening of his prejudices toward the French, he remains largely oblivious to the deceptions and moral wrongs at the foundation of his home life. See Todorov, *On Human Diversity*, 357.

[52] See *EL* 3.15.3. On "destructive prejudices," see also *EL* 3.19.27, 328.

But as I have suggested, in addition to this reflective source of the spirit of tolerance, Montesquieu observes that commerce can also make men tolerant through unreflective habit, giving rise to unreflective commercial tolerance. As the discussion of *la commerce douce* proceeds in chapter 2 of Book 20, Montesquieu follows his familiar acquaintance the Abbé St. Pierre in holding that commerce unites nations through reciprocal dependence, leading to peace.[53] But peace among nations is not the chief concern of this chapter, and he immediately observes that the spirit of commerce "does not unite individuals in the same way [*n'unit pas de même les particuliers*]" (EL 4.20.2). Montesquieu's meaning here is ambiguous. Does he wish to indicate that commerce does not unite individuals *at all*, or that it does indeed unite individuals, albeit in a different way than it unites nations? He explains that,

We see that in countries where one is affected only by the spirit of commerce, there is traffic in all human activities and all moral virtues; the small things, those required by humanity, are done or given for money.

The spirit of commerce produces in men a certain feeling [*sentiment*] for exact justice opposed on the one hand to banditry and on the other to those moral virtues that make it so that one does not always discuss one's own interests alone and that one can neglect them for those of others.

(EL 4.20.2)

We will later revisit Montesquieu's notable misgivings about commercial mores betrayed in this passage. But here we note simply that "the moral virtues," which suffer decline in commercial society, include especially what one might call the generous and unitive virtues – from barbarian hospitality, to pagan public-spiritedness, to Christian charity. From this point of view, it appears that when Montesquieu observes that commerce "does not unite individuals in the same way," he means to say that commerce divides them.

Montesquieu never claims that commercial men fail to do what is "required by humanity." Rather he states that those things required by humanity "are done" – but for a price. Of the commercial Dutch nation, Montesquieu writes, "The heart of the residents of commercial nations is completely corrupted; they will not render the least service to you,

---

[53] In *Pensées* #1940, Montesquieu declares himself a "partisan" of the "sect" of the Abbé de St. Pierre. See also *MP* 1718 and 1876; Céline Spector, "Le Projet de paix perpétuelle: de Saint-Pierre à Rousseau," in *Principes du droit de la guerre, Ecrits sur le Projet de Paix Perpétuelle de l'abbé de Saint-Pierre*, eds. B. Bachofen and Céline Spector (Paris: Vrin, 2008), 229–94.

because they hope that you will purchase it from them ... Everyone pays, everyone asks for something, with every step you take, you find a tax."[54] Men are not united directly through bonds of charity or generosity, but they are united mediately through the rules and spirit of exchange. Montesquieu's thought here is not merely that self-interest replaces nobler, pre-commercial sentiment but rather that the generous sentiments are replaced by a peculiarly commercial sentiment, "a certain feeling of exact justice [*un certain sentiment de justice exacte*]" (*EL* 4.20.2). This sentiment demands the market price, and it pays the market price – not a penny more.

Commercial men are habituated to this sentiment of exact justice by following their own interests in the business of buying and selling. Montesquieu suggests that justice pays in the marketplace; generally speaking, it is easier to make a living through honesty. There are spectacular exceptions, but the moderately risk-averse (that is, the great mass of commercial men) will be just in their commercial dealings because they intuit that a merchant who gains a reputation for dishonesty is ruined. In this connection, Montesquieu explains that the commercial citizens of Marseilles had to be "just, in order to live among the barbarian nations that were to make their prosperity" (*EL* 4.20.5). The habitual observance of justice in the myriad mundane transactions of a commercial society gives rise to the *sentiment de justice exacte*. This is fully consistent with Montesquieu's quasi-Aristotelian understanding of moral development, which he adumbrates in the *Pensées*: "The means of perfecting justice is to make such a habit of it that it is observed even in the smallest things and that one bends to it even in one's manner of thinking" (*MP* 220). Self-interest leads commercial men to a thousand honest transactions. Along the way, a reasonably stable *sentiment de justice exacte* emerges and extends beyond the marketplace to all departments of human life.

While morally ugly, the spirit of commerce thus conduces to peace among individuals just as it does among nations. It unites them not immediately, as men are united in the ancient polis or even within a gang of bandits, but through the mediation of rules of commercial exchange. It similarly renders irrelevant the "destructive prejudices," prejudices that divide generous men in noncommercial societies. In the marketplace, I see before me not a flesh-and-blood human being worthy of my good will or ill will, but rather a potential source of monetary gain winnable only through

---

[54] Montesquieu, "Voyage en Hollande," VF 1:864.

politeness and "exactly just" conduct. Whether it comes from a Protestant, Catholic, or Jew, a profit is a profit. Voltaire's later description of the Exchange of London is illustrative of Montesquieu's meaning: "The Christians deal with one another as if they were of the same religion and reserve the name of infidel for those who go bankrupt. There the Presbyterian trusts the Anabaptist, and the Church of England man accepts the promise of the Quaker."[55] Without any philosophical reeducation, the merchant senses the inaptness of religious intolerance in commercial society.

The sentiment of exact justice may also have a more direct impact on patterns of tolerance and intolerance. As Montesquieu provocatively suggests in his *Pensées*, our understanding of property rights tends to shape our understanding of rights of conscience. Vigilance concerning the former produces vigilance concerning the latter by virtue of a kind of intuitive analogy. Montesquieu writes of men who, while irreligious themselves, respect religious liberty because of their regard for property rights: "[T]hey feel that life and property are no more their own than their religion or manner of thinking, and that whoever can take away the one can even more easily take away the other" (*MP* 727). The commercial spirit produces respect for religious liberty because the commercial man intuits the analogy between property rights and rights of conscience: if the conscience of the religious nonconformist is not secure against state oppression, then how secure is my fortune? One concludes that the latter is most secure when the former is firmly guaranteed. The sentiment of exact justice arises in the context of material property, but it touches our view of intangible "property" such as one's powers of thought and religious conscience. Thus again, the spillover of the economic sentiments into other spheres of life is not altogether regrettable.

Montesquieu deepens the analysis of commercial mores by turning, oddly enough, to the practice of hospitality among "bandit peoples," who make a living by plunder. The sentiment of exact justice, Montesquieu explains, is contrary not only to the generous virtues but also to banditry (*EL* 4.20.2). Bandit peoples are rich in hospitality, for with them there is no *meum* and *tuum*, and thus no sentiment of exact justice. Montesquieu focuses on hospitality as a quintessentially generous virtue. At its best, the spirit of

---

[55] Voltaire, *Philosophical Letters*, ed. John Leigh (Indianapolis: Hackett Publishing Company, 2007), 20. Denis Diderot similarly comments, "But such are the effects of commerce that it silences all national and religious prejudices in the light of that general interest which should be the bond between all men." Quoted in Stanley, *French Enlightenment*, 110.

hospitality turns a stranger into a friend. The commercial spirit, by contrast, can do no such thing. But it makes the innkeeper habitually inclined to treat the stranger justly, uniting the two through the rules of market exchange.

Montesquieu's choice to contrast commercial mores with the practice of hospitality among "bandit peoples" hints at a deficiency in the class of conventional generous virtues that commercial sentiments supplant. He suggests that such generous virtues are not incompatible with injustice. The "spirit" of banditry is "not contrary to certain moral virtues," i.e., the generous virtues (*EL* 4.20.2). This is because the self-forgetfulness of the generous virtues usually stems from a more general forgetfulness about the boundaries, the Lockean "fences," between individuals. Like all fences, these boundaries can both separate each from other, blocking union, and protect each from other, marking out distinct spheres of personal liberty.[56] Forgetfulness of these fences may be noble when it redounds to the benefit of others; but of course, it also leads to banditry. Undermining this self-forgetfulness, the "sentiment of exact justice" magnifies the importance of the rights or fences separating mine from thine. If our goal is the consistent observance of the morally minimal duty of toleration – what Locke calls "the narrow measures of bare justice" in his *Letter Concerning Toleration* – this may count as progress, even if it subverts the morally maximal generous virtues.[57] A Dutchman can "die at the age of eighty without ever doing a good deed," but the same man likely observed exact justice with friend and stranger, Christian and Jew alike (*MP* 592).[58]

---

[56] For an alternative view, see Nicholas Wolterstorff, *Justice in Love* (Grand Rapids, MI: Eerdmans, 2015), and Eleonore Stump, *Aquinas* (London: Routledge, 2005), 309–38.

[57] John Locke, *A Letter Concerning Toleration*, §224. A number of scholars are excessively gloomy about social effects of this sentiment of exact justice. Céline Spector argues that Montesquieu attributes no positive role to commerce in the social life of nations; its benefits obtain only between nations. Céline Spector, "Was Montesquieu Liberal?" 8. Similarly, Christopher J. Kelly writes, "[A]lthough commerce may make nations prefer peaceful pursuit of wealth to war, it makes individuals harsher rather than gentler toward each other by making them concerned exclusively with their own interest." Kelly, "Rousseau and the Illustrious Montesquieu," 24. Such analyses do not sufficiently account for the compatibility of the generous virtues with the "spirit of banditry," a spirit far from gentle and humane. While Montesquieu certainly does not see the sentiment of exact justice as an unalloyed good – standing as it does at no more than a hair's breadth from cupidity – it clearly plays a part in forming the commercial culture of tolerance he portrays in these opening chapters.

[58] It is not quite accurate, therefore, to speak of commercial sentiment "mimicking" virtue. Stanley, *French Enlightenment*, 113. Montesquieu goes further: in its effects, the commercial sentiment improves upon certain virtues inasmuch as it reduces the incidence of violence, injustice, and intolerance.

Moreover, Montesquieu's account underscores the fact that generous virtues tend to be practiced within the bounds of a beloved community – a people united to one another immediately – while injustice is the policy outside that community. Even the most hospitable bandits must rob somebody. By contrast, the sentiment of exact justice has this advantage: it assumes no beloved community and is felt wherever a potential customer or business partner appears. Montesquieu's account suggests that if the aim is religious tolerance outside one's religious community, the more universal scope of commercial sentiments represents a major advantage over the practice of generous virtues within the family circle.

Scholars often locate Montesquieu in a tradition of modern political thinkers who seek "low but solid" alternatives to the practice of noble virtue. As we have seen in previous chapters, this characterization of his strategy is not without merit: in monarchies, for example, "politics accomplishes great things with as little virtue as it can, just as in the finest machines art employs as few motions, forces, and wheels as possible" (*EL* 1.3.5). In the case at hand, the simple "wheel" of commerce accomplishes the work for which the generous virtues had proven unreliable. But it is worth noting that, just as in the case of monarchical honor, Montesquieu's "low but solid" alternative is not as low as his formulation suggests. In lieu of generous virtue, Montesquieu observes not naked self-interest, but the sentiment of exact justice at work. While this sentiment arises as men pursue their material ends, it is not reducible to momentary calculations of self-interest; rather, it is habitual.[59] Granted, it is not a virtue, but merely a sentiment, of exact justice; and it is not a sentiment of justice simply (that is, in a classical or Christian sense that might prove compatible with the moral requisites of human communion), but of *exact justice*, a quality narrower and more cramped than unqualified justice. We may not therefore wish to denominate it a liberal virtue. But these concessions notwithstanding, the sentiment of exact justice, like honor, certainly occupies at least an intermediate station between the low, solid passions and the lofty virtues.[60] The sentiment of exact justice, like

---

[59] Continual, spontaneous calculations of self-interest might allow for violence and intolerance toward those at the margins of commercial concern, but if commerce modifies our *esprit* – our sentiments, mores, and manners – we should expect a more regular observance of exact justice and tolerance toward all.

[60] Monarchical honor is "false honor," one of the better forms of vanity (*EL* 1.3.7). Of course, even noble virtue is less sublime than it appears; Montesquieu famously unmasks it as a byproduct of repression (*EL* 1.5.2), although one is tempted to think he does not quite believe this, for the unmasking does not seem to extinguish entirely his "nostalgia

monarchical honor, ranks among the best of the worst human qualities. Montesquieu trades a world characterized by both the noblest and the most execrable human passions for a world home only to passions of a middling sort. Disillusionment with this moral trade-off, as I will suggest in conclusion, may help to explain the incomplete success of commerce as a source of tolerance. But it is a trade-off Montesquieu made with open eyes.

The pre-commercial models of tolerant culture intrigued Montesquieu, but the revival of either Roman or barbarian tolerance would have required the enervation or elimination of Christian religion in the West, a prerequisite both impracticable and counterproductive on his view. By contrast, the rise of commercial tolerance requires neither the eclipse of piety nor the revision of dogma, for its crucial and direct effects are at the level of "spirits," sensibilities, habits, and sentiments. Indeed, commercial tolerance circumvents doctrine and belief: it gains its end not by changing the content of beliefs but the manner in which we hold them. Commercial tolerance satisfies the need for an "interior" source of tolerant attitudes without producing "interior tolerance" (i.e., approval of other sects) in the terms of the *Mémoire*. Moreover, it avoids a pitfall common to both the Roman and barbarian models – their paradoxical tendency to fuel violent persecution of exclusivist religions (Egyptian, Jewish, Muslim, and Christian), as we have observed here. Because commercial tolerance bypasses doctrine altogether, exclusivist religions present no special obstacle to its operation and are naturally included in the circle of tolerance. The tolerant spirit of commercial society holds out the promise of making all commercial men more tolerant, including members of exclusivist religions. In the very activity scorned by tolerant premodern peoples, Montesquieu believes he has observed the most reliable "spiritual" stanchions for the liberal regimes of toleration.

MONTESQUIEUIAN MISGIVINGS

Was he right? We may justly assert that an extensive analysis of this question goes beyond the bounds of an interpretive study. But even in the absence of such analysis, it is plain to any student of history and current events that if modern commercial activity has indeed contributed to a spirit of tolerance in many societies, its potency is not without limit.

for more heroic times," when men were a full cubit taller. Russo, "Virtuous Economies," 68; *MP*, 1268.

In much of the world that commerce has "penetrated," we have found in the last century or find at present a spirit of intolerance that rivals any precursors in its ferocity (*EL* 4.20.21). Did Montesquieu miss something?

There are discordant notes in his defense of the commercial spirit, as we briefly noted in Chapter 5. Despite his deep moral commitment to religious liberty, Montesquieu seems not fully at home in the modern commercial society he theorizes and champions as a font of soft and tolerant mores. There are notes of resistance to the materialism, rationalism, and alienation that characterize modern commercial life.[61] For all its political and economic advantages over premodern alternatives, its achievement has not come without loss. Not with blithe indifference does Montesquieu darkly observe the "traffic in all human activities and all moral virtues" in commercial society, and that "the small things, those required by humanity, are done or given for money" (*EL* 4.20.2). It is with a genuine sense of loss that he writes of our "our small souls," of the "dregs and corruption of modern times," and of our political men who "speak to us only of manufacturing, commerce, finance, wealth, and even luxury," rather than of virtue (*EL* 1.3.2).[62] Ultimately Montesquieu is a friend of this world of manufactures and finance, but as Elena Russo puts it, he "never abandons some measure of admiration for what he is busy demolishing."[63] Like Tocqueville, Montesquieu stands between two worlds, and in some measure he experiences modernity as a condition of displacement, inquietude, and disunion.[64]

All of this may be edifying to consider as we survey a world in which the reach of tolerant mores is not in fact coextensive with the reach of modern commerce, apparently giving the lie to Montesquieu's observations. Perhaps Montesquieu has given us the resources to understand not

---

[61] "One feels the old abuses and sees their corrections, but one also sees the abuses of the correction itself" (*EL*, "Pref."). Montesquieu's reservations about commercial society are treated thematically in Spector, "Was Montesquieu Liberal?"; Russo, "Virtuous Economies"; and Jean-Fabien Spitz, *La Liberté politique: Essai de généalogie conceptuelle* (Paris: Presses Universitaires de France, 1995), ch. 7. See also Anoush Fraser Terjanian, *Commerce and Its Discontents in Eighteenth-Century French Political Thought* (Cambridge University Press, 2013), 14–16; Daniel Gordon, *Citizens without Sovereignty: Equality and Sociability in French Thought, 1670–1789* (Princeton University Press, 1994), 130–2; Rob Goodman, "Doux Commerce, Jew Commerce: Intolerance and Tolerance in Voltaire and Montesquieu," *History of Political Thought* 37 (2016): 530–55.

[62] On potential for religious attachment to balance or temper the commercial spirit, see Chapter 5 above.

[63] Russo, "Virtuous Economies," 69–70.

[64] Ibid., 69. On inquietude, see Rahe, *Soft Despotism*, ch. 2.

only why commercial tolerance has succeeded, but also why its success is incomplete and must remain so. For if, in this gimlet-eyed analyst of liberal modernity, we discern intimations of discontent with the experience of displacement and disunion in modern commercial society, we may thereby catch sight of the psychic sources of violent, intolerant, and romantic movements that reject the requisites of liberal culture and seek to restore the world to a counterfeit unity – a unity with none of the virtues of the premodern communions, but all of their vices.

These portentous misgivings notwithstanding, Montesquieu saw in commerce the surest means of extending mores of religious tolerance, mores constitutive of political liberty. Over the course of the last three chapters, we have considered his conception of liberal culture from multiple vantages. In lieu of a minimalist conception of the liberal self, Montesquieu dissects not only the requisites of liberal culture but the sources of these requisites, following causes until they reveal themselves as effects of still other causes. Liberal government may be, as we indicated in Chapter 2, natural in respect of its moral foundations. But empirically, it is no less a child of custom than any other regime. Montesquieu's liberalism escapes a naïve reliance on "authentic" human nature or formal institutions to provide the qualities of mind and heart necessary for free and moderate politics. No less than his regime pluralism, this approach to the problem of the liberal self helps us to account for the unity of his liberalism and political particularism, and to judge confidently that there are not two Montesquieus, but one.

Like contemporary treatments of democratic political culture, Montesquieu's account of liberal culture may leave us unsettled for reasons not difficult to discern. To speak of the cultural requisites of liberty is to set up a problem: what of nations that lack them? Our analysis has so far reached this question only indirectly, but Montesquieu is keenly alert to its significance in *Spirit*. To this problem of political change we must now turn in detail. It is the point from which the coherence of Montesquieu's project comes most clearly into view.

7

Political Change and the Psychology of Liberty

Since a particular form of government gives a certain orientation, a certain disposition to minds, you change the former without the latter following you, and you combine the new government with the old manner of thinking, which produces very bad effects.

Montesquieu, *MP* 603

In the last three chapters, we have considered Montesquieu's account of the elements of liberal culture. Liberal government is no exception to the basic principle of his political sociology: every decent regime assumes, and in some measure even consists in, a particular disposition, genius, or manner of thinking among a people. Despotism may require only the passions, and "everyone is good enough for that" (*EL* 1.5.14). But the universal passions of human nature cannot, of themselves, animate and sustain liberal societies and constitutional orders. The maintenance of free and moderate government requires both a "masterpiece of legislation" in the framing of its structure and a foundation of congenial habits, mores, beliefs, maxims, and manners. This understanding of the requisites of liberal culture lies at the center of Montesquieu's critique of political universalism. Of equal significance is his corresponding anxiety about the consequences of installing liberal political institutions in the absence of such requisites. We must now turn our attention to this anxiety and the approach to political change Montesquieu fashions under its influence. Here, we see most vividly the union of his anti-universalism and liberalism.

Mechanistic attempts to universalize liberal political orders, or any particular form of political life, will fail because the matter often resists the form. Montesquieu presents the problem concisely in his *Pensées*: when political actors change the "form of government" without a concomitant change in the "orientation" or "disposition" of mind, "very bad effects" follow (*MP* 603). One might suppose that such "very bad effects" amount simply to institutional instability and social disorder. But while political stability ranks highly among Montesquieu's concerns in *Spirit*, his anxiety about the consequences of rationalistic and universalistic approaches to regime change is more profound, and more firmly rooted in the structure of his normative thought, than one initially imagines. Our task from the beginning has been to understand the theoretical complementarity of Montesquieu's liberalism and political particularism. As we turn now to his explicit counsel on the problem of regime change, we discover that his admonitions against political universalism, and his particularist approach to political change, each follow from the moral logic of his liberalism itself.

When projects of political transformation cut against the grain of a people's *disposition* (*EL* 1.1.1), they also run afoul of Montesquieu's philosophy of liberty. On his view, liberty is not present wherever liberal formal institutions are set in order. Liberty is not simply the condition of men living under a limited government of distributed powers, with legal rights of free speech, free worship, due process, and the like. Although Montesquieu champions the rule of law and civil guarantees, he does not recognize as complete a narrowly procedural and institutional understanding of freedom, shorn of any accounting for the citizen's internal state. Such a formalistic understanding of liberty is common to liberal theories and present, for example, in Locke's original formulation: "[F]reedom of men under government is, to have a standing rule to live by, common to every one of that society, and made by the legislative power erected in it."[1] All things being equal, such a conception of liberty will incline a liberal theory toward political universalism inasmuch as it invites the inference that men can be made free by installing the right

---

[1] Locke, *Two Treatises*, 2.26. Céline Spector correctly sees Montesquieu's definition of liberty as an indication that Montesquieu believes "the Lockean definition of political liberty is insufficient because it fails to account for subjective perception." Spector, *Montesquieu: Liberté, droit et histoire*, 172. See also John Dunn, *Political Obligation in Its Historical Context: Essays in Political Theory* (Cambridge University Press, 2002), 30, on the absence of "complex features of the mind of the agent" in the Lockean account of consent; and Zuckert, "Natural Law, Natural Rights, and Classical Liberalism," on Montesquieu's "subjectivization" of the criterion of political right, in contrast with earlier theories.

formal institutions. On this very point, we find a crucial substitution in Montesquieu's liberalism: in lieu of a formalistic account of liberty, he develops a psychological conception that provides a moral rationale for his warnings against universal politics.

Montesquieu defines liberty in a citizen as a "tranquility of spirit" born of "the opinion each one has of his security" (*EL* 2.11.6). When citizens are prepared to receive and sustain it, free government promotes liberty so understood; it expels the species of fear that dominates men's souls in despotic nations. But when a people is not culturally and socially prepared to receive free political institutions, direct attempts to erect such institutions will likely produce an experience of political disquiet and fear – a "tyranny of opinion" – comparable to the psychological experience of men and women in truly tyrannical states (*EL* 3.19.3). Under these conditions, free institutions are no longer liberal in effect, for they fail to yield the tranquility of spirit that constitutes the "liberty of the citizen." This train of reasoning constitutes what can best be described as a liberal critique of political universalism. When Montesquieu warns against untimely institutional reform in nations culturally unprepared for laws of liberty, he speaks from within the moral logic of his liberalism and not on behalf of prudential considerations external to it.

But Montesquieu's anxiety concerning the moral costs of political universalism does not terminate in a quietistic embrace of the status quo. His liberal and particularist sensibilities together shape a distinctive approach to political and cultural change in *Spirit*. Friends of liberty may pursue two possible courses with respect to nations that are as yet unprepared to receive free and moderate institutions. First, they may acquiesce in despotism. Second, they may seek to transform a nation's cultural life to prepare its people for freer institutions. Montesquieu resists the first path. His political outlook, however pessimistic relative to later liberals, is simply too melioristic to admit of such a solution. This leaves the second path – that of cultural transformation.

But reformers who follow this path must refrain from using coercion to change the nation's culture directly, for such projects transgress the moral limits of state power. This concern is at the heart of Montesquieu's liberalism. Montesquieu therefore sketches an art of political change designed to avoid the twin shoals of quietism and illiberal cultural legislation. He urges reformers to change mores and manners indirectly, not through direct legislation. His initial examples of such indirect means of change appear obscure as the idea first emerges in the "turning point" of his great work, Book 19.[2] But as I argue, we must understand the subsequent books on commerce as an application of this broader counsel. Commerce appears not merely as a technically efficient means of promoting political liberty, but crucially, as a potential path to liberal culture that does not require resort to illiberal methods of coercive cultural transformation. Only in this context can one understand the true moral and political significance of modern commerce for Montesquieu's liberalism. This counsel represents the constructive aspect of Montesquieu's anti-universalist theory of political change, and like the cautionary and critical dimension, it is underwritten by concerns at the center of his normative liberalism.

THE PSYCHOLOGY OF LIBERAL CONSTITUTIONALISM

In Chapter 3, we considered the explicitly regime pluralist character of political liberty in Books 11 and 12 of *Spirit*. But we must now consider Montesquieu's account of the psychological dimension of liberty that emerges in those books. The analysis moves along two fronts. First, in Book 11, Montesquieu promises to approach political liberty in "relation with the constitution" (*EL* 2.11.1). Next, in Book 12, he promises to approach liberty "in relation to the citizen" (*EL* 2.12.1). Though significantly more porous than it first appears, this distinction means that the establishment of liberal or moderate constitutional forms may not fully guarantee the liberty of the citizen (*EL* 2.12.1).

In Book 11, Montesquieu describes the constitutional forms best suited to prevent abuses of power (*EL* 2.11.4). He initially defines political liberty as "the right to do everything the laws permit (*EL* 2.11.3)."[3] When a constitution allows arbitrary constraint or compulsion beyond the scope of settled laws, political liberty is imperiled. In other words, liberty requires the rule of law. Montesquieu therefore proceeds to his discussion of the separation of powers, because this institutional feature preserves the rule of law. It becomes clear that "the laws that form

---

[2] Samuel, "The Design of Montesquieu's *The Spirit of the Laws*," 312. The first edition of *De l'esprit des loix* was published in two volumes, and Book 19 occupied an important place as the final book of the first volume. Montesquieu, *De l'esprit des loix*, 2 vols. (Geneva: Barrillot et fils, 1748).

[3] Compare *EL* 5.26.20: "Liberty consists principally in not being forced to do a thing that the law does not order, and one is in this state only because one is governed by civil laws; therefore, we are free because we live under civil laws."

political liberty in its relation with the constitution" are fundamental laws that secure separation of powers and the rule of law (*EL* 2.11.1).

But what does the "liberty of the citizen" require, beyond the presence of liberal constitutional forms? The liberty of the citizen "consists in security or one's opinion of one's security" (*EL* 2.12.1; 2.11.6). This aspect of liberty has an unmistakably psychological dimension. It matters not only that I am objectively secure but that I consider myself to be secure. This unusual account suggests that the citizen might not experience "liberty" so understood, even when liberal institutions – the separation of powers and the rule of law – are in place. As Montesquieu explains in Book 12,

> It can happen that the constitution is free and that the citizen is not. The citizen can be free and the constitution not. In these instances, the constitution will be free by right and not in fact; the citizen will be free in fact but not by right.
>
> Only the disposition of the laws, and especially of the fundamental laws, forms liberty in relation to the constitution. But in relation to the citizen, mores, manners, and received examples can give rise to it, and certain civil laws can favor it ... "
>
> (*EL* 2.12.1)

The mores, manners, and examples that "give rise" to liberty are what we have called liberal culture. In the absence of such, the citizen is not free even if the "disposition of the laws" forms a constitution that is free de jure.[4] This means, correlatively, that liberal mores, manners, and received examples are nothing less than constitutive causes of the citizen's liberty in free societies.

Montesquieu thus seems to present two views of political liberty: one that is psychological or subjective and another rooted in observable constitutional arrangements and practices. His explicit distinction between Books 11 and 12 suggests as much (*EL* 2.12.1). But at the deepest level, both treatments of liberty are grounded, in part, in the same psychology of political fear. Just after Montesquieu promises to devote Book 11 to "liberty in relation with the constitution" (the "objective" kind of liberty), he inserts his psychological definition of liberty. Appearing to get ahead of himself, he writes, "Political liberty in a citizen is that tranquility of spirit [*tranquillité d'esprit*] which comes from the opinion each one has of his security, and in order for him to have this

---

4 The "disposition of the laws [*disposition des lois*]" refers to the structure of government, while the "disposition of the people [*disposition du peuple*]" in Book 1, chapter 3, refers to other moral and physical causes.

liberty the government must be such that one citizen cannot fear another citizen (*EL* 3.19.6)." From the point of view of the citizen, political liberty is tranquility of spirit.[5] Such a state depends upon his freedom from fear of rulers and fellow citizens alike.

But this reference to "liberty in the citizen," in a chapter purportedly concerned with "liberty in relation to the constitution," is not a Homeric nod. Rather, Montesquieu's psychology of liberty serves as the point of departure for his analysis of the English constitution, and so, of his account of "liberty in relation with the constitution." He continues, "When legislative power is united with executive power in a single person or in a single body of magistracy, there is not liberty, because one can fear that same monarch or senate that makes tyrannical laws will execute them tyrannically (*EL* 2.11.6)." Separation of powers preserves liberty not simply by preventing actual tyrannical deeds, but also by removing the causes of fear – a passion that proves inimical to the human good in despotic regimes. Students of politics cannot fully understand even free and moderate political institutions except in relation to their effects upon

---

[5] Sullivan plausibly suggests that this unusual definition of liberty signals a rejection of the fearful character of Hobbesian sovereignty. Sullivan, *Montesquieu and the Despotic Ideas of Europe*, 53. On subjective or intersubjective conceptions of liberty in the republican tradition, see Philip Pettit, *Republicanism: A Theory of Freedom and Government*, ch. 2, esp. 70ff. Pettit speculates that Montesquieu's definition is a gloss on Machiavelli's association of freedom with the absence of fear in *Discourses*, 1.16. These glosses do not address Montesquieu's particular choice of expression, "*tranquillité d'esprit.*" An overlooked point of reference is the concept of *ataraxia*, the Stoic (and Epicurean) ideal of an absence of psychic disturbance. This concept was commonly rendered as "*tranquillité d'esprit* " and "*tranquillitas animi* " in French and Latin, respectively. A professed admirer of the Stoics (*EL* 4.24.10), Montesquieu owned a copy of Pierre le Charron's widely read *De le Sagesse* (1601), in which the neo-Stoic moral philosopher and political absolutist argues that "*tranquillité d'esprit* " is "*le souverain bien de l'homme,*" the fruit of wisdom, innocence, and a good conscience (433). Minor works by both Seneca and Plutarch bore the Latin title, *De tranquillitate animi*, and Montesquieu owned a French edition of Plutarch's treatise, translated as *De la tranquillité de l'esprit*. Of course, neither Charron nor Plutarch and Seneca treat tranquility of mind as dependent upon political arrangements. Man is to find inner tranquility *despite* the misfortunes that afflict him, including political perils. As Montesquieu appropriates the recognizably Stoic language, he shifts the focus to political sources or prerequisites of tranquility. While Stoic sages may remain tranquil in the face of threats from rulers or neighbors, Montesquieu's ordinary citizens require laws and mores of liberty in order to maintain *tranquillite de l'esprit*. On Charron, see Church, *Constitutionalist Thought*, 306–8; Desgraves and Volpilhac-Auger, *Catalogue*, 102, 344; Pierre Charron, *De la sagesse* (Rouen: Chez L. Costé, [1601] 1614), 456, 459. On tranquility of spirit in Stoic thought, see James Warren, *Epicurus and Democritean Ethics: An Archaeology of Ataraxia* (Cambridge University Press, 2002), 34. See also Larrère, "Montesquieu et le stoïcisme"; Montesquieu, *Considerations*, ch. 16.

the passions and opinions of men. Liberty has an important psychological dimension, and Montesquieu therefore locates the goodness of free institutions largely in their ability to reduce fear. Absent this effect, the institutions are considerably less choiceworthy.

The psychological account of liberty also shapes Montesquieu's defense of the English jury system.[6] Judicial power is "terrible among men" when held by permanent officers, because unlike the legislative and executive, it consists ultimately in the power to condemn (*EL* 2.11.6). The jury trial reduces this terror because it makes the judicial power "invisible and null" (*EL* 2.11.6). When one's judges are not "continually in view," one comes to "fear the magistracy but not the magistrates" (*EL* 2.11.6). Under a jury system, the citizen does not know the identity of his potential judges.[7] The judicial power is composed of all and none. Fear is diffused. Moreover, trial by jury tends to ensure that the accused "does not suppose he has fallen into the hands of people inclined to do him violence" (*EL* 2.11.6). The jury system is a free institution inasmuch as it fosters an "opinion of security" and a tranquility of spirit in the citizen and the accused. Likewise, the fundamental feature of free government – rule by promulgated law – is a free institution not only because it protects the citizen from harm inflicted by arbitrary power, but also because it can liberate the citizen from fear of arbitrary individual wills. We see, therefore, that even Montesquieu's analysis of formal institutional arrangements relies upon the psychological account of liberty – the account he seemed to reserve for Book 12.[8] In this way, Montesquieu places the perceptions of the citizen at the center of his liberalism. He foregoes a merely juridical or formalistic account of political liberty.[9]

Montesquieu's understanding of despotism leads to his emphasis on the psychological dimension of liberty. Fear (*crainte*) is the principle of despotic government (*EL* 1.3.9). Like virtue in a republic or honor in a monarchy, fear sets despotic government in motion and "makes it act" (*EL* 1.3.1). Despotism both produces and feeds upon this passion; as we saw in Chapter 4, Montesquieu surveys the baleful effects of fear.[10] It

---

[6] Montesquieu believed trial by jury was the historic practice in France as well. See *MP* 1184.

[7] See Shklar, *Ordinary Vices*, 214–19, on the depersonalization of politics in *Spirit*.

[8] *EL* 2.11.1; Rahe, *Montesquieu and the Logic of Liberty*, 98.

[9] See Shklar, *Montesquieu*, 91; Mansfield, *Taming the Prince*, 235.

[10] See Sharon R. Krause, "Despotism in the *Spirit of Laws*," in *Montesquieu's Science of Politics: Essays of* The Spirit of Laws, eds. David W. Carrithers, Michael A. Mosher, and

undermines the grounds of political agency – magnanimity, ambition, and honor.[11] It vitiates love within the household (*EL* 1.3.10). Fear colonizes the whole of man's inner life in despotic states, crowding out all other passions; it must reign alone (*EL* 1.6.3). In the presence of habitual fear, reason atrophies and man descends to the level of beasts (*EL* 1.3.10, 1.4.4, 1.5.14).[12] Against the backdrop of this account of despotic fear, Montesquieu offers his definition of liberty as tranquility of spirit. Regimes of liberty afford the citizen relief from this species of fear and its effects upon human well-being.[13] This vision of free government, as we will see, pervades Montesquieu's warnings regarding universalism in politics.

INSTITUTIONAL CHANGE AND THE "TYRANNY OF OPINION"

We find Montesquieu's most explicit warnings against political universalism in his treatment of regime change in the crucial nineteenth book of *The Spirit of the Laws*. As I will show, the particularistic admonitions present in this book are rooted not only in pragmatic reasoning about stability, but also and primarily, in the psychology of liberal constitutionalism.

Book 19 is entitled, "On the laws in their relation with the principles forming the general spirit [*l'esprit général*], the mores, and the manners of a nation." This is the reader's first introduction to the term "general spirit." In previous books bearing obscure titles, Montesquieu opens with brief chapters explaining the terms in doubt.[14] But "What the general spirit is" must wait until chapter 4 of Book 19. Instead, Montesquieu inserts chapter 2: "How much it is necessary for spirits to be prepared for the best laws." Before he turns to the meaning of the general spirit, he offers the reader an indication of its importance. Unlike climate, terrain, and other "physical causes" of laws, the general spirit, together with mores and manners, admits of manipulation by political reformers: it can be "prepared." Montesquieu then provides four examples of

---

Paul A. Rahe (Lanham, MD: Rowman & Littlefield, 2001), 231–73. See generally Corey Robin, *Fear: The History of a Political Idea* (Oxford University Press, 2004), ch. 2.
[11] *EL* 1.5.12, 1.3.8–9; Krause, *Liberalism with Honor*, 1–66.
[12] Shklar, *Montesquieu*, 82; *MP* 1192.
[13] Fear prevents us from enjoying the diverse goods of human life, but liberty is "the good which enables us to enjoy other goods." *MP* 1574, 1797.
[14] Pangle, *Montesquieu's Philosophy of Liberalism*, 193–4.

"unprepared" spirits. He recounts episodes from Roman history in which non-Romans balked at Roman judicial formalities. The Germans found Roman tribunals "intolerable." During one trial, they cut out the lawyers' tongues and demanded, "Viper, stop hissing."[15] Mithradates reproached the Romans for their formal procedures of justice. The Laxians judged the Roman trial of their king's assassin a "horrible and barbarous" affair. Finally, Montesquieu adds that the Parthians were unable to tolerate their king's universal affability and accessibility (*EL* 3.19.2). In the passage from the *Annals* that Montesquieu cites, Tacitus reports that the people took offense at their king's "alien mores [*moribus aliena*]."[16]

In these four examples, Montesquieu shows us nations failing to understand and embrace the mores, tone, and practices of moderate government. As we have seen, he regards the presence of judicial formalities as a hallmark of moderate and free government. Formalities "increase in proportion to the importance given to the honor, fortune, life, and liberty of the citizens" (*EL* 1.6.2). Likewise, accessibility characterizes a monarch, in contradistinction to a cloistered despot (*EL* 4.24.3). Montesquieu therefore means to suggest that the spirits of the Germans, the Laxians, and the Parthians were unprepared for "the best laws."

A summary statement follows these four examples: "Even liberty has appeared intolerable to peoples who were not accustomed to enjoying it. Thus is pure air sometimes harmful to those who have lived in swampy countries" (*EL* 3.19.2). The "best laws" are laws of liberty and political moderation. But absent properly prepared spirits, these best laws are not merely unsustainable, but harmful to a people. The harm these institutions cause springs not from the institutions themselves, but rather from the people's perception of them – from their appearance. Twice in this paragraph, Montesquieu remarks that good laws "appeared unbearable [*paru insupportable*]" to a people. The danger of free and moderate

---

[15] Florus reports of the event, "Never was there slaughter more cruel than took place there in the marshes and woods, never were more intolerable insults inflicted by barbarians, especially those directed against the legal pleaders." Florus, *The Epitome of Roman History*, trans. E. S. Forster (Cambridge, MA: Harvard University Press, 1929), 2:30.37.

[16] Tacitus, "The Annals," in *The Annals and the Histories*, ed. Moses Hadas (New York: Modern Library, 2003), 2:2, 47. The Parthian king, Vonones, was "easy of approach; his courtesy was open to all, and he had thus virtues with which the Parthians were unfamiliar, and vices new to them ... [T]hey hated alike what was bad and what was good in him."

institutions for "unprepared spirits" lies in a problem of opinion or perception, as we shall consider.

Chapter 2 closes with a colorful and revealing anecdote. A Venetian traveler visited the court of the king of Pegu (present-day Bago, Burma). When in the presence of the king this traveler mentioned that Venice had no monarch, the king of Pegu laughed "so much that he began to cough and could scarcely talk to his courtiers" (*EL* 3.19.2). Montesquieu asks, "What legislator could propose popular government to such peoples?" With this final example, Montesquieu suggests that a people may lack the political categories necessary to take new political institutions seriously, much less judge the new institutions legitimate.[17] Book 19 represents a warning for political reformers about the limits and perils of institutional change; yet more than a warning, it represents a guide to the right methods of political change.

The next chapter, "On tyranny," seems at first to be out of place. Tyranny is not a regime type for Montesquieu, and one initially wonders why he takes up the subject in a book on the general spirit. In the original draft of *The Spirit of the Laws*, "On tyranny" is even more strikingly prominent: it appears to have been Book 19's lead chapter (VF 4:462). The chapter's theme was apparently central to the purpose of Book 19 as Montesquieu first conceived it. When we consider this brief treatment of tyranny and its role in the book, we begin to see more clearly the theoretical connection between Montesquieu's liberalism and his particularistic cautions regarding political change.

Montesquieu explains that there are two sorts of tyranny: a real tyranny (*"réelle tyrannie "*) and a tyranny of opinion (*"tyrannie d'opinion "*). Real tyranny "consists in the violence of the government." Tyranny of opinion is "felt when those who govern establish things that run counter to a nation's way of thinking [*la manière de penser d'une nation*]." The introduction of this second variety of tyranny is a true innovation. John Locke offers a single, juridical definition of tyranny – the "exercise of power beyond right."[18] Montesquieu's "real tyranny" answers to Lockean tyranny. But tyranny of opinion is a new political category, forged for this occasion. Montesquieu invites the reader to ask after its significance as he turns to the reign of Augustus to illustrate his meaning.

He explains that when Augustus wanted to be called Romulus, the people "feared that he wanted to make himself king" (*EL* 3.19.3). If he

[17] See also *MP* 699.   [18] Locke, *Two Treatises*, 2.199.

had adopted this name, the Roman people would likely have felt themselves under a tyrant's heel, even in the absence of any acts of violence. The people's fear did not simply flow from an aversion to acts of despotism. Rather, the institution of kingship was opposed to their manners. Montesquieu suggests that though Caesar, the triumvirs, and Augustus "were real kings," the people did not perceive their reigns as tyrannical insofar as they "preserved an appearance of equality" and "seemed opposed to kingly pomp." The perception of tyranny proceeded not from any institutional structure or act of violence but from the rulers' contravention of national manners. The Romans did not want a king because they did not want to "suffer his manners." Montesquieu implies that any political change, if it runs counter to the manners of a people, may be experienced as tyrannical and fear-inducing. Such changes need not come in the form of rulers that covet the name of Romulus.[19]

In time, Augustus enacted truly harsh legislation. He governed violently, as a "real" tyrant (see *EL* 2.12.4). As the Roman people recognized his tyranny, they grew angry and discontent. But as Montesquieu explains,

> Their discontent ceased as soon as [Augustus] brought back the actor Pylades, who had been driven out of the town by the factions. Such a people felt tyranny more vividly when a buffoon was driven out than when all their laws were taken from them.
>
> (*EL* 3.19.3)

The Roman populace was in error, as Montesquieu makes clear. But this episode, together with his previous comments on the reign of Augustus, suggests that just as real tyranny may exist where tyranny of opinion does not, tyranny of opinion may exist where real tyranny does not. The Romans misjudged a real tyrant because he restored their favored celebrity. Another people may misjudge free and moderate government because it runs counter to their mores, manners, and general spirit. Though the institutions of free government may not produce tyrannical violence in Montesquieu's sense, a people may nonetheless experience these institutions as alien, dissonant with their manner of thinking and productive of fear and disquiet.[20] They may endure a *tyrannie d'opinion*.

---

[19] On Romulus and his offense against mores, see *MP* 677. See also Montesquieu, *Considerations*, 210.

[20] See Rahe, *Montesquieu and the Logic of Liberty*, 218–19; and Larrère, "Montesquieu and Liberalism," 291.

In light of this, we see now why Montesquieu introduces the concept of the general spirit as he does. The Germans and Laxians experienced a tyranny of opinion under the Romans' judicial formalities (*EL* 3.19.2). As I have argued, Montesquieu believes that such judicial formalities are essential to the full protection of political liberty. But here, he aims to show that when otherwise moderate, liberal institutions are installed before spirits are prepared to understand them and receive them as legitimate, the people perceive these innovations as tyrannical. No longer liberal in effect, the institutions become despotic in effect. That is, they enflame a people's disquiet and fear – the same pernicious passions that sustains despotic regimes. They disturb and diminish a people's tranquility of spirit and their opinion of their own security (*EL* 2.11.6).[21] While the Germans and Laxians may, in this instance, have been as mistaken as the Romans who felt tyranny when a buffoon was driven out, their perceptions carry moral significance for Montesquieu. The Romans' institutional changes were harmful for the same reason that these liberal institutions are good in nations prepared for them. For on Montesquieu's account, the goodness of these institutions lies substantially in their psychological effects. He teaches the legislator to evaluate political institutions not merely by assessing their merits as abstract forms, but rather by considering their likely effects upon the passions and opinions of a particular people. This is an instance of the paradox Montesquieu alludes to in Book 12. The citizen may be free "by right" (i.e., from a legal and institutional point of view), but not "in fact" (from a psychological point of view) (*EL* 2.12.1).

As we have seen, Montesquieu does not simply approach the legislator with counsels of expedience on the question of matching a regime to a people. He does not merely foretell the difficulties of political change amidst a people unprepared to understand it or receive it. He goes beyond description and prediction. Montesquieu suggests that unseasonable political change represents an injury to a people analogous, though not identical, to the injuries of despotism. Situated in the matrix of Montesquieu's psychology of liberty, this error is not merely technical but also moral. On his view, to seek political liberalization through merely institutional means while neglecting the cultural preconditions of these institutions is to misunderstand and offend against the substance of liberty itself.

---

[21] Pangle aptly hints at a connection between "tyranny of opinion" and liberty defined as an "opinion of security." Pangle, *Montesquieu's Philosophy of Liberalism*, 185.

THE GENERAL SPIRIT AND THE MEANS
OF POLITICAL CHANGE

As Montesquieu cautions against the establishment of liberal institutions in nations not yet prepared for them, he speaks from within the moral logic of his liberalism. This is clear in the foregoing discussion, for his particularistic warnings rely upon his psychological understanding of political liberty. But while this reading confirms the theoretical consistency of Montesquieu's position, the practical harmony of his liberalism and particularism still remains in doubt, for Montesquieu's anxiety about the tyranny of opinion appears to tie the hands of liberal reformers. Yet Book 19 of *Spirit* proceeds to sketch the contours of an approach to political change that seeks to avoid the problem of tyranny of opinion. This approach predictably calls for cultural change as a forerunner to political change. But Montesquieu's liberal commitment to the limited scope of law casts a shadow of moral suspicion over the use of coercive cultural legislation as a means of cultural transformation. Montesquieu therefore seeks to develop an account of indirect, noncoercive cultural change as preparation for political liberalization. Several studies of *Spirit* note that the phenomenon of political change moves to the fore in Book 19.[22] But crucially, this treatment of change represents Montesquieu's attempt to develop a practicable model of political reform within the bounds of his liberal and particularist commitments. This model displays the practical coherence of his liberal constitutionalism and political particularism.

The earliest chapters of Book 19 (1–3) suggest that Montesquieu means to teach the legislator to reshape his nation's general spirit (*EL* 3.19.2) so that, when he finally establishes new civil, political, or fundamental laws, these changes will not run counter to the people's manner of thinking (*EL* 3.19.3). In this way, the people will comprehend the eventual changes and receive them as legitimate, and the legislator will avoid both the "tyranny of opinion" as well as acts of "real tyranny." In chapter 4, "What the general spirit is," Montesquieu appears poised to define Book 19's central concept, but he comes up short. He reports, "Many things govern men: climate, religion, laws, the maxims of government, examples of past things, mores, and manners; a general spirit is formed as

---

[22] Pangle, *Montesquieu's Philosophy of Liberalism*, 195–6; Schaub, *Erotic Liberalism*, 138–44; Larrère, "Montesquieu and Liberalism"; and Samuel, "The Design of Montesquieu's *The Spirit of the Laws*," 312.

a result" (*EL* 3.19.4). This is no definition. To tell the reader what forms the general spirit is not to say what the general spirit is, any more than listing the ingredients in a cake counts as saying what a cake is. However, this may be the point. The general spirit "can be completely decomposed into simple elements" and "contains no 'principle' irreducible to analysis."[23] It is neither an essence nor an organic reality; it bears only superficial resemblance to the later metaphysical concept of the *Volksgeist*.[24] What it signifies, for Montesquieu, is a state of interaction among moral and physical causes in a nation – some yielding, some preponderant – as they combine to shape a people's way of life. The result of this interaction of particular causes exerts a reciprocally causal force of its own upon them. For example, as we have already seen, the general spirit – which is itself "formed" in part by laws – can limit a people's willingness to accept new laws (*EL* 3.19.2). More importantly, according to Montesquieu, a nation's mores "depend" upon its general spirit, even as mores combine with other causes to form that spirit (*EL* 3.19.12).[25]

Because Book 19 is a study of political change, Montesquieu devotes his attention to only a subset of the general spirit's causes: laws, mores, and manners. Unlike physical causes (e.g., geography and climate), these admit of manipulation by the legislator. They are potential sites of human agency. Mores and manners are "usages that laws have not established, or that they have not been able to, or have not wanted, to establish" (*EL* 3.19.16). When laws, mores, and manners are in harmony, "Mores represent laws, and manners represent mores" (*EL* 3.19.16). Mores impress the content of the laws upon man's everyday experience, his judgment, and his passions. Manners represent mores, but in a different way: they are physical and external, consisting in the covering, movements, and postures of the body. Despite their exteriority, manners shape "internal conduct" as habits of the body that reinforce the habits of the

---

[23] Spector, "Spirit, General Spirit." Spector offers a fine account of the development of the concept from Montesquieu's early writings, as does Rahe, *Montesquieu and the Logic of Liberty*, 164–6. See especially the earliest formulation in "De la politique," VF 8:515. See also Francine Markovits, "Montesquieu: l'esprit d'un peuple, une histoire expérimentale," in *Lectures de L'Esprit des lois*, eds. Thierry Hoquet and Céline Spector (Bordeaux: Presses universitaires de Bordeaux, 2004), 65–99.

[24] Richter, *The Political Theory of Montesquieu*, 98.

[25] The term "general spirit" is generally synonymous with "genius" and "character" as applied to nations in *The Spirit of the Laws*. Spector, "Spirit, General Spirit." See, for example, EL 3.19.5.

heart. Given their powerful connection to law and the people's reception of it, mores and manners must lie within the legislator's circle of concern.

Employing these categories, Montesquieu unfolds his art of political change in chapters 5–15 of Book 19. Pangle is correct in dividing the approach of these chapters into two distinct modes.[26] In chapters 5–11, Montesquieu shows how the legislator may sometimes use the existing general spirit of a nation to produce a greater degree of political liberty or to prevent further decline into despotism. This is often possible in Europe. In chapters 12–15, Montesquieu explains how the legislator may bring about political change when the general spirit itself is averse to liberty and moderation, as one finds under profoundly despotic governments. In the first case, the legislator may act with the general spirit and canalize its flow for his political ends. In the second case, the legislator acts not against, but apart from the general spirit to alter it indirectly. Both methods avoid direct manipulation of custom, mores, and manners.

Taken by itself, the title of chapter 5 does not seem to introduce a treatment of political change, for it reads, "How careful one must be not to change the general spirit of a nation." But here Montesquieu does not flatly deny the necessity of changing the general spirit. Rather, he promises a discussion of *how careful* the legislator must be not to change it. He then describes France in terms reminiscent of the account of Paris in *Persian Letters*. The French – especially French women – possess a *joie de vivre*, sociable humor, playfulness, and even frivolity. Men live in the company of women, and each sex desires to please the other. From this desire is born ornamentation and the multiplication of fashions. Montesquieu concludes, "Fashions are an important subject; as one allows one's spirit to become frivolous, one constantly increases the branches of commerce" (*EL* 3.19.8). In light of his teaching on commerce in Books 20 and 21, his meaning is clear. Within the general spirit of the French people, Montesquieu sees the germ of liberty. Their vanity multiplies opportunities for commerce, and commerce conduces to liberty, as we considered in Chapter 6. If the legislator's end is liberalization and moderation, he may find within the vices of the national character a source of political improvement.

But this mode of political reform is not always available. In historically despotic nations, the general spirit offers no support for the work of political liberalization. The legislator finds little or nothing inclined

---

[26] Pangle, *Montesquieu's Philosophy of Liberalism*, 195–6.

toward liberty in the general spirit – no French vanity and no Athenian gaiety. Therefore, if he wishes to liberalize and moderate the state, he must alter the general spirit, together with the causes that form it, to prepare the people.

Montesquieu asserts that in despotic nations, "there are no laws, so to speak; there are only mores and manners" (*EL* 3.19.12). Though he understands that many despotic nations live under nominally legal decrees, he means to suggest that mores and manners are the most powerful forces in these nations. They tend to exert great influence in forming the general spirit. One would therefore suppose that Montesquieu's reforming legislator must act upon mores and manners if he would "prepare spirits" for better laws. But Montesquieu surprises us with an initial warning: "It is a maxim of capital importance that the mores and manners of a despotic regime must never be changed; nothing would be more promptly followed by a revolution" (*EL* 3.19.12). This statement seems to suggest that political reform is impossible in historically despotic states. But we should note that while Montesquieu calls this maxim important, he does not say that it is true without qualification. We should also note that he expects revolution as the consequence of changing mores and manners in a despotic regime; they must "never be changed" if one wishes to avoid a revolution.

Yet chapter 14 is entitled, "What are the natural means of changing the mores and manners of a nation." With this, Montesquieu seems to shunt aside the "capitally important maxim" of chapter 12. If the maxim were unqualifiedly true, he would exclude despotism from the analysis in chapter 14. But instead, he uses the historically despotic government of Russia (or Muscovy) to illustrate the "natural means" of changing mores. Before proceeding to the Russian examples, he writes,

We have said that the laws were the particular and precise institutions of the legislator and the mores and manners, the institutions of the nation in general. From this it follows that when one wants to change the mores and manners, one must not change them by laws, as this would appear to be too tyrannical; it would be better to change them by other mores and other manners.

(*EL* 3.19.14)

The legislator must change mores and manners in order to alter the general spirit and prepare a nation for better laws. But when he crafts new laws aimed at changing mores and manners directly, he errs. He will appear tyrannical because his institutions will run counter to the nation's manner of thinking (*EL* 3.19.1, 2). Instead, he must find a way to effect a change in mores and manners, and so in the general spirit, without opposing them.[27] For as soon as he is seen to oppose them, he will cause the same fear and insecurity – tyranny of opinion – that he would have produced had he simply imposed "the best laws" without preparing spirits (*EL* 3.19.2). Montesquieu's legislator must change mores and manners not by laws, but by new mores, new manners, and fresh examples.

This indirect method takes shape as Montesquieu recounts two episodes from the reign of Peter the Great, the modernizing and westernizing tsar of Russia. First, Peter wanted all Muscovite men to shorten their beards and robes. He passed a law mandating as much. If a long-robed man sought to enter a town, the officer would impose a sartorial penalty, trimming the offending frock (*EL* 3.19.14). Montesquieu calls these sanctions "tyrannical" and "violent means." Such spectacles illustrate the unnatural or tyrannical way to change mores and manners.

We recall here that on Montesquieu's view, real tyranny "consists in the violence of the government" (*EL* 3.19.3). The violence of the government has a specific meaning for Montesquieu. A government does "violence to man" when its punishments proceed from "the legislator's capriciousness" rather than from "the nature of the thing" – that is, the nature of the purported offense (*EL* 2.12.4). Each class of offenses carries a natural, necessary, and reasonable penalty. When the offender meets with his natural penalty, no "violence" is done him; this is the "triumph of liberty" (*EL* 2.12.4). But the imposition of a penalty in excess of an offense's natural penalty constitutes an act of violence. Likewise, the imposition of legal penalties for a deed carrying no natural, necessary penalty constitutes an act of violence (e.g., the execution of heretics). This position, first developed in Book 12, is central to Montesquieu's liberalism.[28] In chapter 14 of Book 19, after discussing Peter's actions, Montesquieu alludes directly to this theory of punishment: "Every penalty that does not derive from necessity is tyrannical. The law is not a pure act of power; things indifferent by their nature are not within its scope [*ressort*]" (*EL* 3.19.14).

The Muscovite manners governing dress and grooming are "indifferent by their nature." To call these manners indifferent is to say that they do not, "by their nature," directly threaten public security or public tranquility. They therefore incur no natural penalty and fall outside the scope of liberal criminal law. Montesquieu certainly does not regard such manners

<hr />

[27] Courtney, *Montesquieu and Burke*, 22–3.   [28] See Chapter 3.

as indifferent in respect of their political effects; on the contrary, he has underscored their political import. Nevertheless, to punish a man for the length of his beard is an act of violence and tyranny. Any use of penal codes to regulate indifferent manners contravenes the "surest rules" of criminal judgments "drawn from nature" (*EL* 2.12.2, 4). To attempt to change such manners by law is not only imprudent; it is immoral and illiberal. Therefore, while Montesquieu's art of political reform often relies upon changes in mores and manners, law ought not directly regulate these conventions to the extent that they are indifferent in themselves. The injunctions of legislators must remain within the natural scope of the law.

Montesquieu uses a second episode from the reign of Peter the Great to illustrate an alternative – what he calls the "natural means" of changing mores and manners. When Peter assumed his rule, Muscovy's women were "enclosed and in a way enslaved" (*EL* 3.19.14). Peter objected to these conditions. He called leading women to his court, had them don German dresses, and sent them new fabrics. The foreign styles were a success. We expect Montesquieu to report that the women appreciated the flattering new style of dress. Instead, he explains that the women "immediately appreciated a way of life that so flattered their taste, their vanity, and their passions, and they made the men appreciate it" (*EL* 3.19.14). The new manners began to transform the mores of the house-hold. Montesquieu leaves it to his reader to discern how this change must have unfolded. But he implies that the charming new attire shifted the balance of power between the sexes by strengthening the men's attach-ments to the women – or, more to the point, by weakening the men. The Muscovite women became more like the alluring and fashionable French women of the *Persian Letters*, who in Rica's assessment had achieved a wholesale capture of authority in their households (*LP* 107).

Montesquieu hypothesizes that the liberalization of mores in the domestic sphere will spur similar effects in the political sphere. In chapter 15, he predicts, "This change in the mores of women will no doubt affect the government of Muscovy very much. Everything is closely linked together: the despotism of the prince is naturally united with the servitude of women; the liberty of women, with the spirit of monarchy" (*EL* 3.19.15). The liberation of women from domestic enslavement opens a pathway to the moderation and liberalization of laws and political insti-tutions.[29] When the husband's authority is absolute and untrammeled,

---

[29] On the domestic sphere, see Chapter 4.

the general spirit is inclined toward despotism. When the husband's authority is checked, softened, moderated, or even undermined by feminine charm, the general spirit is inclined toward monarchy.

With this example, Montesquieu illustrates the "natural means" of changing mores, manners, and, consequently, political institutions. Peter the Great did not "establish" new mores and manners; he did not directly oppose traditional mores and manners. Instead, he "inspired" new mores and manners by insinuating new examples and engaging the people to change their customs themselves (*EL* 3.19.12, 14).[30] Montesquieu calls the method "natural" for two reasons. First, it does not rely upon violence or tyranny. The legislator governs against nature when he dispenses punishments for practices that are by their nature not worthy of punishment. In this way, Peter's treatment of the women is consistent with nature, unlike his earlier treatment of men in overlong frocks. Second, the method is natural because it uses natural passions to achieve its ends. Animated by their passions, the people changed their own mores. So strictly speaking, Montesquieu's "natural means" of changing mores does not contradict the "maxim of capital importance" that mores must never be changed in despotic states (*EL* 3.19.12). This indirect change in mores was not "promptly followed by a revolution" in the conventional sense (*EL* 3.19.12). But Montesquieu predicts that the new manner of dress would begin to leaven the whole lump of state and society, reshaping the general spirit and gradually contributing to the moderation of political and legal institutions. When the legislator follows the natural means of political change, he advances his nation toward freer and more moderate political institutions without revolution. As importantly, he avoids real acts of tyranny and the appearance of tyranny, for he establishes nothing that runs "counter to the nation's way of thinking" and does no violence to man (*EL* 3.19.3, 14; 2.12.4).

This vision of political change is shaped by Montesquieu's commitment to political liberty, his rejection of political universalism, and his liberal understanding of the moral limits of legislation. In view of these considerations, he crafts a coherently *liberal particularist* model of political reform. The Montesquieuian legislator aims to avoid both tyranny of opinion and coercive cultural legislation while still guiding his nation toward a freer and more moderate politics. If liberal institutions are praiseworthy in light of their effects upon the citizen's tranquility of spirit,

---

[30] Cf. *EL*, "Pref.," where Montesquieu wishes to "make it so that men were able to cure themselves of their prejudices," treated in Chapter 5.

then the means of liberalization must be subject to a similar standard of judgment. Through attention to mores, manners, and the general spirit, the legislator may learn to establish bridges to political liberty.

Montesquieu's examples from the reign of Peter the Great may initially strike us as obscure and of limited application outside eighteenth-century Muscovy. But his search for a means of cultural transformation that operates within the bounds of his liberal commitments does not end at the tsar's court. The books on commerce (20–21) immediately follow Book 19's exhortation to employ indirect means of cultural preparation, and they are best understood as a continuation of this theme. Montesquieu looks to commerce not merely as a technically efficient means of promoting political liberty, but crucially, as a way to cultivate mores consonant with "better laws" without resort to illiberal means of coercive cultural transformation, which are beyond the scope of law. The *doux commerce* thesis thus emerges as a distinctively liberal response to a distinctively liberal problem, and one begins to grasp the full moral and political significance of modern commerce in Montesquieu's project.

In short, commerce is a potent means of escaping the trilemma that confronts friends of liberty as they consider the prospect of political change in despotic nations. The first horn of this trilemma is a posture of quietism in the face of despotic rule; the second is a rationalistic, universalistic, and narrowly institutional pursuit of political change that ignores the psychological dimension of liberty and the thick cultural preconditions of "better laws"; the third is the pursuit of direct cultural transformation through the coercive power of the state in violation of moral limits upon the scope of law. None of these choices can emerge from Montesquieu's unified liberal particularist framework. But into this space, commerce enters as an indirect and noncoercive means of liberalizing culture.

Commerce is the most important, though not the only, means of cultural change that could satisfy Montesquieu's standard. The right project of popular education could, in principle, contribute to the erosion of cultural barriers to political liberty without violating the moral limits upon the power of the state. As we considered in Chapter 6, commercial activity will make a *homme d'esprit* of no one, but it can cure destructive prejudices in part by stimulating the activity of comparing mores, a sub-philosophical form of reflection on prejudice (*EL* 4.20.1; VF 9:252). *The Spirit of the Laws* itself similarly invites readers to compare mores, and Montesquieu may expect the same "good things" to result from the broad dissemination of his work (*EL* 4.20.1).[31] Similarly, in Chapter 4, we considered how Montesquieu's political and economic science can reshape the maxims of government by revealing the imprudence of rapine.

It is harder to say how sanguine he was concerning the book's promise as a vehicle of genuine philosophic or scientific enlightenment on a large scale.[32] As we have seen, he judged it difficult to stamp spirits with "something intellectual" and to convince readers of "clear things" through icy moral reasoning (*EL* 3.19.17; 5.25.19). But in an early lecture on "The Motives That Ought to Encourage Us to the Sciences" (1725), he suggests that experience with *belles-lettres* can teach men of science to express themselves "nobly, in a lively manner, with force, grace, order, and a variety that refreshes the spirit."[33] The sciences have much to gain from "from being treated in an ingenious and refined manner; it makes them less dry and wearisome and puts them within reach of all minds." That Montesquieu sought to infuse *Spirit* with grace, order, variety, and liveliness is beyond doubt.[34] Commercial activity bypasses the intellect and leaves its imprint directly upon the mores of men through the enticement of gain. Perhaps Montesquieu entertains the hope that his own graceful science may shape the minds of many through the pleasures of literary excellence.[35]

THE LIMITS OF MODERATION?

We have said little thus far about the agents of political change. To whom does Montesquieu offer his warnings against changing laws and political

---

[31] See Carrese, *The Cloaking of Power*, 75.

[32] On his hope of reaching princes, see *MP* 1864; Montesquieu à Guasco, March 28, 1748, Nagel 3:1112–4; Montesquieu à Charles-Edouard, March 1748, Nagel 3:1114; Montesquieu à l'abbé Venuti, July 22, 1749, Nagel 3:1247–50; Montesquieu à Guasco, 1753, Nagel 3:1471–2; Shackleton, *Montesquieu*, 62, 121, 366.

[33] *VF* 8:500–1; Montesquieu, "Discourse on the Motives That Ought to Encourage Us to the Sciences," trans. Diana J. Schaub, *The New Atlantis* 19 (2008): 36. See also *EL*, Pref.

[34] As Schaub suggests, when he pronounced this 1725 address, Montesquieu may have had his own, immensely popular *Persian Letters* (1721) in mind. Diana J. Schaub, "Montesquieu's Popular Science," *The New Atlantis* 20 (2008): 45–6. See Samuel, "Design of Montesquieu's *The Spirit of the Laws*," 314n.25, on the relationship between *Spirit*'s design and Montesquieu's aesthetic principles as articulated in the "Essay on Taste" (*VF* 10:459–517). He argues that order, variety, symmetry, and contrast in a work of art stimulate natural curiosity, arouse attention, and please the soul. See also *EL* "Pref.," xliv.

[35] See "Invocation to the Muses," *EL* 3.19, p. 337, where Montesquieu reminds the Pierian Muses, "You are never as divine as when you lead to wisdom and truth through pleasure." If they will cast a single glance his way, "everyone will read my works, and what was not intended as an amusement will be a pleasure."

institutions in the absence of prepared spirits? In Book 19, he seems to
have in view a domestic "legislator" (*EL* 3.19.2, 12, 14, 16).[36] At times
this figure appears in the guise of a reform-minded monarch – the "prince
who wants to make great changes in his nation" – or even the Solonic
lawgiver (*EL* 3.19.14, 21). But Montesquieu also occasionally alludes to a
foreign power, especially in the nineteenth book's opening examples of
peoples unprepared "for the best laws" (*EL* 3.19.2). There each of the
four initial examples feature barbarians bristling at Roman procedures
and norms. Thus the counsel in Book 19 seems to apply to both foreign
(i.e., imperial) and domestic "legislators."

This means, in turn, that we must read this counsel against the backdrop of Montesquieu's explicit treatment of conquest and empire in Book
10 of *Spirit*. Though, on the whole, his imperial thought has been relatively neglected, a recent study argues that in chapters 4–5 of Book 10, he
in fact approves of conquest as a vehicle for enlightenment and reform.[37]
If this were true, it would seriously complicate our understanding of
Montesquieu's approach to political change. But this characterization
oversimplifies Montesquieu's position in those chapters. There he offers
no sanction or justification for conquest on liberal or humanitarian
grounds; his focus is not *jus ad bello* but *jus post bello*. He contends that
after one nation has conquered another, whether justly or unjustly, the
conqueror should attempt to do good to the conquered society (e.g.,
freeing slaves), rather than murdering and enslaving the vanquished in
the familiar mode of the conquistador.[38] Notably, Montesquieu's only
approved historical examples of conquerors changing foreign practices by
force concern grave crimes: Alexander prohibited the Bactrians from
feeding their elders to large dogs, and Gelon of Syracuse mandated an
end to child sacrifice among the Carthaginians in the "finest peace treaty"
known to man (*EL* 2.10.5). Montesquieu admires these changes; apparently the crimes were sufficiently heinous to override any consideration of
preparing mores. Certainly, neither Gelon nor Alexander sought to

---

[36] Durkheim, *Montesquieu and Rousseau*, 49–53.

[37] Michael A. Mosher, "Montesquieu on Empire and Enlightenment," in *Empire and
Modern Political Thought*, ed. Sankar Muthu (Cambridge University Press, 2014),
136–9. Cf. Larrère, "L'empire, entre fédération et république," 124–5.

[38] Montesquieu abhorred the methods of the Spanish and Portuguese in South America. See,
for example, VF 8:438, 495–7. On slavery, see Russell Parsons Jameson, *Montesquieu et
l'esclavage: étude sur l'origines de l'opinion antiesclavagiste en France au XVIIIe siècle*
(New York: Burt Franklin, 1911); F. T. H. Fletcher, "Montesquieu's Influence on Anti-
Slavery Opinion in England," *Journal of Negro History* 28 (1933): 414–26.

"fathom by a stroke of genius the whole" of the Bactrian or Carthaginian constitutions before proposing such changes (*EL*, "Pref.").

But Montesquieu's admiration for conquerors who eliminate grave, specific evils does not appear to extend to those who seek to right lesser wrongs or to install improved political and legal systems in subject nations. Alexander himself is Montesquieu's chief example of a conqueror who understood that "things must be left as they were found: the same tribunals, the same customs, the same privileges" (*EL* 2.10.9, 14). The exceptional Bactrian and Syracusan cases proves the rule.[39] It is telling that the lone instance when Montesquieu approvingly discusses a conquest that resulted in the correction of a lesser wrong (oppressive tax-collecting practices), he observes that, "Abuses were corrected even without the conquerors correcting them" (*EL* 2.10.4). The exemplary reform was not, in other words, the result of any deliberate rational plan of the conqueror but rather followed naturally from the conquest itself.

Neither Montesquieu's reasonable preference for humane over inhumane conquerors, nor his approbation of the use of force by conquerors to remedy the most profound insults to humanity, can be taken to indicate a general preference for "liberal imperialism" over the approach outlined in Book 19. Never does he invite foreign powers to search out atrocities abroad as pretexts for war. Only self-defense can justify conquest, as the opening chapters of Book 10 make clear (*EL* 2.10.2–3). Moreover, the evils of conquest itself are usually so vast that a conqueror cannot fully make amends for them even by the finest *post bello* humanitarian deeds (*EL* 2.10.4).

We must also take note of the differences between the kind of changes Montesquieu treats in Book 19 and the kinds of change he takes up in the fourth and fifth chapters of Book 10. In Book 19, the corrections Montesquieu has in view are ultimately broad transformations of political, legal, and social systems. The aims of Peter the Great were grand, as Montesquieu knew well: to westernize and modernize the Russian social and political order. For this, a project of cultural preparation was necessary. As we have seen, Montesquieu suggests that mechanistic efforts to liberalize whole legal and political systems yield "a tyranny of opinion," and such efforts often produce a real tyranny in the long run, as fear must form the basis for obedience when a new rational law code has no foundation in mores. But the "tyranny of opinion" is not an absolute

---

[39] On Montesquieu's admiration for Alexander, see Sullivan, *Montesquieu and the Despotic Ideas of Europe*, 176ff.

evil, and Montesquieu seems to have reasonably held that it can be outweighed by certain grave wrongs that simply must be remedied by those with the power to do so. He therefore does not hesitate to endorse the forcible elimination of the profoundest cruelties in a society, even without recourse to subtle cultural preparation and moderate gradualism. "Even virtue has need of limits"; even moderation has need of limits (EL 2.11.4).

CONCLUSION

Montesquieu's political particularism is not a mere pragmatic rider to his normative liberal project. Rather, by virtue of its very structure, his liberalism demands a careful consideration of culture, place, and circumstance, and it eschews an easygoing confidence in the power of human intelligence to formulate generally applicable political solutions. In *The Spirit of the Laws*, Montesquieu confronts both the moral and practical challenges of political liberalization. He warns against mechanistic efforts to install liberal institutions in nations unprepared to embrace or maintain them. This warning issues from his conviction that, to a significant degree, the goodness of free government is contingent upon the citizens' perception of the regime. Under the right circumstances, free institutions help to promote the "liberty of the citizen," which consists not merely in the presence of liberal formal institutions but also in the citizen's tranquility or belief that he is secure. From this psychological account of liberty, it follows inexorably that conscientious advocates of free and moderate politics must regard as paramount the manner in which a populace perceives institutional changes. Because their perception is largely a function of what we imprecisely call a nation's "culture" – its distinctive mores, manners, and customs – Montesquieu explores the problem of transforming a nation's culture to make it more hospitable to free and moderate government. He concludes, on unmistakably liberal grounds, that while state builders and reformers must often pursue fundamental changes to a people's way of life as preparation for constitutional changes, these actors must not transgress the moral limits of state power. Consistent friends of liberty must indirectly prepare a people for better institutions. In commercial activity, Montesquieu sees one potentially effective and morally legitimate means of promoting mores and manners conducive to, and constitutive of, free and moderate politics.

Montesquieu's framework ultimately provides fresh moral reasons for aspiring liberal reformers and state builders to ask soberly whether cultural conditions will permit their contemplated institutional innovations to produce the benefits they are designed, in theory, to impart. This theoretical founder of the liberal tradition does not deny the possibility of political transformation in nations with illiberal pasts, but especially in such cases, he urges reformers to judge the methods of political liberalization by a moral standard implicit in his theory of liberty and state power. On his view, when theorists and statesmen embrace both liberal constitutionalism and political particularism, their loyalties remain undivided.

Conclusion

Among the earliest and most often rehearsed charges against *The Spirit of the Laws* is that it is a farrago of disconnected, if clever, reflections. The work appears disorderly and even self-contradictory – a "labyrinth without a clue," "an ill-constructed building, built irregularly."[1] The narrower version of this criticism holds that there is no discernable plan or design to justify the divisions and organization of *Spirit*. But in its most significant and interesting form, this line of criticism identifies an incongruence between the principles of Montesquieu's prescriptive or normative political philosophy and the conclusions of his particularistic science of law and politics. As we observed in the introduction to this study, Montesquieu himself imagines the elements of his masterwork as "great gears" that "turn in opposite directions" and seem bound to destroy the grand machine (*MP* 2029). Yet, he avers, "those pieces, which seem at first to be destroying each other, combine together for the proposed purpose." Despite recent fine efforts to make sense of the perplexing design of *Spirit*, we have heretofore lacked an extended, high-resolution account of the relationship between the two great cogs in the machine of Montesquieu's political philosophy: his liberalism and political particularism. This book has developed such an account.

The theoretical, rhetorical, and practical coherence or cooperation of these elements of his thought emerge in several ways. In the first place, we have considered how an appreciation of the intellectual roots of his political particularism sheds light on its relationship to his normative

[1] Voltaire, "L'ABC," in *Philosophical Dictionary*, trans. Peter Gay (New York: Harcourt, Brace and World, 1962) 497–509.

politics of liberty. Montesquieu's particularistic science of law and politics, inspired by a selective appropriation of classical political science, advances his aim of supplanting the classical republic with modern regimes of liberty. Similarly, Montesquieu's inclination to regard the "excess of reason" as a threat to liberty coheres with a tradition of French constitutionalism that culminates in, and is transcended, by *The Spirit of the Laws* (EL 2.11.6).

As we took up the argument of the work itself, this study explored the coherence of Montesquieu's liberalism and political particularism in his treatment of formal legal and political institutions, liberal culture, and political change. Montesquieu's liberalism is regime-pluralistic by virtue of his mode of political theory and the nature of his moral foundations. Because his principles of liberty admit of incorporation in a variety of regimes, his liberal theory is not haunted by the aspiration to raise a single political system to universal status. Turning from his account of liberal political institutions to the problem of culture, we considered how and why Montesquieu rejects the view that the universal human passions or self-interest are sufficient to sustain free and moderate political institutions. He develops an account of the elements of liberal culture, elements necessary for maintenance of liberal political institutions and, indeed, constitutive of the liberty those institutions promise to secure. This leads to his warnings and counsel on the subject of political change, especially regarding transitions to freer and more moderate government. Two elements of Montesquieu's normative liberal theory provide moral grounding for his particularistic approach to political change. His psychological, and not merely formalist, account of political liberty leads him to reject mechanistic attempts to install liberal institutions before "spirits" are prepared. Cultural changes must therefore generally precede political change, and Montesquieu's liberal understanding of the scope of law leads him to favor commerce and other indirect means of "preparing spirits," i.e., shaping culture. Thus in the account of political change, as in the accounts of culture and free institutions, his liberalism and political particularism make common cause. Indeed, it is no exaggeration to say that Montesquieu's political particularism both sustains and flows from the logic of his liberalism and shares with it a common end: the advance of a durable liberty in the world. In fine, "those pieces, which at first seem to be destroying each other, combine together for the proposed purpose" (MP 2092).

Few will doubt that these two elements of Montesquieu's thought secured his place in the history of political philosophy, and an appreciation of their coherence is a crucial step toward understanding his project as a whole – that is, as the *système* he believed it to be, against critics who from the earliest days lamented its apparent disorder and contradictions (*MP* 2092). But even beyond these important interpretive aims, this study's argument has three layers of implications reaching problems in the historiography of Enlightenment political thought, contemporary liberal theory, and contemporary liberal statecraft – our original point of departure.

It is true enough that the foregoing narrative challenges the common tendency to ascribe to Enlightenment liberalism a serial neglect of particularity – what Oakeshott calls the "topical and transitory" – and a corresponding zeal to develop a universal law and regime modeled on transcendent, abstract, rational principles.[2] But this is a bit too easy: even purveyors of such portraits of the Enlightenment have sometimes regarded Montesquieu as exceptional, and as we have seen, several Enlightenment writers similarly doubted his rightful place among their ranks. Yet few have undertaken to explain *how* Montesquieu's liberalism manages to avoid the tendencies of the radical Enlightenment. This study has demonstrated that Montesquieu's liberal particularism owes much to his rejection of minimalistic conceptions of the requisites of liberal citizenship, his dissatisfaction with narrowly formalistic accounts of liberty, and a distinctively regime-pluralistic understanding of the "principles" of liberty (*EL* 2.11.5). This suggests that Enlightenment political universalism, such as it is, owes more to these features than to a moral universalism or political foundationalism that is, in fact, present in Montesquieu's own thought. It is tempting, in an age skeptical of natural law and natural rights reasoning, to ascribe the sane and sensible flexibility of Montesquieu's liberalism to an ironic neglect of foundations. But Montesquieu has not obliged us by crafting such a freestanding liberalism, and part of what makes his place in the tradition of Enlightenment political philosophy so interesting is his simultaneous acceptance of universal moral foundations and antipathy toward universal politics and universal positive law.

The implications of this study for liberal political theory are threefold, and the first concerns this matter of foundationalism. A clearer appreciation of the coincidence, in Montesquieu's thought, of universal moral foundations with a critique of universal politics might serve to rehabilitate

---

[2] Oakeshott, "Rationalism in Politics," 7.

foundationalism in liberal and democratic theory today. The attraction of anti-foundationalism in political theory derives in no small measure from the supposition that it is better accommodated to the fact of cultural diversity and our corresponding understanding of human moral consciousness as conditioned by circumstances.[3] An encounter with Montesquieu's thought will not persuade the convinced liberal ironist or ethical constructivist to sink roots into the soil of natural law reasoning, but it does serve to demonstrate the possibility of a foundationalist liberalism that is yet wholly compatible with a keen attention to the diversity of human culture. The example of Montesquieu's liberalism, properly digested, should cause us to hesitate before ascribing to non-foundationalist political theory the exclusive distinction of being reconciled to the reality of cultural difference.

In this connection, it is important to recall that Montesquieu himself emphasizes the historically particular and contingent character of the English constitution. Like liberal non-foundationalists, Montesquieu recognizes that liberal constitutional government owes its existence to accidents of history. He does not frame a regime *de novo* from an ahistorical account of Nature, nor does he regard the English constitution as occupying an absolute moment in History. He finds political liberty "where it is" – in a historically contingent regime (*EL* 2.11.5). Yet this does not deter Montesquieu from seeking to understand and to lay bare the rationality of the design principles at work in this undesigned regime, nor does it keep him from drawing the conclusion that English civil and constitutional law conform more closely to natural law and natural right than do despotic and immoderate alternatives. We may even be tempted to speak of Montesquieu's interest in the "rationality of the actual," although unlike Hegel, Montesquieu does not regard history as a process whereby the rational becomes actual. As Hegel himself points out, Montesquieu does not "merely abstract [institutions] from experience to raise them thereafter to some universal."[4] History is the ebb and flow of freedom and slavery, and the English constitution represents an especially free regime produced by chance (*EL* 1.5.19; *EL* 2.11.6, 8). While anti-foundationalists might reasonably charge Hegel with universalizing contingent features of his situation, Montesquieu is far less vulnerable to this charge. His is a foundationalist liberalism reconciled to the facts of historical accident and diversity across human communities.

---

[3] See Rorty, *Contingency, Irony, and Solidarity*, chs. 2–3.
[4] Hegel, "Scientific Ways of Treating Natural Law," 128.

In the same vein, and secondly, this study shows why we should not conceive of liberal theory – even foundationalist liberal theory – as essentially consisting in a form of abstract "political geometry" that must be qualified from without by a confrontation with the fact of cultural difference and the concomitant need for prudential flexibility. Were Montesquieu's the only liberal political philosophy we knew, we would be inclined to think of liberalism as having regard for particularity built in at the level of principle, rather than as a political theory in need of restraints imposed by a worldly sobriety foreign to it. As we observed especially in Chapter 7, Montesquieu's art of statesmanship arises from, and certainly not in spite of, his normative understanding of political liberty and the limited "scope of law." While it is certainly true that political stability ranks among the chief concerns in *The Spirit of the Laws*, the critical and constructive elements of his treatment of regime change derive normative force from liberal commitments and not merely from technical concerns about stability.

A third implication for liberal theory, especially in its contemporary incarnations, arises from this problem of stability. As we considered in the introduction to this study, the mode of theorizing adopted by the most influential liberal theorist of the last century led him to the conclusion that we should conceive of just institutions as generating the moral qualities (e.g., a sense of justice, friendship, mutual trust) necessary for their own support. John Rawls writes, "When institutions are just (as defined by this conception), those taking part in these arrangements acquire the corresponding sense of justice and desire to do their part in maintaining them."[5] If institutions do not generate such requisite "moral attitudes," we must conclude that the principle of justice they embody is "unstable" inasmuch as it could not "engender in human beings the requisite desire to act upon it." This treatment of "the problem of stability" was, in the context of *A Theory of Justice*, an attempt by Rawls to insert a dose of realism into his "realistically utopian" system. As he notes, many normative political theories have "flouted" the question of stability entirely, whereas he believes an adequate theory of justice must grapple with it. But ultimately Rawls's insistence on locating the sources of liberal "moral attitudes" in liberal institutions and principles themselves occludes a realistic account of liberal stability.[6] As Samuel Bowles observes, Rawls fails to "provide

---

[5] Rawls, *Theory of Justice*, 454, 399.   [6] Ibid., 399.

reasons or evidence . . . that these mechanisms entrusted with the perpetuation of liberal values would accomplish that end."[7]

In *Liberal Virtues*, which builds upon Rawls's treatment of stability in *Theory of Justice*, Stephen Macedo affords us insight into one of the reasons Rawls (like Macedo himself) is at pains to find in the practices and institutions of a just liberal order the sources of its own stability. Macedo writes,

> Thinkers as diverse as Friedrich Hayek, Irving Kristol, and Jürgen Habermas argue that the legitimacy and stability of liberal regimes is parasitic on the lingering effects of a pre-capitalist or pre-liberal ethic. An appreciation of the values and ideals grounded in liberal justice could help debunk the notion that liberal regimes are incapable of generating a common ethos capable of unifying a society.[8]

Macedo refers to the "parasitic theory of liberalism," as Samuel Bowles has recently called it. On this theory, liberalism depends upon qualities of heart and mind it cannot call forth and may even undermine.[9] The Rawlsian account of liberal stability represents an effort to diminish the power of this critique.

But Montesquieu's approach to the problem of liberal culture suggests that he sees no reason to hold in suspicion a political order that relies upon mores, manners, customs, and tastes that it does not and cannot forge itself. As we have seen, Montesquieu explores the limited ways in which participation in, and life under, liberal institutions shape a people's character and habits of heart. But he does not consider a defense of the viability of free and moderate government to require an account of these forms of rule as entirely self-sustaining. This is nowhere more apparent than in his account of religion as a source of moral restraint that allows the state to govern more mildly, as we observed in Chapter 5. Indeed, free government appears to be uniquely dependent upon a variety of sources of moral attitudes, customs, and habits. Despotism can, at least for a time, generate its own animating passion through "threats and chastisement" (*EL* 1.3.5), and the "singular institutions" of the Ancients can painfully maintain virtue for a season. But an account of the "mores, manners, and received examples" that "can give rise" to political liberty is necessarily

---

[7] Samuel Bowles, "Is Liberal Society a Parasite on Tradition?" *Philosophy and Public Affairs* 39 (2011): 51.

[8] Macedo, *Liberal Virtues*, 285.

[9] Bowles, "Is Liberal Society a Parasite," 48, associates this view with Burke, Bell, Schumpeter, Hayek, and Habermas, among others.

more complex. For liberal legislators can influence, but can never fully control or directly produce, these elements.[10] If this makes liberalism parasitic, then it should embrace parasitism without embarrassment.

Confronting Montesquieu's political science, contemporary liberal theory might find compelling reasons to shed ideal theory's counterproductive, idiosyncratic assumption concerning stability, and to consider realistically how a liberal society's way of life requires and even consists in subpolitical and suprapolitical mores, manners, beliefs, and patterns of thought. As we have considered, this realm of inquiry is particularly important for Montesquieu's political vision because he regards the "liberal disposition" not merely as a "permissive cause" of liberty – rendering it possible for legislators to frame and sustain free institutions – but also as constitutive of liberty. This understanding is on display most vividly in his psychological account of liberty, and it seems to underpin his long-standing interest in the spirit of tolerance. One cannot consider a people free when they have reason to fear the intolerance of their neighbors, even if the state seeks to guarantee freedom of worship by law. Conversely, mores of tolerance constitute liberty of the citizen, understood as both security and the opinion of security (*EL* 2.12.1). This is an especially illustrative example of what Montesquieu means when he claims that the "customs of a free people" are "part of" their liberty, and when he observes that the right mores, manners, and received examples can "give rise to" liberty (*EL* 2.12.1). If Montesquieu is right about the role of such factors in the maintenance and constitution of liberty, an unrealistic approach to these matters should count as a serious deficiency in a liberal theory of politics.

As we considered in the introduction to this study, a number of recent contributions to contemporary liberal theory have appropriately sought to correct the Rawlsian approach by exploring in detail the "dispositions and virtues necessary to preserve and strengthen the institutions and practices that embody liberalism."[11] Much of this work belongs to the school of "virtue liberalism," which understands itself as applying some of the insights of virtue ethics to the study of liberalism while avoiding the perfectionism of classical approaches. Virtue liberals understand

---

[10] It is instructive to note that Montesquieu's intellectual scion, Alexis de Tocqueville, was among the first to articulate a form of the "parasitic theory of liberalism," arguing, for example, that liberal democracy required the aid of religion, "the most precious heritage from aristocratic times." *Democracy in America*, 544. But the "parasitic" character of modern democracy, such as it is, does not count against it for Tocqueville; this is simply a fact of modern politics to which friends of liberty must accommodate themselves.

[11] Dagger, *Civic Virtues*, 182. See the Introduction to this book.

liberalism as consisting partly in a way of life or ethos – concepts to which we have often returned in our account of Montesquieu. On the view of virtue liberals, the success of liberal politics demands more than the construction of the right formal institutions or the promulgation of abstract moral principles; it requires the effective habituation and education of citizens in a set of virtues consistent with the liberal "way of life." In surveying this literature, one is struck by the impressive list of virtues it posits as necessary to a healthy liberal polity: responsible self-reliance, respect for human dignity, self-restraint, democratic humility, democratic magnanimity, reasonableness, good judgment, public-spiritedness, fortitude, prudence, temperance, civility, and many other qualities.[12]

Though Montesquieu's critical unmasking of classical republican virtue has led some to conclude that his thought supports the view that legal and political institutions and procedures are sufficient to sustain liberal politics, he in fact shares more in common with virtue liberalism than with either a Kantian confidence in rational devils or a Rawlsian dependence upon just institutions as sources of liberal moral attitudes. Still, there is light between Montesquieu's approach and recent work on virtue liberalism. For we find in Montesquieu reason to doubt that a search for "liberal virtues" can ever qualify as an exhaustive search for the "dispositions" (Montesquieu's more capacious term) upon which free and moderate governments depend. Why should we assume that the liberal ethos or way of life consists entirely in traits we can justly describe as virtues?

Virtue liberals sometimes invoke Aristotle's teaching that each regime depends on a certain type of citizen.[13] But this also serves to remind us that Aristotle's good man is only a good citizen in the best regime. If a liberal constitutional order is not the best regime – if indeed the best regime is either chimerical or unrealizable – then we should not expect the qualities that sustain liberal constitutional orders to be uniformly admirable. Here we think, for example, of Montesquieu's discussion of the *"sentiment de justice exacte"* (EL 4.20.2). This quality would fit poorly in a glossy portfolio of liberal virtues, and yet as we considered in Chapter 6, it appears to be one of the important though not intrinsically praiseworthy qualities that sustains modern free regimes. This is to say nothing of

---

[12] See, for example, Spragens, *Civic Liberalism*, ch. 8; James T. Kloppenberg, *The Virtues of Liberalism* (Oxford University Press, 2000); Mark Kingwell, *A Civil Tongue: Justice, Dialogue, and the Politics of Pluralism* (University Park, PA: Pennsylvania State University Press, 1995).

[13] Curtis, *Defending Rorty*, 8.

Montesquieu's discussion of matters such as personal orientations toward action and egalitarian attitudes within the household, neither of which rise to the level of virtue but both of which seem to be critical elements in a full account of liberalism as a "way of life." All of this suggests that theorists interested in the habits, attitudes, and character traits that sustain modern liberal orders must cast a wider gaze, looking beyond the liberal virtues.[14]

Thinking about the liberal disposition in this way has an additional advantage: it renders us less hesitant to acknowledge frankly that not all societies possess such a disposition in equal measure. If we imagine the liberal ethos to consist in reasonableness, good judgment, temperance, democratic humility, and other commendable qualities of mind and character, our allergy to claims of cultural superiority may lead us to shrink back from the hypothesis that some nations lack such an ethos. As President George W. Bush urged, "It is not realism to suppose that one-fifth of humanity is unsuited to liberty; it is ... condescension, and we should have none of it."[15] But if we recognize that the liberal disposition is not constituted of wholly admirable qualities, and if we further understand that its emergence may even entail the loss of some estimable moral habits and customs – Montesquieu points to the "generous virtues" as a possible casualty – then we may find ourselves more willing to speak frankly and think clearly about its scarcity in some quarters.

Like liberal theory, liberal statecraft stands to gain from a reclamation of Montesquieu's thought and example. As we considered in the introduction to this book, contemporary liberal statecraft's unseriousness about liberal democracy's preconditions mirrors the deficiencies in liberal theory's treatment of the same. We identified one particularly unsound expectation that has played a role in recent American foreign policy. This is the expectation that human nature, or liberal institutions themselves, or (only slightly more plausibly) a few years of practice with liberal institutions, may furnish a nation with the habits, attitudes, and capacities

---

[14] By the same token, perhaps we may justly charge Montesquieu with neglecting some of the genuine human virtues that strengthen the "liberal disposition"; here Montesquieuian liberalism may have something to gain from virtue liberalism.

[15] Bush, "Remarks at Whitehall Palace," 1576–7. Then-National Security Advisor Condoleezza Rice similarly warned, "[L]et us never indulge the condescending voices who allege that some people are not interested in freedom or aren't ready for freedom's responsibilities. That view was wrong in 1963 in Birmingham and it is wrong in 2003 in Baghdad." Condoleezza Rice, "Remarks by National Security Advisor Condoleezza Rice at the 28th Annual Convention of the National Association of Black Journalists, August 7, 2003." Last accessed March 27, 2017. https://georgewbush-whitehouse.archives.gov/.

needed for the perpetuation of those institutions. The project of regime change in Iraq and the total withdrawal of US forces (predicated on our having left behind a "sovereign, stable, and self-reliant Iraq") each owed something to these misplaced hopes, hopes that would be chastened through an encounter with Montesquieu's liberalism.[16] And even beyond debates concerning the invasions and occupations that followed the September 11th terrorist attacks, revisiting Montesquieu's thought serves to enrich related discussions about the global future of liberal democracy.

Nothing in *The Spirit of the Laws* can relieve us of the need to use our own moral and political judgment in particular cases. Montesquieu himself adverts to this limitation: "I do not speak of particular cases: as mechanics has its frictions which often change or check its theoretical effects, politics, too, has its frictions" (*EL* 3.17.8). Without analyzing such "frictions" in detail, it is difficult to say conclusively whether Montesquieu's liberalism could, for example, underwrite a thoroughgoing critique of any particular point of US foreign policy. Instead, reflection on his political thought commends to our attention several midrange principles that provide practical guidance without yielding determinate answers in specific cases.

First, Montesquieu's liberal particularism suggests reasons for maintaining a presumptive judgment against the initiation of international projects of armed regime change.[17] This is not an absolute negative, but Montesquieu's approach leads us to regard such endeavors with profound moral and practical suspicion. In the eyes of a Montesquieuian liberal, these efforts betray a misunderstanding of the role of culture and character in supporting and constituting liberty. Such projects are likely to produce a psychological simulacrum of the experience of men under despotic regimes, and they tend to yield perpetual instability that can result in the return of "real tyranny." Thus, for example, neither the immediate aftermath of the 2003 American-led invasion of Iraq nor the consequences of the 2011 American withdrawal from Iraq would induce surprise in a Montesquieuian liberal.

---

[16] Obama, "Remarks at Fort Bragg, North Carolina, December 14, 2011."

[17] For contemporary critical perspectives on armed regime change, see Bruce Bueno de Mesquita and George W. Downs, "Intervention and Democracy," *International Organization* 60 (2006): 627–49; Francis Fukuyama, *America at the Crossroads: Democracy, Power, and the Neoconservative Legacy* (New Haven, CT: Yale University Press, 2006). For an alternative view, see James Meernik, "United States Military Intervention and the Promotion of Democracy," *Journal of Peace Research* 33 (1996): 391–402; Mark Peceny, *Democracy at the Point of Bayonets* (University Park, PA: Pennsylvania State University Press, 1999); Paul D. Miller, *Armed State Building: Confronting State Failure, 1898–2012* (Ithaca, NY: Cornell University Press, 2013).

The presumptive judgment against coercive regime change does not extend to prudent foreign aid programs focused on "democracy assistance," which are often regarded as alternatives to forcible state building. While a Montesquieuian liberal will cautiously assess any proposal to improve political institutions in a foreign nation, he does not believe the sources of reform are so inscrutable as to lie beyond the ken of well-taught observers and statesmen. A second midrange principle might inform the allocation of resources for such peaceful democratic assistance: whether domestic or international, private or public, this form of aid should flow not only to programs with obvious links to political or legal institutions (e.g., organizing forums for citizens to debate a proposed constitution or training opposition party leaders), but also to projects aimed at effecting gradual cultural shifts that will have long-term, subterranean political effects.[18] Such projects are on the menu of democracy assistance programs supported by the United States and European Union, but they are by no means the predominant form.[19] Of special interest to a Montesquieuian liberal might be initiatives for the education of women and girls with an eye toward reshaping illiberal patterns in relations between the sexes, which both Montesquieu and contemporary political science identify as politically salient.[20] A more controversial course of action, perhaps reserved for private forms of democracy assistance, would entail the promotion of benign forms of religion as alternatives to violent, antiliberal sects (e.g., funding for construction of houses of worship and

---

[18] Laurence Whitehead, "On 'Cultivating Democracy,'" in *The Conceptual Politics of Democracy*, eds. Christopher Hobson and Milja Kurki (London: Routledge, 2012), 23. On the distinction between developmental and political forms of democracy assistance, see Thomas Carothers, "Democracy Assistance: Political vs. Developmental?" *Journal of Democracy* 20 (2009): 5–19. Even Carothers's developmental approach features programs that would appear narrowly political and institutional in the context of Montesquieu's political science.

[19] For a fine typology of democracy assistance programs now in use, see Sara Sunn Bush, *The Taming of Democracy Assistance* (Cambridge University Press, 2015), 55ff. No extant study compares the effectiveness of all forms of democracy assistance, but Steven E. Finkel, Aníbal Pérez-Liñán, and Mitchell A. Seligson, "The Effects of U.S. Foreign Assistance on Democracy Building, 1990–2003," *World Politics* 59 (2007), 404–39, find that democracy assistance in general has a significant positive impact on democratization.

[20] See especially M. Steven Fish, "Islam and Authoritarianism," *World Politics* 55, (2002), 4–37. Fish concludes that Islam has a democracy deficit, and that this deficit can be explained mainly as a function of the subordination of women. For a critical response, see Daniela Donno and Bruce Russett, "Islam, Authoritarianism, and Female Empowerment: What Are the Linkages?" *World Politics* 56 (2004): 582–607.

religious schools led by moderate clerics supporting secular law).[21] Efforts like these are inevitably difficult to defend to those who take a narrowly institutional view of liberal democracy, but the Montesquieuan liberal understands their political significance just as he perceives, in Peter the Great's importation of German fashions, the seeds of a possible political transition: "*Tout est extrêment lié*" (*EL* 3.19.15).

This underscores an irony in our story. While the political universalist may expect that a natural human desire or capacity for freedom can sustain liberal political forms in any culture, liberal particularism leads us to acknowledge frankly that the global spread of liberal politics requires a significant degree of cultural *convergence* over time. A failure to acknowledge this reality makes transitions to liberal government appear as something short of the monumental undertakings they truly are.

Paradoxically, however, liberalization does not always require the degree of institutional convergence that political universalists assume. Here a third principle emerges: domestic reformers and foreign interveners should not hold too rigidly to any one set of political institutions or form of law as the *sine qua non* of liberal constitutional government. While our discussion of Montesquieu's views on monarchy may at times seem trapped in the tenth century, a lasting implication of those reflections is that political liberty is attainable in a variety of constitutional forms. On Montesquieu's account, constitutional reform does not always require regime change in the strict sense, that is, replacing one regime type with another. It may involve modifying the way in which preexisting powers are combined and balanced. And even when the pace of improvement in constitutional forms is glacial, reformers can cultivate liberty through changes in criminal and civil law – to say nothing of culture – which often admit of fine, gradual emendations with far-reaching effects, as Montesquieu emphasizes. The Montesquieuian liberal recognizes that political liberty comes in degrees, and the task of liberal political reform is to expand the "degree of liberty" present in any given nation (*EL* 1.1.3).

Trade and commerce rise to prominence when Montesquieu turns subtly to the problem of transitions to free and moderate government. He never predicts that political liberty will invariably follow the expansion of commerce, and, as I have suggested in Chapter 6, his misgivings about the dark side of commercial mores may even anticipate the

---

[21] See Angel Rabasa, Cheryl Benard, Lowell Schwartz et al., *Building Moderate Muslim Networks* (Washington, DC: Rand Corporation, 2007).

incomplete success of commerce as an engine of liberal culture. But in the round, history has been kind to the hypothesis that commercial society and political liberty are causally linked.[22] Therefore, while acknowledging the limits of commerce, the Montesquieuian liberal does not weary of pursuing new avenues for economic opening as a prelude to political reform. This would include the encouragement of national and international commerce. Through the lens of Montesquieu's liberal political science, commercial activity appears as a means of changing culture without resort to illiberal regimes of cultural legislation that overshoot the legitimate scope of law (*EL* 3.19.14).

The doctrinaire politics of Montesquieu's critics was more plausible in the mid-eighteenth century than it is in our own day. At the time, it had the advantage of having never been tested by experience. But modern history has not flattered rationalistic strains of liberal and democratic theory, and the events of the last fifteen years have vividly displayed in our lifetime the character of liberal democracy as a distinctive way of life rather than the default setting of humanity. Although modern liberty may not demand the widespread, painful self-sacrifice of ancient virtue, its preconditions do not arise spontaneously from the human heart or finely wrought structures of government. Liberty's preconditions may develop through historical accident or political husbandry, but not by universal nature or manufacture. Too often this truth has been obscured in liberal political theory and discourse. Theorists and citizens keen to consider its implications for modern statesmanship can make a good beginning in the political science and philosophy of the baron de Montesquieu.

---

[22] Consider J. Ernesto López-Córdova and Christopher M. Meissner, "The Impact of International Trade on Democracy: A Long-Run Perspective," *World Politics* 60 (2008): 539–75.

Bibliography

Adams, Geoffrey. *The Huguenots and French Opinion, 1685–1787: The Enlightenment Debate on Toleration.* Waterloo, ON: Wilfrid Laurier University Press, 1991.

Adams, John. *The Works of John Adams.* 6 vols. Ed. Charles Francis Adams. Boston: Little, Brown & Co., 1850–6.

Allen, J. W. *History of Political Thought in the Sixteenth Century.* London: Routledge, 2013.

Allison, Henry E. *Kant's Theory of Freedom.* New York: Routledge, 2002.

Almond, Gabriel. "Comparative Political Systems." *The Journal of Politics* 18, no. 3 (1956): 391–401.

Almond, Gabriel, and Sidney Verba. *The Civic Culture: Political Attitudes and Democracy in Five Nations.* Princeton University Press, 1963.

Althusser, Louis. *Politics and History: Montesquieu, Rousseau, Hegel, and Marx,* trans. Ben Brewster (London: NLB, 1972).

Aquinas, Thomas. *The Summa Theologiae of St. Thomas Aquinas,* trans. Fathers of the English Dominican Province (London: Burns, Oates, and Washbourne, 1911).

Arendt, Hannah. *On Revolution.* New York: Penguin, 1990.

The Promise of Politics. New York: Schocken Books, 2005.

Aristotle. *Politics,* trans. C. D. C. Reeve. Indianapolis: Hackett Publishing Company, 1998.

Aron, Raymond. *Main Currents in Sociological Thought: Montesquieu, Comte, Marx, de Tocqueville, and the Sociologists and the Revolution of 1848,* ed. Brian Anderson and Daniel Mahoney. 2 vols. New Brunswick, NJ: Transaction Publishers, 1999.

Baker, Keith Michael. *Inventing the French Revolution: Essays on French Political Culture in the Eighteenth Century.* Cambridge University Press, 1990.

Bakos, Adrianna E. *Images of Kingship in Early Modern France: Louis XI in Political Thought, 1560–1789.* London: Routledge, 1997.

Barnett, S. J. *The Enlightenment and Religion: The Myths of Modernity.* Manchester University Press, 2004.

Barrel, Rex A. *Bolingbroke and France.* Lanham, MD: University Press of America, 1988.

Barrera, Guillaume. *Les Lois du monde: Enquête sur le dessein politique de Montesquieu.* Paris: Gallimard, 2009.

Barry, Brian. *Culture and Equality: An Egalitarian Critique of Multiculturalism.* Cambridge, MA: Harvard University Press, 2002.

Bart, Jean. "French Law." In *Dictionnaire Montesquieu*, ed. Catherine Volpilhac-Auger. Accessed March 27, 2017. http://dictionnaire-montesquieu.ens-lyon .fr/fr/article/1367163217/en/

"Montesquieu et l'unification du droit." In *Le Temps de Montesquieu: Actes du colloque international de Genève (28–31 octobre 1998)*, ed. Michel Porret and Catherine Volphilhac-Auger. Geneva: Librairie Droz, 2002, 137–46.

Bartlett, Robert C. *The Idea of Enlightenment: A Post-mortem Study.* University of Toronto Press, 2001.

"On the Politics of Faith and Reason: The Project of Enlightenment in Pierre Bayle and Montesquieu." *The Journal of Politics* 63, no. 1 (2001): 1–28.

Bates, Robert H., and Da-Hsiang Donald Lien. "A Note on Taxation, Development, and Representative Government." *Politics & Society* 14, no. 1 (1985): 53–70.

Bates, William David. *A Philosophical Commentary on These Words of the Gospel, Luke 14.23, 'Compel Them to Come In, That My House May Be Full'*, ed. John Kilcullen and Chandran Kukathas. Indianapolis: Liberty Fund, 2005.

States of War: Enlightenment Origins of the Politics. New York: Columbia University Press, 2012.

Bayle, Pierre. *Continuation des Pensées Diverses.* Amsterdam: Herman Uytwerf, 1722.

Political Writings, ed. Sally L. Jenkinson. Cambridge University Press, 2000.

Becker, Carl L. *The Heavenly City of the Eighteenth-Century Philosophers.* New Haven, CT: Yale University Press, 1932.

Beiner, Ronald. *Civil Religion: A Dialogue in the History of Political Philosophy.* New York: Cambridge University Press, 2011.

What's the Matter with Liberalism? Berkeley: University of California Press, 1992.

Belissa, Marc. "Montesquieu, *L'Esprit des Lois* et le droit des gens." In *Le Temps de Montesquieu: Actes du colloque international de Genève (28–31 octobre 1998)*, ed. Michel Porret and Catherine Volpilhac-Auger. Geneva: Librairie Droz, 2002, 171–84.

Benrekassa, Georges. *Montesquieu, la liberté et l'histoire.* Paris: Librairie générale française, 1987.

Berkowitz, Peter. *Virtue and the Making of Modern Liberalism.* Princeton University Press, 1999.

Berlin, Isaiah. "Montesquieu." In *Against the Current: Essays in the History of Ideas*, ed. Henry Hardy. Princeton University Press, 2001, 164–203.

Three Critics of the Enlightenment: Vico, Hamann, Herder. Princeton University Press, 2000.

Beyer, Charles-Jacques. "Montesquieu et la censure religieuse de *L'Esprit des lois.*" *Revue des sciences humaines* 70 (1953): 105–31.

Bianchi, Lorenzo. "'L'auteur a loué Bayle, en l'appelant un grand homme:' Bayle dans la *Défense de L'Esprit des lois.*" In *Montesquieu, oeuvre ouverte? (1748–1755): Actes du colloque de Bordeaux*, ed. Catherine Larrère. Naples and Oxford: Liguori and Voltaire Foundation, 2005, 103–14.

"La funzione della religione in Europa e nei paesi orientali secondo Montesquieu." In *L'Europe de Montesquieu: Actes du olloque de Gêne*, compiled by M. G. Bottaro Palumbo and A. Postigliola. Oxford: Voltaire Foundation, 1995, 375–87.

"Histoire et nature: la religion dans *L'Esprit des Lois.*" In *Le Temps de Montesquieu: Actes du colloque international de Genève (28–31 octobre 1998)*, ed. Michel Porret and Catherine Volpilhac-Auger. Geneva: Librairie Droz, 2002, 289–304.

Binoche, Bertrand. *Introduction* à De l'esprit des lois *de Montesquieu*. Paris: Presses universitaires de France, 1998.

Blitz, Mark. "How to Think about Politics and Culture." *Political Science Reviewer* 25, no. 1 (1996): 5–21.

Bodin, Jean. *Les Six Livres De La République*, ed. Gérard Mairet. Paris: Livre du Poche, [1576] 1993.

Boesche, Roger. "Fearing Monarchs and Merchants: Montesquieu's Two Theories of Despotism." *The Western Political Quarterly* 43, no. 4 (1990): 741–62.

Boone, Rebecca Ard. *War, Domination, and the Monarchy of France: Claude de Seyssel and the Language of Politics in the Renaissance*. Leiden, The Netherlands: Brill, 2007.

Boulainvilliers, Henri de. *Histoire de l'ancien gouvernement de la France*. The Hague and Amsterdam, 1727.

Lettres sur les anciens parlements de France que l'on nomme Etats-généraux. London: Wood and Palmer, 1753.

Bourke, Richard. "Hume's Call to Action." *The Nation*, April 20, 2016. www .thenation.com/article/humes-call-to-action/.

Bowles, Samuel. "Is Liberal Society a Parasite on Tradition?" *Philosophy & Public Affairs* 39, no. 1 (2011): 46–81.

Bradley, Jerry H. *Politics and Culture in Renaissance Naples*. Princeton University Press, 1987.

Brague, Remi. *The Law of God: The Philosophical History of an Idea*. University of Chicago Press, 2007.

Brewer, Daniel. *The Enlightenment Past: Reconstructing Eighteenth-Century French Thought*. Cambridge University Press, 2011.

Brown, Wendy. *Edgework: Critical Essays on Knowledge and Politics*. Princeton University Press, 2005.

Bryan, William Jennings. "Imperialism." In Vol. 2 of *Speeches of William Jennings Bryan*, ed. William Jennings Bryan. New York, London: Funk & Wagnalls Company, 1909, 17–49.

Budé, Guillaume. *Annotationes in quator et viginti Pandectarum libros*. Paris: 1535.

"On the Education of the Prince." In Vol. 2 of *Cambridge Translations of Renaissance Philosophical Texts: Political Philosophy*, trans. Neil Kenny, ed. Jill Kraye. Cambridge University Press, 1997. 258–73.

Bueno de Mesquita, Bruce, and George W. Downs. "Intervention and Democracy." *International Organization* 60, no. 3 (2006): 627–49.

Burgess, Glenn. *Absolute Monarchy and the Stuart Constitution*. New Haven, CT: Yale University Press, 1996.

Bush, George W. "Inaugural Address, January 20, 2005." In *Public Papers of the Presidents of the United States: George W. Bush, 2005, Book 2, Presidential Documents – January 1 to June 30, 2005*. Washington, DC: Government Publishing Office, 2007.

"Remarks on the 20th Anniversary of the National Endowment for Democracy, November 6, 2003." In *Public Papers of the Presidents of the United States: George W. Bush, 2003, Book 2, Presidential Documents – July 1 to December 31, 2003*. Washington, DC: Government Publishing Office, 2006.

"Remarks at Whitehall Palace in London, United Kingdom, November 19, 2003." In *Public Papers of the Presidents of the United States: George W. Bush, 2003, Book 2, Presidential Documents – July 1 to December 31, 2003*. Washington, DC: Government Publishing Office, 2006.

Bush, Sara Sunn. *The Taming of Democracy Assistance*. Cambridge University Press, 2015.

Carcassone, Élie. *Montesquieu et le problème de la constitution française au XVIIIe siècle*. Paris: Presses Universitaires de France, 1927.

Carlyle, R. W., and A. J. Carlyle. *Political Theory from 1300 to 1600*. Vol. 6 of *A History of Medieval Political Theory in the West*. Edinburgh and London: W. Blackwood and Sons, 1936.

Carothers, Thomas. "Democracy Assistance: Political vs. Developmental?" *Journal of Democracy* 20, no. 1 (2009): 5–19.

Carrese, Paul O. *The Cloaking of Power: Montesquieu, Blackstone, and the Rise of Judicial Activism*. University of Chicago Press, 2003.

Democracy in Moderation: Montesquieu, Tocqueville, and Sustainable Liberalism. Cambridge University Press, 2016.

"The Machiavellian Spirit of Montesquieu's Republic." In *Machiavelli's Liberal Republican Legacy*, ed. Paul A. Rahe. Cambridge University Press, 2006, 121–42.

Carrithers, David W. "Introduction." In *The Spirit of Laws: A Compendium of the First English Edition*. Berkeley: University of California Press, 1977, 3–90.

"Introduction: An Appreciation of *The Spirit of Laws*." In *Montesquieu's Science of Politics: Essays on* The Spirit of Laws, eds. David Carrithers, Michael A. Mosher, and Paul A. Rahe. Lanham, MD: Rowman & Littlefield, 2001, 1–40.

"Montesquieu and the Liberal Philosophy of Jurisprudence." In *Montesquieu's Science of Politics: Essays on* The Spirit of Laws, eds. David W. Carrithers, Michael A. Mosher, and Paul A. Rahe. Lanham, MD: Rowman & Littlefield, 2001, 291–334.

"Montesquieu's Philosophy of Punishment." *History of Political Thought* 19, no. 2 (1998): 213–40.

"Montesquieu and Tocqueville as Philosophical Historians: Liberty, Determinism, and the Prospects for Freedom." In *Montesquieu and His Legacy*, ed. Rebecca E. Kingston. Albany, NY: State University of New York Press, 2009, 149–78.

Casson, Douglass. *Liberating Judgment: Fanatics, Skeptics, and John Locke's Politics of Probability*. Princeton University Press, 2011.

Ceaser, James W. "Alexis de Tocqueville and the Two-Founding Thesis." *Review of Politics* 73, no. 2 (2011): 219–43.

Designing a Polity: America's Constitution in Theory and Practice. Lanham, MD: Rowman & Littlefield, 2010.

Liberal Democracy and Political Science. Baltimore: Johns Hopkins University Press, 1990.

Charron, Pierre. *De la sagesse*. Rouen: Chez L. Costé, [1601] 1614.

Chauveau-Maulini, Bruce. "La notion de monarchie tempérée dans les remontrances des parlements au XVIIe siècle: Montesquieu et l'idéologie de robe." In *Annales: Droit, Histoire, Philosophie, Sociologie, Procès*. Paris: École doctorale d'histoire du droit, sociologie du droit, philosophie du droit et droit processuel, Université Panthéon-Assas, 2006, 197–242.

Chevallier, Jean-Jacques. "Montesquieu, ou Le Libéralisme aristocratique." *Revue internationale de la philosophie* 9 (1955): 330–45.

Chinard, Gilbert. *Jefferson et les idéologues*. Baltimore: Johns Hopkins Press, 1925.

"Montesquieu's Historical Pessimism." In *Studies in the History of Culture: The Disciplines of the Humanities*, ed. Gilbert Chinard. Menasha, WI: George Banta, 1942, 161–72.

Church, William Farr. *Constitutional Thought in Sixteenth-Century France: A Study in the Evolution of Ideas*. Cambridge, MA: Harvard University Press, 1941.

"The Decline of French Jurists as Political Theorists." *French Historical Studies* 3 (1967): 1–40.

Cicero. *Les Offices*, trans. Philippe Goibaud du Bois. Paris: 1714.

Cicero. *On Duties*, eds. M. T. Griffin and E. M. Atkins. Cambridge University Press, 1991.

Cohler, Anne M. *Montesquieu's Comparative Politics and the Spirit of American Constitutionalism*. Lawrence, KS: University Press of Kansas, 1989.

Collins, James B. *The State in Early Modern France*. Cambridge University Press, 1995.

Condorcet, Jean Antoine Nicolas de Caritat. "Essay on the Constitution and Functions of the Provincial Assemblies." In *Condorcet, Selected Writings*, ed. Keith Barker. Indianapolis: Bobbs-Merrill, 1976.

"Observations on the Thirty-First Book." In Antoine Louis Claude Destutt de Tracy, *A Commentary and Review of Montesquieu's Spirit of Laws, To Which Are Annexed, 'Observations on the Thirty-First Book,' by the Late M. Condorcet, and Two Letters of Helvétius, On the Merits of the Same Work*, trans. Thomas Jefferson. Philadelphia: William Duane, 1811.

Constant, Benjamin. "The Liberty of the Ancients Compared with That of the Moderns." In *Political Writings*, trans. Biancamaria Fontana. Cambridge University Press, 1988, 307–28.

"The Spirit of Conquest and Usurpation and Their Relation to European Civilization." In *Political Writings*, trans. Biancamaria Fontana. Cambridge University Press, 1988, 43–168.

Cotta, Sergio. "La funzione politica della religione secondi Montesquieu." *Rivista internazionale di filosofia del diritto* 43 (1966): 582–603.

Courtney, C. P. "*L'Esprit des lois* dans la perspective de l'histoire du livre (1748–1800)." In *Le Temps de Montesquieu: Actes du colloque international de Genève (28–31 octobre 1998)*, eds. Michel Porret and Catherine Volpilhac-Auger. Geneva: Librairie Droz, 2002, 65–96.

Montesquieu and Burke. Oxford: Basil Blackwell, 1963.

"Montesquieu and Natural Law." In *Montesquieu's Science of Politics: Essays on* The Spirit of Laws, eds. David W. Carrithers, Michael A. Mosher, and Paul A. Rahe. Lanham, MD: Rowman & Littlefield, 2001, 41–68.

Courtois, Jean-Patrice. *Inflexions de la rationalité dans* L'Esprit des lois – *Écriture et pensée chez Montesquieu*. Paris: Presses Universitaires de France, 1999.

Cox, Iris. *Montesquieu and the History of French Laws*. Oxford: Voltaire Foundation, 1983.

"Montesquieu and the History of Laws." In *Montesquieu's Science of Politics: Essays on* The Spirit of Laws, eds. David W. Carrithers, Michael A. Mosher, and Paul A. Rahe. Lanham, MD: Rowman & Littlefield, 2001, 409–30.

Craiutu, Aurelian. *A Virtue for Courageous Minds: Moderation in French Political Thought, 1748–1830*. Princeton University Press, 2012.

Crevier, J. B. L. *Observations sur le livre de l'Esprit des lois*. Paris: Desaint et Saillant, 1764.

Curran, Mark. *Atheism, Religion and Enlightenment in Pre-Revolutionary Europe*. London: Royal Historical Society, 2012.

Curren, Randall. *Aristotle on the Necessity of Public Education*. Lanham, MD: Rowman & Littlefield, 2000.

Curtis, William. *Defending Rorty: Pragmatism and Liberal Virtue*. New York: Cambridge University Press, 2015.

Dagger, Richard. *Civic Virtues: Rights, Citizenship, and Republican Liberalism*. Oxford University Press, 1997.

Dahlinger, James H. *Etienne Pasquier on Ethics and History*. New York: Peter Lang, 2007.

Dallmyr, Fred. "Montesquieu's *Persian Letters*: A Timely Classic." In *Montesquieu and His Legacy*, ed. Rebecca E. Kingston. Albany, NY: State University of New York Press, 2009, 239–58.

Davis, Michael. *The Politics of Philosophy: A Commentary on Aristotle's Politics*. Lanham, MD: Rowman & Littlefield, [1947] 1996.

Dawson, John P. "The Codification of the French Customs." *Michigan Law Review* 38, no. 6 (1940): 765–800.

Dedieu, Joseph. *Montesquieu*. Paris: F. Alcan, 1913.

Montesquieu et la Tradition Politique Anglaise en France. Paris: Librairie Victor Lecoffre, 1909.

Desgraves, Louis, and Catherine Volpilhac-Auger, eds. *Catalogue de la bibliothèque de Montesquieu à La Brède*. Naples: Liguori Editore, 1999.

Desserud, Donald. "Commerce and Political Participation in Montesquieu's Letter to Domville." *History of European Ideas* 25, no. 3 (1999): 135–51.

Destutt de Tracy, Antoine Louis Claude. *A Commentary and Review of Montesquieu's* Spirit of Laws, To Which Are Annexed, 'Observations on the Thirty-First Book,' by the Late M. Condorcet, and Two Letters of Helvétius, On the Merits of the Same Work, trans. Thomas Jefferson. Philadelphia: William Duane, 1811.

Diamond, Larry. *Developing Democracy: Toward Consolidation.* Baltimore: Johns Hopkins University Press , 1999.

Dictionnaire de L'Académie française, 4th edn. Paris: Veuve Brunet, 1762.

De Dijn, Annelien. *French Political Thought from Montesquieu to Tocqueville: Liberty in a Levelled Society?* Cambridge University Press, 2008.

"Montesquieu's Controversial Context: *The Spirit of the Laws* as a Monarchist Tract." *History of Political Thought* 34 (2013): 66–88.

"On Political Liberty: Montesquieu's Missing Manuscript," *Political Theory* 39, no. 2 (2001): 181–204.

"Was Montesquieu a Liberal Republican?" *Review of Politics* 76 (2014): 21–41.

Dimoff, Paul. "Cicéron, Hobbes et Montesquieu." *Annales Universitatis Saraviensis* 1 (1952): 19–47.

Djaït, Hichem. *Europe and Islam,* trans. Peter Heinegg. Berkeley: University of California Press, 1985.

Donno, Daniela, and Bruce Russett. "Islam, Authoritarianism, and Female Empowerment: What Are the Linkages?" *World Politics* 56, no. 4 (2004): 582–607.

Dos Santos, Antonio Carlos. "L'intolérance dans la Querelle de *L'Esprit des lois.*" In *Montesquieu, Oeuvre ouverte? (1748–1755): Actes du colloque de Bordeaux, 6–8 décembre 2001,* ed. Catherine Larrère. Napoli: Liguori Editore Srl, 2005, 131–40.

Douen, Emmanuel-Orentin. "Le Fondateur de la Caisse des Conversions." *Bulletin de la Société de l'histoire du protestantisme francais* 30 (1853): 145–60.

Douglass, Frederick. *The Narrative Life of Frederick Douglass.* Cambridge, MA: Harvard University Press, 2009.

Dubos, Jean-Baptiste. *Histoire critique de l'établissement de la monarchie française.* Paris, 1742.

Duconseil, Marc. *Machiavel et Montesquieu: recherche sur un principe d'autorité.* Paris: Les Éditions Denoël, 1943.

Dunn, John. *Political Obligation in Its Historical Context: Essays in Political Theory.* Cambridge University Press, 2002.

Durkheim, Émile. *Montesquieu and Rousseau: Forerunners of Sociology,* trans. Ralph Manheim. Ann Arbor, MI: University of Michigan Press, 1960.

Dyck, Andrew R. *A Commentary on Cicero, De Officiis.* Ann Arbor, MI: University of Michigan Press, 1996.

Eagleton, Terry. "Nationalism, Irony, and Commitment." In Terry Eagleton, Fredric Jameson, and Edward W. Said, *Nationalism, Colonialism, and Literature.* Minneapolis: University of Minnesota Press, 1990, 23–42.

Eckstein, Harry. "A Culturalist Theory of Political Change." *American Political Science Review* 82, no. 3 (1988): 789–804.

Ehrard, Jean. *L'idée de Nature en France à l'aube des Lumières*. Paris: Flammarion, 1970.

Politique de Montesquieu. Paris: Armand Colin, 1965.

Ellis, Elizabeth. *Kant's Politics: Provisional Theory for an Uncertain World*. New Haven, CT: Yale University Press, 2005.

Ellis, Harold A. *Boulainvilliers and the French Monarchy*. Ithaca, NY: Cornell University Press, 1988.

"Montesquieu's Modern Politics: *The Spirit of the Laws* and the Problem of Modern Monarchy in Old Regime France." *History of Political Thought* 10, no. 4 (1989): 665–700.

Elster, Jon. *Alexis de Tocqueville: The First Social Scientist*. Cambridge University Press, 2009.

Eisenmann, Charles. "L'Esprit des lois et la séparation des pouvoirs." *Cahiers de philosophie politique* 2–3 (1985): 3–34.

"La pensée constitutionnelle de Montesquieu." *Cahiers de philosophie politique* (1985): 35–66.

Finkel, Steven E., Aníbal Pérez-Liñán, and Mitchell A. Seligson. "The Effects of U.S. Foreign Assistance on Democracy Building, 1990–2003." *World Politics* 59, no. 3 (2007): 404–39.

Fish, M. Steven. "Islam and Authoritarianism." *World Politics* 55, no. 1 (2002): 4–37.

Fletcher, Frank Thomas Herbert. *Montesquieu and English Politics (1750–1800)*. London: Porcupine Press, 1939.

"Montesquieu's Influence on Anti-Slavery Opinion in England." *Journal of Negro History* 28 (1933): 414–26.

Florus. *The Epitome of Roman History*, trans. E. S. Forster. Cambridge, MA: Harvard University Press, 1929.

Force, Pierre. *Self-Interest before Adam Smith: A Genealogy of Economic Science*. Cambridge University Press, 2003.

Ford, Franklin. *Robe and Sword: The Regrouping of the French Aristocracy after Louis XIV*. Cambridge, MA: Harvard University Press, 1962.

Forst, Rainer. *Toleration in Conflict: Past and Present*. Cambridge University Press, 2013.

Franco, Paul N. *Hegel's Philosophy of Freedom*. New Haven, CT: Yale University Press, 1999.

Franklin, Julian H. *Jean Bodin and the Rise of Absolutist Theory*. Cambridge University Press, 1973.

Jean Bodin and the Sixteenth-Century Revolution in the Methodology of Law and History. New York: Columbia University Press, 1963.

Freedom House. "Freedom in the World 2013." Accessed March 27, 2017. https://freedomhouse.org/sites/default/files/FIW%202013%20Booklet.pdf.

"Freedom in the World 2016." Accessed March 27, 2017. https://freedom house.org/sites/default/files/FH_FITW_Report_2016.pdf

Friedrich, Carl Joachim. *The Philosophy of Law in Historical Perspective*. University of Chicago Press, 1963.

Fukuyama, Francis. *America at the Crossroads: Democracy, Power, and the Neoconservative Legacy*. New Haven, CT: Yale University Press, 2006.

The End of History and the Last Man. New York: Free Press, 1992.

Galston, William. *Liberal Purposes: Good, Virtues, and Diversity in the Liberal State*. Cambridge University Press, 1991.

Gay, Peter. *The Enlightenment: The Rise of Modern Paganism*. New York: W. W. Norton & Company, 1966.

The Science of Freedom. Vol. 2 of *The Enlightenment: An Interpretation*. New York: Alfred A. Knopf, 1969.

Gaynor, Tim. "U.S. project flies democracy message on Afghan kites." *Reuters*, September 24, 2010. Accessed March 26, 2017. www.reuters.com/article/us-afghanistan-kites-idUSTRE68N2SS20100924.

Giesey, Ralph E. "The Monarchomach Triumvirs: Hotman, Beza, and Mornay." *Bibliothèque D'Humanisme Et Renaissance* 32, no. 1 (1970): 41–56.

Gill, Christopher. "Personhood and Personality: The Four-Personae Theory in Cicero, *De Officiis* I." In Vol. 6 of *Oxford Studies in Ancient Philosophy*, ed. Julia Annas. Oxford: Oxford University Press, 1988, 169–99.

Gill, Emily R. *Becoming Free: Autonomy and Diversity in the Liberal Polity*. Lawrence, KS: University of Kansas, 2001.

Gilmore, Myron Piper. *Argument from Roman Law in Political Thought 1200–1600*. Cambridge, MA: Harvard University Press, 1941.

Goldschmidt, Victor. "L'état de nature dans *L'Esprit des Lois*." In *Anthropologie et politique: Les principes du système de Rousseau*. Paris: Vrin, 1974, 189–217.

Goldthwaite, Richard A. *The Economy of Renaissance Florence*. Baltimore: Johns Hopkins University Press, 2009.

Goodman, Rob. "Doux Commerce, Jew Commerce: Intolerance and Tolerance in Voltaire and Montesquieu," *History of Political Thought* 37, no. 3 (2016): 530–55.

Gordon, Daniel. *Citizens without Sovereignty: Equality and Sociability in French Thought, 1670–1789*. Princeton University Press, 1994.

Goyard-Fabre, Simone. *Montesquieu, adversaire de Hobbes*. Paris: Lettres Modernes, 1980.

"Montesquieu entre Domat et Portalis." *McGill Law Journal* 35 (1990): 716–45.

Montesquieu: La Nature, les lois, la liberté. Paris: Presses Universitaires France, 1993.

Granato, Jim, Ronald Inglehart, and David Lebland. "The Effect of Cultural Values on Economic Development: Theory, Hypotheses, and Some Empirical Tests." *American Journal of Political Science* 40, no. 3 (1966): 607–31.

John Locke's Liberalism. University of Chicago Press, 1987.

Grant, Ruth W. "John Locke on Custom's Power and Reason's Authority." *The Review of Politics* 74 (2012): 607–29.

Grasso, Christopher. "The Boundaries of Toleration and Tolerance: Religious Infidelity in the Early American Republic." In *The First Prejudice: Religious Tolerance and Intolerance in Early America*, eds. Chris Beneke and Christopher S. Grenda. Philadelphia: University of Pennsylvania Press, 2011, 286–302.

Gray, John. *Enlightenment's Wake: Politics and Culture at the Close of the Modern Age.* New York: Routledge, 1995.

Two Faces of Liberalism. New York: New Press, 2000.

Grenberg, Jeanine. *Kant and the Ethics of Humility.* Cambridge University Press, 2005.

Gressaye, Jean Brethe de la. "Notes." In *Montesquieu, De L'Esprit des Loix,* ed. Jean Brethe de la Gressaye. 4 vols. Paris: Société des Belles Lettres, 1950–1961.

Gutmann, Amy. *Democratic Education.* Princeton University Press, 1987.

Haakonssen, Knud. "Enlightened Dissent: An Introduction." In *Enlightenment and Religion: Rational Dissent in Eighteenth-Century Britain,* ed. Knud Haakonssen. New York: Cambridge University Press, 1996, 1–11.

Habermas, Jürgen. "Modernity versus Postmodernity." In *Modernity: After Modernity,* ed. Malcolm Waters. London: Routledge, 1999, 5–16.

Hamscher, Albert N. *The Parlement of Paris after the Fronde.* University of Pittsburgh Press, 1976.

Hannaford, Ivan. *Race: The History of an Idea in the West.* Washington, DC: Woodrow Wilson Center Press, 1999.

Harrington, James. *The Commonwealth of Oceana and a System of Politics,* ed. J. G. A. Pocock. Cambridge University Press, 1992.

Hegel, G. W. F. *Natural Law: The Scientific Ways of Treating Natural Law, Its Place in Moral Philosophy, and Its Relation to the Positive Sciences of Law,* trans. T. M. Knox. Philadelphia: University of Pennsylvania Press, 1975.

Henshall, Nicholas. *The Myth of Absolutism: Change and Continuity in Early European Monarchy.* London: Longman Group, 1992.

Herodotus. *The Histories,* trans. Robin Waterfield. Oxford University Press, 1998.

Hexter, J. H. "Claude de Seyssel and Normal Politics in the Age of Machiavelli." In *Art, Science, and History in the Renaissance,* ed. Charles S. Singleton. Baltimore: Johns Hopkins University Press, 1967, 389–415.

Hirschman, Albert O. "The Concept of Interest: From Euphemism to Tautology." In *Rival Views of Market Society and Other Recent Essays,* ed. Albert O. Hirschman. New York: Viking Penguin, 1986, 35–55.

The Passions and the Interests: Political Arguments for Capitalism before Its Triumph. Princeton University Press, 1977.

Hobbes, Thomas. *Opera philosophica, quae Latine scripsit omnia.* Amsterdam: Apud J. Blaev, 1668.

Honig, Bonnie. *Political Theory and the Displacement of Politics.* Ithaca, NY: Cornell University Press, 1993.

Hotman, François. *Antitribonian.* Paris: 1603; facsimile ed. in *Images et temoins de l'age classique,* no. 9 [Publications de L'Université de Saint-Etienne, 1980].

Francogallia, ed. Ralph Giesey and J. H. M. Salmon. Cambridge University Press, 1972.

Hoquet, Thierry, and Céline Spector. "Comment lire Montesquieu?" In *Lectures de l'*Esprit des lois, eds. Thierry Hoquet and Céline Spector, 7–33. Bordeaux: Presses Universitaires de Bordeaux, 2004.

Hulliung, Mark. *Montesquieu and the Old Regime.* Berkeley: University of California Press, 1977.

Huppert, George. *The Idea of Perfect History*. Urbana, IL: University of Illinois Press, 1970.

Hurt, John. J. *Louis XIV and the Parlements: The Assertion of Royal Authority*. Manchester, UK: Manchester University Press, 2002.

Irwin, Terence. *Aristotle's First Principles*. Oxford; New York: Clarendon Press, 1988.

Ivison, Duncan. *Postcolonial Liberalism*. Cambridge University Press, 2002.

Jackman, Robert W., and Ross A. Miller. "The Poverty of Political Culture." *American Journal of Political Science* 40, no. 3 (1996): 697–716.

Jameson, Russell Parson. *Montesquieu et l'esclavage: étude sur l'origines de l'opinion antiesclavagiste en France au XVIIIe siècle*. New York: Burt Franklin, 1911.

Jefferson, Thomas. *Political Writings*, eds. Joyce Appleby and Terence Ball. Cambridge University Press, 1999.

"Thomas Jefferson to William Duane, September 16, 1810." In Vol. 11 of *The Writings of Thomas Jefferson*, ed. Albert Ellery Bergh. Washington, DC: Thomas Jefferson Memorial Association, 1907, 413.

Johnson, James. "Conceptual Problems as Obstacles to Progress in Political Science: Four Decades of Political Culture Research." *Journal of Theoretical Politics* 15, no. 1 (2003): 87–115.

Jones, Jr., James F. "Montesquieu and Jefferson Revisited: Aspects of a Legacy." *The French Review* 51, no. 4 (1978): 577–85.

Kagan, Robert. *The Return of History and the End of Dreams*. New York: Vintage Books, 2009.

Kant, Immanuel. "Perpetual Peace: A Philosophical Sketch." In *Kant's Political Writings*, 2nd edn., ed. H. S. Reiss. Cambridge University Press, 1991, 93–130.

Kassem, Badreddine. *Décadence et absolutism dans l'oeuvre de Montesquieu*. Geneva: Librairie Droz, 1960.

Kelley, Donald R. *Foundations of Modern Historical Scholarship: Language, Law, and History in the French Renaissance*. New York: Columbia University Press, [1931] 1970.

François Hotman: A Revolutionary's Ordeal. Princeton University Press, 1973.

The Human Measure: Social Thought in the Western Legal Tradition. Cambridge, MA: Harvard University Press, 1990.

"Legal Humanism and the Sense of History." *Studies in the Renaissance* 13 (1966): 184–99.

"Louis Le Caron Philosophe." In *Philosophy and Humanism: Renaissance Essays in Honor of Paul Oskar Kristeller*, ed. Edward Patrick Mahoney. Leiden: Brill, 1976, 30–49.

"'Second Nature': The Idea of Custom in European Law, Society, and Culture. In *The Transmission of Culture in Early Modern Europe*, eds. Anthony Grafton and Ann Blair. Philadelphia: University of Pennsylvania Press, 1990, 131–72.

Kelly, Christopher J. "Rousseau and the Illustrious Montesquieu." In *The Challenge of Rousseau*, eds. Eve Grace and Christopher J. Kelly. Cambridge University Press, 2013, 19–33.

Kenshur, Oscar. *Dilemmas of Enlightenment.* Berkeley: University of California Press, 1993.

Keohane, Nannerl O. *Philosophy and the State in France: The Renaissance to the Enlightenment.* Princeton University Press, 1980.

"Virtuous Republics and Glorious Monarchies: Two Models in Montesquieu's Political Thought." *Political Studies* 20, no. 4 (1972): 383–96.

Kesler, Charles R. "Democracy and the Bush Doctrine." In *Life, Liberty, and the Pursuit of Happiness: Ten Years of the Claremont Review of Books,* eds. Charles R. Kesler and John B. Kienker. Lanham, MD: Rowman & Littlefield, 2012, 167–75.

Kessler, Sanford. "Religion and Liberalism in Montesquieu's *Persian Letters.*" *Polity* 15, no. 3 (1983): 380–96.

Kingston, Rebecca E. *Montesquieu and the Parlement of Bordeaux.* Geneva: Librairie Droz, 1996.

"Montesquieu on Religion and the Question of Toleration." In *Montesquieu's Science of Politics: Essays on* The Spirit of Laws, eds. David W. Carrithers, Michael A. Mosher, and Paul A. Rahe. Lanham, MD: Rowman & Littlefield, 2001, 375–408.

Public Passion: Rethinking the Grounds for Political Justice. Montreal: McGill-Queen's University Press, 2014.

"Religion." In *Dictionnaire Montesquieu,* ed. Catherine Volpilhac-Auger. Accessed March 27, 2017. http://dictionnaire-montesquieu.ens-lyon.fr/en/art icle/1377637039/en/.

Kingwell, Mark. *A Civil Tongue: Justice, Dialogue, and the Politics of Pluralism.* University Park, PA: Pennsylvania State University Press, 1995.

Kloppenberg, James T. *The Virtues of Liberalism.* Oxford University Press, 2000.

Koganzon, Rita. "Contesting the Empire of Habit: Habituation and Liberty in Lockean Education," *American Political Science Review* 110, no. 3 (2016): 547–58.

Krause, Sharon R. "Despotism in the *Spirit of Laws.*" In *Montesquieu's Science of Politics: Essays on* The Spirit of Laws, eds. David W. Carrithers, Michael A. Mosher, and Paul A. Rahe. Lanham, MD: Rowman & Littlefield, 2001, 231–72.

Liberalism with Honor. Cambridge, MA: Harvard University Press, 2002.

"The Spirit of Separate Powers in Montesquieu." *The Review of Politics* 62, no. 2 (2000): 231–65.

"The Uncertain Inevitability of Decline in Montesquieu." *Political Theory* 30, no. 5 (2002): 702–27.

Labrousse, Élizabeth. "Calvinism in France, 1598–1685." In *International Calvinism,* ed. Menna Prestwich. Oxford: Clarendon, 1986, 285–314.

Lange, Tyler. *The First French Reformation: Church Reform and the Origins of the Old Regime.* Cambridge University Press, 2014.

Lane, Melissa. "Claims to Rule: The Case of the Multitude." In *The Cambridge Companion to Aristotle's Politics,* eds. Marguerite Deslauriers and Pierre Destrée. Cambridge; New York: Cambridge University Press, [1956] 2013, 247–74.

Larmore, Charles. *Patterns of Moral Complexity.* Cambridge University Press, 1987.

Larrère, Catherine. *Actualité de Montesquieu*. Paris: Presses de Sciences Po, 1999.

"L'empire, entre fédération et république." *Revue Montesquieu* 8 (2005–2006): 111–36.

"Montesquieu and Liberalism: The Question of Pluralism." In *Montesquieu and His Legacy*, ed. Rebecca E. Kingston. Albany, NY: State University of New York Press, 2009, 279–302.

"Montesquieu et le stoïcisme." In *Stoïcisme antique et droit naturel moderne*, ed. Jean Terrel. Bordeaux: Presses Universitaires de Bordeaux, 2003, 59–84.

"Les typologies des gouvernements chez Montesquieu." In *Études sur le XVIIIe siècle*, ed. Jean Ehrard. Clermont-Ferrand: Association des publications de la Faculté des Lettres, 1979, 87–103.

Launay, Robert. "Montesquieu: The Specter of Despotism and the Origins of Comparative Law." In *Rethinking the Masters of Comparative Law*, ed. Annelise Riles. Oxford: Hart Publishing, 2001, 22–39.

Lemarié, Louis. *Les Assemblées franques et les historiens réformateurs du XVIIIe siècle*. Paris: Imprimerie Bonvalot-Jouve, 1906.

Levine, Alan. "The Idea of Commerce in Enlightenment Political Thought." In *Rediscovering Political Economy*, eds. Joseph Postell and Bradley C. S. Watson. Lanham, MD: Lexington Books, 2011, 53–82.

Levin, Lawrence M. *The Political Doctrine of Montesquieu's* Esprit des Lois: *Its Classical Background*. New York: Publications of the Institute of French Studies, Columbia University, 1936.

Levy, Jacob T. "Montesquieu's Constitutional Legacies." In *Montesquieu and His Legacy*, ed. Rebecca E. Kingston. Albany, NY: State University of New York Press, 2009, 115–38.

Rationalism, Pluralism, and Freedom. Oxford University Press, 2015.

Linton, Marisa. "Citizenship and Religious Toleration in France." In *Toleration in Enlightenment Europe*, eds. Ole Peter Grell and Roy Porter. Cambridge University Press, 2000, 157–74.

Locke, John. *Two Treatises of Civil Government*, ed. Ian Shapiro. New Haven, CT: Yale University Press, 2003.

Loirette, Gabriel. "Montesquieu et le problème de France: Du bon Gouvernement." In *Actes du Congrès Montesquieu*. Bordeaux: Impriméries Delmas, 1956, 219–39.

López-Córdova, J. Ernesto, and Christopher M. Meissner. "The Impact of International Trade on Democracy: A Long-Run Perspective." *World Politics* 60, no. 4 (2008): 539–75.

Lowenthal, David. "Book 1 of Montesquieu's *The Spirit of the Laws*." *American Political Science Review* 53 (1959): 488–91.

"Montesquieu." In *History of Political Philosophy*, eds. Leo Strauss and Joseph Cropsey. University of Chicago Press, 1987, 513–58.

"Montesquieu and the Classics." In *Ancients and Moderns: Essays on the Tradition of Political Philosophy in Honor of Leo Strauss*, ed. Joseph Cropsey. New York: Basic Books, 1964, 258–87.

Le Roy, Loys. *Les Politiques d'Aristote: Esqvelles est monstree la science de gouuerner le genre humain en toutes especes d'estats publics*. 1568.

Lutz, Donald. *Principles of Constitutional Design.* Cambridge University Press, 2006.

MacDonald, Sara. "Problems with Principles: Montesquieu's Theory of Natural Justice." *History of Political Thought* 24, no. 1 (2003): 109–30.

Machiavelli, Niccolò. *Discourses on Livy,* trans. Harvey C. Mansfield and Nathan Tarcov. University of Chicago Press, [1517] 1995.

The Prince, 2nd edn., trans. Harvey C. Mansfield. University of Chicago Press, [1532] 1998.

MacIntyre, Alasdair. *After Virtue: A Study in Moral Theory.* South Bend, IN: University of Notre Dame Press, 1981.

Macedo, Stephen. *Liberal Virtues: Citizenship, Virtue, and Community in Liberal Constitutionalism.* Oxford: Clarendon Press, 1990.

Markovits, Francine. *Montesquieu: Le droit et l'histoire.* Paris: Vrin, 2008.

"Montesquieu: l'esprit d'un peuple, une histoire expérimentale." In *Lectures de l'Esprit des lois,* eds. Thierry Hoquet and Céline Spector. Bordeaux: Presses Universitaires de Bordeaux, 2004, 65–9988

Madison, James, Alexander Hamilton, and John Jay. *The Federalist Papers,* ed. Clinton Rossiter. New York: Mentor, 1999.

Maletz, Donald. "Tocqueville on Mores and the Preservation of Republics." *American Journal of Political Science* 49, no.1 (2005): 1–15.

Manent, Pierre. *The City of Man,* trans. Marc A. LePain. Princeton University Press, 1998.

Manin, Bernard. "Montesquieu et la politique moderne." In *Lectures de l'*Esprit des lois, eds. Thierry Hoquet and Céline Spector. Bordeaux: Presses Universitaires de Bordeaux, 2004, 171–232.

Mansfield, Harvey C. *Taming the Prince: The Ambivalence of the Executive Power.* Baltimore: Johns Hopkins University Press, 1993.

Martin, Cristophe. "Une apologétique 'moderne' des Anciens: la querelle dans les *Pensées.*" *Revue Montesquieu* 7 (2003–2004): 67–83.

Martin, Kingsley. *French Liberal Thought in the 18th Century.* London: E. Benn., 1929.

Martino, Pierre. "De quelques résidus métaphysiques dans l'*Esprit des lois.*" *Revue d'histoire de la philosophie et d'histoire générale de la civilisation* 43 (1946): 235–43.

Mathiez, Albert. "La place de Montesquieu dans l'histoire des doctrines politiques du XVIIIe siècle." *Annales Historiques de la Révolution Française* 7 (1930): 97–112.

McAdam, Doug, Sidney Tarrow, and Charles Tilly. "Toward an Integrated Perspective on Social Movements and Revolution." In *Comparative Politics: Rationality, Culture, and Structure,* eds. Mark Irving Lichbach and Alan S. Zuckerman. Cambridge University Press, 1997, 142–73.

McCrea, Adriana. "Sixteenth- through Eighteenth-Century Philosophy of Law." In Vol. 2 of *The Philosophy of Law: An Encyclopedia,* ed. Christopher Gray, 799–803. New York: Garland Publishing, 1999.

McIlwain, Charles Howard. *Constitutionalism Ancient and Modern.* Ithaca, NY: Cornell University Press, 1947.

McNeil, David M. *Guillaume Budé and Humanism in the Reign of Francis I.* Geneva: Librairie Droz, 1975.

Meernik, James. "United States Military Intervention and the Promotion of Democracy." *Journal of Peace Research* 33, no. 4 (1996): 391–402.

Mentzer, Jr., Raymond A. *Blood and Belief: Family Survival and Confessional Identity among the Provincial Huguenot Nobility.* West Lafayette, IN: Purdue University Press, 1994.

Mill, John Stuart. *Basic Writings of John Stuart Mill: On Liberty, The Subjection of Women and Utilitarianism.* New York: Modern Library: 2002.

On Liberty and Other Writings, ed. Stefan Collini. Cambridge University Press, 2003.

Miller, David. *Justice for Earthlings: Essays in Political Philosophy.* Cambridge University Press, 2013.

Miller, Paul B. *Elusive Origins: The Enlightenment in the Modern Caribbean Historical Imagination.* Charlottesville, VA: University of Virginia Press, 2010.

Miller, Paul D. *Armed State Building: Confronting State Failure, 1898–2012.* Ithaca, NY: Cornell University Press, 2013.

Montesquieu, Charles Louis de Secondat, baron de. *The Complete Works of M. de Montesquieu.* 4 vols. London: T. Evans, 1777.

Considerations on the Causes of the Greatness of the Romans and their Decline, ed. David Lowenthal. Ithaca, NY: Cornell University Press, 1968.

De l'esprit des loix. 2 vols. Geneva: Barrillot et fils, 1748.

Montesquieu, Charles Louis de Secondat, baron de. "Discourse on the Motives That Ought to Encourage Us to the Sciences." *The New Atlantis,* trans. Diana J. Schaub, no. 20 (2008): 35–63.

My Thoughts, ed. Henry C. Clark. Indianapolis: Liberty Fund, 2012.

Oeuvres Complètes de Montesquieu, eds. Jean Ehrard and Catherine Volpilhac-Auger, et al. Oxford: Voltaire Foundation, 1998–.

Oeuvres Complètes de Montesquieu, ed. André Masson. 3 vols. Paris: Les Éditions Nagel, 1950–55.

Persian Letters, ed. Andrew Kahn. Oxford University Press, 2008.

The Spirit of the Laws, eds. Anne M. Cohler, Basia C. Miller, and Harold S. Stone. Cambridge University Press, 1989.

Mosher, Michael A. "Free Trade, Free Speech, and Free Love: Monarchy from the Liberal Prospect in Mid-Eighteenth Century France." In *Monarchisms in the Age of Enlightenment: Liberty, Patriotism, and the Common Good,* eds. Hans Blom, John Christian Laursen, and Luisa Simonutti. University of Toronto Press, 2007, 101–18.

"Monarchy's Paradox: Honor in the Face of Sovereign Power." In *Montesquieu's Science of Politics: Essays on* The Spirit of Laws, eds. David W. Carrithers, Michael A. Mosher, and Paul A. Rahe. Lanham, MD: Rowman & Littlefield, 2001, 41–68.

"Montesquieu on Empire and Enlightenment." In *Empire and Modern Political Thought,* ed. Sankar Muthu. Cambridge University Press, 2014, 112–54.

Mousnier, Roland E. *The Institutions of France under the Absolute Monarchy, 1598-1879: The Organs of State and Society,* trans. Arthur Goldhammer. University of Chicago Press, 1984.

Murphy, Andrew R. "Tolerance, Toleration, and the Liberal Tradition." *Polity* 29 (1997): 595–602.

Murphy, Stephen. *The Gift of Immortality: Myths of Power and Human Poetics.* London: Associated University Presses, 1997.

Muthu, Sankar. *Enlightenment against Empire.* Princeton University Press, 2003.

Nelson, Eric. *The Greek Tradition in Republican Thought.* Cambridge University Press, 2004.

   The Hebrew Republic: Jewish Sources and the Transformation of European Political Thought. Cambridge, MA: Harvard University Press, 2010.

Nordland, Rod. "Afghan Equality and Law, but with Strings Attached." *New York Times*, September 24, 2010. Accessed April 30, 2018. www.nytimes.com/2010/09/25/world/asia/25kite.html.

Oakeshott, Michael. *Morality and Politics in Modern Europe*, ed. Shirley Robin Letwin. New Haven, CT: Yale University Press, 1993.

   On Human Conduct. Oxford University Press, 1991.

   "Rationalism in Politics." In *Rationalism in Politics and Other Essays*, ed. Timothy Fuller. Indianapolis: Liberty Fund, 1991, 5–42.

Obama, Barack. "Remarks at Fort Bragg, North Carolina, December 14, 2011." In *Public Papers of the Presidents of the United States: Barack Obama, 2011, Book 2, Presidential Documents – July 1 to December 31, 2011.* Washington, DC: Government Publishing Office, 2015.

Oresme, Nicole. *Politiques d'Aristote.* Philadelphia: American Philosophical Society, [1374] 1970.

Orwin, Clifford. "'For Which Human Nature Can Never Be Too Grateful': Montesquieu as the Heir of Christianity." In *Recovering Reason: Essays in Honor of Thomas L. Pangle*, ed. Timothy Burns. Lanham, MD: Lexington Books, 2010, 269–82.

Palmer, R. R. *The Age of the Democratic Revolution.* 2 vols. Princeton University Press, 1969.

Pangle, Thomas L. *Aristotle's Teaching in the* Politics. University of Chicago Press, 2013.

   Montesquieu's Philosophy of Liberalism: A Commentary on The Spirit of the Laws. University of Chicago Press, 1973.

   The Theological Basis of Liberal Modernity in Montesquieu's Spirit of the Laws. University of Chicago Press, 2010.

Pasquier, Étienne. *L'interprétation des Institutes de Justinian.* Paris, 1847.

   Les Lettres. 2 vols. Paris, 1619.

   Les Oeuvres d'Estienne Pasquier. 2 vols. Amsterdam, 1723.

Peceny, Mark. *Democracy at the Point of Bayonets.* University Park, PA: Pennsylvania State University Press, 1999.

Peterson, Michael D. "Fasting: Eastern Christian." In *Encyclopedia of Monasticism.* Chicago: Fitzroy Dearborn Publishers, 2000, 468–70.

Pettit, Philip. *Republicanism: A Theory of Freedom and Government.* Oxford University Press, 1997.

Plamenatz, John. *Man and Society: Machiavelli through Rousseau.* New York: McGraw-Hill, 1963.

Plato. *Divini Platonis Opera Omnia quæ Extant*, trans. Marcilio Ficino. Lyon: Apud Franciscum le Preux, 1590.

   The Laws of Plato, ed. Thomas L. Pangle. University of Chicago Press, 1988.

Pliny the Younger. *Complete Letters*, trans. P. G. Walsh. Oxford University Press, 2006.

Pocock, J. G. A. *The Ancient Constitution and the Feudal Law: A Study of English Historical Thought in the Seventeenth Century, A Reissue with a Retrospect.* Cambridge University Press, 1987.

Barbarism and Religion. 2 vols. Cambridge University Press, 1999.

Commerce, Virtue and History: Essays on Political Thought and History, Chiefly in the Eighteenth Century. Cambridge University Press, 1985.

"Editor's Introduction." In *James Harrington: The Commonwealth of Oceana and A System of Politics*, ed. J. G. A. Pocock. Cambridge University Press, 1992, vii–xxiii.

The Machiavellian Moment: Florentine Political Thought and the Atlantic Republican Tradition. Princeton University Press, 2003.

"The Origins of Study of the Past: A Comparative Approach." *Comparative Studies in Society and History* 4 (1962): 209–46.

Politics, Language, and Time: Essays on Political Thought and History. University of Chicago Press, 1989.

Pope, Alexander. *An Essay on Man: Moral Essays and Satires.* London: Cassell & Company, 1906.

Poujol, Jacques. "Jean Ferrault on the King's Privileges." *Studies in the Renaissance* 5 (1958): 15–17.

Prélot, Marcel. "Montesquieu et les formes de gouvernement." In *La pensée politique et constitutionnelle de Montesquieu: bicentenaire de L'Esprit des lois, 1748–1948*, 2nd edn., eds. Boris Mirkene-Guetzévitch and Henri Puget. Paris: Scientia Verlag Aalen, 1988, 119–32.

Pseudo-Helvétius. "Letters of Helvétius, Addressed to President Montesquieu and M. Saurin, on Perusing the Manuscript of *The Spirit of Laws*." In Antoine Louis Claude Destutt de Tracy, *A Commentary and Review of Montesquieu's Spirit of Laws, To Which Are Annexed, 'Observations on the Thirty-First Book,' by the Late M. Condorcet, and Two Letters of Helvétius, On the Merits of the Same Work*, trans. Thomas Jefferson. Philadelphia: William Duane, 1811, 283–92.

Radasanu, Andrea. "Montesquieu on Moderation, Monarchy and Reform." *History of Political Thought* 31, no. 2 (2010): 283–307.

"Polishing Barbarous Mores: Montesquieu on Liberalism and Civic Education." In *Civic Education and the Future*, eds. Elizabeth Kaufer Busch and Jonathan W. White. Lanham, MD: Lexington Books, 2013, 49–65.

Rahe, Paul A. "Forms of Government: Structure, Principle, Object, and Aim." In *Montesquieu's Science of Politics: Essays on The Spirit of Laws*, eds. David W. Carrithers, Michael A. Mosher, and Paul A. Rahe. Lanham, MD: Rowman & Littlefield, 2001, 69–108.

"Introduction." In *Machiavelli's Liberal Republican Legacy*, ed. Paul A. Rahe. Cambridge University Press, 2006, xix–xxx.

Montesquieu and the Logic of Liberty: War, Religion, Commerce, Climate, Terrain, Technology, Uneasiness of Mind, the Spirit of Political Vigilance, and the Foundations of the Modern Republic. New Haven, CT: Yale University Press, 2009.

Republics Ancient and Modern: Classical Republicanism and the American Revolution. Chapel Hill, NC: University of North Carolina Press, 1992.

Soft Despotism, Democracy's Drift: Montesquieu, Rousseau, Tocqueville, and the Modern Prospect. New Haven, CT: Yale University Press, 2009.

Randall, Michael. *The Gargantuan Polity: On the Individual and the Community in the French Renaissance.* University of Toronto Press, 2008.

Rasmussen, Dennis. *The Pragmatic Enlightenment: Recovering the Liberalism of Hume, Smith, Montesquieu, and Voltaire.* Cambridge University Press, 2014.

Rawls, John. *Political Liberalism,* 2nd edn. New York: Columbia University Press, 2005.

A Theory of Justice. Cambridge, MA: Harvard University Press, 1971.

Régaldo, Marc. *Montesquieu et la Religion.* Bordeaux: Académie Montesquieu, 1998.

Rice, Condoleezza. "Remarks by National Security Advisor Condoleezza Rice at the 28th Annual Convention of the National Association of Black Journalists, August 7, 2003." Accessed March 27, 2017. https://georgewbush-white house.archives.gov/news/releases/2003/08/20030807-1.html.

Richelieu, Cardinal. *The Political Testament,* trans. Henry Bertram Hill. Madison, WI: University of Wisconsin Press, 1961.

Richter, Melvin. "Comparative Political Analysis in Montesquieu and Tocqueville." *Comparative Politics* 1 (1969): 129–60.

"An Introduction to Montesquieu's 'An Essay on the Causes That May Affect Men's Minds and Characters.'" *Political Theory* 4, no. 2 (1976): 132–8.

The Political Theory of Montesquieu. Cambridge University Press, 1977.

Robin, Corey. *Fear: The History of a Political Idea.* Oxford University Press, 2004.

Roelker, Nancy Lyman. *One King, One Faith: The Parlement of Paris and the Religious Reformations of the Sixteenth Century.* Berkeley: University of California Press, 1996.

Rogowski, Ronald. *Rational Legitimacy: A Theory of Political Support.* Princeton University Press, 1974.

Rorty, Richard. *Contingency, Irony, and Solidarity.* Cambridge University Press, 1989.

Rosenblatt, Helena. *Rousseau and Geneva: From the First Discourse to the Social Contract, 1749–1762.* New York: Cambridge University Press, 1997.

Ross, Michael L. "Does Taxation Lead to Representation?" *British Journal of Political Science* 34, no. 2 (2004): 229–49.

Rousseau, Jean-Jacques. "Discourse on the Origin and Foundations of Inequality among Mankind." In *The Social Contract and the First and Second Discourses,* ed. Susan Dunn. New Haven, CT: Yale University Press, 2002, 69–148.

Emile, or On Education, trans. Allan Bloom. New York: Basic Books, 1979.

Russo, Elena. "Virtuous Economies: Modernity and Noble Expenditure from Montesquieu to Caillois." In *Postmodernism and the Enlightenment: New Perspectives in Eighteenth-Century French Intellectual History,* ed. Daniel Gordon. London: Routledge, 2001, 67–116.

Sabine, George H. *A History of Political Theory,* 3rd edn. New York: Holt, Rineart, and Winston, 1961.

Salkever, Stephen. "Aristotle's Social Science." In *Aristotle's Politics: Critical Essays*, eds. Richard Kraut and Steven Skultety, 27–64. Lanham, MD: Rowman & Littlefield, 2005.

Sales, Francis de. *Introduction to the Devout Life*. New York: Vintage Books, 2002.

Samuel, Ana. "The Design of Montesquieu's *The Spirit of the Laws*: The Triumph of Freedom over Determinism." *American Political Science Review* 103, no. 2 (2009): 305–21.

Sandel, Michael. *Liberalism and the Limits of Justice*. Cambridge University Press, 1998.

Saugera, Éric. *Bordeaux port négrier: XVIIe–XIXe siècles*, 2nd edn. Paris: Karthala, 2002.

Schaub, Diana J. *Erotic Liberalism: Women and Revolution in Montesquieu's Persian Letters*. Lanham, MD: Rowman & Littlefield, 1995.

"Montesquieu's Popular Science," *The New Atlantis*, no. 20 (2008): 37–46.

"Of Believers and Barbarians: Montesquieu's Enlightened Toleration." In *Skepticism and the Origins of Toleration*, ed. Alan Levine. Lanham, MD: Lexington Books, 1999, 225–48.

Schiffman, Zachary S. *The Birth of the Past*. Baltimore: Johns Hopkins University Press, 2011.

"Humanism and the Problem of Relativism." In *Humanism in Crisis: The Decline of the French Renaissance*, ed. Philippe Desan. Ann Arbor, MI: University of Michigan Press, 2016, 69–83.

"Estienne Pasquier and the Problem of Historical Relativism." *The Sixteenth Century Journal* 18, no. 4 (1987): 505–17.

Schofield, Malcolm. *Plato: Political Philosophy*. Oxford University Press, 2006.

Schwartz, Stuart B. *All Can Be Saved: Religious Tolerance and Salvation in the Iberian Atlantic World*. New Haven, CT: Yale University Press, 2008.

Scott, James Brown. *Law, the State, and the International Community*. New York: Columbia University Press, 1939.

Scoville, Warren. *The Persecution of Huguenots and French Economic Development 1680–1720*. Berkeley: University of California Press, 2006.

Scruton, Roger. *The Uses of Pessimism: And the Danger of False Hope*. Oxford University Press, 2010.

Seyssel, Claude de. *The Monarchy of France*, ed. Donald R. Kelley. New Haven, CT: Yale University Press: [1519] 1981.

Shackleton, Robert. "Bayle and Montesquieu." In *Pierre Bayle, le philosophe de Rotterdam*, ed. P. Dibon. Amsterdam: Elsevier, 1959, 142–9.

"La genèse de *L'Esprit des lois*." *Revue d'histoire littéraire de la France* 52 (1952): 425–38.

"Montesquieu's Correspondence: Additions and Corrections." *French Studies* 12 (1958): 324–45.

Montesquieu: A Critical Biography. Oxford University Press, 1961.

Sherman, Charles P. *Roman Law in the Modern World*. Boston Book Company, 1917.

Shklar, Judith. *Freedom and Independence: A Study of the Political Ideas of Hegel's* Phenomenology of Mind. Cambridge University Press, 1976.

"The Liberalism of Fear." In *Liberalism and the Moral Life*, ed. Nancy L. Rosenblum. Cambridge, MA: Harvard University Press, 1989, 21–38.

Montesquieu. Oxford and New York: Oxford University Press, 1987.

Ordinary Vices. Cambridge: Belknap, 1984.

"Virtue in a Bad Climate: Good Men and Good Citizens in Montesquieu's *L'Esprit des lois*." In *Enlightenment Studies in Honour of Lester G. Crocker*, eds. Alfred J. Bingham and Virgil W. Topazio. Oxford: Voltaire Foundation, 1979, 315–28.

Siculus, Diodorus. *The Library of History*, trans. Charles H. Oldfather. Cambridge, MA: Loeb Classical Library, 1933–1967.

Sidney, Algernon. *Discourses Concerning Government*. Indianapolis: Liberty Fund, [1704] 1996.

Skinner, Quentin. *The Foundations of Modern Thought*. 2 vols. Cambridge University Press, 1978.

"A Genealogy of the Modern State." *Proceedings of the British Academy* 162 (2009): 325–70.

Smith, Steven B. *Reading Leo Strauss: Politics, Philosophy, Judaism*. University of Chicago Press, 2006.

Sowerby, Scott. "Tolerance and Toleration in Early Modern England." In *A Lively Experiment*, eds. Chris Beneke and Christopher S. Grenda. Lanham, MD: Rowman & Littlefield, 2015, 58–68.

Spector, Céline. "Le fait religieux dans *L'Esprit des lois*." In *Montesquieu, L'État et la Religion*, ed. Jean Ehrard. Sofia, BG: Éditions Iztok-Zapad, 2007, 40–78.

"Le Projet de paix perpétuelle: de Saint-Pierre à Rousseau." In *Principes du droit de la guerre, Ecrits sur le Projet de Paix Perpétuelle de l'abbé de Saint-Pierre*, eds. B. Bachofen and Céline Spector. Paris: Vrin, 2008, 229–94.

Montesquieu et l'émergence de l'économie politique. Paris: Honoré Champion, 2006.

Montesquieu: Liberté, droit et histoire. Paris: Éditions Michalon, 2010.

Montesquieu. Pouvoirs, richesses et société. Paris: Presses Universitaires de France , 2004.

"Quelle justice? Quelle rationalité? La mesure du droit dans *L'Esprit des lois*." In *Montesquieu en 2005*, ed. Catherine Volpilhac-Auger. Oxford: Voltaire Foundation, 2005, 219–42.

"Spirit, General Spirit," trans. Philip Stewart. In *Dictionnaire Montesquieu*, ed. Catherine Volpilhac-Auger. Accessed March 27, 2017. http://dictionnaire-montesquieu.ens-lyon.fr/en/article/1376474276/en/.

Spector, Céline. *Le vocabulaire de Montesquieu*. Paris: Ellipses, 2001.

"Was Montesquieu Liberal? *The Spirit of the Laws* in the History of Liberalism." In *French Liberalism from Montesquieu to the Present Day*, eds. Raf Geenens and Helena Rosenblatt. Cambridge University Press, 2012, 57–72.

Spitz, Jean-Fabien. *La liberté politique: Essai de généalogie conceptuelle*. Paris: Presses Universitaires de France , 1995.

Spragens, Thomas A. *Civil Liberalism: Reflections on Our Democratic Ideals*. Lanham, MD: Rowman & Littlefield, 1999.

Stankiewicz, W. J. *Politics and Religion in Seventeenth-Century France*. Berkeley: University of California Press, 1960.

Stanley, Sharon A. *French Enlightenment and the Emergence of Modern Cynicism*. Cambridge University Press, 2014.

Stein, Peter. *Roman Law in European History*. New York: Cambridge University Press, [1926] 1999.

Stewart, Iain. "Montesquieu in England: his 'Notes on England,' with Commentary and Translation." *Oxford University Comparative Law Forum* 6 (2002). Accessed March 27, 2017. ouclf.iuscomp.org.

Storing, Herbert, ed. *The Complete Anti-Federalist*. University of Chicago Press, 1981.

Strauss, Leo. *The City and Man*. Charlottesville, VA: University of Virginia Press, 1964.

Natural Right and History. University of Chicago Press, 1965.

Seminar on Aristotle, Politics, spring 1960, ed. Joseph Cropsey. Accessed March 27, 2017. https://leostrausscenter.uchicago.edu/course/aristotle-politics-spring-quarter-1960.

Seminar on Montesquieu II, spring 1966, ed. Thomas L. Pangle. Accessed April 30, 2018. https://leostrausscenter.uchicago.edu/course/montesquieu-ii-spring-quarter-1966.

What Is Political Philosophy? and Other Studies. University of Chicago Press, 1959.

Stroumsa, Guy G. *A New Science: The Discovery of Religion in the Age of Reason*. Cambridge, MA: Harvard University Press, 2010.

Stump, Eleonore. *Aquinas*. London: Routledge, 2005.

Sullivan, Vickie B. *Montesquieu and the Despotic Ideas of Europe: An Interpretation of* The Spirit of the Laws. University of Chicago Press, 2017.

Tacitus. *Agricola*. Oxford University Press, 2009.

Tacitus. *The Annals and The Histories*, ed. Moses Hadas. New York: Modern Library, 2003.

Tarcov, Nathan. *Locke's Education for Liberty*. Lanham, MD: Lexington Books, 1999.

Taylor, Mark C. *Confidence Games: Money and Markets in a World without Redemption*. University of Chicago Press, 2004.

Taylor, Robert S. "Democratic Transitions and the Progress of Absolutism in Kant's Political Thought." *The Journal of Politics* 68, no. 3 (2006): 556–70.

Terjanian, Anoush Fraser. *Commerce and Its Discontents in Eighteenth-Century French Political Thought*. Cambridge University Press, 2013.

Tholozan, Olivier. *Henri de Boulainvilliers: L'anti-absolutisme aristocratique légitimé par l'histoire*. Marseille: Presses universitaires d'Aix-Marseille, 2015.

Tillet, Édouard. "*Collectio juris, Oeuvres complètes de Montesquieu*, t. 11 et 12." *Revue Montesquieu* 8 (2005–2006): 215–22.

Tocqueville, Alexis de. *Democracy in America*, ed. J. P. Mayer. New York: HarperCollins, 1988.

The Tocqueville Reader, eds. Oliver Zunz and Alan S. Kahan. Oxford: Blackwell Publishers, 2002.

Todorov, Tzvetan. "Droit naturel et formes de gouvernement dans *L'Esprit des lois*." *Esprit* 75 (1983): 35–48.

On Human Diversity: Nationalism, Racism, and Exoticism in French Thought. Cambridge, MA: Harvard University Press, 1993.

Tomaselli, Sylvana. "Intolerance, the Virtue of Princes and Radicals." In *Toleration in Enlightenment Europe*, eds. Ole Peter Grell and Roy Porter. Cambridge University Press, 2000, 86–101.

"The Spirit of Nations." In *The Cambridge History of Eighteenth-Century Political Thought*, eds. Mark Goldie and Robert Wolker, 9–39. Cambridge University Press, 2006.

Tomasi, John. *Free Market Fairness*. Princeton University Press, 2012.

Liberalism beyond Justice. Princeton University Press, 2001.

Toulmin, Stephen. *Cosmopolis: The Hidden Agenda of Modernity*. New York: Free Press, 1990.

Tuck, Richard. *Natural Rights Theories: Their Origin and Development*. Cambridge University Press, 1979.

Tully, James. *Strange Multiplicity: Constitutionalism in an Age of Diversity*. Cambridge University Press, 1995.

Utt, Walter C., and Brian E. Strayer. *The Bellicose Dove: Claude Brousson and Protestant Resistance to Louis XIV*. Brighton, UK: Sussex Academic Press, 2003.

Valerius Maximus. *Memorable Deeds*, trans. Henry John Walker. Indianapolis: Hackett Publishing Company, 2004.

Van Ruymbek, Bertrand. *New Babylon to Eden: The Huguenots and the Migration to Colonial South Carolina*. Columbia, SC: University of South Carolina Press, 2006.

Vile, M. J. C. *Constitutionalism and the Separation of Powers*. Indianapolis: Liberty Fund, 1998.

Volpilhac-Auger, Catherine, ed. *Dictionnaire Montesquieu*. Accessed March 27, 2017. http://dictionnaire-montesquieu.ens-lyon.fr.

Voltaire. *Oeuvres complètes de Voltaire*. Paris: Garnier, 1880.

Voltaire. *Philosophical Letters*, ed. John Leigh. Indianapolis: Hackett Publishing Company, 2007.

Vyerberg, Henry. *Historical Pessimism in the French Enlightenment*. Cambridge, MA: Harvard University Press, 1958.

Waddicor, Mark H. *Montesquieu and the Philosophy of Natural Law*. The Hague: Martinus Nijhoff, 1970.

Walsh, David. *The Growth of the Liberal Soul*. Columbia, MO: University of Missouri Press, 1997.

Warburton, William. *The Divine Legation of Moses*. London, 1846.

A Selection from the Unpublished Papers of the Right Reverend William Warburton, ed. Francis Kilvert. London: John Bowyer Nichols & Son, 1841.

Ward, Lee. "Montesquieu on Federalism and Anglo-Gothic Constitutionalism." *Publius: The Journal of Federalism* 37, no. 4 (2007): 551–77.

Politics of Liberty in England and Revolutionary America. Cambridge University Press, 2010.

Warren, James. *Epicurus and Democritean Ethics: An Archaeology of Ataraxia*. Cambridge University Press, 2002.

Watson, John Selby. *The Life of William Warburton*. London: Longman, Green, Longman, Roberts, & Green, 1863.

Werlin, Herbert H. "Political Change and Political Culture." *American Political Science Review* 84, no. 1 (1990): 249–59.

West, Thomas G. "The Political Theory of the Declaration of Independence." In *The American Founding and the Social Compact*, eds. Thomas G. West and Ronald J. Pestritto. Oxford: Lexington Books, 2003, 95–146.

Whitehead, Laurence. "The International Politics of Democratization from Portugal (1974) to Iraq (2003)." In *The International Politics of Democratization: Comparative Perspectives*, ed. Nuno Severiano Teixeira. London: Routledge, 2008, 8–25.

"On 'Cultivating' Democracy: Enlivening the Imagery for Democracy Promotion." In *The Conceptual Politics of Democracy Promotion*, eds. Christopher Hobson and Milja Kurki. London: Routledge, 2012, 19–37.

Wiley, James. "Sheldon Wolin on Theory and the Political." *Polity* 38, no. 2 (2006): 211–34.

Williams, David. *Condorcet and Modernity*. Cambridge University Press, 2004.

Williams, David Lay. "Political Ontology and Institutional Design in Montesquieu and Rousseau." *American Journal of Political Science* 54, no. 2 (2010): 525–42.

Wolin, Sheldon. *The Presence of the Past: Essays on the State and the Constitution*. Baltimore: Johns Hopkins University Press, 1989.

Wolterstorff, Nicholas. *Justice in Love*. Grand Rapids, MI: Eerdmans, 2015.

Wright, Johnson Kent. "A Rhetoric of Aristocratic Reaction? Nobility in *De l'Esprit des Lois*." In *The French Nobility in the Eighteenth Century: Reassessments and New Approaches*, ed. Jay M. Smith. University Park, PA: Pennsylvania State University Press, 2006, 227–51.

Young, B. W. *Religion and Enlightenment in Eighteenth-Century England: Theological Debate from Locke to Burke*. Oxford: Clarendon Press, 1998.

Young, David. "Montesquieu's View of Despotism and His Own Use of Travel Literature." *Review of Politics* 40 (1978): 392–405.

Zanin, Sergey. "Rousseau, Montesquieu et la 'religion civile.'" In *Montesquieu, L'État et la Religion*, ed. Jean Ehrard. Sofia, BG: Èditions Iztok-Zapad, 2007, 186–212.

Zuckert, Michael. "Natural Law, Natural Rights, and Classical Liberalism: On Montesquieu's Critique of Hobbes." In *Natural Law and Modern Moral Philosophy*, eds. Ellen Frankel Paul, Fred D. Miller, Jr., and Jeffrey Paul. Cambridge University Press, 2001, 227–51.

Index